The S.A.P.I.E.N.T. Being

A Critical Thinking Guide to Help Stop & Prevent Academia's Neo-Marxist & Racist Progressivist Agenda

By

Corey Lee Wilson

The S.A.P.I.E.N.T. Being

The S.A.P.I.E.N.T. Being

Fratire Publishing books can be purchased in bulk with special discounts for educational purposes, association gifts, sales promotions, and special editions can be created to specifications. All inquiries for such can be made below.

FRATIRE PUBLISHING LLC
4533 Temescal Canyon Rd. # 308
Corona, CA 92883
www.FratirePublishing.com
FratirePublishing@att.net
(951) 638-5502

FratirePublishing
Relevant Books for **SAPIENT** Beings

Fratire Publishing is all about common sense and relevant books for sapient beings. If this sounds like you and you can never have enough common sense, wisdom and relevancy, then visit us and learn more about the 40 *MADNESS* series of book titles at www.FratirePublishing.com.

Printed paperback and eBook ePUB by Ingram Spark in La Vergne, Tennessee, USA
Copyright © 2020 and 2023: 1st Edition Nov. 2020; 2nd Edition Sep. 2023
ISBN 978-1-953319-00-5 (Paperback)
ISBN 978-1-953319-33-3 (eBook)
TSB-02-PDF (pdf)
TSB-02-EPUB (epub)
LCCN 2020919633

Special thanks for the cover and logo designs by Jenny Barroso at j20graphics@gmail.com and ebook conversion by Jahurul Md. Islam at Upwork.

The S.A.P.I.E.N.T. Being

Contents

Acknowledgements

We owe a debt of gratitude to the following for "heavily" borrowing at times pieces of their and/or outright sections. We do this unashamedly to use the sapient phrase, "if it ain't broke—don't try to fix it." Most of the borrowed works and research cannot be improved upon—so why try? It's better to assemble these meaningful parts, profound messages, and eloquent arguments into a cohesive whole, told with high school and college students in mind, and that's what we've done and where our talent lies.

Below in alphabetical order are the major contributors to *The SAPIENT Being* that we borrowed verbatim, quoted, and conceptualized much of their content from a little to a lot. Wherever this happened, we did our best to acknowledge the source. If we didn't at times within the 25 chapters, it was done intentionally because doing so would have distracted from their message. Nonetheless, they are more than referenced in the Resources and Index sections.

City Journal: Is a public policy magazine and website, published by the Manhattan Institute for Policy Research, that covers a range of topics on urban affairs, such as policing, education, housing, and other issues. The *City Journal* and its authors were the most widely used resource for *The SAPIENT Being.*

Epoch Times, The: Is America's fastest-growing independent news media, founded in 2000, and their mission is to bring readers a truthful view of the world free from the influence of any government, corporation, or political party. Contrary to fake news organizations, their aim is to tell readers what they see, not how to think; and they strive to deliver a factual picture of reality that lets readers form their own opinions.

Haidt, Dr. Jonathan: Centrist and co-founder of the Heterodox Academy and its biggest advocate, spokesperson, and leader in the field of viewpoint diversity, he wrote the 2012 book, *The Righteous Mind: Why Good People Are Divided by Politics and Religion*. Haidt co-wrote *The Coddling of the American Mind: How Good Intentions and Bad Ideas Are Setting Up a Generation for Failure* in 2018 with Greg Lukianoff.

Heritage Foundation, The: Is an American conservative think tank that is primarily geared toward public policy and the foundation took a leading role in the conservative movement during the presidency of Ronald Reagan, whose policies were taken from Heritage's policy study Mandate for Leadership. The Heritage Foundation has had a major influence in U.S. public policy making and is among the most influential conservative public policy organizations in America.

Lukianoff, Greg: President and CEO, Foundation for Individual Rights and Expression (FIRE) and co-wrote *The Coddling of the American Mind: How Good Intentions and Bad Ideas Are Setting Up a Generation for Failure* in 2018 with Dr. Jonathan Haidt.

Mac Donald, Heather: Is an American political commentator, essayist, attorney, author, a Thomas W. Smith Fellow of the Manhattan Institute, and a contributing editor of the institute's *City Journal*. She has written numerous editorials and is the author of several books like the bestseller *The Diversity Delusion: How Race and Gender Pandering Corrupt the University and Undermine Our Culture*.

Manhattan Institute: Is a think-tank and community of scholars, journalists, activists, and civic leaders dedicated to advancing opportunity, individual liberty, and the rule of law in America and its great cities.

National Association of Scholars: Is an American non-profit politically conservative advocacy organization, with a particular interest in education, utilizing a network of scholars and citizens united by a commitment to academic freedom, disinterested scholarship, and excellence in American higher education. They have published a quarterly magazine titled *Academic Questions* since 1988.

***National Review*:** Is an American semi-monthly editorial magazine, focusing on news and commentary pieces on political, social, and cultural affairs and its authors contributed a considerable number of articles to this book. The magazine was founded by the author William F. Buckley Jr. in 1955 and has played a significant role in the development of conservatism in the United States, and is a leading voice on the American right.

Pew Research Center: The Pew Research Center is a nonpartisan American think tank based in Washington, D.C. It provides information on social issues, public opinion, and demographic trends shaping the United States and the world.

Randall, David: Is the Director of Research at the National Association of Scholars and a Policy Advisor to The Heartland Institute and leads research studies on education and trends in the curriculum.

Rufo, Christopher F.: Is leading the fight against critical race theory and progressivism madness in American institutions. His research and activism inspired a presidential order and legislation in 15 states, where he has worked closely with lawmakers to craft successful public policy. Rufo is a contributing editor of *City Journal* and director of the Discovery Institute's Center on Wealth & Poverty.

Salzman, Philip Carl: Is a professor emeritus of anthropology at McGill University, senior fellow at the Frontier Centre for Public Policy, fellow at the Middle East Forum, and president of Scholars for Peace in the Middle East.

A SAPIENT Being's Preface

In the 21st century, an ever growing number of academic Progressives have innovated in ideology, jettisoning the economic class struggle of Marxism and replacing it with identity classes: gender, race, sexuality, religion, nationality, and ableness. Now it's (allegedly) whites (including "white adjacent" Asians and "hyperwhite" Jews), males, and Christians who are oppressors—and people of color, women, LGBTQ++, Muslims, and the disabled who are the oppressed victims.

With the "social justice" trinity of "diversity, equity, and inclusion," academic Progressives have returned us to the days of deep Jim Crow, with some races seen as virtuous and others as evil, the only difference being that the colors have changed. Progressive "inclusion" means including preferred races and genders, and excluding the others, as we see in hiring, college admissions, funding, promotions, and awards.

Equity, meaning the statistical equivalence of races and genders, in practice means more of the preferred and fewer of the despised. Objective measures, such as standardized tests, and advanced education programs, are being cancelled by the academy, because they don't produce the desired "equity" results. Now institutionalized DEI racism and discrimination are regarded as desirable by so-called Progressive academia, as long as preferred categories benefit.

Enough of this madness! Now is the time to wake up to this enormous problem before we do even graver damage—not only to ourselves individually but to our country as a whole. It's a bitter irony that those academics and their proponents who want to drive us into this new hysteria often claim to be "woke."

But there is no awakening in woke. It's the sleep of reason that produces monsters, and it poses a profound peril to our republic.

The second edition of *The S.A.P.I.E.N.T. Being* offers an opportunity to be part of the solution to these many Progressivist induced maladies. However, for some of you this book will be a revelation, an epiphany, a sapient being moment. For others, it will be a triggering event, denial of truth, and a painful intervention.

Are you interested in learning all about the hypocrisy and idiocracy of today's academically driven illiberal and retrogressive Progressivism movement, their destructive DEI policies and programs, Marxist foundations of Critical Race Theory (CRT), reverse racism, cancel culture, social injustice—and how to work together to defeat this movement before it destroys our republic?

If yes, please read on and if you also believe in the message of this ground breaking book and willing to fight for it—please considering joining or participating in one of these SAPIENT Being programs.

Sapient Conservative Textbooks (SCT) Program is a relevant and current events textbooks program (published by Fratire Publishing LLC) to help return conservative values, viewpoint diversity, and sapience to high school and college campuses—and enlighten them on the many blessings to humankind that are the direct result of Western European culture, American exceptionalism, and Judeo-Christian values.

Free Speech Alumni Ambassador (FSAA) Program helps create faculty and administrative positions, throughout America's predominantly liberally staffed college campuses, that can serve as much needed conservative club advisors—because conservative students are facing many obstacles when they attempt to start and charter a right-leaning student organization on campus due to faculty members fearful of losing their jobs or tenure for becoming these organization's advisors.

Make Free Speech Again On Campus (MFSAOC) Program is an interactive opportunity and nexus for high school and college students to start SAPIENT Being campus clubs, chapters, and alliances where independent, liberal, and conservative minded students can meet, discuss, and debate important issues by utilizing the sapient principles of viewpoint diversity, freedom of speech, and intellectual humility—and develop sapience in the process.

Are You a Sapient Being or Want to Be One?

Sapience, also known as wisdom, is the ability to think and act using knowledge, experience, understanding, common sense and insight. Sapience is associated with attributes such as intelligence, enlightenment, unbiased judgment, compassion, experiential self-knowledge, self-actualization, and virtues such as ethics and benevolence.

Being a sapient being is not about identity politics, it's about doing what is right and borrows many of the essential qualities of Centrism that supports strength, tradition, open mindedness, and policy based on evidence not ideology.

Sapient beings are independent minded thinkers that achieve common sense solutions that appropriately address America's and the world's most pressing issues. They gauge situations based on context and reason, consideration, and probability. They are open minded and exercise conviction and willing to fight for it on the intellectual battlefield. Sapient beings don't blindly and recklessly follow their feelings or emotions.

Their unifying ideology is based on truth, reason, logic, scientific method, and pragmatism—and not necessarily defined by compromise, moderation, or any particular faith—but is considerate of them.

The love of truth and the desire to attain it should motivate you to think for yourself. The crucial point of a college education is to seek truth and to learn the skills and acquire the virtues necessary to be a lifelong truth-seeker. Open-mindedness, critical thinking, and debate are essential to discovering the truth. Moreover, they are our best antidotes to bigotry.

In today's climate, it's all-too-easy to allow your views and outlook to be shaped by dominant opinion on your campus or in the broader academic culture. The danger any student—or faculty member—faces today is falling into the vice of conformism, yielding to groupthink, the orthodoxy.

At many colleges and universities what John Stuart Mill called "the tyranny of public opinion" does more than merely discourage students from dissenting from prevailing views on moral, political, and other types of questions. It leads them to suppose that dominant views are so obviously correct that only a bigot or a crank could question them.

Since no one wants to be, or be thought of as, a bigot or a crank, the easy, lazy way to proceed is simply by falling into line with campus orthodoxies. Don't do it!

To be sure, our overly-politicized culture has a tough time viewing any "verbal cacophony" as a sign of strength and vibrancy. And perhaps nowhere is this truer than on many college campuses where political correctness is rampant, groupthink is common, and social media "mobs" arise in a flash to intimidate anyone who openly strays from the prevailing orthodoxy.

At the SAPIENT Being we're not intimidated—and our primary purpose is to seek the truth by enhancing viewpoint diversity, promoting intellectual humility, protecting freedom of speech and expression while developing sapience in the process—no matter what the cost on the intellectual battlefield, campus classroom, and marketplace of ideas. This is our ethos! Is it yours?

Best regards and sapiently yours,

Corey Lee Wilson

Corey Lee Wilson

S.A.P.I.E.N.T. Being

1 – What is 21st Century Progressivism & Who Are These So-Called Progressives?

Credit: Chad Crowe.

Historically, the United States has possessed a single dominant ideology of liberalism "classical" liberalism, not to be confused with today's neo-liberalism, that sustained itself from previous ideological challengers. As noted by Bradley A. Thayer's January 2022 "Our 1776 Moment: Either a Liberal or Progressive America" *Epoch Times* article:

Classical Liberalism is a political ideology that promises liberty for the individual. It employs the concept of inalienable rights and individual freedoms. These ideas and principles are expressed in America's founding documents—the Declaration of Independence, the Constitution, and the Bill of Rights—and have been echoed in American political ideas, practices, tradition, and culture since the American Revolution of 1776.

Opposed to classic liberalism, Western leftists like to refer to themselves as "Progressives," and their worldview most closely resembles an evolving fascism, differing only in degree—so far. Their programs include increased government control, the reduction of civil liberties, and the transfer of power from the people, state governments, and Congress to federal bureaucrats, courts, and international institutions. None of these goals, when compared to classical liberalism, are "Progressive" – but "regressive" to the very foundations of the United States of America.

If we take a unbiased look at every major problem or issue facing America in the 21st century, as this book will show, each and every one of them, to one degree or another, is being created by Progressive ideology or negatively impacted by Progressive polices, programs, or agenda.

Today's Progressivism in 21st Century America

American leftists like to call themselves "progressive" as a form of self-praise, a state of being, an assertion that their politics represent a higher consciousness than the prejudices of the mob of unthinking deplorables and will lead mankind to a sunny upland where human nature will transcend its baser impulses, and peace and harmony will reign. The hypocrisy of their belief structure will unfold as we learn more about the Progressivism ideology.

Furthermore, Progressivism Isn't progressive—it's recycled and repackaged Marxism for a 21st century audience as you will see as we learn more about it in the following articles.

Conservatives, independents, and sapient beings should not indulge so-called "Progressives" in this self-deception. We should stop using "Progressive" as a synonym for the noun "Left" or the adjective "left-wing" and use "regressive" or "regressivism" instead. At first, you might be wondering why this antonym is being used—but as we move through this book, chapter by chapter, it will become clearly evident there is no progress for Americans from Progressivism's regressivism—only an Orwellian *1984* future that will fundamentally change America for the worse.

Make no mistake: This neo-Marxist assault has been planned and coordinated for years to strike America where she is weakest: in her innate sense of rightness and fair play. Under so-called Progressive pedagogy, you'll see how quickly we have moved from Dr. Martin Luther King, Jr.'s plea that we judge a man by "the content of his character" and back to "the color of his skin." It's regressivism madness— and if Dr. King could see what is happening to his dream—he would be rolling in his grave.

Progressivism's Long March Through America's Institutions

As in Karl Marx's older drama, the moral imperative of Progressives is to once again "set things right." In Marx's time this was the task of revolutionaries. Today this task falls to Progressive politicians and activists, social justice reformers, civil rights workers, cultural appropriation enforcers, diversity, and inclusion warriors and the like who have spread into the media, government, college campuses, neighborhood organizations and workplaces.

In the past, Marxist revolutionaries sought to set things right by leading a revolution to overthrow the capitalist system and replace it with a just economic system. Progressives want to set things right through social change in order to create a "just" society. In a just society everyone is equal: men and women, immigrants and native-born, persons of various racial and ethnic groups, heterosexuals, and homosexuals, first and third world people, disabled and able-bodied.

Progressives feel (and "feel" may be a more appropriate verb than "think") that because they want to do something that is so obviously good (i.e., help the poor, fight racism, climate justice, etc.), their policy recommendations must necessarily be the right and best solutions—and that anyone who disagrees with them is, a bad or hateful person.

Thus, for example, these naive U.S. Progressives are convinced that because they have good intentions, they can make Socialism work. They think socialism hasn't succeeded elsewhere because the leaders either didn't implement socialism thoroughly enough or because those leaders weren't good people.

Or, they champion the myth of Scandinavian "democratic socialism" as proof it can work—when in fact, it's a Progressive myth, false narrative, a hypocrisy—because these countries are just as capitalist as the USA but with larger welfare programs paid for by highly progressive tax rates. These Nordic countries are not socialist, but the ones who most certainly are, and have failed miserably across the world stage, are the Soviet Union, Cuba, Mao's China, North Korea, and most recently, Venezuela.

However, what the Soviet Union failed to do economically and militarily during its losing 20th-century confrontation with the West, cultural Marxism, by way of 21st century Progressivism, are coming closer to realizing the collapse of Western Civilization at the hands of young Progressives via the destruction of what the Russian communists used to refer to as the "principal enemy"—the United States.

Revolutionary Justice and the 'Progressive' Terror

Per the Harley Price "From Mao to Now: A 'Progress' Report on the New Millennium" *Epoch Times* December 2020 article:

Having inherited from their Communist totalitarian forbears the self-righteous certitude that they have proprietary rights to virtue and truth, contemporary Progressives continue to occult a Nietzschean will to power behind a nimbus of moral superiority. In the good old days of Lenin, Stalin, and Mao, non-conforming opinion was condemned as "bourgeois," "anti-revolutionary." Today, the enemies of "so-called" progress are denounced as "bigoted," "racist," "sexist," or "homophobic," and thereupon subjected to all the latest instruments of revolutionary justice from Generations X, Y and Z, the overwhelming demographic of Progressivism.

Non-Progressive opinion—i.e., any criticism of homosexuality, transgenderism, radical feminism, or Black Lives Matter—is criminalized as "hate speech;" ideological censorship is now euphemized as academic "trigger warnings," "speech codes," or Big Tech "fact-checking," or effected by political mobs who have exchanged the brown and black shirts of last century's utopian fanatics for the more fashionable hoodies and balaclavas of the millennial social justice movement.

Lenin's and Mao's paranoid loathing of the bourgeoisie, moreover, has once again mutated, as it did a century ago, from class hatred into race hatred, in the post-modernist diabolization of whites as the inheritors of "privilege," and along with it a collective guilt transmitted through the blood, demanding rituals of expiation. Whites are now considered the racial bogeymen responsible for the world's social and economic woes (as the Jews were for the National Socialists {Nazis}, who had learned from their communist tutors the political usefulness of scapegoating a collective enemy).

Who Are the Progressive Left?

Who are the Progressive Left? Answer: They are typically very liberal, highly educated, and majority White—and most say U.S. institutions need to be completely rebuilt because of racial bias per the Pew Research Center.

Reflecting their name, Progressive Left have very liberal views across a range of issues—including the size and scope of government, foreign policy, immigration and race. A sizable majority (79%) describe their views as liberal, including 42% who say their views are very liberal—double the share of the next largest group (20% of Outsider Left).

Roughly two-thirds of Progressive Left (68%) are White, non-Hispanic, by far the largest share among Democratic-aligned groups. Progressive Left are the second youngest typology group—71% are ages 18 to 49, primarily Gens X, Y and Z. Progressive Left are also highly educated, with about half (48%) holding at least a four-year college degree, making it one of the two most highly educated groups overall.

Their liberal outlook is not limited to issues related to the size and scope of government. Their views on race and racial equality also distinguish them from other typology groups: Sizable majorities say White people benefit from societal advantages that Black people do not have and that most U.S. institutions need to be completely rebuilt to ensure equal rights for all Americans regardless of race or ethnicity.

Progressive Left broadly support substantial hikes in tax rates for large corporations and high-income households. They are the only typology group in which a majority express positive views of political leaders who describe themselves as democratic socialists. And Progressive Left are more likely than any other typology group to say there are other countries that are better than the U.S.

Although they are one of the smallest political typology groups, Progressive Left are the most politically engaged group in the Democratic coalition. No other group turned out to vote at a higher rate in the 2020 general election, and those who did nearly unanimously voted for Joe Biden. They donated money to campaigns in 2020 at a higher rate than any other Democratic-oriented group.

Politically, the Progressive Left is overwhelmingly Democratic and nearly unanimous in their support for Joe Biden in 2020. Nearly all Progressive Left (98%) either identify with or lean toward the Democratic Party: 46% say they strongly identify with the party. About a third (32%) are independents who lean toward the Democratic Party.

To Understand and Oppose Progressivism Madness, Their Ideals Must be Clearly Identified

To understand and oppose the post-modernists (i.e., Progressives), the ideas by which they orient themselves must be clearly identified.

First is their new unholy trinity of diversity, equity and inclusion (DEI). Diversity is defined not by opinion, such as viewpoint heterodoxy, but by race, ethnicity or gender identity; equity is no longer the laudable goal of equality of opportunity, but the insistence on equality of outcome; and inclusion is the use of identity-based quotas to attain this misconceived state of equity.

All the classic rights of the West are to be considered secondary to these new values.

Take, for example, freedom of speech—the very pillar of democracy. The post-modernists refuse to believe that people of good will can exchange ideas and reach consensus.

Their world is instead a Hobbesian nightmare of identity groups warring for power. The Hobbesian Nightmare refers to a chaotic, conflict-torn society in which social strata are immersed in a self-centered perpetual antagonism that culminates in widespread violence in which the state apparatus fails to enforce law and order across its territory.

Second is rejection of the free market—of the very idea that free, voluntary trading benefits everyone. They won't acknowledge that capitalism has lifted up hundreds of millions of people so they can for the first time in history afford food, shelter, clothing, transportation—even entertainment and travel. Those classified as poor in the US (and, increasingly, everywhere else) are able to meet their basic needs. Meanwhile, in once-prosperous Venezuela—until recently the poster-child of the campus radicals—the middle class lines up for toilet paper.

Third, and finally, are the politics of identity. Post-modernists don't believe in individuals. You're an exemplar of your race, sex, or sexual preference. You're also either a victim or an oppressor. No wrong can be done by anyone in the former group, and no good by the latter. Such ideas of victimization do nothing but justify the use of power and engender intergroup conflict.

All these concepts originated with Karl Marx, the 19th-century German philosopher. Marx viewed the world as a gigantic class struggle—the bourgeoisie against the proletariat; the grasping rich against the desperate poor. But wherever his ideas were put into practice—in the Soviet Union, Cuba, Mao's China, Vietnam, and Venezuela, to name just a few—whole economies failed, and tens of millions were killed. We fought a decades-long cold war to stop the spread of those murderous notions. But they're back, in the new guise of identity politics.

The corrupt ideas of the post-modern neo-Marxists should be consigned to the dustbin of history. Instead, we underwrite their continuance in the very institutions where the central ideas of the West should be transmitted across the generations. Unless we stop, post-modernism will do to America and the entire Western world what it's already done to its universities.

You may not realize it, but you might be currently funding some dangerous people according to the Jordan Peterson "Who Is Teaching Your Kids?" Prager U video: Academia is indoctrinating young minds throughout the West with their resentment-ridden ideology. They have made it their life's mission to undermine Western civilization itself, which they regard as corrupt, oppressive and "patriarchal."

If you're a taxpayer—or paying for your kid's liberal arts degree—you're underwriting this gang of nihilists. Nihilism is a philosophy, or family of views within philosophy, that rejects generally accepted or fundamental aspects of human existence, such as objective truth, knowledge, morality, values, or meaning. Supporting ideologues who claim that all truth is subjective; that all sex differences are socially constructed; and that Western imperialism is the sole source of all Third World problems—is problematic.

Many academics and college faculty are post-modernists, pushing "Progressive" activism at a college near you. They produce the mobs that violently shut down campus speakers; the language police who enshrine into law the use of fabricated gender pronouns; and the deans whose livelihoods depend on madly rooting out discrimination where little or none exists.

Their thinking took hold in Western universities in the '60s and '70s when the true believers of the radical left became the professors of today. And now we rack up education-related debt—not so that our children learn to think critically, write clearly, or speak properly, but so they can model their mentors' destructive agenda.

Hate and Fear Are Now Major Motivators on Campus

Also per the Philip Carl Salzman "Hate and Fear Are Now Major Motivators on Campus" *Epoch Times* October 2022 report: Almost every university in North America has committed to what is called "social justice," which is the implementation of identity politics through the mechanisms of "diversity, equity, and inclusion." Identity politics divides everyone into one of two categories: evil oppressor or innocent victim.

Through official mandatory policies, universities have transformed academic culture from a quest to discover truth about the world and its beings, to the indoctrination of identity politics and enforcement of "social justice" policies.

In practice, this means the adoption of identity ideology to the exclusion and suppression of other views. An elaborate bureaucracy of "diversity and inclusion" officers are charged with policing thought, speech, and action. Activists, and those who support them, encourage active hate against their alleged oppressors: males, whites, Christians and Jews, heterosexuals, and cis-normal individuals.

How do we know this? Three ways: First, the vehement rejection of any criticism of or counter-argument to their neo-sexist/racist/bigoted ideological positions, and complete unwillingness to entertain any alternative position to their narratives. Second, the immediate use of the most hateful rhetoric imaginable to designate anyone challenging their position. Third, their immediate and unrestrained demands that the challenger be severely punished and preferably destroyed. Let us take these in order.

In response to any opinion contrary to their own, these activists do not offer counterarguments and contrary evidence. They do not claim that the facts are wrong or the position is untrue. No, they reject the opinion on identity grounds, saying that the challenge denies their existence as people, and that it makes them feel unsafe. Or just that it denies the truth of their sacred narrative, and that the complainant is therefore a heretic, any of whose words must be rejected.

The response on campus to this identity-fueled mob hate and its manifestation in attacks, condemnations, and cancellations is fear. Students fear bad grades if they do not repeat identity politics talking points, and they fear social isolation if they are attacked as enemies of "social justice." Professors fear both students and administrators, especially the "diversity and inclusion" officials whose job it is to weed out dissenters for re-education, punishment, and exile.

Self-censorship by college students is well documented in multiple surveys. A survey by the Foundation for Individual Rights and Expression (FIRE) reported that 83 percent engaged in self-censorship.

How far our colleges and universities have come! From open fellowships of research inquiry and intellectual exchange, they have become seminaries of true believers and doctrine enforcers. Identity politics has divided students, professors, and administrators into warring sexes, races, sexualities, genders, ethnicities, and ablenesses, and mandated hate between them. Admission and success, once based on academic achievement, merit, and potential, is now based on one's sex, race, sexuality, etc., and one's devotion to the identity politics "social justice" narrative. We have regressed from Enlightenment openness back to a Medieval religious order.

Safeguarding Our Republic From Progressivism Madness

From the Philip Carl Salzman "Safeguarding Our Republic From Progressivism Madness" *Epoch Times* October 2022 article: Radical activists now confront America with a host of unsapient policies, subversive activism, and false narratives like the 1619 Project, Black Lives Matter (BLM), and Critical Race Theory (CRT). The Progressives who champion these false and woke critiques threaten who we are as a nation, accompanied by equally radical proposals to remake our basic institutions.

Furthermore, the Progressive activists who lead these woke movements have targeted America's schools to impose a revolutionary transformation on our country and they also seek to transform the family, work, the marketplace, government, law, religion, entertainment, sports—all of American society with neo-Marxist ideologies. This cannot be allowed to happen and now is the time to wake up to this woke Progressivism madness before it's too late to stop it.

America is exceptional not least because of its long traditions of antislavery, abolition, and dedication to civic equality that transcends race. It is one of the least racist countries in the world and its citizens of all races have achieved extraordinary prosperity and liberty. The peoples of the world seek to become American because our nation offers opportunity to all. Woke radical activists must engage in hallucinatory defamation to erase these facts.

Shall We Surrender to Marxist CRT?

The Progressive activists who lead these movements have targeted America's schools as the means by which to impose a revolutionary transformation on our country. These activists believe not only that our schools are the linchpin of our apparatus of racial injustice and oppression but also the means by which to force their so-called "liberation" on America. They will seize our children's minds to seize America's future.

As previously noted, these radical activists seek to transform the family, work, the marketplace, government, law, religion, entertainment, sports—all of American society with neo-Marxist ideologies. Their proposals to accomplish this are sweeping. They include a call to establish "equity" that requires a quasi-totalitarian imposition of job quotas and the suppression of all opposing speech as part of Diversity, Equity, and Inclusion (DEI) programs.

But every such proposal is ultimately a plan to change the way Americans think. They require a transformation of our schools from places that teach students to seek out truth to places that teach students to seek out power so as to revolutionize America. No free people would accept the radicals' plans, so they wish to teach our children to embrace tyranny, by persuading them that tyranny is actually fairness or justice. How does this happen?

- They abuse the authority delegated to the schools to propagandize and coerce a captive audience, who must assent to indoctrination or risk all the damage to career prospects that follows from poor grades.

- They exploit the innocence and naiveté of the impressionable young Americans who are in no position to recognize the falsehoods and distortions embedded in these appeals.

- The proponents of neo-racism—to give this collection of radical critiques a unifying name—most of all wish to impose their theory as a curriculum.

- They intend to compel every person to study that curriculum, from early childhood education through high school, college, graduate study, vocational training, and on-the-job instruction.

Or Shall We Stand and Fight For Our Republic?

We approve wholeheartedly MLK's equality of opportunity—but oppose emphatically neo-racism's forced equity of outcomes (the "equity" portion of DEI) because we uphold the value of human freedom. Freedom is an intellectual as well as a political virtue: the freedom to think for oneself and the freedom of a people to govern themselves are distinguishable but interdependent. Intellectual freedom allows us to pursue the truth, which entails encountering and weighing the validity of conflicting views.

Political freedom is the attempt to frame laws and reach decisions through orderly and peaceful processes that give due weight to the many and often conflicting judgments of the governed. There can be no political freedom without intellectual freedom.

And yet this is exactly what neo-racism demands—the end of intellectual freedom. The proponents of so-called "Antiracism" state this most explicitly when they assert that anyone who dissents from their view that America is a systemically racist nation perpetuates racism and deserves to be silenced.

Neo-racism's proponents explicitly advocate for censorship. Their doctrines brook no disagreement, dissent, skepticism, or demand for evidence. Their position is that the only allowable intellectual position is enthusiastic assent to their dogma.

This sort of intellectual totalitarianism is not new. Neo-racism imitates the logic of Marxism, which uses opposition to its arguments to confirm them. Only a class traitor would doubt the necessity of the revolution. The same self-confirming circularity always accompanies movements that suppress intellectual and political freedom.

Only witches would doubt the prevalence of witches, and therefore the witch-deniers must be condemned as witches. Neo-racism at its core is yet another of the witchcraft hysterias that chronically afflict society. America has never been immune to these disorders. We feel ashamed when we awake from them, but we forget our better selves while we are in the midst of them.

Now is the time to wake up before we do even graver damage—not only to ourselves individually but to our country as a whole. It is a bitter irony of our moment that those who want to drive us into this new hysteria often claim to be "woke." There is no awakening in woke. It is the sleep of reason that produces monsters, and it poses a profound peril to our republic.

The Increasing Intolerance of the Left Must Stop

In the past decade, the Democratic Party has moved further and further to the Progressive left, while claiming the labels of diversity, inclusion and tolerance per the Bill Connor "The increasing intolerance of the left must stop" *Charleston Mercury* March 2023 story: Just more than a decade ago, Democratic candidates were not credible without voicing support for traditional marriage, as was the case with both Barack Obama and Hillary Clinton in the 2008 election.

The Democratic Party was solidly against words like "socialism," or of any support for defunding the police. As we have all seen in the recent election cycle, the party has morphed to the far Progressive left, both economically and socially. Although it continues to label itself the party of diversity, inclusion and tolerance, the reality is the opposite and must change. Let me explain.

Despite calls for national unity after many media outlets "called" the 2020 presidential election, Joe Biden's rhetoric was countered by the shrill calls from his party. For example, around the time of Joe Biden's "victory speech" (held before Trump's concession and while votes were being counted and legal challenges made) Rep. Alexandria Ocasio-Cortez tweeted a disturbing question: Whether or not someone was "archiving" Trump supporters to prevent them from being able to "downplay or deny their complicity" of their political support.

Immediately, a group called the "Trump Accountability Project" answering AOC and made clear the blacklisting of Trump supporters was well underway. This is a group, by the way, supported by Buttigieg and Obama aides. CNNs Jake Tapper warned Trump supporters that future "employers" would likely question their "character" for Trump support. "The View's" Sunny Hostin justified the blacklist because "past is prologue" and would not concede the obvious comparison of this to McCarthyism.

The primary means of intolerance of conservatism by the Progressive Left has taken the form of the ultimate stigma in modern America: Racism. Stigmatizing with the charge of racism has become ubiquitous from the Left. As Zachary Leeman has written: "They constantly slam the opposition as white supremacists, misogynists, fascists, etc. Even someone like rapper Ice Cube simply admitting to working with the administration on legislation to help black communities was enough to get him called a racist and labeled a Trump supporter."

Conservatives in Hollywood, like James Woods and others, have expressed how conservative politics have kept them out of certain jobs. As Leeman also wrote: "The president himself accused the industry of blacklisting conservatives after 'Will & Grace' stars Debra Messing and Eric McCormack demanded knowing who was attending a Hollywood fundraiser for the president."

Progressive Left have very cold feelings about Republicans

Average ratings for _____ on a 'feeling thermometer' from 0 (coldest) to 100 (warmest)

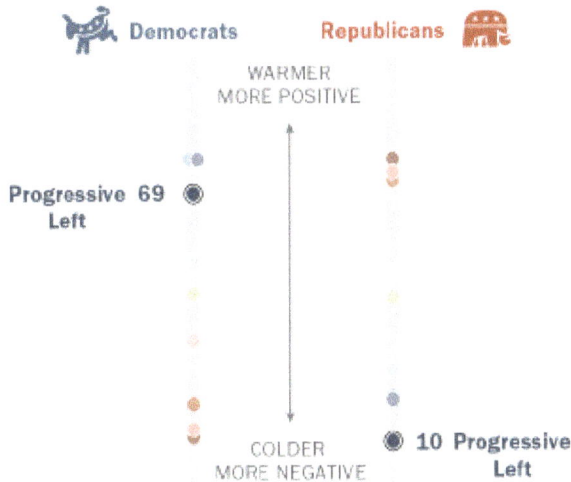

Democrats   Republicans

WARMER
MORE POSITIVE

Progressive 69
Left

10 Progressive
Left

COLDER
MORE NEGATIVE

Source: Surveys of U.S. adults conducted June 14-27 and July 8-18 2021.

PEW RESEARCH CENTER

In a twisted irony, the left has even begun to argue that silencing and blacklisting conservative viewpoints is part of creating a more tolerant, diverse and inclusive viewpoint. On our nation's campuses, silencing and ostracism of conservatives is rampant. As published in *Atlantic Magazine* in February 2020 (about the University of North Carolina): 68 percent of conservative students self-censor their conservative views due to fear of retribution (compared with under a quarter of liberal students).

More than six times more liberal students than conservative students agreed with shutting down speech students found objectionable. Better than eight times more liberal students than conservative students would refuse to be friends with someone across the political divide. Those numbers are worse at the elite Ivy League schools and across the nation's universities, intolerance of conservatism grown.

2 – How Woke Are America's High School, Community College & University Systems?

Credit: EAG.

Learning has been replaced by an aggressive political agenda designed to instill doubt, mental pain, and low expectations in students. According to government statistics, America's education system is failing. According to one expert, lower expectations and the shift in focus from academic excellence in mathematics, science, reading, and history toward the implementation of social constructs like critical race theory equals fewer literate graduates.

As noted by Thomas Sowell, a senior fellow at the Hoover Institution, Stanford University, decades of dumbed-down education no doubt have something to do with this, but there is more to it than that. Education is not merely neglected in many of our schools today, but is replaced to a great extent by ideological indoctrination. Moreover, it is largely indoctrination based on the same set of underlying and unexamined assumptions among teachers and institutions.

If our educational institutions—from the schools to the universities—were as interested in a "diversity of ideas" as they are obsessed with racial diversity, students would at least gain experience in seeing the assumptions behind different visions and the role of logic and evidence in debating those differences.

The failure of our educational system goes beyond what they fail to teach. It includes what they do teach, or rather indoctrinate, and the graduates they send out into the world, incapable of seriously weighing alternatives for themselves or for American society.

"Public records and other evidence show that state-level and some local education officials are no longer focused on maintaining high academic standards and providing the best public education possible to students," Liv Finne wrote in her September 2021 report regarding the lowering of academic standards by school officials in Washington state as they implement CRT.

"Instead, a concern for learning has been replaced by an aggressive political agenda designed to instill doubt, mental pain and low expectations in students. This race-centered agenda also seeks to divide children from teachers, their own communities and from each other. This harmful trend can only be resolved through policies that return high-quality academic standards to public education and well-funded and supportive education-choice programs that allow families to access alternatives services to meet the learning needs of all children."

Statistics Show America's Education System is Failing

Per the Patricia Tolson "Statistics Show America's Education System is Failing: CRT and Lower Expectation Equals Fewer Literate Graduates, Expert Says" *Epoch Times* article in January 2022:

Liv Finne, a former adjunct scholar now serving as Director of the Center for Education at Washington Policy Center, has been analyzing education policy for the past 13 years. Her research suggests the unmistakable decline in the literacy of America's students from fourth to twelfth grade is a direct result of the shift from academic excellence toward social constructs such as CRT.

"Internationally, we do pretty well at the fourth grade," Finne told *The Epoch Times*, "but we decline from there." Recent statistics support her claim.

Government data for 2019 shows the average fourth grader has a 41 percent proficiency level in mathematics. By the eighth grade, the proficiency level drops to 34 percent. By the twelfth grade, America's students have an average math proficiency level of only 24 percent. In reading, fourth graders have an average proficiency rate of 35 percent. By eighth grade, the proficiency level drops to 34 percent, and by the twelfth grade, America's average student shows only a slight proficiency improvement to 37 percent. In writing, the proficiency levels are 28 percent in fourth grade with eighth and twelfth graders sharing a score of 27 percent.

America's students fare worse in science, with fourth-graders having only a 36 percent proficiency rate and eighth-graders dropping to 35 percent. Twelfth-graders have only a 22 rate of proficiency in science. The worst scores come in history, with fourth-graders starting out with only 20 percent proficiency and dropping to 15 percent by the eighth grade. By grade 12, America's students have a paltry 12 percent proficiency level in history.

Recent numbers from USA Facts show similar results. According to Finne, there are a number of reasons for the steady decline in literacy among America's students the longer they remain in school. Number one is "the low expectations we have of our teachers."

Lowering the Academic Achievement Bar

Rather than develop curriculum that provides students with the qualifications needed to graduate high school, Liv Finne says the education system has opted to lower the bar of academic standards.

"They're lowering the bar in a couple of ways," Finne explained. "Like the Ethnic Studies framework passed by the State of Washington in 2019, critical race theory concepts are now woven into the learning standards of all of the different subjects."

As Finne explains, traditional educational standards have been reorganized into systems of oppression and the whole CRT construct—a "false philosophy from radical professors in higher education" is now being "imposed as the truth" in the standards of learning in K-12 schools.

"When you take attention away from the basics, and focus on teaching this ideology, you're going to get a lowered level of knowledge and skill acquisition of the basics in reading, math, history, and science; not to mention learning falsehoods in history like the 1619 Project," Finne insisted. "It's astonishing."

The Status Quo System

According to Liv Finne, the new push by the school system to abandon efforts of academic achievement and shift toward social constructs like CRT is an effort to hide the fact that they have failed in their jobs to educate our children.

"The whole idea is that if the community knew that their schools are not educating their children to basic levels they would rise up," Finne said. "Just look what's happening now with the uprising of parents against CRT in places like Loudoun County [Virginia] and they're still going forward with it. It's a huge uphill battle for parents."

"The whole system has promoted children whether they learn the content or not," Finne said. "So why should they care if a whole generation of children lost the content of a year (from the pandemic)? It's consistent with their practice. They do not individualize education. They don't make sure each individual child is ready to go on to the next grade. They move them along, especially minority children. The only people blocking real reform are the defenders of the status quo, the ones who like it just the way it is."

Teachers Unions are indeed the ones who fight against charter schools, school choice, and parental involvement and fought to keep kids out of classrooms during the COVID-19 outbreak. According to Finne, "if they really cared about black lives, they would be expanding their options for charter schools. But they're not. If these critical race theorists are truly intent on helping the children, they would be going after the unions. But they're not."

The Silver COVID-19 Lining

Ironically, Liv Finne believes the greatest hope for the education of America's children will rise from the ashes of the COVID-19 school lockdowns.

"The silver lining is we will eventually figure out how terrible it has been," Finne said. "Through the COVID shutdowns it has become clear how far behind so many kids are and the movements to expand school choice is not going away, because parents have woken up. That's what's so exciting about the COVID school shutdowns. Together with the takeover of the schools by this crazy critical race theory idea that children are bad and if they're white they're racist and if they're not white they're victims, that is going to lead to lawsuits.

"Maybe out of the ashes of this, school choice will arise," Finne opined of the educational chaos that ensued during the lockdowns. "This is still a democracy. The exchange of ideas is still happening in education because we do care about our children. That's what I'm hoping; that people will see the wisdom of giving parents real control, not just window dressing like involving parents and having parent involvement coordinators, but real control."

What Are Public Schools For?

From the Oren Cass "What Are Public Schools For?" *City Journal* article in December 2021:

Recent battles over racially divisive curricula prompted Virginia gubernatorial candidate Terry McAuliffe to remark, "I don't think parents should be telling schools what they should teach." But those battles, and the peculiar response that parents are best kept away from the process of educating their children, are signs of a much larger crisis. The gap in perspective between professional educators and the communities they serve about what public education is for has grown unsustainably large.

The gap is most evident, and costly, on the question of what outcome a good education should lead toward. For the current generation of reformers, the answer is simple: a college degree.

Embracing this college-for-all mentality, secondary schools have become college-prep academies held accountable to rigorous testing regimes and college-going rates, while policymakers have plowed hundreds of billions of dollars into subsidizing higher education. Leading proposals for "free college" and student-loan forgiveness reinforce those commitments.

American parents disagree. In partnership with YouGov, the organization, American Compass, surveyed 1,000 American parents with a child between the ages of 12 and 30 about their priorities for the public education system. We asked: Which is more important, helping students "maximize their academic potential and gain admission to colleges and universities with the best possible reputations," or helping them "develop the skills and values to build decent lives in the communities where they live?" By more than two to one, parents chose life preparation over academic excellence.

Uncommon for contentious issues in American life, this opinion holds across all the usual divisions. "Build decent lives" earns 68 percent among Democrats, 69 percent among Republicans, and 77 percent among Independents. It earns 68 percent among lower-class parents (defined by education level and income), 69 percent in the working class, 75 percent in the middle class, and 71 percent in the upper class; 68 percent with women and 74 percent with men, 76 percent with whites, and 63 percent with nonwhites.

Parents also express this view across various experiences for their own children. While having a child drop out of college is correlated most strongly with a preference for life preparation (79 percent), parents whose children have completed college still choose it over academic excellence 69 percent of the time. The preference also holds by similar margins regardless of whether parents report their children are "living the American dream," "getting by," or "struggling."

An optimistic educator might argue that developing the skills and values to build decent lives is what public schools already do, but parents would again disagree. Most rate their school system's performance as good or excellent at teaching students academic skills and engaging students in extracurriculars, but not on life preparation. In a parallel survey, young people aged 18–30 were even more frustrated with their schools' academic focus. They gave priority to life preparation by a four-to-one margin; fewer than one-third rated their school's performance on that task positively.

College isn't always the answer.

Parents and young people with recent experience in America's education system seem to understand something that the experts designing it do not: college isn't always the answer. Nationwide, only one in five young people moves smoothly from high school to college to career. Twice as many never enroll in college at all; twice as many enroll in college but drop out, or graduate into a job that doesn't require a degree.

The main constituency for the college fixation is Democrats with postgraduate degrees, who prefer the idea of full-tuition scholarships by more than two-to-one. Yet that perspective seems to dominate public debates. For all the political energy expended on college costs and college debt, meaningful non-college programs that would help students develop the skills to build decent lives in the communities where they live are scarce.

Most parents want options that meet the needs of their children; this means not only that high schools should cater to the majority of students who will not succeed in college, but also that public education should offer as much after high school to this non-college majority as it offers those fortunate enough to pursue a college degree.

In *The Making of Americans*, education scholar E. D. Hirsch observes that our tradition of public education began with an emphasis on "common knowledge, virtue, skill, and an allegiance to the larger community shared by all children no matter what their origin." Our schools were "the central and main hope for the preservation of democratic ideals and the endurance of the nation as a republic."

Today, they resemble strip-mining operations—serving the needs of the academically talented by extracting them from their hometowns to ivory towers in faraway lands from which they will never return. Some go on to run the education system and see nothing wrong with this state of affairs. For reformers to succeed in improving public education, they will need to remember what public education is for.

Universities Breed Anger, Ignorance, and Ingratitude

As per the Victor Davis Hanson "Universities Breed Anger, Ignorance, and Ingratitude" *National Review* article in October 2019:

In turning out woke and broke graduates, our higher education system has a lot to answer for like the question of: What do widely diverse crises such as declining demography, increasing indebtedness, Generation Z's indifference to religion and patriotism, static rates of home ownership, and a national epidemic of ignorance about American history and traditions all have in common?

Answer: 21st-century higher education.

A pernicious cycle begins even before a student enroll.

A typical college-admission application is loaded with questions to the high-school applicant about gender, equality, and bias rather than about math, language, or science achievements.

How have you suffered rather than what you know and wish to learn seems more important for admission. The therapeutic mindset preps the student to consider himself a victim of cosmic forces, past and present, despite belonging to the richest, most leisured, and most technologically advanced generation in history.

Without a shred of gratitude, the young student learns to blame his ancestors for what he is told is wrong in his life, without noticing how the dead made sure that almost everything around him would be an improvement over 2,500 years of Western history.

Once admitted, students take classes from faculty who, polls reveal, are roughly 90 percent liberal. According to one recent survey, Democrat professors on average outnumber Republican faculty by a 12-to-1 ratio on the nation's supposedly diverse campuses.

But such political asymmetries are magnified by a certain progressive messianic self-righteousness that turns the lectern into the pulpit, the captive class into a congregation. The rare conservative professor is more resigned to the tragedy of the universe and, in live-and-let-live fashion, vacates the campus arena to the left-wing gladiators who wish to slay any perceived heterodoxy.

Campus activism has replaced the old university creed of disinterested inquiry.

Students are starting to resemble military recruits in boot camp, prepping to become hardened social-justice warriors on the frontlines of America's new wars over climate change, gun control, abortion, and identity politics. In Camp Yale or Duke Social Warrior Base, they learn just enough about purported historical oppression to make them dangerous, as they topple statues, demand the renaming of streets and buildings, and swarm professors deemed politically incorrect.

No wonder that certain issues—abortion, global warming, illegal immigration— are mostly off-limits to campus disagreement. Safe spaces, racial theme houses, and censorship have replaced the 1960s ideals of unfettered free speech and racial and ethnic integration and assimilation.

Today's students often combine the worst traits of bullying and cowardice.

They are quite ready as a mob to dish it out against unorthodox individuals, and yet they're suddenly quite vulnerable and childlike when warned to lighten up about Halloween costumes or a passage in *Huckleberry Finn*. The 19-year-old student is suddenly sexually mature, a Bohemian, a cosmopolitês when appetites call—only to revert to Victorian prudery and furor upon discovering that callousness, hurt, and rejection are tragically integral to crude promiscuity and sexual congress without love.

The curricula in the social sciences and humanities are largely politicized.

Culture, history, and literature are often taught through the binary lenses of victims and victimizers, as a deductive zero-sum melodrama. There is little allowance for tragedy, irony, and paradox or simply the complexities of the human experience. That preexisting slavery, imperialism, and atrocity were as common in the New World, Asia, and Africa as in Europe is rarely mentioned in the boilerplate campus indictment of the West.

Regarding the cost of a university education, the federal government guarantees student loans to pay skyrocketing tuition, room, and board. That guarantee has empowered crony-capitalist universities to hike their annual costs far above the rate of inflation—without much worry over what happens to their customers when and if they graduate.

Eighteen-year-olds entering college are seldom warned by campus financial officers exactly how long their debt obligations will last—or which majors are likely to lead to better salaries after graduation. None are given itemized bills that are broken down to show where their money is going. Many who will remain in debt for years might have wished to know how much they paid for the vast swamp of non-teaching facilitators and high-paid administrators.

Colleges today can never assure students that after graduation they will at least test higher on the standardized tests than when they entered.

If colleges could do that, they'd long ago have required exit examinations to boast of their success. Instead, the higher-education industry insists that almost any baccalaureate degree is a good deal, without worrying about how much it costs or whether their brand certifies any real knowledge. Again, the logic is that of consumer branding—as we see with Coca-Cola, Nike, and Google—in which status rather than cost-benefit efficacy is purchased. Does anyone believe that a graduating senior of tony Harvard, Yale, or Stanford knows more than a counterpart at Hillsdale or St. John's?

The net result is the current generation that owes $1.6 trillion in college loans to the federal government. And that debt is now affecting the entire country, including those who never went to college, who as taxpayers eventually may be asked to forgive some if not all the debt. An entire generation of Americans has costly degrees; many cannot use them to find well-paying jobs, and they increasingly forgo or delay marriage, child-rearing, and buying a car or home until their mid-twenties or thirties. All that pretty much sums up the profile of Antifa, Black Lives Matter, and Occupy Wall Street adherents—or the environmental-studies major who is shocked that a skilled electrician makes three times more than he does.

Colleges are turning out woke and broke graduates.

They are not up to ensuring the country that they will pass on to the next generation an America that's as prosperous, secure, and ethical as what they inherited and have so often faulted.

Ignorance, arrogance, and ingratitude are now the brands of the undergraduate experience. No wonder a once duly honored institution, higher education, is now either the butt of jokes or cynically seen as a credentialing factory.

National Suicide by Education

Per the Philip Carl Salzman "National Suicide by Education" Minding the Campus story in September 2022:

It's true that children are our future, for good or ill, depending on their education. Ill-educate children, as we are doing in the United States and Canada, and the result will be cultural decay, social breakdown, and political decline.

We now teach our children that our country is illegitimate, based on genocide and racism, and is systemically evil. Will this lead the next generation to love or despise their country? Who will volunteer for the military, to risk their lives to protect their evil country? When generals assert that the military is racist and sexist, homophobic and transphobic, and harbors white supremacists and domestic terrorists, who will volunteer for the military, to risk their lives to protect their country? Recruitment for the military in both the United States and Canada is severely down, and no one can figure out how to increase it.

We teach our children that our society is divided between helpless victims and cruel oppressors. BIPOC (black, indigenous, people of color) and females are all and everywhere oppressed, and whites and males, Christians and Jews, and (astonishingly) Asians are privileged, evil villains. Children learn to fear and hate their fellow citizens of other races, sexes, religions, and ethnicities. What kind of society will we have when we teach children that race hatred, sexism, and ethno-supremacy are justified and virtuous?

Children are taught that speaking and writing correct English is racist, and so they must not learn correct English.

Math too is racist, when really, there are no correct answers, and to deny that two plus two can equal anything is oppressive. The demand for correct answers, logic, and scientific proof are sins of "whiteness" that must be eradicated from the socially just society. Thus, it isn't a weakness that American children perform poorly on international tests of reading, math, and science, but a demonstration of virtue, of social justice.

When schools teach the counterfactual lie that police every day murder innocent black and brown people, a lie refuted by every serious study, is it a surprise that police are viewed by black and brown children with fear and hatred? The constant insults and attacks on police by BIPOC children as well as adults are a predictable result of such inculcation. So too is the low morale of police in almost all urban jurisdictions, their unwillingness to engage in proactive policing, the flood of resignations, early retirements, transfers to rural jurisdictions, and suicides, and the lack of recruits to fill the large gaps in almost every urban police force. It's no surprise that the crime rate has shot up in every urban jurisdiction.

Race and gender disparities in academic participation and performance are explained by one and only one possible factor: racist and sexist discrimination. The other likely causes—family weakness in single-parent homes, community pathologies, and individual choices—may not be mentioned or investigated. In this way, disparities in participation or performance are deemed illegitimate, and therefore must be wiped out in order to achieve "equity," that is, equal results among census categories of the population, and "social justice."

Thus, poor performers are "victims," and measures must be taken to ensure that outcomes are the same.

This is done by giving preferences to underperforming BIPOC pupils and students, canceling accelerated programs for which they do not qualify, canceling examinations in which they do poorly, and setting aside performance standards. Programs in which females are underrepresented must prioritize recruiting females through special preferences and benefits.

BIPOC pupils and students are taught that their academic participation and performance is not their responsibility, but the responsibility of others who victimize them, and who owe them preference, benefits, and reparations. This is the perfect pedagogical plan for destroying individual motivation and a sense of responsibility. There's always someone else to blame.

In order to advance "equity," based on demographic "representation" of race, sex, ethnicity, etc., alternative criteria for judgment, such as individual achievement, merit, and potential, are denounced as, you know, "racist," and rejected. So recruitment to academia, science, media, professions, and government will be of the demographically underrepresented, not of the most capable candidates.

The foundation of this plan is the racism of low expectations, assuming that people from BIPOC categories could never make it on merit. This guarantees mediocrity or complete incompetence throughout our institutions: in medical care, scholarship and teaching, engineering, the press, law, and governance. The consequent trajectory is a societal decline and decay.

Female pupils and students are taught that they are being excluded due to sexist discrimination.

This counterfactual claim ignores the reality that females are the majority in universities and in most schools and programs. Those few programs where they are not, in spite of all of the heavy recruiting—physical sciences, mathematics, computer science—is a result of the choices of females who prefer to enter other fields. Yet females are continually told that they are victims of sexist discrimination. And male pupils and students are told that non-existent female victimhood is their fault.

Given the understanding that reason, logic, the search for evidence and correct answers, and science are taught as features of oppressive "whiteness," it should come as no surprise that schools discourage students from basing their understandings on scientific facts. A particular focus of teaching from kindergarten through graduate studies is the rejection of biology and its knowledge of biological factors in human life. Biological sex is now taught to be irrelevant to human life; the only thing that counts is one's feelings about gender.

Children are taught that they can be any of a hundred genders that they choose. Some teachers groom children to be supporters and "allies" of LGBTQ+, and to join in wherever they choose. Some children who are uncomfortable with their sex or confused about it are in some schools recruited into the trans community. Schools funnel pupils to sex transition clinics run by people, who still call themselves doctors, where children are subjected to life-changing chemical treatments and surgical mutilation in the futile effort to transform children from their biological sex to a replica of the other.

What devious force brought all of this cultural destruction into being?

Who injected this destructive poison into our educational system? The source, of course, is our universities. They were taken over by grievance studies advanced by various particular interest groups. First and most decisive were the feminists who established women's and gender studies to advance what they defined as the narrow interests of women.

They adopted the Marxist model of society divided into two warring classes; in place of the proletariat versus the bourgeoisie, they defined the conflicting classes as females versus the patriarchy, all men. The feminists inspired queer studies and LGBTQ+ activism. Black studies, Latinx studies, and Asian studies all championed their races in alleged conflict with the other races. Universities no longer were about what can we learn about the world and its people, but about what you could do through propaganda and activism to advance the narrow interests of your category.

All of these activisms were absorbed in social science and humanities programs, often by joint appointed professors with one or another grievance study. Administrators were either activists themselves or were won over and instituted "social justice" measures of "diversity, equity, and inclusion," hiring "diversity officers" to police the staff and students to ensure that no "wrong think" was allowed to flourish.

Faculties of education, being weak in academic content and lax in pursuing that, adopted grievance theory with a vengeance, and trained their students, the future school administrators and teachers, in the most radical forms of grievance activism. The faculties of education have contaminated our K-12 schools and made them what they are now.

3 – Academic Intellectual Diversity vs. Freedom of Expression

Apparently ideological "groupthink" isn't just confined to the student admissions process; it also appears to pervade the faculty hiring and tenure-granting processes as well. According to longitudinal nationwide data collected by UCLA's Higher Education Research Institute, a dramatic leftward shift in the composition of university faculty occurred between 1989 and 2014.

As far back as October 29, 2003, a special Senate report concluded after a hearing before the Committee on Health, Education, Labor, and Pensions, United States Senate, One Hundred Eighth Congress titled: *Is Intellectual Diversity an Endangered Species on America's College Campuses?* and was it becoming more scarce and beginning to lean heavily leftward.

Whereas progressives comprised roughly 40 percent of the professoriate in the late 1980s, they comprise 60 percent today. Moderates (at 28 percent) and conservatives (at twelve   percent) not only account for a smaller share of today's faculty, but conservatives have practically reached "endangered species" status (a mere five percent) in the humanities and social sciences.

There is no denying the left-leaning political bias on American college campuses. As data from UCLA's Higher Education Institute show, the professoriate has moved considerably leftward since the late 1980s, especially in the arts and humanities. In New England, liberal professors outnumber their conservative colleagues by a ratio of 28:1. This ratio is liberal madness!

Lack of Viewpoint Diversity in the Academy

Professors are getting more liberal

Ideology among college and university professors, 1990 – 2014

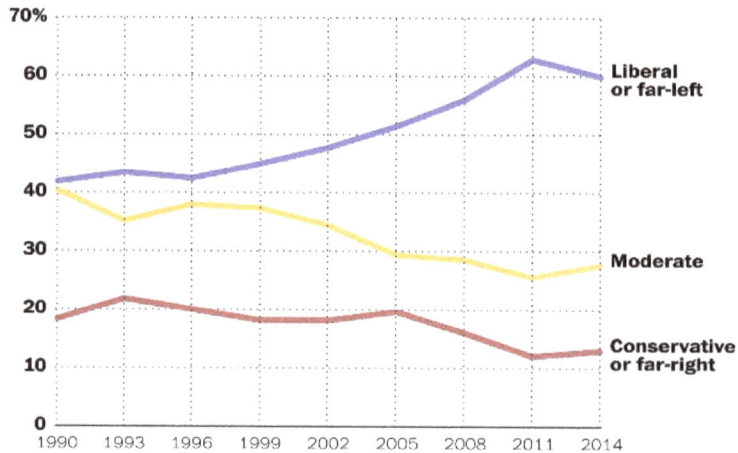

WAPO.ST/**WONKBLOG**   Source: Higher Education Research Institute

Growing skepticism about the current direction of American higher education isn't just found among those on the center-right. For example, a center-left New York University professor named Dr. Jonathan Haidt teamed with Greg Lukianoff, a former ACLU attorney who now heads the Foundation for Individual Rights and Expression (FIRE), to write a 2015 article for *The Atlantic* magazine entitled, "The Coddling of the American Mind." The essay, which became the second-most-cited article in the long history of *The Atlantic*, directed heavy criticism at "microaggressions," "safe spaces," "trigger warnings," "speech codes," and other attempts to narrowly define the boundaries of acceptable discourse in higher education.

In this chapter the focus is on academia's intellectual viewpoint orthodoxy which is mostly discriminating against conservative viewpoints. It's a growing problem and both the dramatic leftward shift in the composition of university faculty are interconnected and issues of enormous concern.

The leftward tilt of today's academic life hurts scholars–and would-be scholars–of a more conservative bent. Most all the modern arguments of progressivism, post-modernism, and the New Left fail the basic tenants of practical logic, common sense, and sapience.

Without viewpoint diversity and intellectual humility acting as the checks and balances essential to validate the academic standards, truth and logic behind new causes, issues, and programs can degrade and diminish and in turn academic and ideological orthodoxy become the norm with our academic institutions as well as the student bodies that determine the limits of free speech on campus.

Campuses that are overwhelmingly dominated by one ideological perspective are much more vulnerable to violations of free speech (and the embarrassing public relations problems that go with them) since the absence of viewpoint diversity can lead to the trampling of First Amendment rights. Put another way, free speech is more likely to be defended vigorously when more viewpoint diversity is present—the latter is perhaps the best guarantee of the former's defense.

Truth is a process, not just an end-state. *The Righteous Mind: Why Good People are Divided by Politics and Religion* is a 2012 social psychology book by Haidt, is about the obstacles to that process, such as confirmation bias, motivated reasoning, tribalism, and the worship of sacred values. Given the many ways that our moral psychology warps our reasoning, it's a wonder we've gotten as far as we have, as a species.

That's what's so brilliant about science: it is a way of putting people together so that they challenge each other and cancel out each other's confirmation biases and tribal commitments. The truth emerges from the interaction of flawed individuals.

The Dramatic Shift That's Hurting Students' Education

Something alarming has happened to the academy since the 1990s. As the graph below shows, it has been transformed from an institution that *leans* to the left, which is not a big problem, into an institution that is almost *entirely* on the left, which is a noticeably big problem. This phenomena are shown on the graph above and the one below.

If you've spent time in a college or university any time in the past quarter-century you probably aren't surprised to hear that professors have become strikingly more liberal. In 1990, according to survey data by the Higher Education Research Institute (HERI) at UCLA, 42 percent of professors identified as "liberal" or "far-left." By 2014, that number had jumped to 60 percent and represents a much higher percentage as opposed to the student body they teach.

Over the same period, the number of academics identifying as "moderate" fell by thirteen percentage points, and the share of "conservative" and "far-right" professors dropped nearly six points. In the academy, liberals now outnumber conservatives by roughly five to 1. Among the general public, on the other hand, conservatives are considerably more prevalent than liberals and have been for some time.

Students aren't as liberal as professors

Ideology among college freshmen, 1990 – 2014

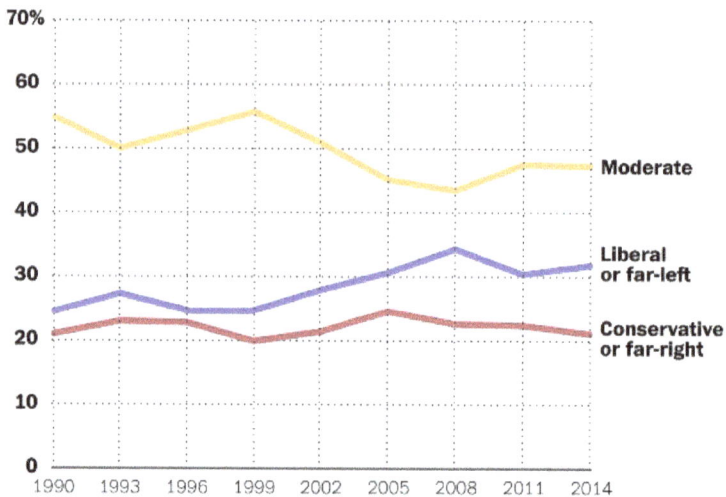

WAPO.ST/WONKBLOG   Source: Higher Education Research Institute

Nowadays there are no conservatives or libertarians in most academic departments in the humanities and social sciences. The academy has been so focused on attaining diversity by race and gender (which are valuable) that it has created a hostile climate for people who *think* differently.

The American academy has–arguably–become a politically orthodox and quasi-religious institution. When everyone shares the same politics and prejudices, the disconfirmation process breaks down. Political orthodoxy is particularly dangerous for the social sciences, which grapple with so many controversial topics (such as race, gender, poverty, inequality, immigration, and politics).

Can a Social Science That Lacks Viewpoint Diversity Produce Reliable Findings?

America needs innovative and trustworthy research on all these topics, but can a social science that lacks viewpoint diversity produce reliable findings?

But the folks that first put these numbers together, a group of academic faculty calling themselves Heterodox Academy, argue that homogeneity in higher education is a bigger problem than it is in other areas. "With relatively few right-leaning voices in the professoriate, particularly in the humanities and the social sciences where ideas matter most, many college students receive less than the intellectually rigorous education they deserve," some of the group's members recently wrote.

Dr. Samuel Abrams explored how the left-to-right ratio has increased over the past 25 years, particularly at colleges and universities in New England. He also reviewed work by Honeycutt and Freberg (2016) which suggested that conservatives experience a more hostile climate in academia than moderates or progressives.

A quarter-century ago, college professors were about sixteen percentage points more likely to identify as "liberal" or "far-left" than their first-year students. By 2014, professors were close to 30 percentage points more likely than freshmen to call themselves liberal.

Among the college class of 2009, 39.1 percent identified as liberals, 38.5 percent called themselves moderates, and 22.5 percent said they were conservatives. While more liberal and less conservative than the general public, the seniors were also considerably *less* liberal and *more* conservative than the people who taught them.

Faculty Voter Registration in Economics, History, Journalism, Law and Psychology

Recently, Mitchell Langbert, Anthony Quain, and Daniel Klein published their findings on faculty voter registration in the fields of economics, history, journalism, law, and psychology. Their work is now the most recent snapshot we have of the politics of American professors. This blog post briefly summarizes their methodology, findings, and conclusions.

To explore the politics of faculty members in the United States, Langbert, Quain, and Klein obtained the voter registrations of all faculty in five kinds of departments at 40 leading universities. Voter registration is public information and was obtained in this study through the Aristotle database. Due to differences in state policy over the storage of voter registration in a database such as Aristotle, their analysis was limited to universities within 30 states. Nonetheless, check out these disturbing findings:

- Registered Democrats outnumber registered Republicans in the academic departments of Economics, History, Journalism, Law, and Psychology. In most cases the discrepancies were higher than previously reported (see Klein & Stern, 2005; Klein & Stern, 2009).

- The discrepancy was lowest for Economics departments (4.5:1) and highest for History departments (33.5:1).

- A good number of departments have no registered Republicans.

- Discrepancies are higher at more prestigious universities.

- Assistant professors are least likely to be Republicans; thus, discrepancies are lower among older professors and among higher-ranked professors.

- Consistent with the findings of Abrams, discrepancies were higher at universities in New England.

- The overall ratio across all departments was roughly ten Democrats to one Republican.

- In total, Langbert et al. looked up the voter registration of 7,243 professors. They found 3,623 registered Democrats and 314 Republicans.

Increased Discrepancy Due to These Specific Mechanisms in Academia

Langbert et al. finds the overall ratio of registered Democrats to Republicans has increased over time, from roughly 3.5:1 in 1970 to roughly 8:1 in 2004 to roughly

10:1 in 2016. They further suggest that one of the reasons for this increased discrepancy may be due to three specific mechanisms present in academia:

1. Sacred values are likely to impact a given professor's political outlook. Typically, these values cannot be divorced from that professor's scholarship and may impact what is considered a worthy topic of study, what methods to employ in one's investigation, and how one interprets their findings. The role of sacred values makes groupthink theory applicable to the professoriate.

2. Academia is made up of distinct disciplinary pyramids that are sustained as departments within a university. The apex of these pyramids consists of the top departments for a given discipline. These departments typically produce most of the Ph.D.'s and then subsequently place those Ph.D.'s in other top departments.

3. The success of an individual research career is linked to one's department. The members of a department vote on who to hire, how much to pay that hire, and ultimately whether that new hire, if they accept the job, will be promoted, and receive tenure.

"Once the apex of the disciplinary pyramid becomes predominantly left leaning, it will sweep left-leaners into positions throughout the pyramid (or, at least, it will exclude vibrant dissenters). At the micro level of a particular university department—no matter where in the pyramid—once it has a majority of left leaners, it will, in serving, enjoying, protecting, advancing, and purifying sacred values, tend to hire more left leaners (or at least not vibrant dissenters)" (Langbert et al., 2016, p. 428).

The increasing sweep of left-leaners into positions throughout the pyramid is evident when, on the one hand, one considers that only ten universities had an overall ratio of Democrat to Republican of less than 9:1. On the other hand, fourteen universities had an overall ratio of Democrat to Republican of greater than 20:1.

The Discrepancy Between Democrats and Republicans at American Universities

The presence of the three prevalent mechanisms noted above continues to increase the discrepancy between Democrats and Republicans at American Universities.

One pundit on higher education has described our colleges and universities as islands of oppression in a sea of freedom. While the comment is humorous, the observation is quite serious. The lack of intellectual diversity on our college and university campuses is increasingly troublesome and of profound concern and interest to educators, next generation of leaders and the SAPIENT Being.

As early as 1991, Yale President Benno Schmidt warned that, "The most serious problems of freedom of expression in our society today exist on campuses. The assumption seems to be that the purpose of education is to induce correct opinion rather than to search for wisdom and liberate the mind."

In his last report to the Board of Overseers, retiring Harvard president Derek Bok similarly warned: "What universities can and must resist are deliberate, overt attempts to impose orthodoxy and suppress dissent. … In recent years, the threat of orthodoxy has come primarily from within rather than outside the university."

The American Council of Trustees and Alumni (ACTA) was founded in 1995 and is a bipartisan network of college and university trustees and alumni across the country dedicated to academic freedom and excellence. Since their founding, they've had occasion to evaluate colleges and universities in terms of academic freedom and academic offerings and what they discovered confirms these eminent university presidents' worst fears.

A Robust Exchange of Ideas is the Essence of a College Education

Rather than fostering intellectual diversity—the robust exchange of ideas traditionally viewed as the very essence of a college education—our colleges and universities are increasingly bastions of political correctness, hostile to the free exchange of ideas.

Threats to the robust exchange of ideas on our college and university campuses come in many forms, but typically manifest themselves in the following ways:

- Disinviting of politically incorrect speakers.

- Mounting of one-sided panels, teach-ins, and conferences.

- Sanctions against speakers who fail to follow the politically correct line.

- Instruction that is politicized.

- Virtual elimination of broad-based survey courses in favor of trendy, and often politicized, courses.

- Reprisal against or intimidation of students who seek to speak their mind.

- Political discrimination in college hiring and retention.

- Speech codes and campus newspaper theft and destruction.

Why Campus Concepts Creep to the Left

Nick Haslam's 2016 paper, titled "Concept Creep" shows that many concepts in psychology have changed over time (e.g., bullying, trauma, addiction). As reported by Conor Friedersdorf in the April 19, 2016 issue of *The Atlantic*, "Meanings shift so that these concepts apply to more phenomena and smaller phenomena."

He explains in more detail using Dr. Jonathan Haidt's 2015 paper, "Why Concepts Creep to the Left," that extends Haslam's analysis to explain why they change in one direction only: they "creep to the left." As psychology has become politically purified, its concepts have morphed to make them more useful to social justice advocates trying to prosecute and convict their opponents. This political shift poses a grave danger to the credibility of psychology.

In the process of writing a political diversity paper, Haidt learned that psychology is not unique in undergoing a political purification process with rising hostility toward political minorities. Most fields in the social sciences and humanities seem to be experiencing these trends (Klein & Stern, 2009).

As Friedersdorf reports in *The Atlantic*: Psychology (like almost all of the other social sciences and humanities) has a serious problem. Haslam (2016) has shown that their concepts are creeping to the left in ways that make psychology ever more appealing to the left and ever less appealing to the right. Haslam has shown that their membership is creeping to the left as well, as part of a broad national trend of rising affective polarization.

In brief, the loss of political diversity in many universities--and in psychology in particular--at a time of rising cross-partisan hostility has amplified the already powerful process of motivated reasoning. Concepts are morphing to become ever more useful to "intuitive prosecutors" (Tetlock, 2002) who are prosecuting their enemies in the culture war.

It's problematic when an academic field leans left, as psychology did before the 1990s. In a free society few fields will end up with perfectly proportional representation by politics, gender, race, or other criteria. As long as there are sure to be some conservatives (or women, or African Americans) to review papers, speak at symposia, and otherwise challenge the biases and prejudices of the dominant group, the scientific process of institutionalized questioning can function.

But when the ratio of liberals to conservatives rises above a certain point (Five-to one? Ten-to-one?) we get a phase change. People start to assume that everyone in the room shares their politics. They start making jokes, from the lectern, about conservatives. They create a hostile climate, and the few remaining non-liberals begin to hide their views. Non-liberal graduate students and assistant professors are particularly vulnerable to discrimination, as many have told Haidt (see their stories at Haidt, 2011).

The Heterodox Academy is a Champion of Viewpoint Diversity

Dr. Jonathan Haidt and two others founded Heterodox Academy in 2015 just before a wave of student protests at Yale and other schools increased pressures toward political orthodoxy. Heterodox Academy (HxA) describes itself as "a politically diverse group of social scientists, natural scientists, humanists, and other scholars" concerned about "the loss or lack of 'viewpoint diversity'" on campuses. As Haidt puts it: "When a system loses all its diversity, weird things begin to happen."

As Haidt explains in the rest of this section, in order to address society's most intractable problems, learners must weave together the best ideas from a range of perspectives, often times, called the marketplace of ideas.

In many fields, scholars' backgrounds and commitments are insufficiently diverse. As a result, important questions and ideas may go unexplored, key assumptions can go unchallenged, and the natural human tendencies towards motivated reasoning, confirmation bias, and tribalism can go unchecked. This undermines research quality and the impartiality of peer review; it can also corrupt committee decisions about admissions, hiring, promotion, and curriculum design.

Simultaneously, institutional policies, procedures and incentive models of colleges and universities are changing. The needs, priorities, and expectations among new cohorts of students are evolving—even as the political climate in the United States (and beyond) has grown increasingly polarized and toxic.

The result is a highly-combustible campus environment. Professors and students alike describe the toll self-censoring and the ever-present threat of social or bureaucratic censure have taken on learning, discovery, and growth.

These problems have not gone unnoticed by lawmakers, the media, or the general public. Many fields and institutions where these trends are most pronounced have faced declining enrollments and budget cuts. Meanwhile, trust in universities, expertise, and scientific research has eroded—reducing the impact and continued viability of many lines of inquiry.

What It Does and Why the Heterodox Academy Necessary

As a collaborative of academic insiders, the Heterodox Academy, led by President John Tomasi, D.Phil., is deeply committed to the continued flourishing of colleges and universities—and deeply concerned about the current state of affairs, which is not sustainable. They aspire to help chart a different path forward by:

- Increasing public awareness of these issues, to spur action among faculty, staff, students, alumni, and donors.

- Conducting, disseminating, and facilitating research to better understand the nature of the challenges facing institutions of higher learning—and how they can be effectively addressed.

- Developing tools and resources that professors, administrators, and others can deploy to assess and then improve their own pedagogical, disciplinary, and broader campus cultures.

- Cultivating communities of practice among teachers, researchers, and administrators to help accelerate the process of reform.

- Identifying and celebrating institutions that make progress on these matters.

Haidt (like the SAPIENT Being) is a non-partisan centrist, and genuinely concerned about the loss of viewpoint diversity in the academy. He believes the problem is amplified by the rising political polarization of the United States more generally. Haidt teamed up with two dozen professors in psychology and other disciplines (most of whom are not conservative) to make the case, consistently and forcefully, that the academy must increase viewpoint diversity in order to function effectively.

How Heterodox Is Your University?

The Heterodox Academy ratings reveal the good, the bad and the ugly about the intellectual diversity on 150 leading campuses and published a rating of the intellectual diversity and free speech friendliness of 150 of America's more prominent universities and colleges. The goal of the Heterodox Academy group is to find "ways of improving the academy by enhancing viewpoint diversity and the conditions that encourage free inquiry." The founding academicians of the Heterodox Academy all endorse this statement:

"University life requires that people with diverse viewpoints and perspectives encounter each other in an environment where they feel free to speak up and challenge each other. I am concerned that many academic fields and universities currently lack sufficient viewpoint diversity—particularly political diversity. I will support viewpoint diversity in my academic field, my university, my department, and my classroom."

Why Does This Matter?

Most people know that professors in America, and in most countries, generally vote for left-leaning parties and policies. But few people realize *just how fast things have changed since the 1990s*. An academic field that leans left (or right) can still function, as long as ideological claims or politically motivated research is sure to be challenged.

But when a field goes from leaning left to being entirely on the left, the normal safeguards of peer review and institutionalized disconfirmation break down. Research on politically controversial topics becomes unreliable because politically favored conclusions receive less-than-normal scrutiny while politically incorrect findings must scale mountains of motivated and hostile reasoning from reviewers and editors.

When it comes to measuring the true quality of a learning institution, conventional measures of academic quality are relatively useless if the intellectual life of the university is skewed in a manner that (intentionally or unintentionally) suppresses unfashionable ideas and alternative points of view.

Countering campus "groupthink" is part of what led to the creation of Heterodox Academy. "When nearly everyone in a field shares the same political orientation, certain ideas become orthodoxy, dissent is discouraged, and errors can go unchallenged," they write.

President Roth Calls on Universities to Promote Intellectual Diversity

On May 11, 2017, Wesleyan President Michael Roth's statement about heterodoxy was published in *The Wall Street Journal* regarding the need for colleges and universities to proactively cultivate intellectual diversity on campus. While student protests over controversial speakers have dominated headlines of late, he writes:

The issue, however, isn't whether the occasional conservative, libertarian or religious speaker gets a chance to speak. That is tolerance, an appeal to civility and fairness, but it doesn't take us far enough. To create deeper intellectual and political diversity, we need an affirmative-action program for the full range of conservative ideas and traditions, because on too many of our campuses they seldom get the sustained, scholarly attention that they deserve.

Our present political circumstances should not prevent us from engaging with a variety of conservative, religious, and libertarian modes of thinking, just as they shouldn't prevent us from engaging with modes of thinking organized under the banner of progressivism or critical theory. Such engagement might actually lead to greater understanding among those who disagree politically, and it might also allow for more robust critical and creative thinking about our histories, our present and the possibilities for the future.

.

4 – Campus Illiberalism & Intolerance vs. Freedom of Speech & Viewpoint Heterodoxy

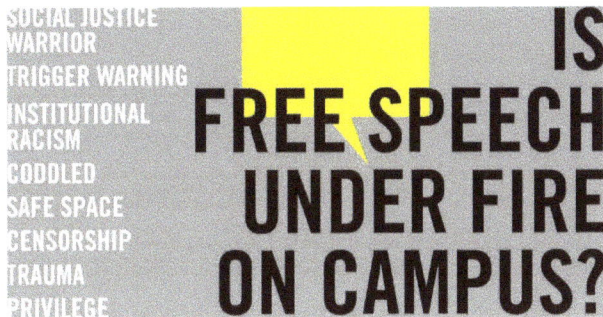

Credit: A Moment Symposium.

Webster's Dictionary defines illiberalism as "opposition to or lack of liberalism." In popular usage, the word is used to describe an attitude that is close-minded, intolerant, and bigoted. Furthermore, from *Free Speech Madness: A SAPIENT Being's Guide to the War Against Truth, Conservative Ideals & Freedom of Speech:*

The pursuit of knowledge and the maintenance of a free and democratic society require the cultivation and practice of the virtues of intellectual humility, openness of mind, and, above all, love of truth. These virtues will manifest themselves and be strengthened by one's willingness to listen attentively and respectfully to intelligent people who challenge one's beliefs and who represent causes one disagrees with and points of view one does not share.

That's why all of us should seek respectfully to engage with people who challenge our views. And we should oppose efforts to silence those with whom we disagree—especially on college and university campuses. As John Stuart Mill taught, a recognition of the possibility that we may be in error is a good reason to listen to and honestly consider—and not merely to tolerate grudgingly—points of view that we do not share, and even perspectives that we find shocking or scandalous.

All of us should be willing—even eager—to engage with anyone who is prepared to do business in the currency of truth-seeking discourse by offering reasons, marshaling evidence, and making arguments. The more important the subject under discussion, the more willing we should be to listen and engage—especially if the person with whom we are in conversation will challenge our deeply held— even our most cherished and identity-forming—beliefs.

Intolerance as Illiberalism

"We live in intolerant times" notes Dr. Kim R. Holmes of The Heritage Foundation from his 2014 article in Public Discourse "Intolerance as Illiberalism." All across America, this illiberal mindset is spreading, corrupting our culture and our politics. It is evident in the mendacity with which opposing opinions are attacked and in the way that state and federal governments conduct their business.

This mindset turns ideas like tolerance and liberalism on their heads. It weakens the checks and balances that have long protected our rights and freedoms. As a result, illiberalism threatens not only the social peace of our country, but the very future of freedom and democracy in America. We ignore this growing phenomenon at our peril.

It's all-too-common these days for people to try to immunize themselves from criticism opinions that happen to be dominant in their particular communities. Sometimes this is done by questioning the motives and thus stigmatizing those who dissent from prevailing opinions; or by disrupting their presentations; or by demanding that they be excluded from campus or, if they have already been invited, disinvited.

Sometimes students and faculty members turn their backs on speakers whose opinions they don't like or simply walk out and refuse to listen to those whose convictions offend their values. Of course, the right to peacefully protest, including on campuses, is sacrosanct. But before exercising that right, each of us should ask: Might it not be better to listen respectfully and try to learn from a speaker with whom I disagree? Might it better serve the cause of truth-seeking to engage the speaker in frank civil discussion?

The Culture of Illiberalism

The S.A.P.I.E.N.T. Being's *Free Speech Madness: A SAPIENT Being's Guide to the War Against Truth, Conservative Ideals & Freedom of Speech* has shown the roots of modern American illiberalism lie in the trauma experienced by liberals in the 1960s. The rise of the New Left and its sister movement, the Counter-Culture, changed how liberals viewed not only culture but also politics. As described in *Rebound: Getting America Back to Great*, by Dr. Kim R. Holmes, rebellion for New Left liberals moved beyond mere economic class issues to ones involving gender, sex, and race.

Politics became cultural, and Marxist assumptions about the irreconcilability of class conflict were transferred to the culture wars over gender, race, and sexual identity. Channeling the ideas of philosopher Herbert Marcuse, the New Left dismissed old-fashioned liberalism that preached individualism and moral responsibility as "repressive tolerance." Liberation focused now on groups, not on individuals, and dissent was seen not as an individual right of conscience, but as a political weapon to overthrow traditional morality.

Since the 1960s, the radical egalitarianism of the New Left has fused with traditional progressive ideas about state and society. Feminism is no longer about giving women equal political and legal rights—it's about confronting the male power structure and the "rape" culture. Fighting racism is no longer about ensuring that African-Americans and minorities are treated equally before the law—it's about eradicating "systemic" racism and promoting affirmative action. Environmentalism is no longer about conserving natural resources—it's about "saving" the planet from overpopulation and climate change.

With such utopian causes, it seems perfectly acceptable to "break a few eggs" to make a new liberal omelet.

Traditional American Liberalism Has Changed in Three Important Ways

The first change involves the understanding of tolerance. The old Jeffersonian notion, rooted in debates over religious freedom, holds that individual conscience is sacrosanct. This has given way to the notion that certain ideas (e.g., racism or sexism) are so heinous that no one should be allowed to hold, much less express, any idea about race or women or sexuality that proponents believe is socially oppressive. In other words, intolerance is now seen as a good thing—if it serves the purpose of a certain definition of social liberation.

The second change involves the idea of dissent. Historically, respect for dissent had its roots in debates over religious freedom and freedom of conscience. But the New Left took an entirely different view of dissent. Rather than an expression of individual conscience, dissent was now seen as a weapon to overthrow the old order. The end justified the means. It was perfectly justifiable, according to the New Left, to shut out the views of the ruling class, defined now along race, gender, and sexual orientation lines.

The third idea that has undergone a radical change is our conception of virtue. Historically, virtue has been understood as a positive habit that forms one's personal character. In this view, one acquires virtue by repeatedly choosing to treat others well and act in accord with objective standards of morality, even when it is difficult.

Today, people who see themselves as "liberal-minded" have come to justify the most illiberal of ideas—namely, curbing freedom of expression and using the power of the state to deny equal rights to Americans with whom they disagree.

Modern liberalism thus does not merely flirt with intolerance. It is now fundamentally based on it. And that is largely because it has become accepted by the culture as a good thing to employ in the service of a cause you believe in. Whatever you may call this new American culture, you cannot call it liberal, for tolerance is the acid test of true liberalism.

This is where the culture stands today. The thinkers of the New Left infect it with illiberal values consciously designed to destroy classic liberalism. It may be true that illiberalism always lurked on the edges of American progressivism in the various ideologies associated with socialism.

But for most of history, progressives had tried to keep their distance from the more blatantly illiberal values of the far Left. That resistance started breaking down in the sixties. As a result, American liberalism today has a decidedly illiberal wing eating away at its purported core values.

Free Speech Zone Policies

Free speech zones have repeatedly been struck down by courts or voluntarily revised by colleges as part of settlements to lawsuits brought by students. The

FIRE's Stand Up For Speech Litigation Project has included successful challenges to free speech zone policies at eight colleges and universities and includes an ongoing challenge to a free speech zone policy at Pierce College in Los Angeles.

Additionally, state legislatures have continued to take action to prohibit public colleges and universities from maintaining free speech zones. Currently, twelve states have enacted laws prohibiting these restrictive policies: Virginia, Missouri, Arizona, Kentucky, Colorado, Utah, North Carolina, Tennessee, Florida, Georgia, Louisiana and Alabama.

Based on the Campus Free Expression (CAFE) Act model legislation from the FIRE, Florida's bill, which was signed into law in March 2018, states:

A person who wishes to engage in an expressive activity in outdoor areas of campus may do so freely, spontaneously, and contemporaneously as long as the person's conduct is lawful and does not materially and substantially disrupt the functioning of the public institution of higher education or infringe upon the rights of other individuals or organizations to engage in expressive activities … A public institution of higher education may not designate any area of campus as a free-speech zone or otherwise create policies restricting expressive activities to a particular area of campus …

The law also provides a right to sue a public institution of higher education in Florida if the institution violates the expressive rights guaranteed by the law.

Furthermore, the Student Press Law Center (SPLC) has worked to support, promote and defend the First Amendment and freedom of expression rights of student journalists at the high school and college level, and the advisers who support them. Working at the intersection of law, journalism and education, SPLC runs the nation's only free legal hotline for student journalists.

Universities Must Choose One Telos: Truth or Social Justice

On the Heterodox Academy website, Dr. Jonathan Haidt explains eloquently why universities must choose one telos: truth or social justice. Furthermore, he elaborates that Aristotle often evaluated a thing with respect to its "telos"—its purpose, end, or goal. The telos of a knife is to cut. The telos of a physician is health or healing. What is the telos of university?

The most obvious answer is "truth"—the word appears on so many university crests. But increasingly, many of America's top universities are embracing social justice as their telos, or as a second and equal telos. But can any institution or profession have two teloses (or teloi)? What happens if they conflict?

Haidt believes that the conflict between truth and social justice is likely to become unmanageable. Universities will have to choose, and be explicit about their choice, so that potential students and faculty recruits can make an informed choice. Universities that try to honor both will face increasing incoherence and internal conflict.

To further illuminate his point, consider two quotations:

The philosophers have only interpreted the world, in various ways; the point is to change it.– Karl Marx, 1845

He who knows only his own side of the case knows little of that. His reasons may be good, and no one may have been able to refute them. But if he is equally unable to refute the reasons on the opposite side, if he does not so much as know what they are, he has no ground for preferring either opinion...– John Stuart Mill, 1859

As Haidt puts it: Marx is the patron saint of what he calls "Social Justice U," which is oriented around changing the world in part by overthrowing power structures and privilege. It sees political diversity as an obstacle to action.

Mill is the patron saint of what he calls "Truth U," which sees truth as a process in which flawed individuals challenge each other's biased and incomplete reasoning. In this process, all become smarter. However, Truth U dies when it becomes intellectually uniform or politically orthodox.

One Telos: Truth or Social Justice?

Truth is paramount to sapience, and the antithesis to sapience is modern progressivism. Not only does progressivism deny commonly held truths across all cultures of the world, today's progressivism has evolved to many degrees into a twentieth century version of Marxism lite—without the horrific calories of human sacrifice, failed regimes, and economic ruin.

When progressivism madness is incubated in the right condition on campus, illiberalism will follow, and when illiberalism follows, so do social justice warriors and campus radicals. Put simply enough by Haidt, "no university can have Truth and Social Justice as dual teloses. Each university must pick one.

Say NO to Campus Mob Fascism With the Chicago Statement

In response to the Berkeley riot incident in 2017, the Foundation for Individual Rights in Education (FIRE) issued this statement:

No university may be considered "safe" if speakers voicing unpopular ideas on its campus incur a substantial risk of being physically attacked. A university where people or viewpoints are likely to be opposed with fists rather than argumentation is unworthy of the name. Granting those willing to use violence the power to determine who may speak on campus is an abdication of UC Berkeley's moral and legal responsibilities under the First Amendment.

Strong-arming one's belief onto others is just a form of mob fascism—no matter what side of a political spectrum you are coming from. If the Chicago Principles support allowing any invited speaker, as the statement does, then great. We must value our wonderful educational space, framed by laws and policies on one side and supported by documents like the Chicago Principles on the other. We need students to feel free to offer any viewpoint and likewise to offer any challenge, both within the context of our curriculum and on campus, to open up a discourse, and to learn from the engagement.

Let's underscore that point at the beginning: the Chicago Principles envision and protect both controversial viewpoints and protests against those viewpoints, with the proviso that protesters "may not obstruct or otherwise interfere with the freedom of others to express views they reject or even loathe."

Any statement or policy that supports students' freedom of speech rights is welcomed. Below is an excerpt from the Chicago Statement as a reference if there is ever a question or push-back about allowing a controversial speaker on campus because someone finds some topic of inquiry distasteful.

"Because the University is committed to free and open inquiry in all matters, it guarantees all members of the University community the broadest possible latitude to speak, write, listen, challenge, and learn . . . . [I]t is not the proper role of the University to attempt to shield individuals from ideas and opinions they find unwelcome, disagreeable, or even deeply offensive."

The "Chicago Statement" refers to the free speech policy statement produced by the Committee on Freedom of Expression at the University of Chicago. In July of 2014, University of Chicago President Robert J. Zimmer and Provost Eric D. Isaacs tasked the Committee with "articulating the University's overarching commitment to free, robust, and uninhibited debate and deliberation among all members of the University's community." The Committee, which was chaired by esteemed University of Chicago Law School professor Geoffrey Stone, released the report in January of 2015.

Here are several tips for ensuring that your university will be the next institution to stand in solidarity with the Chicago Statement's principles:

- Work to pass a student government resolution calling on the university to adopt its own version of the Chicago Statement.

- Reach out to faculty members and work with faculty governing bodies on campus.

- Build a broad coalition of students and groups, particularly across the ideological spectrum, to support the Chicago Statement and raise awareness on campus.

- Publish articles and op-eds in student newspapers and other outlets.

- Host events on campus, such as debates, speakers, and panels to discuss the principles supported by the Chicago Statement.

- Communicate and collaborate with members of your university's administration.

- Host a petition drive, asking students to pledge their support for the Chicago Statement's principles in a petition that will go to the administration.

Why Today's Students Are Less Tolerant Than Before

The resurgence of influence of Herbert Marcuse's New Left, who argued in the 1960s that true "liberating" tolerance requires suppressing all non-progressive voices is problematic with Millennials and college students. April Kelly-Woessner shows the big split in American opinion on matters of free speech:

Millennials, Zillennials and college students embrace Marcusian ideals much more than did previous generations, and it is this moralistic illiberalism that leads to the witch-hunts and ultimatums that are sweeping across American college campuses since Halloween 2015.

Millennials Are Less Politically Tolerant Than Their Parents

First, Kelly-Woessner makes the case that young people are less politically tolerant than their parents' generation and that this marks a clear reversal of the trends observed by social scientists for the past 60 years. Political tolerance is generally defined as the willingness to extend civil liberties and basic democratic rights to members of unpopular groups.

Second, Kelly-Woessner argues that youthful intolerance is driven by different factors than old fashioned intolerance, and that this change reflects the ideology of the New Left. Herbert Marcuse considered "The Father of the New Left," articulates a philosophy that denies political expression to those who would oppose today's progressive social agenda. In his 1965 essay "Repressive Tolerance," Marcuse (1965) writes:

"Tolerance is extended to policies, conditions, and modes of behavior which should not be tolerated because they are impeding, if not destroying, the chances of creating an existence without fear and misery. This sort of tolerance strengthens the tyranny of the majority against which authentic liberals protested… Liberating tolerance, then, would mean intolerance against movements from the Right and toleration of movements from the Left."

The Orwellian Argument of Liberating Tolerance

The idea of "liberating tolerance" then is one in which ideas that the left deems to be intolerant are suppressed. It is an Orwellian argument for an "intolerance of intolerance" and it appears to be gaining traction in recent years, reshaping our commitments to free speech, academic freedom, and basic democratic norms.

If we look only at people under the age of 40, intolerance is correlated with a "social justice" orientation. That is, I find that people who believe that the government has a responsibility to help poor people and blacks get ahead are also less tolerant. Importantly, this is true even when we look at tolerance towards groups other than blacks. For people over 40, there is no relationship between social justice attitudes and tolerance. I argue that this difference reflects a shift from values of classical liberalism to the New Left.

For older generations, support for social justice does not require a rejection of free speech. Thus, this tension between leftist social views and political tolerance is something new.

Third, Kelly-Woessner states that intolerance itself is being reclassified as a social good. For six decades, social scientists have almost universally treated intolerance as a negative social disease. Yet now that liberties are surrendered for equality rather than security, the Left seems less concerned about the harmful effects of intolerance. In fact, they have reframed the concept altogether. For example, political scientist Allison Harell (2010) uses the term "multicultural tolerance," which she defines as the willingness to "support speech rights for objectionable groups" but not for "groups that promote hatred."

In other words, multicultural tolerance allows individuals to limit the rights of political opponents, so long as they frame their intolerance in terms of protecting others from hate. This is what Marcuse refers to as "liberating tolerance."

In fact, the idea that one should be "intolerant of intolerance" has taken hold on many college campuses, as exemplified through speech codes, civility codes, and broad, sweeping policies on harassment and discrimination. Students now frequently lead protests and bans on campus speakers whom they believe promote hate.

While this may have the effect of creating seemingly more civil spaces, it has negative consequences. In fact, tolerance for all groups is positively correlated. It is not simply the fact that leftists oppose the expression of right-wing groups. Rather, those who are intolerant of one group tend to be intolerant of others and of political communication in general.

When colleges fail to represent the full measure of political ideas, students are less likely to learn to tolerate those unlike themselves. This combined with the New Left's legacy of "liberating tolerance," creates an environment that values anger and orthodoxy over inquiry, debate and viewpoint diversity.

Laying Siege to the Institutions

The lesson we've drawn from reporting on institutions that promote ideologies such as critical race theory and radical gender theory is that they have been captured at the structural level and can't be reformed from within. So the solution is not a long counter-march through the institutions. You can't replace bad directors of diversity, equity, and inclusion with good ones. The ideology is baked in. That's why we call for a siege strategy.

As laid out by Christopher F. Rufo's "Laying Siege to the Institutions" *Imprimis* April/May 2022 Volume 51, Issue 4/5 report:

This means, first, that you have to be aggressive. You have to fight on terms that you define. In responding to opponents of the Florida bill, for instance, don't argue against "teaching diversity and inclusion," but against sexualizing young children. And don't pull your punches. We will never win if we play by the rules set by the elites who are undermining our country. We can be polite and lose every battle or we can be impolite and actually deliver results for the great majority of Americans who are fighting for their small businesses, fighting for their jobs, fighting for their families.

Second, you have to mobilize popular support. This requires ripping the veil off of what our institutions are doing through real investigation and reporting so that Americans can make informed choices. We live in an information society, and if we don't get the truth out, we will never gain traction against the narratives being constantly refashioned and pushed by the Left.

Less than two years ago, an infinitesimal number of Americans knew about critical race theory. Through investigation and reporting, we've brought that number up to 75 percent. The public now opposes critical race theory by a two-to-one margin, and it is being hounded out of schools and other places. This kind of action is a model for dealing with every ideology and institution that is undermining the public good and America's future.

Remember that institutions don't choose these ideologies democratically—they don't ask people or employees to vote for them. They impose them by fiat, through bureaucratic, not democratic rule. So it isn't surprising that the institutions lose big when we force their agendas into the political arena. What politician or campaign manager in their right mind would ignore an issue that is supported by a two-to-one margin? So-called conservative politicians who do ignore such issues—or who oppose bringing them up out of a false sense of decorum—aren't on the people's and the country's side.

With public institutions like K-12 education, another crucial step is to decentralize them. It is centralization and bureaucratization that makes it possible for a minority of activists to take control and impose their ideologies. Decentralizing means reducing federal and state controls in favor of local control—and it ultimately means something like universal school choice, placing power in parents' hands. Too many parents today have no escape mechanism from substandard schools controlled by leftist ideologues. Universal school choice—meaning that public education funding goes directly to parents rather than schools—would fix that.

Conservatives have for too long been resistant to attacking the credibility of our institutions. Trust in institutions is a natural conservative tendency. But conservatives need to stop focusing on abstract concepts and open their eyes. Our institutions are dragging our country in a disastrous direction, actively undermining all that makes America great.

To some extent, the institutions are now destroying their own credibility. Look at the public health bureaucracy and teachers' unions, which acted in concert to shut down schools and keep children needlessly masked—and for far too long. As a result, there has been an explosion in homeschooling, as well as in the number of alternative K-12 schools such as the ones Hillsdale College is helping to launch around the country. What is needed is to build alternative or parallel institutions and businesses in all areas. There is no reason, for example, why plenty of high production value children's entertainment can't be produced outside the ideological confines of the Walt Disney Company.

5 – The Rise of Academia, Mainstream & Social Media Illiberalism & Intolerance

Credit: Reuters.

The pursuit of knowledge and the maintenance of a free and democratic society require the cultivation and practice of the virtues of intellectual humility, openness of mind, and, above all, love of truth. These virtues will manifest themselves and be strengthened by one's willingness to listen attentively and respectfully to intelligent people who challenge one's beliefs and who represent causes one disagrees with and points of view one does not share.

That's why all of us should seek respectfully to engage with people who challenge our views. And we should oppose efforts to silence those with whom we disagree—especially on college and university campuses. As John Stuart Mill taught, a recognition of the possibility that we may be in error is a good reason to listen to and honestly consider—and not merely to tolerate grudgingly—points of view that we do not share, and even perspectives that we find shocking or scandalous.

None of us is infallible. Whether you are a person of the left, the right, or the center, there are reasonable people of goodwill who do not share your fundamental convictions. This does not mean that all opinions are equally valid or that all speakers are equally worth listening to. It certainly does not mean that there is no truth to be discovered. Nor does it mean that you are necessarily wrong. But they are not necessarily wrong either.

"The person you are now only exists because the person you were was willing to grow into something new." - John Templeton.

All of us should be willing—even eager—to engage with anyone who is prepared to do business in the currency of truth-seeking discourse by offering reasons, marshaling evidence, and making arguments. The more important the subject under discussion, the more willing we should be to listen and engage—especially if the person with whom we are in conversation will challenge our deeply held— even our most cherished and identity-forming—beliefs.

Consider These Disturbing Trends

Given the current undergraduate tendency toward intellectual orthodoxy, one wonders: Would the advances of the feminist movement even have happened, had the campus conformists of a half-century ago had their way?

- A recent study found that 68 percent of college students "largely agree" the campus climate today prevents some of them from speaking their minds for fear of offending someone.

- In a 2016 Gallup survey, one in four college students felt their schools should be able to restrict students from "expressing political views that are upsetting or offensive to certain groups."

- Shockingly, the Foundation for Individual Rights and Expression (FIRE, for short) rated the level of freedom of speech permitted at 466 major universities in America. They found that 19 percent received a "red light' rating, 68 percent a "yellow light" rating, and only 13 percent received a "green light" rating.

Regarding the lack of viewpoint diversity needed to burst the prevailing ideological bubbles on campus, consider these alarming statistics:

- More than 50 percent of students surveyed reported that they do not think their college frequently encourages students to consider a wide variety of viewpoints and perspectives.

- UCLA's Higher Education Institute shows that the faculty has moved considerably leftward since the late 1980s, especially in the Arts and Humanities. In New England alone, liberal professors outnumber conservative ones by an astonishing ratio of 28:1.

- A large student and faculty sampling by the American Association of Colleges and Universities reported only 18 percent of the faculty and staff strongly agreed that it was "safe to hold unpopular positions on campus."

And the third major concern is a lack of intellectual humility from students, administrators, and faculty. Consider these examples:

- The first is the rise of Intolerance: Since 2000, the FIRE has recorded 379 instances of disinvitations, with nearly a quarter of those occurring between 2016 to 2018. In those two years, 82 percent of these disinvitations have been because of the Left's doing.

- The second is the lack of Constructive Disagreement: The concept centers around creating a dynamic where key stakeholders in the faculty and student body are compelled to disagree. The word "constructive" alludes to the need to raise issues, debate, and resolve them reasonably. In the academy, this rarely happens--but it does so in the corporate world—successfully.

- And the third concerns the prevalence of Confirmation Bias: The 2008 paper, "Estimating the reproducibility of psychological science" describes the replication failure rate being as high as one-half to two-thirds of 100 sampled experiments published in 2008 in three high-ranking psychology journals.

The 'Heckler's Veto' on America's University and High School Campuses

There is a George Orwell statue at the headquarters of the BBC and the Orwell quote on the wall reads: "If liberty means anything at all, it means the right to tell people what they do not want to hear."

The *Economist* reports, "People as different as Condoleezza Rice, a former secretary of state, and Bill Maher, a satirist, have been dissuaded from giving speeches on campuses, sometimes on grounds of safety … Fifty years ago, student radicals agitated for academic freedom and the right to engage in political activities on campus. Now some of their successors are campaigning for censorship and increased policing by universities of student activities. The supporters of these ideas on campus are usually described as radicals. They are, in fact, the opposite."

Our society, it seems, has failed to transmit our values, in particular free speech, to the next generation. According to a new survey by the Pew Research Center, 40 per cent of Millennials support government censorship of speech offensive to minority groups. The poll found that Millennials were the most likely of any age group to agree that government should have the authority to stop people from saying things that offend minorities.

There can be little doubt that our society is not doing a particularly good job in transmitting our history and values to the next generation. A recent survey of 1,100 colleges and universities found that only eighteen percent require American history or government, where the foundations of our society, such as the First Amendment, can be explained.

The survey, by the American Council of Trustees and Alumni (ACTA), found that at the universities where free speech is now under attack, such as the University Missouri, Amherst, and Yale, very little is being done to transmit our history and values.

Those in Charge Tend to Recoil From the Defense of Free Speech

With few defenders in today's academic world, the future of academic freedom looks increasingly bleak. Hopefully, alumni will rally to restore the universities they once knew, a genuine marketplace of ideas where "political correctness," "safe zones" and "microaggression," were terms yet to be coined. But if they and others in positions of influence prove unwilling or unable to address this growing problem, "academic freedom" will begin to reflect with what *The SAPIENT Being* has pointed out.

The seriousness of freedom of speech suppression was recently investigated in 2017 by the House of Representatives Joint Hearing Before the Subcommittee on Healthcare, Benefits and Administrative Rules and the Subcommittee on

Intergovernmental Affairs of the Committee on Oversight and Government Reform titled *Challenges to Freedom of Speech on College Campuses*.

The issues with trigger warnings, safe spaces, safe zones, shout-downs, microaggressions, bias response teams, and riots on campuses were discussed and debated regarding their impact of campus freedom of speech suppression.

Herbert Marcuse Wrote That Conservative Ideas Should be Repressed

Indeed, in 1968, Critical Theorist Herbert Marcuse wrote that society should only be tolerant of the ideas from oppressed groups, and that conservative ideas should be repressed. Marcuse wrote:

It should be evident by now that the exercise of civil rights by those who don't have them presupposes the withdrawal of civil rights from those who prevent their exercise, and that liberation of the Damned of the Earth presupposes suppression not only of their old but also of their new masters....Withdrawal of tolerance from regressive movements before they can become active; intolerance even toward thought, opinion, and word, and finally, intolerance in the opposite direction, that is, toward the self-styled conservatives, to the political Right— these anti-democratic notions respond to the actual development of the democratic society which has destroyed the basis for universal tolerance.

CRT writers applied this idea to their area of study. Richard Delgado wrote in 1994, "We are raising the possibility that the correct argument may sometimes be: the First Amendment condemns [the suppression of speech, even hate speech], therefore the First Amendment (or the way we understand it) is wrong."

Still more pointedly, Delgado and Jean Stefancic write in Critical Race Theory: An Introduction, "If one is an idealist, campus speech codes, tort remedies for racist speech, diversity seminars, and increasing the representation of black, brown, and Asian actors on television shows will be high on one's list of priorities."

Again, remember CRT founder Derrick Bell's comment cited earlier in this Backgrounder that CRT scholarship should incite rebellion and "most critical race theorists are committed to a program of scholarly resistance, and most hope scholarly resistance will lay the groundwork for wide-scale resistance."

In addition to CRT's central tenets of disrupting systems of power and destabilizing classical liberal civil and political structures, CRT and Critical Theory object to free speech as a cornerstone of society. The themes and logical responses from CRT proponents are echoed by students who shout down professors, guest speakers, and even other students at colleges across the country.

Spotlight on Speech Codes 2022: Major Findings

From the Spotlight on Speech Codes F.I.R.E. 2022 report from the Foundation for Individual Rights and Expression (FIRE):

The percentage of colleges and universities earning an overall "red light" rating in FIRE's Spotlight database has gone down for the fourteenth year in a row—this year to 19%. This is approximately a three percentage point drop from last year, and is more than 50 percentage points lower than the percentage of red light institutions in FIRE's 2009 report.

- 68% of institutions now earn an overall "yellow light" rating. Though less restrictive than red light policies, yellow light policies still restrict expression that is protected under First Amendment standards and invite administrative abuse.

- 13 %, or a total of 58 colleges and universities now earn an overall "green light" rating, up from 56 schools as of last year's report. Policies earn a green light rating when they do not seriously threaten protected expression. Significantly, there are now more public schools earning a green light rating (54) than there are earning a red light rating (45).

- 5.2% of institutions surveyed maintain "free speech zone" policies, which limit student demonstrations and other expressive activities to small and/or out-of-the-way areas on campus. A 2013 FIRE survey of these institutions found roughly triple that percentage.

- Eighty-two university administrations or faculty bodies have now adopted policy statements in support of free speech modeled after the "Report of the Committee on Freedom of Expression" at the University of Chicago (the "Chicago Statement"), released in January 2015.

Executive Summary

Most college students in the United States should be able to expect that freedom of expression will be upheld on their campuses. After all, public institutions are legally bound by the First Amendment, and the vast majority of private colleges and universities promise their students commensurate free speech rights.

Nevertheless, far too many colleges across the country fail to live up to their free speech obligations in policy and in practice. Often, this occurs through the implementation of speech codes: university policies that restrict expression protected by the First Amendment.

For their 2022 report, FIRE surveyed the written policies of 481 colleges and universities, evaluating their compliance with First Amendment standards. Overall, 18.5% of surveyed colleges maintained at least one severely restrictive policy that earned FIRE's worst, "red light" rating, meaning that the policy both clearly and substantially restricts protected speech. This is the fourteenth year in a row that the percentage of schools earning a red light rating has gone down; last year, 21.3% of schools earned a red light rating.

The majority of institutions surveyed (68%) earned an overall "yellow light" rating, meaning they maintained at least one yellow light policy. Yellow light policies are either clear restrictions on a narrower range of expression or policies that, by virtue of vague wording, could too easily be applied to restrict protected expression. While the steady decline in red light institutions is cause for optimism, FIRE will continue to work with colleges and universities to ensure that yellow light institutions improve to earn our highest, "green light" rating.

A green light rating indicates that none of a university's written policies seriously imperil protected expression. A total of 58 colleges and universities (12.1% of those surveyed) earned an overall green light rating, up from 56 schools as of last year's report.

In further good news, a growing number colleges and universities are adopting policy statements in support of free speech modeled after the "Report of the Committee on Freedom of Expression" at the University of Chicago (the "Chicago Statement"). As of this writing, 82 universities, university systems, or faculty bodies have endorsed a version of the "Chicago Statement," with seven adoptions since last year's report.

Though these improvements in policy are heartening, free speech on campus remains under threat. Demands for censorship of student and faculty speech—

whether originating on or off campus—are common, and universities continue to investigate and punish students and faculty over protected expression.

In that year, schools across the country continued to grapple with challenges presented by the COVID-19 pandemic. During the spring semester, and before COVID-19 vaccines became widely available, many classes continued to be conducted remotely, making the concerns presented by policies that govern online speech that much greater.

It is imperative that those who care about free speech on campus stay vigilant. The decrease in restrictive speech codes and the proliferation of free speech policy statements are the result of the tireless work of free speech advocates at FIRE and elsewhere. But we must ensure that new national and global challenges do not result in such progress being lost. We must continue to work to ensure that students have the opportunity to pursue their education and that faculty are able to teach with the greatest possible foundation for free expression in place.

Methodology

For this report, FIRE surveyed publicly available policies at 374 four-year public institutions and 107 of the nation's most prestigious private institutions. Our research focuses in particular on public universities because, as explained in detail below, public universities are legally bound to protect students' right to free speech and can be successfully sued in court when they do not.

FIRE rates colleges and universities as "red light," "yellow light," or "green light" institutions based on how much, if any, protected expression their written policies governing student conduct restrict. The speech code ratings do not take into account a university's "as-applied" violations of student speech rights or other cases of censorship, student- or faculty-led calls for punishment of protected speech, and related incidents and controversies. Monitoring and rating such incidents consistently across 481 institutions with accuracy is not feasible and is beyond the scope of this report.

The speech code ratings are defined as follows:

Red Light: A red light institution maintains at least one policy that both clearly and substantially restricts freedom of speech, or bars public access to its speech-related policies by requiring a university login and password for access.

A "clear" restriction unambiguously infringes on protected expression. In other words, the threat to free speech at a red light institution is obvious on the face of the policy and does not depend on how the policy is applied. A "substantial" restriction on free speech is one that is broadly applicable to campus expression. For example, a ban on "offensive speech" would be a clear violation (in that it is unambiguous) as well as a substantial violation (in that it covers a great deal of what is protected under First Amendment standards). Such a policy would earn a university a red light.

When a university restricts access to its speech-related policies by requiring a login and password, it denies prospective students and their parents the ability to weigh this crucial information prior to matriculation. At FIRE, we consider this denial to be so deceptive and serious that it alone warrants an overall red light rating.

Yellow Light: A yellow light institution maintains policies that could be interpreted to suppress protected speech or policies that, while clearly restricting freedom of speech, restrict relatively narrow categories of speech.

For example, a policy banning "verbal abuse" has broad applicability and poses a substantial threat to free speech, but is not a clear violation because "abuse" might refer to unprotected speech and conduct, such as threats of violence or unlawful harassment. Similarly, while a policy banning "profanity on residence hall door whiteboards" clearly restricts speech, it is relatively limited in scope. Yellow light policies are typically unconstitutional when maintained by public universities, and a rating of yellow light rather than red light in no way means that FIRE condones a university's restrictions on speech. Rather, it means that in FIRE's judgment, those restrictions do not clearly and substantially restrict speech in the manner necessary to warrant a red light rating.

Green Light: If FIRE finds that a university's policies do not seriously threaten campus expression, that college or university receives a green light rating. A green light rating does not necessarily indicate that a school actively supports free expression in practice; it simply means that the school's written policies do not pose a serious threat to free speech.

Warning: FIRE believes that free speech is not only a moral imperative, but an essential element of a college education. However, private universities, as private associations, possess their own right to free association, which allows them to prioritize other values above the right to free speech if they wish to do so. Therefore, when a private university clearly and consistently states that it holds a certain set of values above a commitment to freedom of speech, FIRE gives it a Warning rating in order to warn prospective students and faculty members of this fact. Seven schools surveyed for this report meet these criteria

Overall ratings: To determine overall ratings, FIRE does not produce an "average" of an institution's policy ratings; a school with five yellow light policies and one red light policy earns an overall red light rating, just as a school with one yellow light policy and five red light policies earns an overall red light rating.

Findings

Of the 481 schools reviewed by FIRE, 89, or 18.5%, received a red light rating. 327 schools received a yellow light rating (68%), and 58 received a green light rating (12.1%). Seven schools earned a Warning rating (1.5%).

This marks the fourteenth year in a row that the percentage of universities with an overall red light rating has fallen, this year from 21.3% to 18.5%. The continued reduction in red light institutions is encouraging: Just over a decade ago, red light schools encompassed about 75% of the report's findings.

However, this year's numbers also reveal an increase in yellow light institutions, as 65.3% of schools earned an overall yellow light last year, compared to 68% this year. While yellow light policies are not as clearly and substantially restrictive as red light policies on their face, they nevertheless impose impermissible restrictions on expression.

The number of green light institutions has continued to rise this year, though only slightly, from 56 institutions last year to 58 now. At 12.1%, the percentage of green light schools is at an all-time high, with more than one million students across the country enrolled at green light colleges and universities.

In total, 20 schools improved their overall ratings for that year.

Public Colleges and Universities

The percentage of public schools with a red light rating dropped again, from 14.5% last year to 12% this year. Overall, of the 374 public universities reviewed for this report, 45 received a red light rating (12%), 273 received a yellow light rating (73%), and 54 received a green light rating (14.4%). As a result, public colleges and universities have reached a significant turning point: There are now more public institutions earning an overall green light rating than an overall red light rating. As just nine public schools earned the green light rating a decade ago, this milestone reveals significant progress.

This year, FIRE was pleased to welcome Elizabeth City State University and the University of North Carolina School of the Arts to the list of green light institutions.

Notably, 13 of the 16 institutions in the University of North Carolina System currently earn an overall green light rating, making North Carolina the state in the country with the greatest number of green light schools. We hope to use North Carolina as a model, working with governing bodies of other public university systems across the country to adopt similar, sweeping reform in other states.

Private Colleges and Universities

Of the 107 private colleges and universities reviewed, 44 received a red light rating (41.1%). 54 received a yellow light rating (50.5%), four received a green light rating (3.7%), and five earned a Warning rating (4.7%).

The percentage of private universities earning a red light rating, which stood at 44.3% last year, continued to decrease, coming in at 41.1% this year. This progress, albeit slight, is hard-earned, given that private universities are not legally bound by the First Amendment, which regulates only government actors. For this reason, it is gratifying that these colleges are closer to fulfilling their institutional commitments to free expression.

FIRE will continue to work with private colleges and universities to improve policies so that they better meet institutional commitments to protecting students' free speech rights.

Speech Codes on Campus: Background and Legal Challenges

Speech codes—university regulations prohibiting expression that would be constitutionally protected in society at large—gained popularity with college administrators in the 1980s and 1990s. As discriminatory barriers to education declined, female and minority enrollment increased. Concerned that these changes would cause tension and that students who finally had full educational access would arrive at institutions only to be offended by other students, college administrators enacted speech codes.

In the mid-1990s, the phenomenon of campus speech codes converged with the expansion of Title IX, the federal law prohibiting sex discrimination in educational institutions receiving federal funds. Under the rationale of the obligation to prohibit discriminatory harassment, unconstitutionally overbroad harassment policies banning subjectively offensive conduct proliferated.

In enacting speech codes, administrators ignored or did not fully consider the philosophical, social, and legal ramifications of placing restrictions on speech, particularly at public universities. As a result, federal courts have overturned speech codes at numerous colleges and universities over the past several decades.

Despite the overwhelming weight of legal authority against speech codes, a large number of institutions—including some of those that have been successfully sued on First Amendment grounds—still maintain unconstitutional and illiberal speech codes. It is with this unfortunate fact in mind that we turn to a more detailed discussion of the ways in which campus speech codes violate individual rights and what can be done to challenge them.

Public Universities vs. Private Universities

With limited, narrowly defined exceptions, the First Amendment prohibits the government—including governmental entities such as state universities—from restricting freedom of speech. A good rule of thumb is that if a state law would be declared unconstitutional for violating the First Amendment, a similar regulation at a state college or university is likewise unconstitutional.

The guarantees of the First Amendment generally do not apply to students at private colleges because the First Amendment regulates only government conduct. Moreover, although acceptance of federal funding does confer some obligations upon private colleges (such as compliance with federal anti-discrimination laws), compliance with the First Amendment is not one of them.

This does not mean, however, that students and faculty at all private schools are not entitled to free expression. In fact, most private universities explicitly promise freedom of speech and academic freedom in their official policy materials.

Howard University, for example, provides in its student handbook that "all students are guaranteed freedom of expression, inquiry and assembly." Likewise, the University of Tulsa states that "[t]he rights of free inquiry and free expression, both public and private, are essential to the learning process," and that these rights "shall not be infringed upon."

Yet both of these institutions, along with most other private colleges and universities, maintain policies that prohibit the very speech they promise to protect.

This year, both private and public institutions, including statewide systems, have continued to adopt policy statements in support of free speech modeled after the one produced in January 2015 by the Committee on Freedom of Expression at the University of Chicago. Since our last report, seven more institutions have adopted policy statements in support of free speech modeled after the "Chicago Statement."

Notably, earlier this year the University of Virginia convened a Committee on Free Speech and Inquiry, tasked with drafting a statement of principles affirming the university's strong commitment to freedom of expression. Following significant community engagement, the Board of Visitors officially adopted the Committee's statement over the summer, becoming the sixteenth green light institution to adopt a version of the Chicago Statement.

Overwhelming Majority of Speech is Protected by the First Amendment

Over the years, the Supreme Court has carved out a limited number of narrow exceptions to the First Amendment, including speech that incites reasonable people to immediate violence; so-called "fighting words" (face-to-face confrontations that lead to physical altercations); harassment; true threats and intimidation; obscenity; and defamation. If the speech in question does not fall within one of these exceptions, it most likely is protected.

The exceptions are often misapplied and abused by universities to punish constitutionally protected speech. There are instances where the written policy at issue may be constitutional—for example, a prohibition on "incitement"—but its application may not be. In other instances, a written policy will purport to be a legitimate ban on a category of unprotected speech like harassment or true threats, but (either deliberately or through poor drafting) will encompass protected speech as well. Therefore, it is important to understand what these narrow exceptions to free speech actually mean in order to recognize when they are being misapplied.

Speech Codes—university regulations prohibiting expression that would be constitutionally protected in society at large—gained popularity with college administrators in the 1980s and 1990s. Utilizing the Foundation for Individual Rights in Education's (FIRE) extensive website, reports, and statistics, most of the content for this chapter is borrowed from these ground breaking resources in the arena of free speech rights and protections.

As discriminatory barriers to education declined in the Sixties and Seventies, female and minority enrollment increased substantially starting in the Eighties. Concerned that these changes would cause tension and that students who finally had full educational access would arrive at institutions only to be offended by other students, college administrators enacted speech codes.

In the mid-1990s, the phenomenon of campus speech codes converged with the expansion of Title IX, the federal law prohibiting sex discrimination in educational institutions receiving federal funds. Under the guise of the obligation to prohibit discriminatory harassment, unconstitutionally overbroad harassment policies banning subjectively offensive conduct proliferated. Given the current undergraduate tendency toward intellectual orthodoxy, one wonders: Would the advances of the feminist movement even have happened, had the campus conformists of a half-century ago had their way?

Respect for freedom of speech and diversity of thought are essential for achieving civil and thoughtful discourse, but also for enabling societal progress itself. Progress relies on early agitators, who are willing to speak out and press forward, no matter the backlash they engender. Many ideas once considered heretical have become accepted wisdom, thanks to early dissenters challenging the tide.

Real change relied on the courage of young women during the 1960s and 1970s, who stood up for equal opportunity in higher education and the workforce. They faced vocal opposition from many college alumni, professors, and fellow students. Nevertheless, these women persisted, no matter how "problematic" their efforts may have been considered. Their determined activism paved the way for the generations to come.

6 – How Did Freedom of Speech Suppression Happen?

Speech codes—university regulations prohibiting expression that would be constitutionally protected in society at large—gained popularity with college administrators in the 1980s and 1990s. Utilizing the Foundation for Individual Rights in Education's (FIRE) extensive website, reports, and statistics, most of the content for this chapter is borrowed from these ground breaking resources in the arena of free speech rights and protections.

As discriminatory barriers to education declined in the Sixties and Seventies, female and minority enrollment increased substantially starting in the Eighties. Concerned that these changes would cause tension and that students who finally had full educational access would arrive at institutions only to be offended by other students, college administrators enacted speech codes.

In the mid-1990s, the phenomenon of campus speech codes converged with the expansion of Title IX, the federal law prohibiting sex discrimination in educational institutions receiving federal funds. Under the guise of the obligation to prohibit discriminatory harassment, unconstitutionally overbroad harassment policies banning subjectively offensive conduct proliferated. Given the current undergraduate tendency toward intellectual orthodoxy, one wonders: Would the advances of the feminist movement even have happened, had the campus conformists of a half-century ago had their way?

Respect for freedom of speech and diversity of thought are essential for achieving civil and thoughtful discourse, but also for enabling societal progress itself. Progress relies on early agitators, who are willing to speak out and press forward, no matter the backlash they engender. Many ideas once considered heretical have become accepted wisdom, thanks to early dissenters challenging the tide.

Real change relied on the courage of young women during the 1960s and 1970s, who stood up for equal opportunity in higher education and the workforce. They faced vocal opposition from many college alumni, professors, and fellow students. Nevertheless, these women persisted, no matter how "problematic" their efforts may have been considered. Their determined activism paved the way for the generations to come.

Campus Speech Codes Converged With the Expansion of Title IX

Colleges and universities that receive federal funding must be in compliance with new rules by August 14, 2020. The regulations rebalance "scales of justice," says Betsy DeVos, former Secretary of Education. "The new regulation will secure due process rights for students who report sexual misconduct and for those accused of it, by requiring colleges to provide live hearings and allowing students' advisers to cross-examine parties and witnesses involved."

Under the new rules, institutions must presume that those accused of sexual misconduct are innocent prior to the investigative and decision-making process, addressing a repeated criticism of 2011 guidance issued by the Obama administration. Those in favor of a Title IX overhaul say the Obama guidance, referred to as the Dear Colleague letter, caused colleges to over enforce campus sexual misconduct and led to students being unjustly removed from campuses for false accusations. DeVos rescinded the letter in 2017.

In enacting speech codes, administrators ignored or did not fully consider the philosophical, social, and legal ramifications of placing restrictions on speech, particularly at public universities. As a result, federal courts have overturned speech codes at numerous colleges and universities over the past three decades.

Despite the overwhelming weight of legal authority against speech codes, a large number of institutions—including some of those that have been successfully sued on First Amendment grounds—still maintain unconstitutional speech codes. It is with this unfortunate fact in mind that FIRE turns to a more detailed discussion of the ways in which campus speech codes violate individual rights and what can be done to challenge them.

The Campus Expression Survey (CES) was developed by members of Heterodox Academy in response to students and professors who say they feel like they are "walking on eggshells," not just in the classroom but in informal interactions on campus as well.

Q2: WHY are they afraid? WHAT potential consequences are they most concerned about?

- Students are concerned about their views being criticized as offensive by other students. This concern was higher on all three controversial issues of gender, race, and politics, than any of the other concerns assessed.

What Exactly Is "Free Speech," And How Do Universities Curtail It?

With limited, narrowly defined exceptions, the First Amendment prohibits the government—including governmental entities such as state universities—from restricting freedom of speech. A good rule of thumb is that if a state law would be declared unconstitutional for violating the First Amendment, a similar regulation at a state college or university is likewise unconstitutional.

The guarantees of the First Amendment generally do not apply to students at private colleges because the First Amendment regulates only government conduct. Moreover, although acceptance of federal funding does confer some obligations upon private colleges (such as compliance with federal anti-discrimination laws), compliance with the First Amendment is not one of them.

This does not mean, however, that students and faculty at all private schools are not entitled to free expression. In fact, most private universities explicitly promise freedom of speech and academic freedom in their official policy materials. Lehigh University, for example, promises students "free inquiry and free speech and expression, including the right to open dissent."

Similarly, according to Middlebury College's student handbook, students "are free to examine and discuss all questions of interest to them and to express opinions publicly and privately." Yet both of these institutions, along with most other private colleges and universities, maintain policies that prohibit the very speech they promise to protect.

Encouragingly, more colleges than ever before, including private institutions, have adopted policy statements in support of free speech modeled after the one produced in January 2015 by the Committee on Freedom of Expression at the University of Chicago.

Think about being at your school in a class that was discussing a controversial issue about GENDER. How comfortable or reluctant would you feel about speaking up and giving your views on this topic?

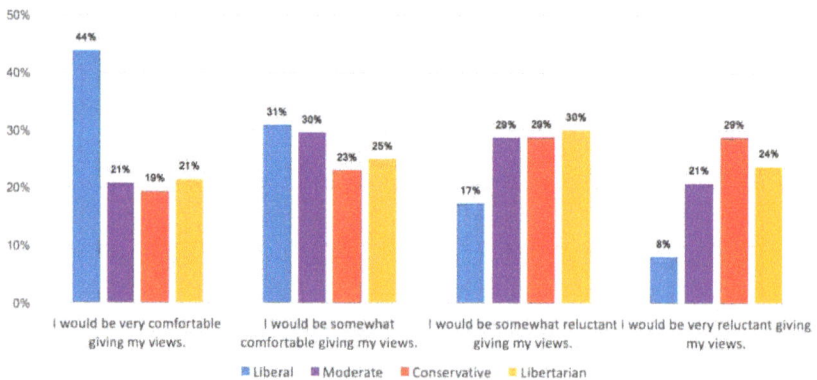

Credit: The Heterodox Academy.

What Does FIRE Mean When They Say That a University Restricts "Free Speech"?

Do people have the right to say absolutely anything, or are certain types of expression unprotected?

Simply put, the overwhelming majority of speech is protected by the First Amendment. Over the years, the Supreme Court has carved out a limited number of narrow exceptions to the First Amendment, including speech that incites reasonable people to immediate violence; so-called "fighting words" (face-to-face confrontations that lead to physical altercations); harassment; true threats and intimidation; obscenity; and defamation. If the speech in question does not fall within one of these exceptions, it most likely is protected speech.

The exceptions are often misapplied and abused by universities to punish constitutionally protected speech. There are instances where the written policy at issue may be constitutional—for example, a prohibition on "incitement"—but its application may not be. In other instances, a written policy will purport to be a legitimate ban on a category of unprotected speech like harassment or true threats, but (either deliberately or through poor drafting) will encompass protected speech as well.

Therefore, it is important to understand what these narrow exceptions to free speech actually mean in order to recognize when they are being misapplied.

Q3: WHO is afraid to speak up? WHAT topics are they afraid of speaking up about? WHAT potential consequences are they most concerned about?

- Almost half of the male students surveyed (49%, compared to 34% of female students surveyed) reported they were reluctant to give their views on gender in the classroom.

- Over half of the male students surveyed (57%, compared to 40% of female students surveyed) reported that they were concerned about criticism from other students if they shared their views on gender in the classroom.

- Almost half of the female students surveyed (47%) and half of the male students surveyed (50%) reported that they were reluctant to give their views on race in the classroom.

- Almost half of the female students surveyed (49%) and over half of the male students surveyed (54%) reported that they were concerned about criticism from other students if they shared their views on race in the classroom.

- Almost half of female students surveyed (47%, compared to 42% of male students surveyed) reported they were reluctant to give their views on politics in the classroom.

- Slightly more than three in five conservative students surveyed (63%, compared to 38% of liberal students surveyed) reported they were reluctant to discuss race in the classroom.

- Almost half of moderate students surveyed (47%) reported they were reluctant to discuss race in the classroom.

- Overall, liberal students surveyed were more comfortable discussing gender (75%), race (63%), and politics (66%) in the classroom than any other ideological group.

- Liberals were also less concerned about every potential consequence than the other ideological groups.

Policies on Tolerance, Respect, and Civility

The Foundation for Individual Rights and Expression (FIRE) has done extensive research as outlined in the following sections and the majority of following content in also from the FIRE website.

Many schools invoke laudable goals like respect and civility to justify policies that violate students' and faculty members' free speech rights. While a university has every right to promote a tolerant and respectful atmosphere on campus, a university that claims to respect free speech must not limit discourse to only the inoffensive and respectful. And although pleas for civility and respect are often initially framed as requests, many schools have speech codes that effectively turn those requests into requirements.

While respect and civility may seem uncontroversial, most uncivil, or disrespectful speech is protected by the First Amendment and is indeed sometimes of great political and social significance. Some of the expression employed in the civil rights movement of the 1950s and 60s, for example, would violate campus civility codes today. Colleges and universities may encourage civility, but public universities—and those private universities that purport to respect students' fundamental free speech rights—may not require it or threaten mere incivility with disciplinary action.

Bias and Hate Speech

In recent years, the FIRE explains how colleges and universities around the country have instituted policies and procedures specifically aimed at eliminating "bias" and "hate speech" on campus. These sets of policies and procedures, frequently termed "Bias Reporting Protocols" or "Bias Incident Protocols," often include bans on protected expression.

While speech or expression that is based on a speaker's prejudice may be subjectively offensive, it is nonetheless protected unless it rises to the level of harassment, true threats, or other unprotected speech.

Bias incident protocols often also infringe on students' right to due process, allowing for anonymous reporting that denies students the right to confront their accusers. Moreover, universities are often heavily invested in these bias incident policies, having set up extensive regulatory frameworks and response protocols devoted solely to addressing them.

While many bias incident protocols do not include a separate enforcement mechanism, the mere threat of a bias investigation will likely be sufficient to chill speech on controversial issues. When the only conduct at issue is constitutionally protected speech, even investigation is inappropriate.

Threats and Intimidation

The Supreme Court has defined "true threats" as "statements where the speaker means to communicate a serious expression of an intent to commit an act of unlawful violence to a particular individual or group of individuals." *Virginia v. Black*, 538 U.S. 343, 359 (2003). The Court also has defined "intimidation," of the type not protected by the First Amendment, as a "type of true threat, where a speaker directs a threat to a person or group of persons with the intent of placing the victim in fear of bodily harm or death." Id. at 360. Neither term would encompass, for example, a vaguely worded statement that is not directed at anyone in particular.

Nevertheless, as the FIRE points out, universities frequently misapply policies prohibiting threats and intimidation so as to infringe on protected speech.

As a result, students will likely refrain from speaking rather than risk investigation or discipline—the very definition of the impermissible chilling effect on protected speech. Indeed, Venigalla has expressed to the FIRE that the meeting gave him the impression that, going forward, he must be careful about what he says.

The FIRE does not mean to suggest that *Long Island University (LIU) Post* must ignore true threats or statements implying the possibility of harm. However, without more, students cannot be summoned for questioning every time they post a photo of themselves engaging in recreational firearm use.

The controversy *at LIU Post* is just one example of a common misapplication of the legal standards for threats and intimidation, in which universities cite generalized concerns about safety with no regard to the boundaries of protected speech. Instead, universities must revise policies so that they track these legal standards and enforce the policies accordingly.

Incitement

There is also a propensity among universities to restrict speech that offends other students on the basis that it constitutes "incitement." The basic concept, as administrators too often see it, is that offensive or provocative speech will anger those who disagree with it, perhaps so much so that it moves them to violence. While preventing violence is necessary, this is an impermissible misapplication of the incitement doctrine.

Incitement, the FIRE explains in the legal sense, does not refer to speech that may lead to violence on the part of those opposed to or angered by it, but rather to speech that will lead those who agree with it to commit immediate violence. In other words, the danger is that certain speech will convince sympathetic, willing listeners to take immediate unlawful action.

The paradigmatic example of incitement is a person standing on the steps of a courthouse in front of a torch-wielding mob and urging that mob to burn down the courthouse immediately. To misapply the doctrine to encompass an opposing party's reaction to speech they dislike is to convert the doctrine into an impermissible "heckler's veto," where violence threatened by those angry about particular speech is used as a reason to censor that speech.

As the Supreme Court has said, speech cannot be prohibited because it "might offend a hostile mob" or because it may prove "unpopular with bottle throwers."

The legal standard for incitement was announced in the Supreme Court's decision in *Brandenburg v. Ohio*, 395 U.S. 444 (1969). There, the Court held that the state may not "forbid or proscribe advocacy of the use of force or of law violation except where such advocacy is directed to inciting or producing imminent lawless action and is likely to incite or produce such action." Id. at 447 (emphasis in original).

Obscenity

The Supreme Court has held that obscene expression, to fall outside of the protection of the First Amendment, must "depict or describe sexual conduct" and must be "limited to works which, taken as a whole, appeal to the prurient interest in sex, which portray sexual conduct in a patently offensive way, and which, taken as a whole, do not have serious literary, artistic, political, or scientific value." *Miller v. California*, 413 U.S. 15, 24 (1973).

Per the FIRE, this is a narrow definition applicable only to some highly graphic sexual material. It does not encompass profanity, even though profane words are often colloquially referred to as "obscenities." In fact, the Supreme Court has explicitly held that profanity is constitutionally protected. In *Cohen v. California*, 403 U.S. 15 (1971), the defendant, Paul Robert Cohen, was convicted in California for wearing a jacket bearing the words "Fuck the Draft" in a courthouse. The Supreme Court overturned Cohen's conviction, holding that the message on his jacket, however vulgar, was protected speech.

Similarly, in *Papish v. Board of Curators of the University of Missouri*, 410 U.S. 667 (1973), the Court determined that a student newspaper article entitled "Motherfucker Acquitted" was constitutionally protected speech. The Court wrote that "the mere dissemination of ideas—no matter how offensive to good taste— on a state university campus may not be shut off in the name alone of 'conventions of decency.'" Id. at 670.

Nonetheless, many colleges erroneously believe that they may lawfully prohibit profanity and vulgar expression.

Harassment

Hostile environment harassment, properly defined, is not protected by the First Amendment. In the educational context, the Supreme Court has defined student-on-student harassment as discriminatory, unwelcome conduct that is "so severe, pervasive, and objectively offensive that it effectively bars the victim's access to an educational opportunity or benefit." *Davis v. Monroe County Board of Education*, 526 U.S. 629, 633 (1999).

This is not simply expression; it is conduct far beyond the protected expressive activities that are too often deemed "harassment" on today's college campus. Harassment is extreme and usually repetitive behavior—behavior so serious that it would interfere with a reasonable person's ability to receive his or her education. For example, in Davis, the conduct found by the Court to be harassment was a months-long pattern of conduct including repeated attempts to touch the victim's breasts and genitals, together with repeated sexually explicit comments directed at and about the victim.

For decades now, as noted by the FIRE, many colleges and universities have maintained policies defining harassment too broadly and prohibiting constitutionally protected speech. And years of Title IX enforcement by the Department of Education's Office for Civil Rights (OCR) that neglected to fully protect First Amendment rights, including an unconstitutionally broad definition of sexual harassment promulgated by OCR, led numerous colleges and universities to enact overly restrictive harassment policies in an effort to avoid an OCR investigation.

It will likely take a great deal of time and effort by free speech advocates to undo this damage.

Colleges and universities often fail to limit themselves to the narrow definition of harassment that is outside the realm of constitutional protection. Instead, they expand the term to prohibit broad categories of speech that do not even approach actionable harassment, despite similar policies having been struck down by federal courts years earlier.

Having discussed the most common ways in which universities misuse the narrow exceptions to the First Amendment to prohibit protected expression, the FIRE turns to the innumerable other types of university regulations that restrict free speech on their face. Such restrictions are generally found in several distinct types of policies.

Anti-Bullying Policies

Over the past decade, the FIRE has found that more and more colleges and universities have adopted policies on "bullying" and "cyberbullying." On October 26, 2010, OCR issued a letter on the topic of bullying, reminding educational institutions that they must address actionable harassment, but also acknowledging that "some conduct alleged to be harassment may implicate the First Amendment rights to free speech or expression."

For such situations, OCR's letter refers readers back to the 2003 "Dear Colleague" letter stating that harassment is conduct that goes far beyond merely offensive speech and expression. However, because it is primarily focused on bullying in the K–12 setting, the letter also urges an in loco parentis (in place of a parent) approach that is inappropriate in the college setting, where students are overwhelmingly adults.

Court decisions and other guidance regarding K–12 speech have a way of "trickling up" to the collegiate setting, and indeed, FIRE has come across numerous university policies prohibiting bullying in a problematic manner.

But as courts have held in rulings spanning decades, speech cannot be prohibited simply because someone else finds it offensive, even deeply so. Offensive speech, if it does not rise to the level of harassment or one of the other narrow categories of unprotected speech and conduct, is entitled to constitutional protection (and, accordingly, to protection at private institutions that claim to uphold the right to free speech.

Internet Usage Policies

University policies regulating online expression, while perhaps appearing to be narrow, can have a significant impact on students' and faculty members' free speech rights.

Policies Governing Speakers, Demonstrations, and Rallies

Universities have a right to enact reasonable, narrowly tailored "time, place, and manner" restrictions that prevent demonstrations and other expressive activities from unduly interfering with the educational process.

They may not, however, regulate speakers and demonstrations on the basis of content or viewpoint, nor may they maintain regulations that burden substantially more speech than is necessary to maintain an environment conducive to education. Such regulations can take several forms, as discussed in the sections below.

Security Fee Policies

In recent years, FIRE has seen a number of colleges and universities hamper— whether intentionally or just through a misunderstanding of the law—the invitation of controversial campus speakers by levying additional security costs on the sponsoring student organizations.

The Supreme Court addressed a similar issue *in Forsyth County v. Nationalist Movement*, 505 U.S. 123 (1992), where it struck down an ordinance in Georgia that permitted the local government to set varying fees for events based upon how much police protection the event would need.

Invalidating the ordinance, the Court wrote that "the fee assessed will depend on the administrator's measure of the amount of hostility likely to be created by the speech based on its content. Those wishing to express views unpopular with bottle throwers, for example, may have to pay more for their permit." Id. at 134.

Deciding that such a determination required county administrators to "examine the content of the message that is conveyed," the Court wrote that "listeners' reaction to speech is not a content-neutral basis for regulation. … Speech cannot be financially burdened, any more than it can be punished or banned, simply because it might offend a hostile mob." Id. at 134–35 (emphasis added).

Despite this precedent, the impermissible use of security fees to burden controversial speech is all too common on university campuses.

Prior Restraints

The Supreme Court has held that "it is offensive—not only to the values protected by the First Amendment, but to the very notion of a free society—that in the context of everyday public discourse a citizen must first inform the government of her desire to speak to her neighbors and then obtain a permit to do so." *Watchtower Bible and Tract Society of NY, Inc. v. Village of Stratton*, 536 U.S. 150, 165–66 (2002).

Yet many colleges and universities enforce prior restraints, requiring students and student organizations to register their expressive activities well in advance and, often, to obtain administrative approval for those activities

Free Speech Zone Policies

Of the 466 schools surveyed for the FIRE's report, 49 institutions (10.5%) have "free speech zone" policies—policies limiting student demonstrations and other expressive activities to small and out-of-the-way areas on campus. Despite being inconsistent with the First Amendment, free speech zones are more common at public universities than at private universities: 12.7% of public universities surveyed maintain free speech zones, while just 2.9% of private universities do.

Free speech zones have repeatedly been struck down by courts or voluntarily revised by colleges as part of settlements to lawsuits brought by students. The FIRE's Stand Up For Speech Litigation Project has included successful challenges to free speech zone policies at eight colleges and universities and includes an ongoing challenge to a free speech zone policy at Pierce College in Los Angeles.

Additionally, state legislatures have continued to take action to prohibit public colleges and universities from maintaining free speech zones. Currently, eleven states have enacted laws prohibiting these restrictive policies: Virginia, Missouri, Arizona, Kentucky, Colorado, Utah, North Carolina, Tennessee, Florida, Georgia, and Louisiana.

Based on the Campus Free Expression (CAFE) Act model legislation from the FIRE, Florida's bill, which was signed into law in March 2018, states:

A person who wishes to engage in an expressive activity in outdoor areas of campus may do so freely, spontaneously, and contemporaneously as long as the person's conduct is lawful and does not materially and substantially disrupt the functioning of the public institution of higher education or infringe upon the rights of other individuals or organizations to engage in expressive activities. … A public institution of higher education may not designate any area of campus as a free-speech zone or otherwise create policies restricting expressive activities to a particular area of campus …

The law also provides a right to sue a public institution of higher education in Florida if the institution violates the expressive rights guaranteed by the law.

Despite the unpopularity of free speech zones with judges and lawmakers, too many universities still maintain them.

7 – Viewpoint Diversity, Intellectual Humility & Sapience

Credit: Minding the Campus.

The Campus Expression Survey (CES) from 1,078 currently enrolled college students in the United States was developed by members of Heterodox Academy in response to students and professors who say they feel like they are "walking on eggshells," not just in the classroom but in informal interactions on campus as well.

This chapter captures their report and presents a summary of all of the CES data Heterodox Academy has obtained to date. These analyses revealed a number of interesting findings, including:

- 53% of students surveyed reported that they do not think their college or university frequently encourages students to consider a wide variety of viewpoints and perspectives.

- 32% of conservatives (vs. 8% of liberals) were very reluctant to discuss politics in the classroom.

- 29% of conservatives (vs. 8% of liberals) were very reluctant to discuss gender in the classroom.

- 30% of conservatives (vs. 15% of liberals) were very reluctant to discuss race in the classroom.

- When discussing potentially controversial topics (politics, race, and gender), the students surveyed were most concerned about criticism from their peers followed by criticism or a lower grade from their professor. They were least concerned about criticism on social media or the potential for a harassment complaint against them.

In the intellectual sphere, as it turns out, ideological intolerance is not the monopoly of any particular party. Rather, what we are seeing is a wider, systemic pattern. Oliver Traldi locates it in belief-intensity or "zealousness"—in which the long-documented polarization of the political climate is bleeding into a polarization of the academic sphere. That polarization is being expressed at different levels of the university, against different groups, in different ways.

Bipartisan Problem, Transpartisan Solutions

The academic freedom crisis is multifaceted, covering multiple dimensions of the intensely complicated social fabric of the modern campus. Dr. Jonathan Haidt has focused particularly on students; others have persuasively argued that administrations are a more potent variable; still others have emphasized the role professors have played in the changing campus climate—or the pernicious influence of outside groups.

If approached in a partisan way, it's easy to cherry-pick individual dimensions of the crisis to support a grievance politics that one's own side is being systematically wronged (or wronged more): the Right will point to patterns of disinvitation and a perceived hostile climate for conservative students and faculty driven by left-leaning activists. The Left will point to patterns of faculty dismissal, as well as the professional and media harassment of professors, especially by the Far Right. The result is a systematic, partisan missing of the forest for the trees.

For a principled commitment to speech rights and intellectual pluralism, all of those levels need to be treated with care, judicious examination of data, and appropriate concern. And concern is appropriate—regardless of one's political or ideological commitments.

Cultivate a Campus Culture That Welcomes Diverse Thought and Open Discussion

Given the importance of intellectual inquiry, of subjecting ideas to rigorous back-and-forth testing, it is critically important for universities to cultivate a campus culture that welcomes diverse thought and open discussion–even, or perhaps especially, on controversial topics. And while removing any and all restrictive speech codes is an important first step towards cultivating such a culture, FIRE's ratings don't tell us everything we might like to know about the intellectual "openness" of any school.

After all, just because a particular university has no speech code restrictions does not necessarily mean that its students will feel free to exercise their First Amendment rights–especially if they sense that viewpoints other than their own are "privileged" on campus. Accordingly, it may be useful to think of campus speech having a "hierarchy of needs" similar in some ways to those Abraham Maslow identified for the individual.

That is, at the most basic "survival" level, students need legal protections that ensure their right to free expression; but building on this, students need an intellectually-rich environment that fosters respect for diverse viewpoints and allows them to engage in spirited intellectual debate without feeling like they must constantly "walk on eggshells."

Sadly, Haidt and the Heterodox Academy reports that a growing number of the college students he encounters say they pointedly avoid engaging in such spirited discourse–and that this self-censorship often begins in high school.

Unfortunately, when they graduate the most effective policymakers that weave together the best ideas from a range of perspectives in order to address society's most intractable problems will be lacking.

The Campus Expression Survey (CES) was developed by members of the Heterodox Academy in response to students and professors who say they feel like they are "walking on eggshells," not just in the classroom but in informal interactions on campus as well. For example:

Q1: WHAT topics are students afraid to speak up about?

- Almost half of students surveyed reported they were reluctant discussing race (48%) and politics (46%) in the classroom.

- Students surveyed also expressed reluctance discussing gender (41%) in the classroom.

What are students concerned about?

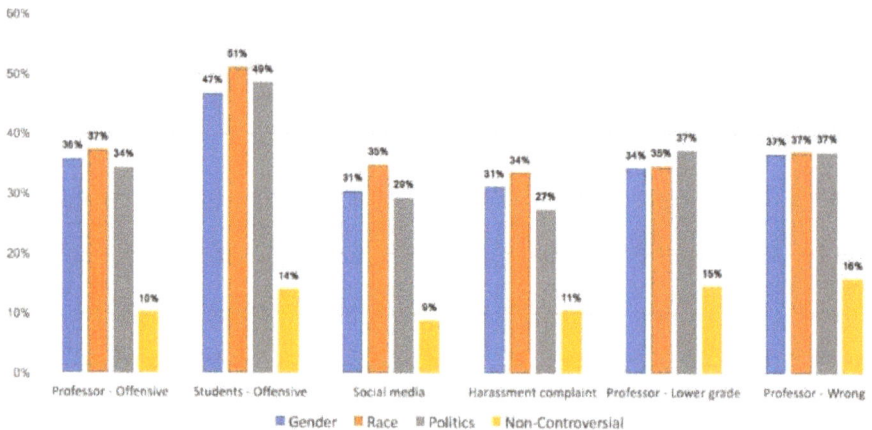

Credit: The Heterodox Academy - Note: In the figure above (and all subsequent figures in this report) the Y-axis depicts the total percentage of respondents for each issue and category.

When College Students Self-Censor, Society Loses

Colleges—the intended training ground for the sort of creative and integrative thinking such problem-solving requires—have become increasingly characterized by orthodoxy in what types of questions can be asked and what sort of comments can be shared in the classroom and around campus.

As a result, many students and even some faculty elect to self-censor. As citizens who are counting on students' future contributions to our shared social and civic endeavors, we all suffer when students elect to sit on the sidelines of their own learning or opt-out of scholarship because they feel they do not "belong" at institutions of higher learning.

Indeed, it is vital for America's future to encourage a diversity of opinions on college campuses. But what will it take to achieve that goal?

Academic stakeholders must create campuses eager to welcome professors, students and speakers who approach problems and questions from different points of view, explicitly valuing the role such diversity plays in advancing the pursuit of knowledge, discovery, and innovation.

Rather than merely tolerating fellow learners whose views are wildly different from one's own, all should seek out and cherish that difference.

Because we see things differently, we will be better able to explore the nuances of the topics we study, deepening our understanding and thus equipping us to be better able to move the needle on those issues we care about most.

This is Not a Left-Right Issue

This is about creating intellectual institutions where learners can come together, humbled by their incomplete knowledge, curious what they can learn from others, able to share their own ideas and perspectives and eager to think together with nuance, open minds, respect and goodwill—all in service to understanding the complexities of our world more deeply.

The concept of constructive disagreement centers around creating a dynamic where key stakeholders in an organization can and are compelled to disagree. The word constructive alludes to the need to raise issues, debate, and resolve them. In the academy, this no longer or rarely happens--but it does in the corporate world.

To achieve that goal in academia where it's sorely lacking, academic stakeholders must enact policies and practices that support heterodox classrooms and campuses. This requires three ingredients:

First, stakeholders must value open inquiry and constructive disagreement. The good news is the available data suggest students, faculty and administrators overwhelmingly do value these things (in principle).

Second, stakeholders must have access to, or be willing to create, effective strategies for enacting these values. For students, this could mean forming or participating in freedom of speech organizations or related initiatives.

For professors, it could be about strategies they deploy in the classroom to create an environment conducive to open inquiry and constructive disagreement or signaling a desire for viewpoint diversity in job ads during faculty searches.

In other cases, it's as simple as the chief academic officer being a vocal and visible cheerleader for the role constructive disagreement across lines of difference plays in realizing the very mission of the institution.

Other interventions are a heavier lift, like actually following through on the consequences stated in an existing policy even when there's tremendous social pressure to do otherwise. Organizations like Heterodox Academy, OpenMind and Village Square continue to design and distribute tools and resources to support these efforts of administrators and faculty.

Third, stakeholders must perceive social permission to act on these values. This is a tougher nut to crack. For instance, even if professors set a good tone, students could be concerned about social sanction from peers.

Many of America's colleges and universities have fallen into a narrow orthodoxy in what is acceptable to say and to think on campus. Now is the time for all of us who value the pursuit of knowledge to support a new heterodoxy that welcomes, supports, and encourages a diversity of viewpoints.

The concept of constructive disagreement centers around creating a dynamic where key stakeholders in the faculty and student body are compelled to disagree. The word constructive alludes to the need to raise issues, debate, and resolve them reasonably. In the academy, this no longer or rarely happens--but it does so in the corporate world.

Our future as the world's leader in higher-education innovation depends on it.

Viewpoint Diversity on Campus is Essential

Viewpoint diversity refers to the state of a community or group in which members approach questions or problems from multiple perspectives. When a community is marked by intellectual humility, empathy, trust, and curiosity, viewpoint diversity gives rise to engaged and civil debate, constructive disagreement, and shared progress towards truth. Viewpoint diversity enables colleges and universities to realize their twin goals of producing the best research and providing the best education.

As citizens who are counting on students' and researchers' future contributions to our shared social, civic, moral, and scientific endeavors, we all suffer when orthodoxies distort and limit understanding of the social, aesthetic, and natural world—or when institutions of higher learning are unable to draw in perspectives from the whole of society. To help solve this problem we need heterodox academies.

To make headway on solving the world's most complex problems, scholars and policy makers must deploy the best ideas. This typically requires consulting a wide range of perspectives.

While a community of inquiry defined by intellectual humility, curiosity, empathy, and trust may hold many beliefs in common, few ideas will be beyond discussion, revision, or good-faith debate.

The Surest Sign of an Unhealthy Scholarly Culture is the Presence of Orthodoxy

Orthodoxies are most readily apparent when people fear shame, ostracism, or any other form of social or professional retaliation for questioning or challenging a commonly held idea.

The best way to defend against orthodoxies—or to neutralize them—is to foster commitment to open inquiry, viewpoint diversity and constructive disagreement. When these elements are missing, orthodoxies can take root and thrive.

Viewpoint diversity occurs when members of a group or community approach problems or questions from a range of perspectives. Institutions of higher learning face several interrelated viewpoint diversity deficits including:

- Racial/Ethnic
- Socioeconomic
- Geographical
- Religious
- Political
- And in many fields, Gender

Academic freedom demanded a respect for a diversity of views. During the Vietnam War years, college campuses were alive with debates about the war and a host of other subjects. There was no effort to silence diverse points of view.

Per Haidt, the future of liberal democracy depends in no small measure on empathy—the ability to humanize and understand others and tolerance. Students need to see those with whom they disagree politically as people—or else they risk alienating and demonizing the other side, which only leads to further conflict and highly-limited understanding.

A culture that will not tolerate divergence of opinion harms students, but academic research is also at risk when dominant theories and opinions no longer encounter counterclaims that test their validity.

Viewpoint Diversity Deficits Can Lead to Intolerance

When environments lack sufficient viewpoint diversity, problematic assumptions can go unchallenged, promising ideas and methods can go underexplored, and it can be difficult to effectively understand or engage with others who have different backgrounds, priors, and commitments.

For instance, to the extent that institutions of higher learning lack viewpoint diversity (and are thus not representative of the broader societies in which they are embedded), scholars may struggle to communicate the value and relevance of their work to people outside the academy in an accessible and compelling way.

Well-intentioned social programs can fail in their stated aims—or even cause harm—when the people designing policies are too far removed from the populations their interventions are intended to serve. Meanwhile, young people from underrepresented groups may come to feel as though they don't belong in the academy—and decline to apply to college, drop out midway through, or pursue non-academic paths if they push through to graduation.

In short, we would have reasons to recruit and retain a more diverse pool of faculty, staff, and students even if the lack of viewpoint diversity were purely the result of differences in interests and priorities among members of various groups.

However, we know that many disparities are also—at least in part—the result of a hostile atmosphere, discrimination, a lack of access or institutional dynamics that tend to privilege certain groups for reasons other than the quality of their research or ideas. It seems important to rectify these imbalances for moral as well as practical reasons.

Challenges and Threats to Free Speech From Social Psychology

What does the science of social psychology have to tell us about the current challenges and threats to free speech? A great deal, according to Dr. Jonathan Haidt, Thomas Cooley Professor of Ethical Leadership at New York University's Stern School of Business.

Haidt is one of three co-founders of Heterodox Academy (HxA) in 2015, an exciting new alliance of academics seeking to expand support for political diversity and highlight the challenges of ideological orthodoxy in higher education. ACTA's *The Forum* sat down with Haidt and his team at Heterodox Academy to discuss this innovative organization's approach to changing the culture in higher education and expanding viewpoint diversity:

The Heterodox Academy's membership has grown to 3,200 plus "In the wake of the Middlebury protests and violence, we're seeing a lot of liberal-left professors standing up against illiberal-left professors and students," Haidt says. Less than a fifth of the organization's members identify as "right or conservative;" most are centrists, liberals, or progressives.

By giving more academic jobs and tenure to outspoken libertarians and conservatives seems like the most effective way to change the campus culture, if only by signaling to self-censoring students that dissent is acceptable.

The Problem: Orthodoxy in the Academy

The Forum: Freedom of expression and diversity of opinion are under attack on many college campuses. What prompted Heterodox Academy's founding in this environment, and what do you hope to achieve?

Dr. Jonathan Haidt: In September 2015, a few weeks before the wave of student protests began, Heterodox Academy was founded to address a very specific problem: the loss of viewpoint diversity, especially political diversity, among the faculty in colleges and universities across America.

But as campus debate heated up in the fall of 2015, political passions rose and students who dissented from the prevailing orthodoxy found themselves increasingly under attack. Why should students feel like they cannot express themselves? Why should any subgroup of students be able to deem what is appropriate speech and which speaker is worthy of being heard? Are we engineering a climate where students will graduate without any exposure to contrasting viewpoints? What does that mean for businesses who hire grads unable to deal with those with whom they disagree politically?

A culture that will not tolerate divergence of opinion harms students, but academic research is also at risk when dominant theories and opinions no longer encounter counterclaims that test their validity.

The Heterodox Academy's goal is to create a network of academic stakeholders united in their intent to see the university live up to its ideals of truth, civil disagreement, and intellectual discovery. We want administrators and professors to stand up for free speech and free inquiry. We envision a campus where ideas can be expressed, beliefs challenged and theories critically analyzed so as to help students develop a more comprehensive and valid understanding of varied social and political perspectives, freed from the fear of intimidation by peers.

The Case for Intellectual Humility

The Templeton Foundation is leading research in intellectual humility and its many benefits. Psychologists and philosophers are working to tease apart the ways we respond to new ideas and information—and the possible benefits of a humble approach. Over the last decade, psychologists, philosophers, and other researchers have begun to explore intellectual humility, using analytical and empirical tools aimed at understanding its nature and implications.

At once theoretically fascinating and practically weighty, the study of intellectual humility calls for collaboration among researchers from fields of inquiry including psychology, epistemology, neuroscience, and educational research. In recent reviews of research commissioned by the John Templeton Foundation, Fordham University philosopher Nathan Ballantyne and Duke University psychologist Mark Leary synthesized findings from dozens of recently published articles on the topic, highlighting both the answers, and the questions, they raise.

From the 2018 paper by Leor Zmigrod, et. al., titled, "The psychological roots of intellectual humility: The role of intelligence and cognitive flexibility," intellectual humility has been identified as a character virtue that allows individuals to recognize their own potential fallibility when forming and revising attitudes. Intellectual humility is therefore essential for avoiding confirmation biases when reasoning about evidence and evaluating beliefs.

The present study investigated the cognitive correlates of intellectual humility. The results indicate that cognitive flexibility, measured with objective behavioral assessments, predicted intellectual humility. Intelligence was also predictive of intellectual humility.

Let's Embrace Constructive Disagreement

Constructive Disagreement occurs when people who don't see eye-to-eye are committed to exploring an issue together, alive to their own fallibility and the limits of their knowledge—and open to learning something from others who see things differently than they do.

When people lack the skill or the will to disagree constructively, disputes about theories, methods, data, analysis, or solutions can take on the character of zero-sum power struggles rather than opportunities for mutual growth and discovery. People become more polarized and closed-minded. They grow less likely to share and cooperate, and more likely to withhold key information, or engage in bad-faith for competitive advantage.

Mistakes and failures are more likely to be weaponized against scholars rather than being understood as an unavoidable part of the iterative process of exploration, trial, error, discovery, and revision that lies at the core of the scientific method. People grow less likely to take risks or tolerate uncertainty. Under these circumstances, increased diversity can become a liability—a source of additional paranoia and strife—rather than an asset.

Many students, faculty and staff have insufficient training in how to constructively engage across difference—especially as it relates to fundamental ideological commitments. To help resolve this campus wide problem, the Heterodox Academy that partners with professors, administrators, and others to create an academy eager to welcome people who approach problems and questions from different points of view, has a set of tools and ten steps professors can take to promote open inquiry and constructive disagreement in their classrooms.

Engaging With Underrepresented Perspectives Meaningfully and Charitably in the Curriculum

However, constructive disagreement cannot simply be taught from the armchair—it's a skill people refine through real-world engagement. In many contexts this is difficult due to the aforementioned demographic and ideological distortions within institutions of higher education.

Many students lack opportunities to engage with underrepresented perspectives meaningfully and charitably in the curriculum. Many professors who are concerned about this problem don't know where or how to begin introducing missing perspectives, as they often do not have a solid foundation in them either.

In many academic contexts, from class discussions to academic research, there are apparent incentives towards competition which can be counterproductive to learning and growth. It often seems easier to build a reputation by attacking others—to elevate oneself at the expense of others—than to seek opportunities for mutual growth and collaborative discovery among people who seem to be on opposite sides of an issue.

The background political culture in the contemporary United States is highly polarized and increasingly toxic. In such an environment, differences of opinion are more likely to be attributed to moral or intellectual defects in one's interlocutors. People are easily branded as sellouts or traitors for collaborating with "the enemy"—or providing ammunition for the "enemy" by defying the consensus of their tribe known as identify politics.

We All Suffer From Confirmation Bias

Per Dr. Jonathan Haidt, "We all suffer from confirmation bias—the tendency to use all of our powers of reasoning to seek out proof of why we are right. The only known cure for confirmation bias is engaging with other people who see things differently. Only they can find reasons why you might be wrong. Only they can help you improve your thinking. Therefore, an orthodox university cannot make you smarter, it can only confirm the prejudices you brought with you."

A heterodox university, in contrast, elevates everyone's ability to reason and sets students up with more realistic expectations about the world they will enter after commencement. In an interview with ACTA's *The Forum* he continues:

The Forum: What are the effects on individuals who live, work, and study in an environment that tolerates only one viewpoint—or orthodoxy?

Haidt: In such an environment, individuals with contrasting views are silenced either by peers or—more often—through self-censorship, walking on eggshells. What we want to break is the echo chamber in which people who have the same perspective endlessly reinforce each other, deepening orthodoxy and lessening the potential for cross-partisan conversations and empathy.

The future of liberal democracy depends in no small measure on empathy—the ability to humanize and understand others. Students need to see those with whom they disagree politically as people—or else they risk alienating and demonizing the other side, which only leads to further conflict and highly-limited understanding.

8 – Civil Debate, Discourse and Critical Thinking

Our society, it seems, has failed to transmit our values, in particular free speech, to the next generation. According to a new survey by the Pew Research Center, 40 per cent of Millennials support government censorship of speech offensive to minority groups. The poll found that Millennials were the most likely of any age group to agree that government should have the authority to stop people from saying things that offend minorities.

There can be little doubt that our society is not doing a very good job in transmitting our history and values to the next generation. A recent survey of 1,100 colleges and universities found that only eighteen percent require American history or government, where the foundations of our society, such as the First Amendment, can be explained.

The survey, by the American Council of Trustees and Alumni (ACTA), found that at the universities where free speech is now under attack, such as the University Missouri, Amherst, and Yale, very little is being done to transmit our history and values. There seems to be a correlation.

Is it any wonder that at such institutions, those in charge tend to recoil from any defense of free speech?

Measuring the Freedom of Expression Climate on Campus

Civil debate, discourse and critical thinking are perfectly consistent with an environment where people are talking *past* one-another, or *at* one-another, yet more effective when we speak *with* one-another, and work collaboratively and iteratively to understand and address difficult problems. This requires institutional norms and culture based on mutual respect—and a commitment to constructive disagreement. These cultural components cannot be effectively legislated or imposed, but they can be measured.

Simultaneously, institutional policies, procedures and incentive models of colleges and universities are changing. The needs, priorities, and expectations among new cohorts of students are evolving—even as the political climate in the United States (and beyond) has grown increasingly polarized and toxic. The result is a highly-combustible campus environment. Professors and students alike describe the toll of self-censoring and the ever-present threat of social or bureaucratic censure have taken on learning, discovery, and growth.

An effective assessment of a campuses' intellectual climate would, therefore, require an evaluation of:

1. Whether or not a school's policies protect or undermine free expression.

2. How diverse the intellectual community is, and...

3. How free students and faculty from different groups feel to share their views or express disagreement.

Americans used to frequently quote Voltaire's declaration: "I disapprove of what you say, but I will defend to the death your right to say it." This is no longer the case at too many of our colleges and universities. We have entered the era of what has been called "the heckler's veto."

Nat Hentoff, a long-time eloquent advocate for free speech, said, "First Amendment law is clear that everyone has the right to picket a speaker, and go inside a hall and heckle him or her—but not to drown out the speaker, let alone rush the stage and stop the speech before it starts. That's called the 'heckler's veto.'"

Universities Are Becoming Increasingly Hostile to Diverse Ideas

A recent study by the American Association of Colleges and Universities (AACU) of 24,000 college students and 9,000 faculty and staff members found that only eighteen per cent of the faculty and staff strongly agreed that it was "safe to hold unpopular positions on campus."

There is a difference between an opinion and an argument. An opinion is an expression of preference; it does not require any support (although it is stronger with support). An opinion is only the first part of an argument and to be complete, arguments should have three parts: an assertion, reasoning, and evidence (easily remembered with the mnemonic ARE).

We live in a climate ripe for noise: Media outlets and 24-hour news cycles mean that everyone with access to a computer has access to a megaphone to broadcast their views. Never before in human history has an opinion had the opportunity to reach so many so quickly regardless of its accuracy or appropriateness. This is a huge problem!

Educators are well positioned to provide a counterweight to this loudest-is-best approach. Speaking in a classroom or school environment is different from speaking in the outside world. Schools and classrooms strive to be safe places where students can exchange ideas, try out opinions and receive feedback on their ideas without fear or intimidation.

Children, of course, often come to school with opinions or prejudices they have learned in their homes or from the media. This means that it is also possible for schools to become places of intolerance and fear, especially for students who voice minority opinions.

Schools must work to be sites of social transformation where teachers and young people find ways to communicate effectively.

The Heckler's Veto and Squelching Speech

The sad reality is that many college campuses today have become hotbeds of bullying and intimidation. Speech which challenges "politically correct" doctrine is often shouted down. Or relegated to tightly-restricted "free speech zones." Or deemed unworthy of respectful consideration—even if presented by someone who grew up under Jim Crow (see, for example, the protests against Condoleezza

Rice's invitation to be Rutgers' 2014 commencement speaker).

The point here is that all of us (whether on the Left or the Right) are capable of trampling on the freedoms of others. And the danger appears to be particularly great when one holds considerable power—as the white supremacists did in the Jim Crow South and as progressives do on today's college campuses.

Now, none of this would surprise our nation's founders (who had their own shortcomings, lest we forget). As James Madison famously said, "If men were angels, no government would be necessary." And part of the reason Madison penned the First Amendment is so that the public square could be filled with the vigorous exchange of (both popular and unpopular) ideas.

To be sure, few Americans have ever exercised their free speech rights as effectively as Patricia Stephens and her fellow FAMU students. Which is why all of us should seek to learn from—and follow—these college students' courageous example.

Cancel Culture is All Around Us

Think about being at your school in a class that was discussing a controversial issue about POLITICS. How comfortable or reluctant would you feel about speaking up and giving your views on this topic?

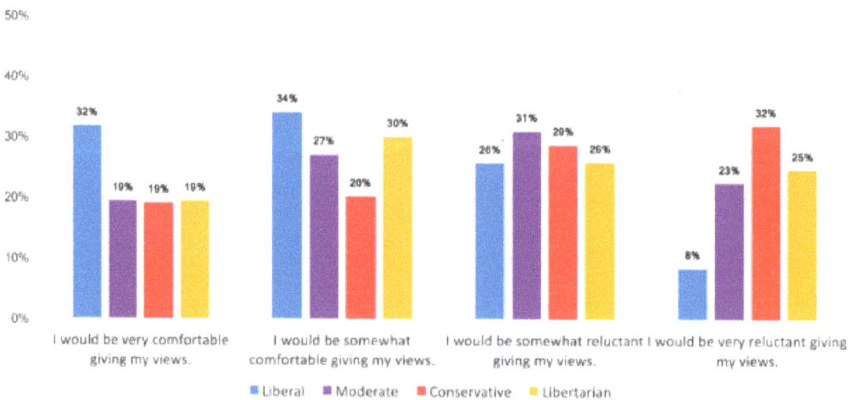

Credit: The Heterodox Academy.

American thought leader Scott Adams,' the *Dilbert* creator, satirist, and cartoonist, was interviewed by the *Epoch Times* in 2019 and from that article is some great advice to live by regarding cancel culture:

The "48-hour" rule says that if you've done something dumb–usually you've misspoken, or maybe you said exactly what you meant but it was a bad thing to say–you have 48 hours to clarify and/or apologize. If you hit that, (if) it's a reasonable apology, has to be a pretty good one, or a reasonable clarification, (then) we as a society should say: 48 hours–(he) saw a problem. (He) did what he could do.

Now the other rule is the "20-year" rule. I suggest the "20-year" rule. If something happened more than twenty years ago–unless you're a pedophile, or a murderer or something–that we let it go, because you're just not the same person. It's very close to blaming a different person for your crime because every cell in your body has been replaced. The way you think, the way you act, is almost certainly different over twenty years.

Criticisms of cancel culture centered on the feeling that people were becoming too keen to ruin lives over mistakes made many years ago. That people didn't get a second chance. That social media is too quick to pile on and police increasingly high standards of political correctness and do so in a way that simply is virtue signaling and performatively woke.

That canceling has gone too far and simply become a way of rejecting anyone you disagreed with or someone who did something you didn't like. Former President Barack Obama notably criticized cancel culture (though not using the words as such), arguing that easy social media judgments don't amount to true social activism.

Ground Rules for Respectful Public Discourse & Behavior

Being concerned about growing incivility in our civic and public settings we can learn from the people of Utah to return to fundamental principles that will lead to greater civility and a new spirit of community. In 2008, they reaffirmed their "inherent and inalienable" Constitutional rights is the fundamental right "to communicate freely about our thoughts and opinions," and yet they are also "responsible for the abuse of that right" Constitution of Utah Article I Section 1. In that context they believe that there must be a renewal of respectful discourse and behavior in civic and public settings in Utah.

This is not an appeal for us all simply to get along. We recognize that there are profound differences among us, and that spirited debate is a vital part of American democracy. Participation in American civic and public life does not require us to sacrifice our deepest convictions; rather we best protect our own rights by protecting the rights of others and adhering to high ethical standards.

With that in mind lets propose the following ground rules of civic and public engagement that recognize the important place of the rights, responsibilities, and respect inherent in our civic and constitutional compact.

1. Remember the Importance of Rights and the Dignity of Each Individual. Our society is founded upon the proposition that all people are born free and equal in dignity and rights, and that freedom of conscience and expression are at the foundation of our rights.

2. Responsibly Exercise your Rights While Protecting the Rights of Others. Each of us should be responsible both in the exercise or our rights and in protecting the rights of others. Especially on matters of personal faith, claims of conscience, and human rights, public policy should seek solutions that are fair to all.

3. Respect Others. All people—especially our leaders and the media—should demonstrate a commitment to be respectful in discourse and behavior, particularly in civic and public forums. Respect should also be shown by being honest and as inclusive as possible, by mindfully listening to and attempting to understand the concerns of others, by valuing their opinions even when there is disagreement, and by addressing their concerns when possible.

4. Refrain from Incivility. Public discourse can be passionate while maintaining mutual respect that reaches beyond differing opinions. Intimidation, ridicule, personal attacks, mean spiritedness, reprisals against those who disagree, and other disrespectful or unethical behaviors destroy the fabric of our society and can no longer be tolerated. Those who engage in such behavior should be brought to light, held accountable and should no longer enjoy the public's trust.

5. Rekindle Building Community. Our social compact "of the people" and "by the people" is "for the people." Each one of us has a responsibility to build

community. On divisive issues, areas of common ground should first be explored. Effort should be given to building broad-based agreement, giving due regard to the concerns of minority points of view.

A Plea for Civil Discourse: Needed, the Academy's Leadership

The United States of America—that inspiring experiment in democratic government—was founded on compromise; the Constitution, one of the greatest give-and-take documents, describes a government with multiple loci of power. The bicameral makeup of Congress ensures the rights of small and large states alike, a solution reached during the republic's creation.

The United States came into existence because of religious and heritage plurality. The country's plurality in the twenty-first century includes an entire spectrum of skin colors, ethnic groups, beliefs, languages, and cultures. In a pluralistic society, people hold varying views, and that very diversity is an inherent strength. In a country anchored in compromise and diversity, discourse among people of good faith should flourish.

A Crucible Moment: College Learning and Democracy's Future, commissioned by the US Department of Education, was published by the American Association of Colleges and Universities (AACU) in 2012.

Representing the work of the National Task Force on Civic Learning and Democratic Engagement (2012), the report builds a strong case for higher education's responsibility, in collaboration with the larger society, for assuring that all students have the skills and knowledge they need to become informed, civically engaged citizens. The section below is intended to complement *A Crucible Moment* by focusing in greater depth on civil discourse and the crucial need for colleges and universities to commit strongly to its survival.

Defining Civil Discourse

What is civil discourse? A 2011 conversation among national leaders from many fields, held at the US Supreme Court, defined civil discourse as "robust, honest, frank and constructive dialogue and deliberation that seeks to advance the public interest" (Brosseau 2011).

James Calvin Davis, in his book *In Defense of Civility*, proposes "the exercise of patience, integrity, humility and mutual respect in civil conversation, even (or especially) with those with whom we disagree" (2010, 159).

National Public Radio journalist Diane Rehm, during an event at Oberlin College, said simply: our ability to have conversation about topics about which we disagree, and our ability to listen to each other's perspectives (Choby 2011).

Civil discourse is discourse that supports, rather than undermines, the societal good. It demands that democratic participants respect each other, even when that respect is hard to give or to earn. Democratic societies must be societies where arguments are tolerated and encouraged, but this is not always easy.

"To engage in a healthy political argument is to acknowledge the possibility that one's own arguments could be falsified or proven wrong," says Thomas Hollihan, professor at the University of Southern California's Annenberg School of Communication. "This demands that citizens listen respectfully to the claims made by others. Name-calling, threats and bullying behaviors do not meet the demands of effective deliberation."

For the purposes of this article, discourse that is civil means that those involved:

- Undertake a serious exchange of views.

- Focus on the issues rather than on the individual(s) espousing them.

- Defend their interpretations using verified information.

- Thoughtfully listen to what others say.

- Seek the sources of disagreements and points of common purpose.

- Embody open-mindedness and a willingness change their minds.

- Assume they will need to compromise and are willing to do so.

- Treat the ideas of others with respect.

- Avoid violence (physical, emotional, and verbal).

While some consider politeness and good behavior as essential to civil discourse, Ahrens (2009) argues that civil discourse must accommodate offensive expression, with the latter term capturing the harshness of many public debate conflicts. Leach (2011) says that civility "is not simply or principally about manners. It doesn't mean that spirited advocacy is to be avoided. Indeed, argumentation is a social good.

Without (it) there is a tendency to dogmatism, even tyranny." Herbst (2010, 148) suggests that "even some incivility can move a policy debate along. Creating a culture of argument, and the thick skin that goes along with it, are long-term projects that will serve democracy well." One should not expect civil discourse to create a feeling of comfort; discord causes uneasiness, and a challenge to deeply held opinions induces pain.

Wegge (2013) distinguishes two elements in civil discourse: (1) the emotive, as expressed through manners and norms of behavior (moderating or failing to moderate self-control), and (2) "constructive confrontation" or civility demonstrated through argument and deliberation. In any case, civil discourse goes beyond courtesy. It involves committing to an informed, frank exchange of ideas, along with an understanding of complexity and ambiguity.

Koegler (2012) clarifies that "civil" refers not to mannered conduct but to membership in a civil society. He suggests that civil discourse has both a process ("a pragmatic and open dialogue of the issues themselves, based on evidence and argument, coupled with the willingness to learn from the other") and content ("serious conversation about public matters of common concern").

As used here, the term civil discourse includes speaking or writing knowledgeably about a topic and harkens back to the definition of discourse as the process or power of reasoning. It is this basis in reasoned inquiry that affords one essential hook for holding higher education accountable.

Civil Discourse in Civic Learning

A Crucible Moment advocates for adding to college study a third nationwide educational priority, complementing those of increased access and career preparation: the graduation of responsibly engaged citizens.

These graduates will need to be informed through knowledge, including knowledge of the political process and the major issues of current and former times. They will also need to be empowered by possessing a range of intellectual and practical skills. Civil discourse, a central skill of such civic learning, itself rests on core intellectual abilities at the very heart of powerful education:

- Critical inquiry.

- Analysis and reasoning.

- Information retrieval and evaluation.

- Effective written communication.

- Effective oral communication that includes listening as well as speaking.

- An understanding of one's own perspectives and their limitations.

- The ability to interact constructively with a diverse group of individuals holding conflicting views.

Civil discourse also embodies the very values of civic learning: open-mindedness, compromise, and mutual respect.

Participants in civil discourse need to learn about the issue at hand, critically weigh the information's veracity and validity, build a logical argument, and present it in a convincing but nondoctrinaire manner to individuals who might not share the same views. They need to be respectfully attentive to alternative interpretations—weighing them, too, analytically—and be willing to alter positions based on convincing argument and evidence.

Educators will recognize these skills and values as those of any serious intellectual undertaking, which is why civil discourse is not limited to political science or the political arena. It figures centrally in any field with controversies—science, art, or philosophy, for example—and, therefore, can be learned and practiced in most disciplines.

Just like the core intellectual and practical abilities of liberal learning, civil discourse is transferable across disciplines and outside the academy, to the workplace and civic life. While concern about the harsh tenor of interchanges in the political arena catalyzed this article, as a democratic approach to handling controversy, civil discourse has broad applicability. Referencing Diane Rehm again, civil dialogue and discourse begin at home.

Promoting Civil Discourse in Undergraduate Education

Once we accept that students need to become adept civil discoursers—for their own and democracy's good—how can college education foster this important skill?

First, civil discourse must be addressed at the heart of undergraduate education. It cannot be relegated to student affairs or simply embodied in codes of conduct or speech, nor can it remain the purview of a department of politics or communications. Civil discourse needs to be addressed in general education for all students and embraced by the various majors, across the curriculum. Given the swirl of many students among institutions, commitment will be needed in all high schools, colleges, and universities.

Second, students need to be taught (and not simply exposed to or asked to use) civil discourse, which means giving them both a theoretical basis of the concept and practical tools for using it.

Theory could include, for example, definitions and rules, cultural variations, and norms, plus analysis of the consequences of dogmatism. Practical tools might involve applying to contentious issues skills learned elsewhere in the curriculum: active listening, debating techniques, public speaking, as well as the basics of persuasive writing (turning opinions into arguments, refuting the arguments of others).

Pedagogy is at least as important here as curricular design. Useful non-subject-specific classroom practices (discussed by Shuster but applicable to the university level) include intentionally teaching controversy or turning classroom discussion into a pedagogical strategy: consciously attending to the conduct of discussions, setting goals, having students summarize discussions, and requiring meta-analysis.

Third, we know from much formal research and informal observation that deep learning occurs cumulatively and progressively, whether the learning is of information or of skills. One-time exposure only initiates the process. Learners also progress better when exposed to multiple modalities, including active involvement.

Therefore, college curricula and cocurricula should provide students the opportunity to study about, reflect on, and practice civil discourse in a purposeful manner at several points and in increasingly sophisticated ways. The process might start in a first-year seminar, continue in an introduction to the major where civil discourse could be applied to the controversies of the field, and form part of a senior seminar or thesis defense.

Fourth, as with any important learning outcome, the ability to engage in civil discourse needs to be assessed at least at the individual student and the program levels, formatively and summatively. How well do students understand the concept? How skillfully do they practice discourse that is effective and responsible? How successfully does the program (be it for a degree or not) meet its objectives and in what ways can it be improved? For such an assessment, rubrics for civil discourse would need to be developed.

Fifth, given that the ability to engage in civil discourse has rarely figured as an institutional learning outcome (Roger Williams University is one notable exception), most professors will be ignorant of ways to include it in their courses—or even how to model it. Therefore, faculty development will be vital; fortunately, most campuses have internal expertise upon which to draw (e.g., their own political scientists, linguists, philosophers, debate coaches, rhetoric teachers, and those from any field who teach controversy in the classroom).

Open Inquiry

A world-class academic community depends on an open society to thrive; it also models an ideal culture of discourse. Questioning and argument, weighing evidence and analyzing alternative interpretations—such values are at the core of teaching and scholarship.

Open Inquiry is the ability to ask questions and share ideas without risk of censure.

In an environment that is insufficiently open, facts can be corrupted or suppressed for the benefit of special interests. Important innovations can be set back or outright snuffed out. Avoidable problems can fester and spread. Personal and intellectual growth can be stunted.

Open inquiry is threatened on several fronts. Across the political spectrum there are people who make it their business to surveille and mob scholars who threaten their preferred narratives.

Expanding bureaucracies at many colleges and universities subject ever more of campus life to administrative oversight—and encourage people to resolve disputes through reporting, investigations, and academic reprisals rather than good-faith debate and discussion.

Concerns about placating donors, ensuring high enrollments or positive course evaluations can distort research and pedagogy—especially for the growing numbers of contingent faculty whose careers and livelihoods can be threatened by a single upset student, donor, or colleague.

And, of course, many fear losing the esteem of, or being ostracized by, one's peers for saying the "wrong" thing (a risk which is more pronounced in highly-homogenous environments). Even in the absence of formal sanctions, social and professional isolation can make academic life extremely difficult and unpleasant—and many reasonably prefer to self-censor rather than risk it. This is a significant concern among students, faculty, and administrators.

Academics worried about attacks on free speech have felt the need to respond, and they have articulated sound principles. Princeton professors Robert P. George and Cornel West recently attracted lots of supporters for a statement underscoring that "all of us should seek respectfully to engage with people who challenge our views" and that "we should oppose efforts to silence those with whom we disagree—especially on college and university campuses."

Trying to understand the logic of someone else's arguments is a core skill that schools should be paying more attention to, and it doesn't always require elaborate new programs. The group Heterodox Academy, which includes faculty from many universities and from across the political spectrum, has recently launched the "Viewpoint Diversity Experience," an online effort to combat "the destructive power of ideological tribalism." The aim is "to prepare students for democratic citizenship and success in the political diverse workplaces they will soon inhabit."

Such efforts are sorely needed, but they can succeed only if we do a better job of bringing underrepresented points of view into the mix. Simply relying on the marketplace of ideas isn't enough. We need an affirmative-action program for conservative, libertarian, and religious modes of thinking.

The Failure to Improve Critical-Thinking Skills

As noted by Dr. April Kelly-Woessner, Professor of Political Science and Chair of the Department of Politics, Philosophy and Legal Studies at Elizabethtown College, "What we find is that confidence in civic knowledge correlates pretty strongly and is a good predictor of political tolerance.

So, if you think you know a lot relative to other people, if you think you can hold your own in a political conversation, you're more tolerant than people who are insecure about their civic knowledge. The perception of these college students protestors is that they're ideological radicals who have these strong opinions, and yet what the data shows is wanting to shut down other voices reflects an insecurity to defend your own. The decline in civic knowledge is a big factor in political intolerance."

Results of a standardized measure of reasoning ability show many students fail to improve over four years—even at some flagship schools, according to *The Wall Street Journal* analysis of nonpublic results

Students at Plymouth State University in New Hampshire showed extensive progress in critical thinking over four years, as measured by a test called the College Learning Assessment Plus, (CLA+). Freshmen and seniors at about 200 colleges across the U.S. take this little-known test every year to measure how much better they get at learning to think. The results are discouraging.

At more than half of schools, at least a third of seniors were unable to make a cohesive argument, assess the quality of evidence in a document or interpret data in a table. *The Wall Street Journal* found after reviewing the latest results from dozens of public colleges and universities that gave the exam between 2013 and 2016.

For prospective students and their parents looking to pick a college, it is almost impossible to figure out which schools help students learn critical thinking, because full results of the standardized test, called the CLA+, are seldom disclosed to the public. This is true, too, of similar tests.

Some academic experts, education researchers and employers say *The Wall Street Journal's* findings are a sign of the failure of America's higher-education system to arm graduates with analytical reasoning and problem-solving skills needed to thrive in a fast-changing, increasingly global job market. In addition, rising tuition, student debt and loan defaults are putting colleges and universities under pressure to prove their value.

A survey by PayScale Inc., an online pay and benefits researcher, showed 50% of employers complain that college graduates they hire aren't ready for the workplace. Their No. 1 complaint? Poor critical-reasoning skills.

"At most schools in this country, students basically spend four years in college, and they don't necessarily become better thinkers and problem solvers," said Josipa Roksa, a University of Virginia sociology professor who co-wrote a book in 2011 about the CLA+ test. "Employers are going to hire the best they can get, and if we don't have that, then what is at stake in the long run is our ability to compete."

International rankings show U.S. college graduates are in the middle of the pack when it comes to numeracy and literacy and near the bottom when it comes to problem solving.

CLA+ Test Raises Questions About the Purpose of a College Degree

The CLA+ test raises questions about the purpose of a college degree and taps into a longstanding debate about the role of colleges: Are they are designed to raise students' intellectual abilities or to sort high-school graduates so they can find the niche for which they are best suited?

The role of a diploma as signal of ability has been in the ascendancy recently, given how having a degree is closely related to graduates' lifetime earnings. The test data, by contrasl, show that many students earn their degrees without improving their ability to think critically or solve problems.

Tests such as the CLA+ can be used to fulfill a mandate by accreditors for schools to show that they are trying to assess and improve the education they provide.

The CLA+ measures critical thinking, analytical reasoning, problem solving and writing because it demands students manipulate information and data in real-world circumstances that require different abilities. It has been lauded by a federal commission that studied higher education in the U.S.

Students Who Perform Well on the Test Say It's an Accurate Gauge of Their Academic Programs

The CLA+ requires students to use spreadsheets, newspaper articles, research papers and other documents to answer questions, make a point or critique an argument. Colleges pay about $35 a student to the test's creator and administrator, the Council for Aid to Education, a nonprofit group in New York.

At each college, the roughly 90-minute test is given to one group of freshmen in the fall of their freshman year and to a separate group of seniors in the spring of the same academic year. A statistical analysis of the difference between the average scores of the two groups is considered a valid way to reflect the value added during four years of college.

Overall, a majority of students at colleges that took the CLA+ made measurable progress in critical thinking, the *Journal* found. Colleges that added the most value aren't necessarily highly ranked in areas that more often build a college's reputation, such as faculty research, graduate programs, on-campus amenities, sports programs, and the selectivity of the freshmen class.

9 – Social Justice, Woke Schooling & Critical Pedagogies Are Ruining U.S. Education

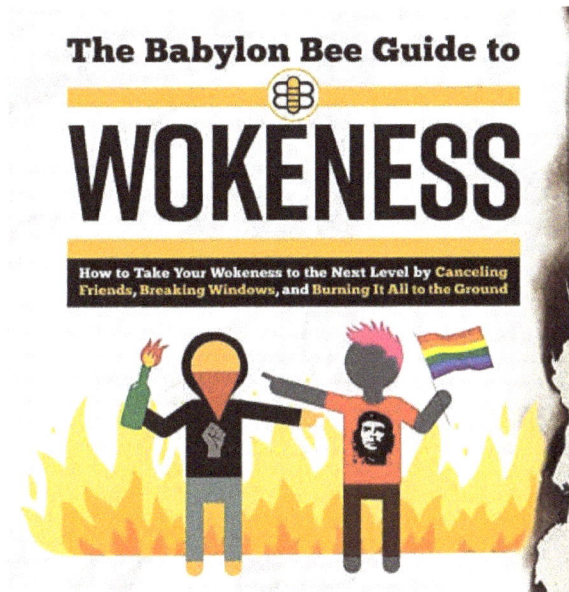

Credit: Babylon Bee.

Social-justice ideology is turning higher education into an engine of progressive political advocacy, according to a new report by the National Association of Scholars. Left-wing activists, masquerading as professors, are infiltrating traditional academic departments or creating new ones—departments such as "Solidarity and Social Justice"—to advance their cause.

They are entering the highest rung of college administration, from which perch they require students to take social-justice courses, such as "Native Sexualities and Queer Discourse" or "Hip-hop Workshop," and attend social-justice events—such as a Reparations, Repatriation, and Redress Symposium or a Power and Privilege Symposium—in order to graduate.

But social-justice education is merely a symptom of an even deeper perversion of academic values: the cult of race and gender victimology, otherwise known as "diversity." The diversity cult is destroying the very foundations of our civilization. It is worth first exploring, however, why social-justice education is an oxymoron.

Why shouldn't an academic aspire to correcting perceived social ills? The nineteenth-century American land-grant universities and the European research universities were founded, after all, on the premise that knowledge helps society progress. But social justice is a different beast entirely.

When a university pursues social justice, it puts aside its traditional claim to authority: the disinterested search for knowledge. We accord universities enormous privileges. Their denizens are sheltered from the hurly-burly of the marketplace on the assumption that they will pursue truth wherever it will take them, unaffected by political or economic pressures.

The definition of social justice, however, is deeply political, entailing a large number of contestable claims about the causes of socioeconomic inequality. Social-justice proponents believe that those claims are settled, and woe to anyone who challenges them on a college campus. There are, however, alternative explanations—besides oppression and illegitimate power—for ongoing inequalities, taboo though they may be in academia—they are fully covered in *Education Madness*.

The Cost of America's Cultural Revolution

From the Heather Mac Donald "The Cost of America's Cultural Revolution" *City Journal* report in December 2019:

Social-justice pedagogy is driven by one overwhelming reality: the seemingly intractable achievement gap between whites and Asians on the one hand, and blacks and Hispanics on the other. Radical feminism, as well as gay and now trans advocacy, are also deeply intertwined with social-justice thinking on campus and off, as we have just seen. But race is the main impetus. Liberal whites are terrified that the achievement and behavior gaps will never close. So they have crafted a totalizing narrative about the racism that allegedly holds back black achievement.

What are the "white norms" and "culture" that "race talk" seeks to deconstruct? Objectivity, a strong work ethic, individualism, a respect for the written word, perfectionism, and promptness, according to legions of diversity trainers and many humanities, social sciences, and even STEM faculty. Any act of self-discipline or deferred gratification that contributes to individual and generational success is now simply a manifestation of white supremacy.

The *New York Times* recently singled out parents who had queued up hours early to visit a sought-after public school in New York City. "Why were white parents at the front of the line for the school tour?" asked the *Times* headline. The article answered: their white privilege, not their dedication to their children's schooling.

The test for whether a norm is white and thus illegitimate is whether it has a disparate impact on blacks and Hispanics. Given the behavioral and academic skills gaps, every colorblind standard of achievement will have a disparate impact.

The average black 12th-grader currently reads at the level of the average white eighth-grader. Math levels are similarly skewed. Truancy rates for black students are often four times as high as for white students. Inner-city teachers, if they are being honest, will describe the barely controlled anarchy in their classrooms—anarchy exacerbated by the phony conceit that school discipline is racist.

In light of such disparities, it is absurd to attribute the absence of proportional representation in the STEM fields, say, to bias. And yet, STEM deans, faculty, and Silicon Valley tech firms claim that only implicit bias explains why 13 percent of engineering professors are not black. The solution to this lack of proportional representation is not greater effort on the part of students, according to social-justice and diversity proponents.

Instead, it is watering down meritocratic standards.

Professors are now taught about "inclusive grading" and how to assess writing without judging its quality, since such quality judgments maintain white language supremacy. The social-justice diversity bureaucracy has constructed a perpetual-motion machine that guarantees it eternal life.

Minority students who have been catapulted by racial preferences into schools for which they are not academically prepared frequently struggle in their classes. The cause of those struggles, according to the social-justice diversity bureaucracy, is not academic mismatch; it is the lack of a critical mass of other minority students and faculty to provide refuge from the school's overwhelming bigotry. And so, the school admits more minority students to create such a critical mass.

Rather than raising minority performance, however, this new influx of diverse students lowers it, since the school has had to dig deeper into the applicant pool. The academic struggles and alienation of minority students will increase, along with the demand for more diversity bureaucrats, more segregated safe spaces, more victimology courses, more mental health workers, more diverse faculty, more lowered standards, and of course, more diversity student admits.

And the cycle will start all over again.

The only precedent for our current resentment-driven war on the West's magnificent achievements is the Chinese Cultural Revolution, and that didn't turn out well. The Cultural Revolution, however, was waged mostly by the less educated against the more educated.

The oddest feature of today's social-justice crusade is that it is being prosecuted by the elites against themselves. Every college president, law firm managing partner, and Fortune 500 CEO would rather theatrically blame himself and his colleagues for phantom bigotry than speak honestly about the real causes of ongoing racial inequality: family breakdown and an underclass culture that mocks learning and the conformity to bourgeois values as acting "white."

Anti-racism has become the national religion, with the search for instances of racism to back up that religion becoming ever more desperate.

In fact, America is among the least racist countries on the planet.

There is not a single mainstream institution not trying to hire and promote as many underrepresented minorities as possible. Conservative philanthropists and corporations spend billions each year on social-uplift programs to close the achievement gap. Taxpayer dollars are liberally distributed from government coffers. We so take these efforts for granted that we don't even see them; they have no effect on the dominant narrative about white indifference and exploitation.

We are in uncharted territory. How a civilization survives with so much contempt for itself is an open question.

Social Justice Education in America

Per the David Randall "Social Justice Education in America" National Association of

Scholars report in November 2019:

American universities have drifted from the political center for fifty years and more. By now scarcely any conservatives or moderates remain, and most of them are approaching retirement. The radical establishment triumphed on campus a generation ago. What they have created since is an even more disturbing successor to the progressive academy of the 1990s.

In the last twenty years, a generation of academics and administrators has emerged that is no longer satisfied with using the forms of traditional scholarship to teach progressive thought. This new generation seeks to transform higher education itself into an engine of progressive political advocacy, subjecting students to courses that are nothing more than practical training in progressive activism. This new generation bases its teaching and research on the ideology of social justice.

What we may call radical social justice theory, which dominates higher education, adds to broader social justice theory the belief that society is divided into social identity groups defined by categories such as class, race, and gender; that any "unfair distribution" of goods among these groups is oppression; and that oppression can only— and must—be removed by a coalition of "marginalized" identity groups working to radically transform politics, society, and culture to eliminate privilege.

A rough, incomplete catalogue of the social justice movement's political goals includes increased federal and state taxation; increased minimum wage; increased environmental regulation; increased government health care spending and regulation; restrictions on free speech; restrictions on due process protections; maximizing the number of legislative districts that will elect racial minorities; support for the Black Lives Matter movement; mass release of criminals from prison; decriminalizing drugs; ending enforcement of our immigration laws; amnesty for illegal aliens; open borders; race and sex preferences in education and employment; persecution of conscientious objectors to homosexuality; advocacy for "transgender rights"; support for the anti- Israeli Boycott, Divest, and Sanction movement; avowal of a right to abortion; and mob violence to enforce the social justice policy agenda.

Social justice advocates' emphasis on words such as justice, equity, rights, and impact all register social justice's fundamental goal of acquiring governmental power. Social justice advocates tend to dedicate any activity in which they engage to the effort to achieve the political ends of social justice.

Activism is the Exemplary Means to Forward Social Justice

This word signifies the collective exertion of influence via social justice nonprofit organizations. Activism may take the form of organization-building (staff work, fundraising, membership recruitment), publicity, lobbying, and actions by responsible officials in pursuit of social justice. It may also take the form of "protest"— assembling large numbers of people on the streets to "persuade" responsible officials into executing the preferred policies of social justice advocates. Social justice activism formally eschews violence, but far too many social justice advocates are willing to engage in all "necessary" violence.

Social justice activists in the university are subordinating higher education toward the goal of achieving social justice. Social justice education takes the entire set of social justice beliefs as the predicate for education, in every discipline from accounting to zoology. Social justice education rejects the idea that classes should aim at teaching a subject matter for its own sake, or seek to foster students' ability to think, judge, and write as independent goods.

Social justice education instead aims directly at creating effective social justice activists, ideally engaged during class in such activism. Social justice education transforms the very definitions of academic disciplines—first to permit the substitution of social justice activism for intellectual endeavor, and then to require it.

Social justice advocates' most important curricular tactic within higher education is to insert one or more social justice requirements into the general education requirements. They give these requirements different names, including Diversity, Experiential Learning, Sustainability, Global Studies, and, forthrightly, Social Justice. This tactic forces all college students to take at least one social justice course, and thereby maximizes the effect of social justice propaganda.

The common practice of double counting a social justice requirement so that it also satisfies another requirement powerfully reinforces the effect of social justice requirements. These requirements also effectively reserve a large number of teaching jobs and tenure-track lines for social justice educators. No one but a social justice advocate, after all, is really qualified to teach a course in social justice advocacy. The direct financial burden of social justice general education requirements is at least $10 billion a year nationwide, and rising fast.

The direct financial burden of social justice general education requirements is at least $10 billion a year nationwide, and rising fast.

Social justice advocates have also taken over or created a substantial portion of the academic departments in our universities. The departments most likely to advertise their commitment to social justice are those most central to the social justice educators' ideological vision, political goals, and ambition for employment. The heaviest concentrations of social justice departments are the Identity Group Studies, Gender Studies, Peace Studies, and Sustainability Studies pseudo-disciplines; the career track departments of Education, Social Work, and Criminology; and the departments dedicated to activism such as Civic Engagement, Leadership, and Social Justice.

Social Justice's Dizziest Success Has Been Its takeover of the University Administration

While social justice education has made great strides among university professors, its dizziest success has been its takeover of the university administration. Higher education administration is now even more liberal than the professoriate. The training of higher education administrators, especially within the labyrinth of "co-curricular" bureaucracies, increasingly makes commitment to social justice an explicit or an implicit requirement. These administrators insert themselves into all aspects of student life, both outside and inside the classroom. Overwhelmingly, they exercise their power to promote social justice.

Social justice administrators catechize students in social justice propaganda; select social justice advocates as outside speakers; funnel students to off-campus social justice organizations that benefit from free student labor; and provide jobs and money for social justice cadres among the student body. The formation of social justice bureaucracies also serves as an administrative stepping stone to the creation of social justice departments. Perhaps most importantly, university administration provides a career for students specializing in social justice advocacy.

Higher education's administrative bloat has facilitated the growth of social justice bureaucracies—among them, Offices of Diversity and Multicultural Affairs; Title IX coordinators; Offices of First-Year Experience and Community Engagement; Offices of Student Life and Residential Life; Offices of Service-Learning and Civic Engagement; Offices of Equity and Inclusion; Offices of Sustainability and Social Justice; and miscellaneous institutes and centers.

These bureaucracies focus on co-curricular activities, which consist largely of social justice activities such as Intersectionality Workshops and Social Justice Weekend Retreats. Social justice administrators aim to subordinate the curriculum to the co-curriculum, as the practical way to subordinate the pursuit of truth to social justice advocacy.

Social Justice Administrators Have Set Up Institutions That Make Social Justice Advocacy Inescapable

Offices of Residential Life have turned large amounts of housing into venues for social justice advocacy. The most intensive advocacy proceeds through Living Learning Communities—housing units dedicated to themes such as Global Citizenship, Gender and Social Justice, and Social Justice Action.

Bias Incident Response Teams, which rely on voluntary informers ("active bystanders") throughout campus, dedicate themselves to gathering reports of "bias incidents"—which, practically speaking, can include any word or action that offends social justice advocates. Bias Incident Response Teams act as enforcers of social justice orthodoxy on campus. Break and Study Abroad programs have also been largely taken over by social justice advocates, and are now frequently exercises in service-learning and social justice advocacy.

Offices of Residential Life subject students to social justice education even while they are eating and sleeping, Bias Incident Response Teams monitor every private social interaction, and Study Abroad and Break programs subject students to social justice education even while they are away from campus.

Social Justice Bureaucracies Sponsor a Large Number of Social Justice Events on Campus

These events are the actual substance of social justice education on campus. The varieties of social justice events include activism programs, commencements, community mobilizations, conferences, dialogues, festivities, films, fine arts performances, hunger banquets, lectures, projects, residence hall programs, resource fairs, retreats, roundtables, student education, student training, workshops, and youth activities.

The subjects of these events have included activism, ally education, Black Lives Matter, civic engagement, community organizing, diversity, food, gender identity, health care, illegal aliens, implicit bias, leadership, LGBTQ, mental illness, policing, power, prisons, racial identity, social justice, and sustainability.

Social Justice Bureaucracies Also Engage in Large Amounts of Student Training

This student training identifies, catechizes, and provides work experience for the next generation of social justice advocates. This student training is especially useful for training the next generation of social justice educators. By scholarships, the provision of student jobs, and linking social justice cadres to careers, social justice educators ensure that social justice education is linked to social justice jobs for graduates. The Diversity Peer Educator of today is the Dean of Diversity of tomorrow. Today's Social Justice Scholar will become tomorrow's Dean of Student Affairs. Student training provides the cadres for social justice activism.

"During a Hunger Banquet, each group experiences the wealth or poverty of their representative group. The very rich dine on a meal that most North Americans would consider standard: meat, vegetables, side dishes and clean water. The middle class receives a small bowl of rice and beans, typical of the meal that middle-class households often consume around the world. The poorest group sits on the floor, receiving only a communal pot of rice that leaves them all hungry

The Diversity Peer Educator of today is the Dean of Diversity of tomorrow. Today's Social Justice Scholar will become tomorrow's Dean of Student Affairs.

Social justice education, in addition, prepares students for positions in private industry (human resources, diversity associates), progressive nonprofit organizations, progressive political campaigns, progressive officials' offices, government bureaucracies, K-12 education, social work, court personnel, and the professoriate. University administration and faculty directly provide a massive source of employment for social justice advocates: the total number of social justice advocates employed in higher education must be well above 100,000.

Soon All of Higher Education May Be Reserved For Social Justice Advocates

Before we know it, all of higher education may be reserved for social justice advocates since university job advertisements have begun explicitly to require affirmations of diversity and social justice. These ideological loyalty oaths will effectively reserve higher education employment to the 8% of Americans who are progressive activists.

Since social justice educators have to publish a minimum amount of peer-reviewed academic research to receive tenure, they have also created an apparatus of journal and book publication as cargo-cult scholarship—an imitation of the form of academic research, largely consisting of after-action reports on social justice activism on campus.

The core of this cargo-cult apparatus is a network of hundreds of academic journals dedicated to social justice scholarship, whose editors and peer reviewers are also social justice educators.

Their specializations mirror the range of social justice education—ethnic studies and gender studies, education journals and sustainability journals, journals devoted to critical studies, dialogue, diversity, equity, experiential education, inclusive education, intercultural communication, multicultural education, peace, service-learning, social inclusion—and, of course, social justice.

The bureaucracy of accreditation plays an important role in forwarding social justice advocacy at America's colleges and universities. Some accreditation bureaucracies require diversity, or other keywords that can be used to justify the creation of social justice requirements, programs, or assessments. Where accreditation bureaucracies do not explicitly require social justice advocacy, college bureaucrats often justify social justice advocacy as a way to fulfill other accreditation requirements. In both cases, social justice advocates within colleges and universities twist accreditation to advance their own agenda.

Education reformers must disrupt higher education's ability to provide stable careers for social justice advocates. These reforms cannot be aimed piecemeal at individual campuses. Social justice education is a national initiative, which has taken over entire disciplines and professions. Social justice's capture of higher education must be opposed on a similarly national scale. Above all, the opposition must aim at cutting off the national sources of funding for social justice education. A priority should be to deny public tax dollars for social justice education.

Nine General Reforms Would Severely Disrupt Social Justice Education:

1. Eliminate experiential learning courses;

2. Remove social justice education from undergraduate general education requirements;

3. Remove social justice education from introductory college courses;

4. Remove social justice requirements from departments that provide employment credentials;

5. Remove social justice positions from higher education administration;

6. Restrict the power of social justice advocates in higher education administration;

7. Eliminate the "co-curriculum;"

8. Remove social justice requirements from higher education job advertisements; and

9. Remove social justice criteria from accreditation.

Most importantly of all, college students must cease cooperating with social justice requirements. A mass coordinated campaign of civil disobedience, in which students simply stop taking social justice classes, attending social justice events, or obeying social justice administrators, would deal a body-blow to social justice education.

The Art of Teaching and the End of Wokeness

Per the Adam Ellwanger "The Art of Teaching and the End of Wokeness" National Association of Scholars paper in the Winter of 2021:

Any enthusiast of classical liberal education will be much dismayed at the current state of education in America, both in K-12 schools and our colleges and universities. In addition to the schools' incessant propagation of the modern leftist worldview, there is the new war against standardized means of assessing student performance—and even a growing conviction that any formal measure of academic success is a way of perpetuating the injustices of the "status quo."

For over thirty years, when surveying the unfolding crisis in the nation's schools, conservatives and their allies have centered their critique on matters of curriculum. Almost without exception their arguments revolve around the conviction that we are teaching the wrong things, and the solutions that they propose usually consist of recommitting ourselves to teaching the right things.

These critics aren't wrong. American students are being taught the wrong things. History has been reduced to a cataloguing of Euro-American failure, injustice, and violence. Literature serves as a springboard from which to launch attacks on "uninterrogated" traditional values and "assumptions." Social studies are now a vehicle for gender ideology and Critical Race Theory, which teaches a moralistic race essentialism where whites are de facto bigoted oppressors and minorities are virtuous victims of "systemic" brutality and hatred. In the wake of the racial unrest in the summer of 2020, some public schools have abandoned advanced mathematics courses on the grounds that they marginalize minorities.

Suffice it to say, then, that there are many ways in which the curriculum can be improved. Nevertheless, focusing on curricular concerns as a way to "reclaim" the schools is a deeply misguided approach. The conservative fetishization of the what's of American education (i.e., considerations of what is being taught) is largely responsible for the success of the left in conquering these institutions.

Put simply, an exclusive focus on the what's has been self-defeating, because the left's successes in turning schools into houses of political indoctrination were largely achieved by ignoring the question of content: their victory was secured through an elevation of style over substance, of form over content. Their conquest was achieved through a resolute dedication to the how's of schooling; that is, the methods by which content is conveyed to students and how teaching techniques and strategies can be instrumentalized to serve ideological ends.

They also devoted themselves to changing how the schools are run at the administrative and procedural levels. This elevation of the how's over the what's allowed the political left to take over education at a time when their activists were a minority within what was then a culturally conservative institution. This hostile takeover was consolidated mainly throughout the 1980s.

Sounding the alarm that American schools were in intellectual decline.

By the time that educational reformer William Bennett was appointed to the post of Secretary of Education by Ronald Reagan in 1985, many were sounding the alarm that American schools were in intellectual decline. But by then, the left's alternate model of education had already substantially dislodged the older model that had been defined by strict standards and rigorous monitoring of student performance. By the mid-1990s, the new educational order had received the tacit (if oft-unspoken) approval of administrators and school boards.

If we are to redirect the trajectory of American education, there is only one viable form of recourse: we must temporarily abandon the concern with content and dedicate ourselves to developing teaching techniques that might cultivate a disposition and style of thinking that will encourage students to view current institutional politics and official ideology with skepticism and hostility.

This reorientation will require dissident teachers to give significant thought to "mundane" aspects of teaching that were previously viewed as frivolous and subordinate to the issue of curricular content. Some progress can be made simply by refusing the innovations and commonplaces of modern education. Re-centralize the classroom, for example. Give lectures (rather than holding open-ended "discussions"). Stand at the front of the room when lecturing. Maintain an attendance policy and insist upon punctuality. Penalize plagiarism. Insist upon the existence of objective truth: maintain that there are correct and incorrect answers and that knowledge is not contingent upon the "lived experience" of the individual.

The left's annexing of the schools was achieved by attending to the how's of education more than to the what's. Formulating a complete pedagogical model for reclaiming American education will be an involved process that will require sustained dialogue and collaboration between dissident teachers across the country. This dialogue—which demands a focus on tactics rather than texts—is our most urgent task. Together, we must develop strategies to form a much different sort of citizen than the schools are now producing. Nothing less will be sufficient for our aims.

10 – Progressivism's Multiculturalism + Wokeness + Cancel Culture = Free Speech Intolerance

Credit: The Economist.

The term "cancel culture" has hurtled into popular use as a way of identifying instances of social justice mobbing—essentially, the attack on a person, place, or thing that is perceived as inconsonant with "woke" ideological narratives. When a "cancel culture" event takes place the complainants demand—and often get— offenders fired, shut down, silenced, or otherwise removed from the public eye.

In *Cancel Culture: The Latest Attack on Free Speech and Due Process*, Alan Dershowitz—*New York Times* bestselling author and one of America's most respected legal scholars—makes an argument for free speech, due process, and restraint against the often overeager impulse to completely cancel individuals and institutions at the ever-changing whims of social media-driven crowds.

Alan Dershowitz has been called "one of the most prominent and consistent defenders of civil liberties in America" by Politico and "the nation's most peripatetic civil liberties lawyer and one of its most distinguished defenders of individual rights" by *Newsweek*. Yet he has come under intense criticism for his steadfast and consistent championing of those same principles, and his famed "shoe-on-the-other-foot test," to those who have been "cancelled" for any number of faults, both real and imagined.

Cancel Culture is a defense of due process, free speech, and even-handedness in the application of judgment. It makes the case for restraint and care in decisions about whom and what to cancel, boycott, deplatform, and bar from public life, and offers recommendations for when, why, and to what degree these steps may be appropriate, as long as objective, fair-minded criteria can be determined and met.

While Dershowitz argues against the worst excesses of cancel culture—the rush to judgment and the devastating results it can have on those who may be innocent, the power of social media to effect punishment without a thorough examination of evidence, the idea that historical events can be viewed through the same lens as actions in the present day—he also acknowledges that its defenders ostensibly try to use it to create meaningful, positive change, and notes that cancelling may itself be a constitutionally protected form of free speech.

In the end, Cancel Culture represents an icon in the defense of free speech and due process reckoning with the greatest challenge and threat to these rights since the rise of McCarthyism. It is essential reading for anyone interested in or concerned about cancel culture, its effects on our society, and its significance in a greater historical and political context.

Taking on the 'Wokeism' Movement

John McWhorter, an African-American, teaches at Columbia University and has been published in the nation's leading left-wing journals. But he is not your typical liberal. The Woke antiracism "we're being sold," he believes, "isn't the path to a more just and equitable world for all. It's the barrier."

McWhorter's thesis: Wokeism "has come to excite a grievous amount of influence over American institutions to the point that we are beginning to accept, as normal, the kinds of language, policies, and actions that Orwell wrote of as fiction."

He argues that Woke ideology "is one under which white people calling themselves our saviors make Black people look like the dumbest, weakest, most self-indulgent human beings in the history of our species, and teach Black people to revel in the status and cherish it as making us special."

The Woke movement has morphed into a modern secular religion that does not tolerate dissent. Dissenting is a form of "environmental pollution" for disciples. Hence, Woke inquisitors, or the "Elect," as McWhorter calls them, demand white people submit to self-mortification because of their "original sin," namely white privilege.

According to their catechism, for a white person to say "I don't see color" is racist. To assert one is not racist proves one is racist. Racism is "what makes one white." And for black kids to "embrace school" is bad because it is "acting white." To hold a contrary view is "heresy" and any black thinkers who dare to "question the Elect orthodoxy are traitorous Judases out to make a buck."

Elect ideology, McWhorter concludes, ...teaches black people that cries of weakness are a form of strength. It teaches us that in the richness of this thing called life, the most interesting thing about you is that the ruling class doesn't like you enough. It teaches us that to insist that black people can achieve under less than perfect conditions is ignorant slander. It teaches us that we are the first people in the history of the species for whom it is a form of heroism to embrace the slogan "Yes, we can't!" Elect philosophy is, in all innocence, a form of racism in itself. Black America has met nothing so disempowering—including the cops—since Jim Crow.

McWhorter calls for the Elect "anti-white" ideology to be exorcised from school curriculums and calls for commonsense programs to tackle black America's problem.

These include making sure kids "not from book-lined homes" learn to read via phonics, ending the war on drugs, and advocating "vocational training for poor people," and battling "the idea that 'real' people go to college."

Such modest proposals may put the nation on the road to "saving Black America for real." McWhorter concedes that if a white man wrote Woke Racism, he would be dismissed as racist. He also expects to be labeled a traitor and self-hating. Nevertheless, the fearless McWhorter dedicates his book "to each who find it within themselves to take a stand against the detour in humanity's intellectual, cultural, and moral development."

During the fall campaign, we witnessed the beginning of a movement dedicated to taking a stand against Woke's disordered ideology that divides us as a people. And touting Professor McWhorter's prescriptions may help in the battle to restore unity and the cogency of our Nation's original motto, "E pluribus unum"—"Out of many, one."

Progressivism Isn't Progressive: It's Recycled Marxism

According to historian William Leuchtenburg: The Progressives believed in the Hamiltonian concept of positive government, of a national government directing the destinies of the nation at home and abroad. They had little but contempt for the strict construction of the Constitution by conservative judges, who would restrict the power of the national government to act against social evils and to extend the blessings of democracy to less favored lands. The real enemy was particularism, state rights, limited government.

However, an entrenched and growing bureaucracy, without drastic measures, becomes an entrenched and immovable force, whether it's in American government or our educational systems. And because the intellectual capital of our educational institutions is so heavily weighted with liberal and leftist ideals, it appears they've become a safe haven for today's progressivism movement, starting with the Frankfurt School at Columbia established in 1934 during the midst of the Great Depression.

The Frankfurt School's biggest intellectual creation was Critical Theory, an approach to cultural analysis that focuses on criticizing existing social structures. To counter Critical Theory, Social Justice, and Progressivism, I argue that the message, goals, and sapience from organizations like the Heterodox Academy, FIRE, and the Templeton Foundation and their "progressive" programs, trump critical theory.

Along with sapience, they are creating a reasonable and illuminating path for second age of enlightenment on campus to follow that promotes viewpoint diversity, cherishes intellectual humility and fights for freedom of speech. To understand and appreciate this second age of campus enlightenment, we need to first understand and identify Critical Theory, New Modernism, and Progressivism.

Understanding Critical Theory and the Frankfurt School

Critical Theory is a social theory oriented toward critiquing and changing society as a whole. It differs from traditional theory, which focuses only on understanding or explaining society. Critical theories aim to dig beneath the surface of social life and uncover the assumptions that keep human beings from a full and true understanding of how the world works.

Over the years, many social scientists and philosophers who rose to prominence after the Frankfurt School have adopted the goals and tenets of critical theory. We can recognize critical theory today in many feminist theories and approaches to conducting social science. It is also found in critical race theory, cultural theory, gender, and queer theory, as well as in media theory and media studies.

Critical theory as it is known today can be traced to Karl Marx's critiques of the economy and society. It is inspired greatly by Marx's theoretical formulation of the relationship between economic base and ideological superstructure and focuses on how power and domination operate.

Following in Marx's critical footsteps, Hungarian György Lukács and Italian Antonio Gramsci developed theories that explored the cultural and ideological sides of power and domination. After seeing that wealth and quality of life for workers was increasing after his imprisonment from the Italian fascist regime, Gramsci theorized from his many letters published in his *Prison Notebooks* written between 1929 and 1935, that traditional Western values must be destroyed in order to promote Communism, because old Marxist economic arguments could no longer be made.

In other words, workers were no longer poor enough and desperate enough for Communism to appeal to them. For these ideas to take hold, cultural structures such as religion (Christianity), the family, and traditional values of personal responsibility must be broken down.

Shortly after Lukács and Gramsci published their ideas, the Institute for Social Research was founded at the University of Frankfurt, and the Frankfurt School of critical theorists took shape. The work of the Frankfurt School members, including Max Horkheimer, Theodor Adorno, Erich Fromm, Walter Benjamin, Jürgen Habermas, and Herbert Marcuse, is considered the heart of critical theory.

One of the most influential members of the Frankfurt School, Herbert Marcuse fled to Columbia University in New York in 1934 following Hitler's rise to power where the new Frankfurt School of Columbia was started. The Frankfurt School, known more appropriately as Critical Theory, is a philosophical and sociological movement spread across many universities around the world.

During the civil rights and antiwar movements against the Vietnam conflict in the 1960s, Marcuse's *One-Dimensional Man: Studies in the Ideology of Advanced Industrial Society*, a 1964 best seller by the philosopher, primarily known by the "power of negative thinking" became the standard for revolutionary speech in the movement he called the "Great Refusal."

His devotees included campus radical Angela Davis, from Brandeis University. Countless students read his books. New Left marchers carried posters of his face, along with images of the Chinese communist leader Mao Tse Tung, the Argentinean guerrilla leader Che Guevara, and the Vietnamese president Ho Chi Minh.

In contrast to orthodox Marxism, Marcuse champions non-integrated forces of minorities, outsiders, and radical intelligentsia, attempting to nourish oppositional thought and behavior through promoting radical thinking and opposition. *One-Dimensional Man* made Marcuse famous for this.

Today's Progressivism as the New Marxism

As in Marx's older drama, the moral imperative of progressives is to once again "set things right." In Marx's time this was the task of revolutionaries. Today this task falls to progressive politicians and activists, social justice reformers, civil rights workers, cultural appropriation enforcers, diversity, and inclusion warriors and the like who have spread into the media, government, college campuses, neighborhood organizations and workplaces.

Marxist revolutionaries sought to set things right by leading a revolution to overthrow the capitalist system and replace it with a just economic system. Progressives want to set things right through social change in order to create a just society. In a just society everyone is equal: men and women, immigrants and native-born, persons of various racial and ethnic groups, heterosexuals, and homosexuals, first and third world people, disabled and able-bodied. This will be a society free from the "isms" of sexism, nativism, racism, heterosexism, colonialism, and ableism.

To the progressive, the success of the newly liberated oppressed person must not be limited by the extent of his talent or effort. Success is merited by the very existence of his membership in an oppressed group. As in Marxist theory—"from each according to his ability, to each according to his needs"—even people of lesser abilities and efforts deserve equal outcomes. The progressive sees anything less than this as failure.

Undergirding all this is the assumption that a just society will be gained through the intervention of government. Only government can force the needed changes. This is achieved through a complex and extensive web of government mechanisms: civil rights laws; affirmative action programs; minimum wage laws; housing assistance; guaranteed income; income maintenance programs that seamlessly transfer wealth from haves to have nots; block grants to states; guaranteed health care for all; national disaster relief...and more.

Per Dr. Raymond M. Berger, "In the progressive view there is little tolerance for government that cannot deliver equal outcomes for all. However, every human being is unique and not standardized widgets, so ultimately, government is incapable of creating a society of equals (which is impossible)."

The Critical Method of the Frankfurt School Fuels Progressivism

Some of the key issues and philosophical preoccupations of the Frankfurt School's Critical Theory and methods involve the critique of modernity and capitalist society, the definition of social emancipation, as well as the detection of the pathologies of society. The academic influence of Critical Theory throughout America's academia provides the foundation for today's progressivism thought, issues, and actions.

These foundations were influenced by Marxism and/or inherently Marxist in nature.

The first generation of Marxist Frankfurt School philosophers, particularly Herbert Marcuse and Jurgen Habermas, have influenced generations within the American academy and its students throughout, and turned global, influencing methodological approaches in other European academic contexts and disciplines after World War II.

It was during this phase that Richard Bernstein, a second generation Frankfurt School philosopher and contemporary of Habermas, embraced the research agenda of Critical Theory and significantly helped its development in American universities (after the initial influence of Marcuse) when he joined in 1989 the graduate faculty at the New School for Social Research in New York.

The Impact of Richard Bernstein: Second Generation Frankfurt School Academic

Prior to that, Richard Bernstein spent 23 years at Haverford College in Pennsylvania where he published some of his most famous books, including *Praxis and Action: Contemporary Philosophies of Human Activity* (1971), *The Restructuring of Social and Political Theory* (1978), *Beyond Objectivism and Relativism: Science, Hermeneutics and Praxis* (1983), and *Philosophical Profiles: Essays in a Pragmatic Mode* (1986).

In his 1983 book *Beyond Objectivism and Relativism: Science, Hermeneutics, and Praxis*, Bernstein diagnosed a serious issue that affects much of modern philosophy as it oscillates unendingly between two untenable positions; on the one hand, the dogmatic search for absolute truths, and on the other, the conviction that "anything goes" when it comes to the justification of our most cherished beliefs and ideas. Progressivism thrives on the later.

The third generation of critical theorists, therefore, arose either from Habermas' research students in the United States and at Frankfurt am Main and Starnberg (1971-1982), or from a spontaneous convergence of independently educated scholars like Bernstein throughout the United States and beyond. Therefore, third generation of Critical Theory scholars consists of two groups.

The first group spans a broad time—denying the possibility of establishing any sharp boundaries. The second group of the third generation is instead composed mostly of American scholars who were influenced by Habermas' philosophy during his visits to the United States. From there on, the philosophical reach of Critical Theory in America's academia, educational institutions and social justice warriors can only be theorized from Bernstein to be outward and beyond.

However, if one were to make a conservative estimate of their combined impact upon America's academia, millions of college students, and Progressivism movement—based on all of the evidence, realizations and conclusions uncovered so far in *The Sapient Being*—Critical Theory and its methods are pervasive, entrenched, and wide spread.

Marxism and Progressivism: A Play in Two Acts

From Dr. Raymond M. Berger, "Marxism and Progressivism: A Play in Two Acts" published 2018 in *The Times of Israel*, about why every Marxist government in history has been a repressive nightmare, the section is drawn from.

Today's progressives believe they are onto something new. But the progressive script is an old theatrical play with the same drama as the earlier communist play. It stars the same protagonists dressed up with different names. And despite the hype of the performance, when the curtain comes down after the finale, both plays are equally unsatisfying.

Yesterday's Communism

Communist theory was first expounded by the nineteenth century philosopher, Karl Marx. Marx crafted a morality play. He observed economic changes wrought by the early industrial revolution in Western Europe, and he correctly perceived the inherent injustice in the evolving economic system.

This was high drama, complete with villains and downtrodden heroes. The villains were the bourgeoisie, the owners of industry or what Marx called the "means of production." The downtrodden heroes were the proletariat or workers.

When the enclosure movement threw the serfs off the manor and into the towns and cities, they were robbed of their former dignity and means of livelihood. Forced to resort to selling their labor as their only means of survival, they became wage slaves. Gone was the pride of craftsmanship and the stability of manor life. As the bourgeoisie exploited the "surplus labor"—that is, the money value created by proletariat labor—the proletarian was robbed of the fruits of his labor.

Even worse, he was now subject to the wild swings of economic expansion and contraction and hence to misery and insecurity. At the same time, societal wealth became increasingly concentrated in the hands of the small bourgeoisie class while the proletariat remained impoverished.

The system was maintained by a false consciousness in which the proletariat failed to recognize the "class structure" of society and the exploitive nature of the bourgeois class and the system of capitalism.

The play's drama was advanced by revolutionaries—like Marx—who alerted the proletariat to their exploitation and encouraged them to overthrow the capitalist system. The workers would inevitably open their eyes. According to Marx, this would lead to a revolution and a "dictatorship of the proletariat."

But despite the dictatorial nature of this transitional phase, the new paradigm would result in a just society in which each contributed according to his ability and took according to his need. Thus, the unjust capitalist society would be replaced by a just and classless society.

The central purpose of twentieth century communism was to "set things right."

Today's Progressivism

Older generations voted mildly net Democratic in Presidential elections when they were young

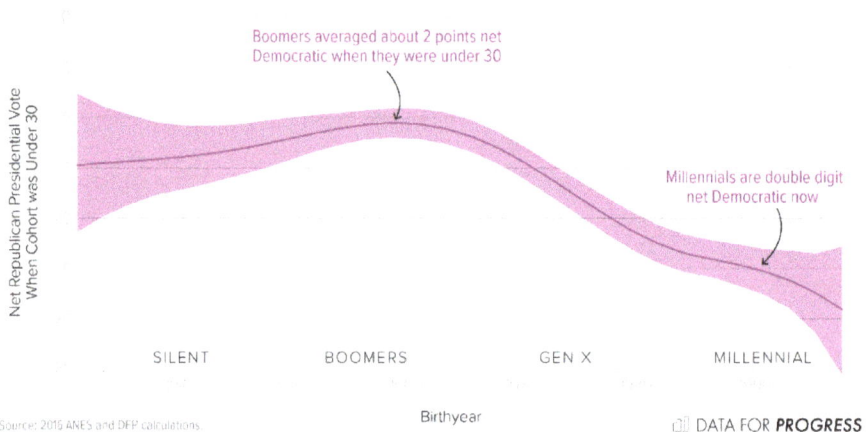

Boomers averaged about 2 points net Democratic when they were under 30

Millennials are double digit net Democratic now

Net Republican Presidential Vote When Cohort was Under 30

SILENT   BOOMERS   GEN X   MILLENNIAL

Birthyear

Source: 2016 ANES and DFP calculations.

DATA FOR **PROGRESS**

Berger continues that today's progressive movement—different from the American Progressive movement of the late nineteenth century—repackaged this Marxist theory with new actors and injustices but the same old drama.

The epic struggle between bourgeoisie and proletariat is replaced by the morally laden struggles between privileged and oppressed actors with new names. In this contemporary version of Marxist drama, people of color are pitted against a white male power structure supported by a mysterious but powerful force of institutional racism. Women are pitted against a male patriarchy that invades not only the workplace but intrudes into the very intimacy of the home to wreak injustice.

As the blinders of the new false consciousness fall from the eyes of the oppressed, new oppressed groups emerge. Some are based on "sexual minority status"—gay people, transsexuals, intersex, non-gender conforming—others on physical traits—the disabled, the unattractive, fat people. In place of an exploitive bourgeoisie there are heterosexists, cis-gender persons, those who exploit the disabled and those who engage in "lookism," that is, those who exploit others due to their appearance.

Added to these colorful actors are the multitude of colonized people of the third world and their exploitive evil colonizers. Because this is a drama, the respective roles of colonizer and colonized are always simplified, with few benefits but much evil attributed to colonization. And even long after the departure of the colonizers from formerly colonized lands, the injustice of the original colonial sin is said to persist, as every problem of the newly independent peoples is attributed to the legacy of colonialism.

In the same way, injustices based on race and ethnicity are said to live on, in the form of the legacy of racism, even after much of the oppression is alleviated.

More recently the world has seen a northward migration of millions from impoverished and violent lands in the south. Amidst the confusion of roles—are these immigrants, migrants, or refugees?—these folks join the long line of oppressed people who are unjustly exploited and abused in their adopted countries. There is nothing more dramatic and poignant than these huddled masses, to use the words of poet Emma Lazarus.

These are new actors in an old drama around the struggle between persecutor and victim, between exploiter and exploited. Marx's focus on labor has now extended to every conceivable human difference, as if the very existence of difference is morally wrong.

The Left Has Undergone an Unsapient Ideological Transformation

Dr. Jonathan Haidt has observed: In the recent past, important social matters were settled though free and open discussion and debate using logic and reason. Our American civil order is predicated on this. It works well when those engaged share a conviction that universal truth exists—regardless of one's beliefs, feelings, and opinions.

For today's campus radicals, feelings have largely replaced logic and reason. A generation ago, social justice was understood as equality of treatment and opportunity. Per Haidt, "… If black people are getting discriminated against in hiring and you fight that, that's justice."

Today justice means equal outcomes. "There are two ideas now in the academic left that weren't there ten years ago," Haidt says. "One is that everyone is racist because of unconscious bias, and the other is that everything is racist because of systemic racism." That makes justice impossible to achieve: "When you cross that line into insisting if there's not equal outcomes then some people and some institutions and some systems are racist, sexist, then you're setting yourself up for eternal conflict and injustice."

Haidt is right. If the goal of this new social justice is equality of outcome, you are setting yourself up for eternal conflict, injustice, and ultimately social disintegration.

Equal outcomes can only be achieved through the tyrannical imposition of power and coercion, with a resulting loss of individual freedom. It results in human beings being objectified, manipulated, and otherwise treated unjustly.

Where it has been attempted—in places like Maoist China and the Soviet Union— the outcomes were utterly destructive. Millions were imprisoned and murdered. Millions more lost their families, livelihoods, and freedoms. These are the facts!

Why Social Justice is Wrong to Demand Equality of Outcomes

A primary objective of the new progressive orthodoxy is to unmask or expose the many oppressive structures that are pervasive in Western civilization. Adherents do this by exposing inequalities and fighting for "social justice." There is a plethora of examples as Scott Allen shows below:

Exhibit A: Laws and regulations that excluded gays and lesbians from the institution of marriage resulted in unequal and discriminatory treatment. Social justice demands that these laws, rooted in Judeo-Christian beliefs about the exclusivity of marriage as one male and one female, be overturned. This notion of marriage was judged to be hateful, homophobic, and bigoted. It needed to be torn down—a dream realized in 2015 when the Supreme Court, by judicial fiat, made homosexual "marriage" legal in all 50 states. Family madness!

Exhibit B: Norms and civic ordinances that exclude transgendered people from using the bathrooms and locker facilities of their choice are discriminatory.

Equality demands that all people, regardless of gender, be able to use the restroom facilities, locker rooms (and eventually, to play on the sports teams) of their choosing. After all, the notion of a simple gender binary male-female reality is oppressive, a legacy of Western, Judeo-Christian beliefs that were structurally imposed on everyone. Sexual madness!

Exhibit C: The percentage of black students expelled from St. Paul Minnesota public schools is greater than the number of white students expelled as a percent of their population. The superintendent cites the cause for this inequality as systemic racism. Others wonder if the actions of black students themselves might be behind their higher rates of expulsion, but the second "core doctrine" of the new religion, multiculturalism, stigmatizes anyone who would ask such a question. Crime rate madness!

To do so would be to commit the cardinal sin of blaming the victim. Blame must be attributed to larger social forces, in this case, structural or systemic racism endemic in American culture. The solution: Require teachers and administrators to bring down the numbers of black expulsions, without regard to the actions of the students themselves. The result: More violent and chaotic schools that make learning almost impossible.

This Un-Sapient Notion of Social Justice is Relatively New

In a previous post, Os Guinness quoted New York University professor Dr. Jonathan Haidt: "A generation ago, social justice was understood as equality of treatment and opportunity… If black people are getting discriminated against in hiring and you fight that, that's justice. Today justice means equal outcomes … an idea that wasn't there ten years ago."

Guinness summarizes this final core doctrine:

Social justice movements must each deconstruct all that oppresses its victims anywhere … They invite an attack on all accepted truths, because unmasking the social fictions is seen as a way of liberating ourselves from the oppression of socially constructed realities that have imprisoned us without our realizing it … It is an open invitation to an assault on tradition and on long-held ways of seeing and doing things. In other words, on Western civilization and Judeo-Christian beliefs.

First, there must be liberation from God and therefore from meaning and ethics, from solid institutions such as marriage and the family, and from all inhibiting categories such as "the binary opposites" of "male" and "female" ... There must be liberation from nature and even from what was considered our own nature.

Guinness puts his finger on an important insight when he says that the new religion is animated by a desire to be "liberated from God." The ideological roots of the new religion, whether Postmodernism, Marxist or Nietzschean, are ultimately atheistic.

The attack on Western civilization is really an indirect way of attacking Judeo-Christian beliefs, which ultimately is a kind of rage and rebellion against God and His created order. In this sense, it isn't new at all. It goes all the way back to Genesis 3 and the fallen heart's desire to overthrow God and assume ultimate authority for ourselves.

Social Justice Warriors' Chilling Effect on Political Correctness Culture

Per Scott Allen: It has gotten to the point where people are fearful of sharing what they think about reality. In an email interview, *The Atlantic's* Conor Friedersdorf engaged a 22-year-old San Francisco resident on the stifling PC culture that has grown up around that city. He made the following observation:

Disagreement gets you labeled fascist, racist, bigoted, etc. It can provoke a reaction so intense that you're suddenly an unperson to an acquaintance or friend. There is no saying 'Hey, I disagree with you,' it's just instant shunning. Say things online, and they'll try to find out who you are and potentially even get you fired for it. Being anti-PC is not about saying 'I want you to agree with me on these issues.' It's about saying, 'Hey, I want to have a discussion and not get shouted down because I don't agree.'

We don't want to end political correctness so that we can say hateful things. We want to stop feeling silenced and condemned for having alternative viewpoints. We want to articulate thought-provoking, uncomfortable truisms, and not be told, 'you can't say that' without even a modest effort at explaining why.

When confronting people who disagree with you, the best tactic is to prove why they're wrong instead of shutting them up. Have enough faith in your own arguments to welcome dissenting opinions; if your ideas are truly superior, it will show. No need to get emotional, indignant, or defensive.

Why is this? Why has this new and expansive sense of student fragility spread so rapidly, but only among Millennials who are currently living or working on college campuses? Lukianoff and Haidt tried to explain the recent spread of trigger warnings and micro-aggression theory by examining broad historical trends, such as increases in protective parenting that began in the 1980s, and we examined more recent changes in federal laws that pressured universities to over-police language use on campus.

How the New Religion of Progressivism Leverages Victimization

According to the tenets of the toxic new religion of progressivism—victimization accrues power. Per Scott Allen, here's how it works:

First, the religion sees reality entirely within the Marxist framework of oppressor and oppressed. Further, the principal oppressors are white, Christian, or Jewish heterosexual males. They are uniquely oppressive, "white supremacists" who have abused cultural power and privilege at the expense of every other group.

These are givens. They function as "core doctrines" of the new religion. Try arguing these points with adherents; they will be incredulous, as if you were asserting a flat earth. These are simply "self-evident" realities. If you are not white, male, Christian/Jewish, heterosexual, you are, by definition, a victim, and victimization accrues power. Ben Shapiro explains how this works:

The toxic new religion ranks the value of a view not based on the logic or merit of the view but on the level of victimization in American society experienced by the person espousing the view. An LGBT black woman is automatically considered more correct than a straight white male, before any speech exits either of their mouths. Progressivism madness!

Shapiro continues, "If a straight white male, or anyone else who ranks lower on the victimhood scale, says something contrary to the viewpoint of the higher ranking intersectionality identity, that person has engaged in a microaggression. They have engaged in hate speech or violence, and violent action is justified to silence them."

The fact that victimization accrues power helps explain the wild exaggeration and hyperbole employed by so-called victim groups. The more victimized and oppressed you paint yourself, the more your voice counts. If you say (of your experience as a black, female student at Yale University) "we are dying here!" you are setting yourself up to be taken more seriously.

But this is a dangerous delusion. Yazidis in Iraq, or Christians in North Korea, or Karin in Myanmar can truthfully claim that "we are dying here" without exaggerating. But to make the same claim as a privileged student at one of America's most prestigious universities is to mock actual violent oppression.

Victimization Warrants Mob Tactics, Riots, and Violence

Examples of this abound in the news. In the past years we've read about mobs of students shouting down those who disagree, almost always combined with vitriol, cursing, property damage, threats of violence and actual violence: Berkeley, Evergreen, Missouri State, Yale, Middlebury, and the list goes on.

According to Deion Kathawa, the students who engage in these mobs,... fervently believe that they are the front-line troops of an infallible moral vanguard, locked in an epic struggle for the very soul of their generation—and of their nation, rotten to the core ... (Given this) it is not quite so shocking that they understand themselves to have entirely legitimate grievances and are accordingly motivated to act in extreme ways.

Another (white female) Evergreen professor wrote about her own experiences of the riots.

Student activists gain license to harass and intimidate members of the Evergreen community in an effort to achieve their ends. Last Wednesday on two separate occasions I was followed by white students who yelled and cursed at me, accused me of not caring about black and brown bodies and claimed that if I did care I would follow their orders and join the protest in the library. They stood in front of me, blocking my way as I attempted to walk across campus.

Here's what jumps out at me: First, the students and faculty behind the riots "ignore (inhumane, totalitarian) tactics for the sake of the goal." Second, this mob behavior is part and parcel of the movement on many US college campuses (not only Evergreen).

This is the same totalitarianism of the Maoist Cultural Revolution or the Russian Revolution!

11 – Marxist, Progressive, Racist, LGBTQ & Ethnic Studies Programs Are Being Exposed

Credit: The Epoch Times.

From the Robert Leroux "Woke Madness and the University" National Association of Scholars article in the Winter of 2021:

On college and university campuses, from where it emerged, the woke ideology has become a powerful instrument of censorship, a particularly clear manifestation of the intellectual terrorism that has reigned there for about half a century. In some cases, such as at Evergreen College in the State of Washington , it even encourages violence. In fact, woke culture is the intellectual plague of our times.

We must say that what we now call the woke culture or movement is nothing new. It is part of a long tradition, influenced by Marxism, feminism, relativism, etc. It is not a scientific approach to reality, but essentially an ideological posture, an attitude, a social movement. The situation is getting worst because most academics are now activists.

As early as the 1980s, in his seminal book *The Closing of the American Mind*, Allan

Bloom analyzed this phenomenon in its first manifestations before the word woke was coined.

It became almost impossible to question the radical orthodoxy without risking vilification, classroom disruption, loss of the confidence and respect necessary for teaching, and the hostility of colleagues. Racist and sexist were, and are, very ugly labels—the equivalents of atheist or communist in other days with other prevailing prejudices—which can be pinned on persons promiscuously and which, once attached, are almost impossible to cast off. Nothing could be said with impunity. Such an atmosphere made detached, dispassionate study impossible."

For Bloom, it became almost impossible to question extremist orthodoxy without running the risk of being vilified as an intolerant person. The situation today is not really different.

New generations of professors have been hired not because they are concerned with and dedicated to science and objective knowledge, but because they are mainly political activists. Everything is wrong with the woke ideology: extreme paranoia, a mistaken view of social life, free speech, and the common man. Listening to the doctrinaires of the woke movement, we see that we are entering an unreal world, based on exaggerations, resolutely closed to dialogue and debate.

With wokeness, we cannot have a better example of the extreme radicalization of the left.

The left, which was once devoted to the fate of the working class and its struggles belongs to a bygone past. At the University of Ottawa, on a job posting one can read this:

The Institute of Feminist and Gender Studies at the University of Ottawa, located on the traditional and unceded territory of the Anishinabe-Algonquin people, is accepting applications for one tenure-track position in Afro-feminist studies. Applications from people who work with an intersectional framework on Islamophobia and anti-black racism, solidarities between Black and Indigenous people, transnational feminisms, Black feminist methodologies and practices, queer of color or black trans studies and/or the history and impacts of slavery in Francophone contexts, are particularly welcome. Community experience is an asset, as is bilingualism . . . Qualified Black applicants from Africa or the African diaspora (descended from the Caribbean, North America, Europe, Latin America, etc.) are invited to apply for this position.

The description is ridiculous!

Wokeness views the world today with great disdain, indeed hates it bitterly. Not only must social distinctions disappear, it is, above all, important that politicized racial, sexual, and gender groups impose their interests and their vision on the world.

Like Marxism, this doctrine delivers the individual to servitude: we flout him, we censor him, we impose a new vocabulary on him, even a new way of thinking. It is clear that many universities have become liberticidal.

How Public Schools Went Woke—and What to Do About It

As per the Daniel Buck and Garion Frankel "How Public Schools Went Woke—and What to Do about It" *National Review* report in March 2022:

A radical theory of education—one that sees the classroom as the locus of societal change, not academic training—dominates our colleges of education. Thus, like a drainage pipe into a common supply, teacher-prep programs around the country dump a politicized approach to education into our schools, and it is here where our reform efforts must focus.

This outsized influence of the university on K–12 schools occurs not without precedent. Once before, our nation's dominant philosophy of education universally altered. Prior to the 20th century, American education was almost universally classical in nature—great books, grammar and rhetoric, direct teacher guidance, a healthy patriotism. However, the establishment of teacher colleges began to change that. Between 1910 and 1930, 88 normal schools—local institutions to train teachers—associated with universities and became teacher colleges.

At the most influential of these, Columbia's Teachers College, John Dewey and William Kilpatrick trained 35,000 students and wrote popular essays that influenced countless more. With such an influence, the progressive pedagogy of Dewey and Kilpatrick—which rejects liberal notions of knowledge worth knowing and direct teacher guidance to instead center a student's personal interests and exploration—supplanted classical education in American schools. The theory's association with colleges of education legitimated progressive education and so flooded American schools with proclamations of "best practices" and "expertise."

The influence of teacher colleges hasn't changed, only the theory within. Today, Teachers College, still one of the most prestigious teacher-prep programs in the country with 90,000 alumni, continues its significant role in determining what occurs in K–12 classrooms. A quick scroll through Columbia's course catalog reveals that teacher-prep programs now look toward "liberation" rather than virtue. A popular curriculum from Teachers College encourages children to read through critical-race lenses and acknowledges its dependence on critical race theory.

The college offers a class in "Black, Latina, and Transnational Feminisms," which seeks to "engage in an interdisciplinary exploration of feminist scholarship located at the intersections of race, class, and culture." In addition, the school offers a class in "Anti-Racist Curriculum, Pedagogy, Leadership and Policy." This trend continues across the college's course offerings, with frequent mentions of gender, race, class, and inclusivity.

Notably, course descriptions rarely if ever mention instruction, curriculum, assessment, or anything having to do with educating children. It amounts to a program in "proper" political opinions, not the practicalities of classroom instruction.

And Teachers College Is No Outlier

An education-policy course at the also influential University of Wisconsin-Madison "[focuses] on the ideas of transformative educators such as Paulo Freire and bell hooks (and yes, her name is all lower case!)." Freire's *Pedagogy of the Oppressed*, an incoherent attempt to explore the parasitic relationship between oppressor and oppressed in the context of the classroom, is considered a seminal work by many teacher-prep programs. References to Freire and other advocates of critical pedagogy appear on the syllabi of Harvard, UC Berkeley, California State-Long Beach, and the University of North Texas.

A UW professor, Gloria Ladson-Billings, is considered one of the single most influential thinkers in education. In 1998, she synthesized CRT and K–12 education, and in 2021, Indianapolis Public Schools hosted her at a racial-equity training for teachers.

Simply look through the DEI offerings at local schools to see that references to Freire, Billings, hooks, and other radical theorists abound. The organization Teachers Without Borders encourages their educators to understand and implement Freire's theory of "peace education"—ironic, considering that Freire cites Che Guevara and Lenin as exemplary teachers. After the passing of bell hooks in 2021, countless testimonials appeared online of how teachers implemented her ideas in their classrooms.

Woke ideas about race and power did not form ex nihilo in the minds of DEI consultants at K–12 schools. They stem from a decades-long process that saw a noteworthy shift in the research interests of education faculty. As the DEI fad caught on, its teachings made their way to both university and K–12 classrooms. Moreover, the transformation of the university's pedagogical environment is not an unprecedented event. Once again, Columbia and universities like it are acting like a superspreader event of critical pedagogy and other radical ideas.

That our teaching force requires their credentials ensures that the drainage pipe will flow on. Even if we ban explicit instruction in something like CRT, its ideas can still influence policy, curricula, behavior plans, and teaching. Even if school-choice bills passed in every state today, the same teaching force trained in the precepts of Freire and other pedagogues would staff our schools tomorrow. We must decouple the colleges of education and schools by ending teacher-licensing requirements.

Thankfully, schools don't seem to need these schools of education. Research into the efficacy of such programs finds "little difference in the average academic achievement impacts of certified, uncertified and alternatively certified teachers." More like a degree in business than medicine, official teacher-training may assist in initial hiring but is no guarantee of effectiveness. In fact, many successful charter schools run on a model that relies on well-educated but untrained recent graduates who then undergo rigorous on-the-job training and constant professional development.

There are other potential knock-on benefits of ending our licensing racket. Burdensome processes that require years of training and financial investment create an opportunity cost that dissuades talented would-be candidates from other professions. Furthermore, fewer regulatory hoops to jump through could encourage entry into the profession and thereby mitigate the teacher-shortage crisis that our schools currently face.

Any attempt at reform—reestablishing classical and liberal conceptions of education in these institutions—would take a 50-year Gramscian countermarch of our universities. As such, our only recourse is to sever the control they have over teacher training.

CRT: The Monster Is in the Classroom

Per the Erika Sanzi "The Monster Is in the Classroom" *City Journal* report in April 2021:

Many American parents may assume that culture-war battles over critical race theory and "wokeness" are fought on legitimate terrain, involving such matters as how high school students can best grapple with our nation's complex past. Perhaps they think that the suddenly ubiquitous topics of gender identity and preferred pronouns rankle only those parents who are old-fashioned in their thinking. If only. America's youngest students are being bombarded with classroom activism and indoctrination that is inappropriate not only developmentally but for public school systems in general.

The contemporary obsession with identity has made its way into elementary school policy, curricula, and standards approved by state boards. While we continue to see poor reading and math scores, schools spend money and time confusing and shaming other people's children. Many educators and elected leaders have good intentions; they believe deeply that they are part of a necessary and long-overdue movement to teach racial literacy, social justice, equity, and antiracism.

But as virtuous as these terms may sound on their face, they mean something else in far too many classrooms. American schools are teaching young children race essentialism: reducing them to identity groups, putting them in boxes labeled "oppressor" and "oppressed," and often inflicting emotional and psychological harm.

If This Sounds Extreme, That's Because It Is

Schools indoctrinate children as young as eight in race and gender essentialism.

It is not happening everywhere—but it is happening enough to have juiced a multibillion-dollar, nationwide industry. Sometimes the source is a rogue teacher whom the principal and superintendent admit they are trying to rein in; but increasingly, it is simply public officials implementing approved policies.

- Consider Bellevue, Washington, home to Cherry Crest Elementary School. The school website indicates that students "will have explicit conversations about race, equity, and access" and "will identify culture and begin to recognize and identify white culture through storytelling, sharing, and conversation." The school promises to hold monthly assemblies that focus on culture, identity, and race, and has created a group called SOAR (Students Organized Against Racism) for fourth- and fifth-graders. These children, who range from ages nine to 11, are tasked with "implementing learning and stratimplementation of school-wide learning and strategies for being anti-racist." Left unclear is whether these students have been made aware that modern antiracism requires discrimination on the basis of race.

- Or take Lexington, Massachusetts, where, in October 2019, fourth-graders were taught to "articulate what gender identity is and why it's important to use nonbinary language in describing people we don't know yet." According to photos shared on Twitter by the district's Director of Equity and Student Supports, students learned about "gender identity," "gender expression," "sexual orientation," and "sex assigned at birth" by examining sticky notes on a "Gender Snowperson" who was drawn in magic marker on a large sheet of paper. The students were also taught that their pronouns had been "assigned at birth."

- In Oregon, teachers can use new state standards in "ethnic studies" starting in September 2021; the standards will become a mandatory part of the curriculum in 2025. The Oregon Department of Education released an update on the standards in 2020. While most Americans may not consider gender an essential component of ethnic studies, the Oregon Department of Education does. The revised recommendations for the standards require kindergartners to "understand their own identity groups, including but not limited to race, gender, family, ethnicity, culture, religion and ability." First-graders will be able to "describe how individual and group characteristics are used to divide, unite, and categorize racial, ethnic and social groups."

- In Rockwood, Missouri, a fifth-grade teacher recently gave students a handout with written excerpts by Alicia Garza, co-founder of Black Lives Matter. The writings included the claim that "Michael Brown was murdered just steps from his mother's home in Ferguson, Missouri." (They did not mention Attorney General Eric Holder's conclusion that "the facts did not support the filing of criminal charges against Officer Darren Wilson.") The handout goes on: "Disruption is the new world order. It is the way in which those denied power assert power. And in the context of a larger strategy for how to contend for power, disruption is an important way to surface new possibilities." When I asked the school principal about the assignment, he said: "This was used by a teacher and is not a Rockwood approved resource. I am working with the teacher to ensure that only Rockwood curricular resources are used when teaching lessons."

- This past February 2021, students in Evanston, Illinois, listened to the book *Not My Idea: A Book About Whiteness*. Parents were asked to discuss the book with their children at home. The book says that "whiteness is a bad deal" and "always was," and that "you can be white without signing on to whiteness." As Conor Friedersdorf reports in *The Atlantic*, Evanston schools ask kindergarten parents to quiz their five- and six-year-olds on whiteness and to give them examples of "how whiteness shows up in school or in the community."

- In Cupertino, California, third-graders at R. I. Meyerholz Elementary School were required to deconstruct their racial identities and then rank themselves according to their "power and privilege." The teacher asked all students to create an "identity map," which required them to list their race, class, gender, religion, family structure, and other characteristics. The teacher explained to students that they live in a "dominant culture" of "white, middle class, cisgender, educated, able-bodied, Christian, English speaker[s]," who, according to the lesson, "created and maintained" this culture in order "to hold power and stay in power." Students were then asked to deconstruct these intersectional identities and "circle the identities that hold power and privilege" on their identity maps, ranking their traits based on the hierarchy the teacher had just explained to them.

Some parents may agree with such content. But public institutions funded with public dollars do not exist to groom activists for particular causes, shame children for their immutable traits, or deny them their agency or their childhood. We are talking about eight- and nine-year-old kids who believe in Santa Claus, hide their lost teeth under their pillow for the tooth fairy, and curl up in their parents' laps for comfort and love. It is immoral—at least—to reduce them to confected racial and gender categories and to teach them to do the same to others. Parents around the country need to understand what is happening in a growing number of elementary classrooms.

"Banging Beyond Binaries"

Per the Christopher F. Rufo "Banging Beyond Binaries" *City Journal* article in May 2022:

In early July 2021, the district's Office of Diversity, Equity, and Inclusion sent invitations to the Philadelphia Trans Wellness Conference to teachers and staff on the SDP Connect mailing list, promoting the conference as a way to "learn more about the issues facing the trans community." The School District of Philadelphia encouraged teachers to attend a conference on "kink," "BDSM," "trans sex," and "banging beyond binaries."

The conference was organized by the Mazzoni Center, an LGBTQ activist organization that has worked with the district on sexual-education programs. (When reached for comment, the School District of Philadelphia described its promotion of the conference as part of its commitment to "creating equitable and inclusive environments," and said it did "not have any information" on the number of teachers who attended the event. The Mazzoni Center did not return request for comment.)

I have obtained videos from a publicly accessible website that show that the conference went far beyond the school district's euphemism about "issues facing the trans community." The event included sessions on topics such as "The Adolescent Pathway: Preparing Young People for Gender-Affirming Care," "Bigger Dick Energy: Life After Masculinizing [Gender Reassignment Surgery]," "Prosthetics for Sex," "The Ins and Outs of Masturbation Sleeves," and "Trans Sex: Banging Beyond Binaries."

The conference attendees included educators, activists, adults, and adolescents. There were graphic sessions on prosthetic penises, masturbation toys, and artificial ejaculation devices, which some hosts explicitly promoted to minors. As one session host explained, "there's no age limit, because I feel like everybody should be able to access certain information."

The conference began with presentations promoting puberty blockers, hormone treatments, breast removals, and genital surgeries. In one session, "The Adolescent Pathway Preparing Young People for Gender-Affirming Care," Dr. Scott Mosser, the principal at the Gender Confirmation Center in San Francisco, explained that he has performed "over two thousand top surgeries," which involve removing girls' breasts, and that there is no age limit for beginning the "gender journey."

"I do not have a minimum age of any sort in my practice," he said, explaining that he would be willing to consult with children as young as ten years old with parental consent. In another session open to children, "Gender-Affirming Masculine and Feminizing Hormones for Adolescents and Adults," Dane Menkin, divisional director of LGBTQ services at Main Line Health, endorsed treatments ranging from puberty-blocking hormones to manual breast-binding for "masculinizing" adolescent girls. "I'm a strong proponent that you can bind for as many hours a day as you can tolerate binding," he said.

Other presentations at the Trans Wellness Conference involved explicit sexual themes.

Two female-to-male trans activists, Kofi Opam, a graduate student at the University of Iowa, and Sami Brussels, a medical illustrator, hosted a presentation called "Bigger Dick Energy," in which they explained the process of phalloplasty and using an artificial penis for "navigating cruising and anonymous/casual sex life."

Chase Ross, a transgender activist and YouTuber, hosted a series of sessions on "packers," "masturbation sleeves," and "prosthetics for sex," demonstrating various devices from his collection of more than 500 genital prosthetics. "I have tried and touched many dicks, right—prosthetics, real dicks, all dicks. This is one of the most realistic feeling in terms of like the inside of a penis," he said during one demonstration. "It's a big boy, this is, like, gigantic. Alright, give me two hours alone and I'll get this in my butt," he said during another.

The most extreme presentation at the three-day conference was "Trans Sex:

Banging Beyond Binaries." Jamie Joy, a self-described "kinky," "polyamorous," "pretty big slut," and Lucie Fielding, a self-described "white, queer, kinky, polyamorous, visibly able-bodied, Jewish, witchy, non-binary, trans femme" led the session.

The women led a presentation on politically correct anatomical language, including terms such as "front hole" and "back hole," and shared personal information about organizing orgies for participants to "explore their fantasies and their perversions in groups." The instructors then discussed various "kink" activities, including fetishes about puppies, Mary Poppins, and spanking. "I haven't gotten to explore a lot of my mommy kink. And I think for tonight I'm really wanting to feel cared for, but also get punished a little bit," said Joy.

It is important to remember that this conference is not a fringe activity.

The Mazzoni Center, which organized it, received more than $5 million in government contracts in 2021 and runs sexuality programs in schools throughout the region. The School District of Philadelphia has partnered with the Center on sexual-health research and student sexual-education programs, and the district's director of teacher leadership, Amy Summa, sits on Mazzoni's board of directors. Despite the school district's euphemisms about "wellness" and "self-esteem," the conference materials reveal a sexual ideology steeped in radical queer theory, not commonsense sex education. Parents and taxpayers should ask why the district's Office of Diversity, Equity, and Inclusion encouraged teachers to participate in such programming.

Radical Gender Lessons for Young Children

Per the Christopher F. Rufo "Radical Gender Lessons for Young Children" *City Journal* article in April 2022:

Evanston–Skokie School District 65 has adopted a radical gender curriculum that teaches pre-kindergarten through third-grade students to celebrate the transgender flag, break the "gender binary" established by white "colonizers," and experiment with neo-pronouns such as "ze," "zir," and "tree.

Rufo has obtained the full curriculum documents, which are part of the Chicago-area district's "LGBTQ+ Equity Week," which administrators adopted in 2021. The curriculum begins in pre-kindergarten, with a series of lessons on sexual orientation and gender identity. The lesson plan opens with an introduction to the rainbow flag and teaches students that "Each color in the flag has a meaning."

The teacher also presents the transgender flag and the basic concepts of gender identity, explaining that "we call people with more than one gender or no gender, non-binary or queer." Finally, the lesson plan has the teacher leading a class project to create a rainbow flag, with instructions to "gather students on the rug," "ask them to show you their flags," and "proudly hang the class flag where they can all see it."

In kindergarten, the lessons on gender and trans identity go deeper.

"When we show whether we feel like a boy or a girl or some of each, we are expressing our GENDER IDENTITY," the lesson begins. "There are also children who feel like a girl AND a boy; or like neither a boy OR a girl. We can call these children TRANSGENDER."

Students are expected to be able to "explain the importance of the rainbow flag and trans flag" and are asked to consider their own gender identity.

The kindergartners read two books that affirm transgender conversions, study photographs of boys in dresses, learn details about the transgender flag, and perform a rainbow dance. At the end of the lesson, the students are encouraged to adopt and share their own gender identities with the class. "Now you have a chance to make a picture to show how YOU identify," the lesson reads. "Maybe you want to have blue hair! Maybe you want to be wearing a necklace. Your identity is for YOU to decide!"

In first grade, students learn about gender pronouns.

The teachers explain that "some pronouns are gender neutral" and students can adopt pronouns such as "she," "tree," "they," "he," "her," "him," "them," "ze," and "zir."

The students practice reading a series of scripts in which they announce their gender pronouns and practice using alternate pronouns, including "they," "tree," "ze," and "zir." The teacher encourages students to experiment and reminds them: "Whatever pronouns you pick today, you can always change!" Students then sit down to complete a pronouns workbook, with more lessons on neo-pronouns and non-binary identities.

In third grade, Evanston–Skokie students are told that white European "colonizers" imposed their "Western and Christian ideological framework" on racial minorities and "forced two-spirit people to conform to the gender binary."

The teacher tells students that "many people feel like they aren't really a boy or a girl" and that they should "call people by the gender they have in their heart." Students are encouraged to "break the binary," reject the system of "whiteness," and study photographs of black men in dresses and a man wearing lipstick and long earrings.

"It is a myth that gender is binary," the lesson explains.

"Even though we are all given a sex assigned at birth, you are NOT given your gender. Only you can know your gender and how you feel inside." At the end of the lesson, students are instructed to write a letter to the future on how they can change society. "Society right now is very unfair," reads a sample letter. "I see a lot of marches on the T.V and I even went to a march last summer."

The curriculum in Evanston–Skokie School District 65 is the perfect illustration of college-level queer theory translated into early-elementary pedagogy. For weeks, as the nation has debated Florida's Parental Rights in Education Act, which prohibits public schools from teaching gender identity and sexual orientation in grades K–3, commentators on the political left have claimed that public schools do not teach this material and have accused conservatives of instigating a "moral panic."

This claim is demonstrably false, and the Evanston–Skokie lesson plans offer additional proof for parents and legislators concerned about gender ideology in American public schools. Queer theory has made its way into public school curriculums for children as young as four. This development should be subject to robust political debate, not denial and dismissal from the political Left.

Sexual Liberation in Public Schools

Per the Christopher F. Rufo "Sexual Liberation in Public Schools" *City Journal* article in July 2022:

Los Angeles Unified School District has adopted a radical gender-theory curriculum encouraging teachers to work toward the "breakdown of the gender binary," to experiment with gender pronouns such as "they," "ze," and "tree," and to adopt "trans-affirming" programming to make their classrooms "queer all school year."

Rufo has obtained a trove of publicly accessible documents from Los Angeles Unified that illustrates the extent to which gender ideology has entered the mainstream of the nation's second-largest school district. Since 2020, the district's Human Relations, Diversity, and Equity department has created an infrastructure to translate the basic tenets of academic queer theory into K-12 pedagogy. The materials include a wide range of conferences, presentations, curricula, teacher-training programs, adult-driven "gender and sexuality" clubs, and school-sponsored protests.

In a week-long conference last fall, titled "Standing with LGBTQ+ Students, Staff, and Families," administrators hosted workshops with presentations on "breaking the [gender] binary," providing children with "free gender affirming clothing," understanding "what your queer middle schooler wants you to know," and producing "counter narratives against the master narrative of mainstream white cis-heteropatriarchy society."

The narrative follows the standard academic slop: white, cisgender, heterosexual men have built a repressive social structure, divided the world into the false binary of man and woman, and used this myth to oppress racial and sexual minorities. Religion, too, is a mechanism of repression. During the conference, the district highlighted how teachers can "respond to religious objections" to gender ideology and promoted materials on how students can be "Muslim and Trans."

In another training program, titled "Queering Culture & Race," the Human Relations, Diversity, and Equity office encouraged teachers to adopt the principle of intersectionality, a key tenet of critical race theory, and apply it to the classroom.

First, administrators asked teachers to identify themselves by race, gender, and sexual orientation, and to consider their position on the identity hierarchy. The district then encouraged teachers to "avoid gendered expressions" in the classroom, including "boys and girls" and "ladies and gentlemen," which, according to queer theory, are vestiges of the oppressive gender binary.

Administrators also warned teachers that they might have to work against the families of their minority students, especially black students, regarding sexuality.

"The Black community often holds rigid and traditional views of sexual orientation and gender expression," the presenters claimed. "Black LGBTQ youth experience homophobia and transphobia from their familial communities."

Finally, Los Angeles Unified has gone all-in on "trans-affirming" indoctrination.

The Human Relations, Diversity, and Equity department has flooded the district with teaching materials, including, for example, videos from the consulting firm Woke Kindergarten encouraging five-year-olds to experiment with gender pronouns such as "they," "ze," and "tree" and to adopt nonbinary gender identities that "feel good to you." The district requires teachers to use a student's desired name and pronoun and to keep the student's gender identity a secret from parents if the student so desires.

In other words, Los Angeles public schools can facilitate a child's transition from one gender to another without notifying parents. And the district is far from neutral: it actively celebrates sexual identities such as "pansexual," "sexually fluid," "queer," "same-gender-loving," and "asexual," and gender identities such as "transgender," "genderqueer," "agender," "bigender," "gender nonconforming," "gender expansive," "gender fluid," and "two-spirit."

The problem with creating a "trans-affirming" culture is obvious.

In one of the district's own materials, "Mental Health Among Transgender Youth," the Human Relations, Diversity, and Equity department cites a survey by Mental Health America pointing out that, among 11-to-17-year-old transgender youth who were screened for mental health issues, 93 percent were at risk for psychosis, 91 percent exhibited signs of posttraumatic stress disorder, 90 percent likely used drugs and alcohol, 90 percent experienced moderate-to-severe anxiety, and 95 percent experienced moderate to severe depression. Additionally, according to a Trevor Project study, 71 percent of transgender youth have been diagnosed with eating disorders, with the ratio even higher for female-to-male transgender children.

These numbers are deeply alarming. But rather than provide a sober assessment of these risks and seek to mitigate them, Los Angeles Unified has adopted a year-round program glamorizing transgender identity and promoting an uncritical, "trans-affirming" culture in the classroom. It is, of course, a noble goal for schools to provide a safe environment for minority groups and to affirm the basic dignity of all children regardless of their sexuality. But Los Angeles Unified's program goes much further, promoting the most extreme strains of transgender ideology, which almost certainly contributes to the "social contagion" effect documented by Abigail Shrier and others.

The Los Angeles Unified School District governs the educational life of more than 600,000 children, the majority of whom are racial minorities from poor families. The implicit cynicism of the district's gender-ideology instruction is sickening: highly educated, well-paid bureaucrats promote fashionable academic programming that will do nothing to provide a basic education for these children or help them move up the economic and social ladder. It will only keep them trapped in a morass of confusion, fatalism, and resentment—while the bureaucrats keep collecting their paychecks.

12 – Universities Have Become Ground Zero for the Progressive Neo-Racism of DEI

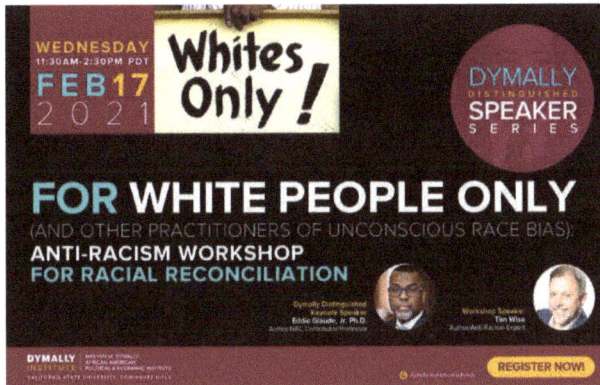

"White People Only: An Anti-Racism Workshop for Racial Reconciliation,"
at California State University, Dominguez Hills (CSUDH).

Critical race theorists have been dominant in colleges and universities for years, but their impact on public policy was limited until recently. The precepts of CRT have now burst outside the universities, affecting K-12 schools, workplaces, state and federal governments, and even the military. This has sparked resistance from Americans who refuse to have their children indoctrinated or to submit to race-based workplace harassment.

As a new tactic against this grassroots opposition, CRT's defenders now deny that the curricula and training programs in question form part of CRT, insisting that the "diversity, equity, and inclusion (DEI)" programs of trainers such as Ibram X. Kendi and Robin DiAngelo are distinct from the academic work of professors such as Derrick Bell, Kimberle Crenshaw, and other CRT architects. While there are many different CRT variations, there are bedrock features that are common to all its theorists and practitioners such as the cult of race and gender victimology, and this diversity cult is systematically destroying the social fabric of our multi-racial society, the equality of opportunity that makes that possible, and America's unifying cultural cohesion. It is worth first exploring, however, why social-justice education is an oxymoron.

This new academic state religion of DEI combines the ideology of intersectionality with strands of radical feminism, anti-imperialism, and gay and transgender activism as noted in the Howard Gold "Opinion: At America's most 'woke' colleges, extreme liberal politics fails students and free speech" Market Watch article published in January 2020:

But it's really about turning the existing power relationships on their head, so that, say, black lesbians or trans women are now at the top of the inverted pyramid and "cis" white males are at the bottom. "Toxic masculinity" and "white privilege" are the roots of all evil. The last shall be first, and the first last.

It's true that men have dominated the world and women lag behind; gay people have been persecuted, trans people continue to be targets of violence, and African-Americans and other people of color are still victims of systemic racism and discrimination in jobs, housing, and policing. But self-righteous undergraduates, backed by professors and administrators, are turning this new campus orthodoxy into a toxic stew. "Four legs good, two legs bad," the sheep brayed in "Animal Farm." Once again, life imitates Orwell.

Without a "Diversity" Leg to Stand On

Every year since 2013, usually during the first week of September, the *Harvard Crimson* publishes survey results profiling the incoming freshman class, including their political and social orientations. These feature-length reports have consistently shown that a dominant majority of Harvard's incoming students identify as politically and socially Progressive, with ever-fewer students identifying as conservative.

In 2022, however, per the Renu Mukherjee "Without a "Diversity" Leg to Stand On" *City Journal* October 2022 article: The *Crimson* didn't publish the feature and didn't reply to my inquiry about whether they would do so. Harvard may have good reasons for wanting to delay such a report, given an upcoming Supreme Court case that ruled against the university on June 29, 2023.

In *Students for Fair Admissions v. President and Fellows of Harvard College*, the Supreme Court reexamined a half-century-old justification for race-based university admissions—namely, that racial diversity generates viewpoint diversity on campus and contributes to the lively exchange of ideas. Past results of Harvard's freshman surveys, which detail growing racial diversity but diminishing viewpoint diversity, discredit this justification.

Harvard's own freshman survey data undermine one of its justifications for affirmative action.

Of the Class of 2025, for example, only 1.4 percent identify as very conservative; only 7.2 percent identify as somewhat conservative; and only 18.6 percent identify as moderate. By contrast, 72.4 percent of freshmen identify as predominantly liberal. Yet this class is the "the most diverse class in the history of Harvard," according to William R. Fitzsimmons, dean of admissions and financial aid.

Other survey responses drive the point home. Of members of the Class of 2025 who supported a candidate in the 2020 presidential election, 87 percent backed Joe Biden. Meantime, 82 percent said they supported the Black Lives Matter protests of 2020, which resulted in at least $1 billion in damages and numerous deaths, while nearly half (49.8 percent) said that they supported defunding the police. This doesn't sound like viewpoint diversity to me.

Without viewpoint diversity as a justification, race-based admissions—that is, affirmative action—may not survive.

Since 2014, Students for Fair Admissions (SFFA), a nonprofit group of more than 20,000 students, parents, and others, has argued that affirmative action violates Title VI of the 1964 Civil Rights Act and the Fourteenth Amendment's Equal Protection Clause, which prohibit public and private universities receiving federal funds from discriminating based on race, color, and national origin.

This straightforward legal argument is likely to play well with a Supreme Court that leans toward originalism, but this doesn't mean that the justices' decision will rest on that philosophy alone. In fact, the Court's jurisprudence on race-conscious admissions has centered predominantly not on the legality of the policy but on its implications for higher education.

In his landmark opinion in *Regents of the University of California v. Bakke*, Lewis Powell argued that the use of race as a factor in college admissions ought to be permitted because it would (presumably) lead to greater student-body diversity.

This was a laudable goal for a university, he said, for it would allow it to achieve "a robust exchange of ideas."

Sandra Day O'Connor recapitulated Powell's argument in her opinion for the Court in *Grutter v. Bollinger*, upholding the University of Michigan Law School's policy of intentionally favoring applicants from certain racial groups over others with similar qualifications. O'Connor justified the decision largely by appealing to its supposed policy implications. She cited several amicus briefs submitted by left-wing academics, corporations, and professional organizations, all of which alleged countless studies showing that racial and ethnic diversity guaranteed greater viewpoint diversity and, in turn, increased tolerance of differing opinions.

But is this true? Has the use of racial preferences in higher education admissions achieved the "robust exchange of ideas" on which it was originally justified by the courts?

In an amicus brief supporting SFFA's challenge to race-conscious admissions policies at Harvard and the University of North Carolina, the Legal Insurrection Foundation (LIF) says "no." In the years since Grutter was decided, "the American university campus," LIF argues, "has become less ideologically diverse and more intolerant of ideas challenging campus dogmas." The group cites several nonpartisan surveys to support the claim. A 2021 survey of 37,104 students conducted jointly by the College Pulse, the Foundation for Individual Rights in Education (FIRE), and RealClearEducation found that more than 80 percent of students reported some amount of self-censorship.

Similarly, LIF notes that a Knight Foundation-Ipsos study released in January 2022 showed that 65 percent of college students felt today's "campus climate prevents people from saying what they believe for fear of offending someone." What's more, less than half of all college students "said they were comfortable offering dissenting opinions to ideas shared by other students or the instructor in the classroom." And 71 percent of students who identified as Republican "felt that the campus climate chilled speech."

The Court now seems likely to strike down the use of race-conscious admissions in higher education next June 2023. Given the originalist-bent of the Court's majority, the decision will rely most heavily on the text of both Title VI and the Equal Protection Clause, which prohibit racial discrimination. But it may also have something to say about the faulty premise underlying race-conscious admissions all these years. Contrary to what O'Connor claimed in Grutter, affirmative action has not led to greater diversity of thought on America's college campuses.

An Overt Political Litmus Test

According to the John D. Sailer and Ray M. Sanchez "An Overt Political Litmus Test" *City Journal* May 2022 report:

On May 5, 2022, the Chancellor's Office of the California Community Colleges (CCC) system amended its proposed diversity, equity, inclusion, and accessibility (DEIA) competencies. Issued in March, the original proposal sought to establish "diversity" and "anti-racism" evaluations for every employee of the 116-college system—a political litmus test. The newly issued changes are merely cosmetic, indicating that, despite notable pushback to the proposal, it will likely become policy.

While DEI requirements are quickly becoming common, CCC's proposal stands out for its thoroughness and ideological aggressiveness. It defines "cultural competency" as "the practice of acquiring and utilizing knowledge of the intersectionality of social identities and the multiple axes of oppression that people from different racial, ethnic, and other minoritized groups face." It calls for all community college districts to "include DEIA competencies and criteria as a minimum standard for evaluating the performance of all employees" and "place significant emphasis on DEIA competencies in employee evaluation and tenure review processes to support employee growth, development, and career advancement."

The Chancellor's Office also provides a list of competencies. Some of them: "Includes a DEI and race-conscious pedagogy," "Contributes to DEI and anti-racism research and scholarship," and "Engages in self-assessment of one's own commitment to DEI and internal biases, and seeks opportunities for growth to acknowledge and address the harm caused by internal biases and behavior."

Requiring faculty to embrace the politically-charged concepts of "intersectionality" and "multiple axes of oppression" clearly violates academic freedom—but the CCC system seems unperturbed by that prospect. A workgroup for the system's curriculum committee created guidelines called "DEI in Curriculum: Model Principles and Practices," which explain what "DEI and race-conscious" pedagogy looks like in practice.

One of the document's recommended "culturally responsive classroom practices" reads: "Protect the cultural integrity of an academic discipline to support equity by no longer weaponizing 'academic integrity' and 'academic freedom' that impedes equity and inflicts curricular trauma on our students, especially historically marginalized students."

Perhaps unsurprisingly, the proposal has gained significant pushback. The Foundation for Individual Rights in Education referred to the policy as "unacceptable and unconstitutional." The Pacific Legal Foundation condemned it in equally strong terms: "The proposed regulation will entrench a political orthodoxy, reduce intellectual diversity on college campuses, threaten First Amendment freedoms, and impair the education of students who deserve exposure to a rich and robust range of viewpoints on the critical issues facing our country."

Even Brian Leiter, law professor at University of Chicago and certainly no conservative, agreed with the Pacific Legal Foundation's First Amendment argument, noting on his blog that the "letter gets it right on the constitutional infirmities."

But the criticism seems to have fallen on deaf ears, as the new amendments are trivial. Per the changes, evaluators should have a "consistent," rather than "uniform," understanding of the DEIA evaluation process. Cultural competency involves "developing cultural knowledge" rather than "learning specific bodies of cultural knowledge." The key thrust of the policy—most notably, that every employee in America's largest system of higher education will be evaluated for his or her political beliefs—remains unchanged.

The California Community Colleges system proposes a diversity, equity, and inclusion system unique for its ideological aggressiveness.

Those concerned with higher education should pay close attention. After all, DEI competencies for promotion and tenure are the next big thing. Recently, the University of Illinois at Urbana-Champaign announced that it will require diversity statements of all faculty members seeking promotion or tenure. The Diversity Strategic Plan at Northern Arizona University promises to embed diversity "as an important component of learning outcomes, professional development, performance expectations, and performance evaluations at all levels."

Even disciplines that seem apolitical, such as medicine, have followed the trend. The UNC-Chapel Hill School of Medicine's new promotion and tenure guidelines require every candidate to submit a diversity statement and include diversity contributions in their CV. (The guidelines provide a list of sample activities.)

Oregon Health and Science University's Diversity, Equity, Inclusion and Anti-Racism Strategic Action Plan establishes a similar promotion and tenure policy, promising to "include a section in promotion packages where faculty members report on the ways they are contributing to improving DEI, anti-racism and social justice. Reinforce the importance of these efforts by establishing clear consequences and influences on promotion packages."

California often functions as a testing ground for the rest of the nation. What happens in California rarely stays in California—especially if it's an "innovation" in Progressive politics. We should hope that this overt political litmus test will be unequivocally rejected. Unfortunately, that does not look likely.

The Highest Principle

As per the Christopher F. Rufo "The Highest Principle" *City Journal* February 2023 article: Left-wing DEI bureaucracy has captured Florida State University and installed radical politics as the governing value.

Florida State University has adopted a series of "diversity, equity, and inclusion" programs that divides Americans along a "matrix of oppression," castigates Christians for their "Christian privilege," and offers a racially segregated scholarship that deliberately bars white students from applying.

Officially, Florida State officials have claimed in a recent report to Governor Ron DeSantis that they support 23 separate DEI programs and initiatives. But beneath the surface, the ideology has embedded itself everywhere in the university.

I have obtained documents through public searches and Sunshine Law requests that reveal a sprawling bureaucracy, dedicated to promoting left-wing racial narratives, including a seemingly endless array of programs, departments, trainings, certificates, committees, statements, grants, groups, clubs, reports, and initiatives.

One representative program is "Social Justice Ally Training," hosted by Student Equity & Inclusion Director Sierra Turner and the Center for Leadership & Social

Change. The program provides a basic recapitulation of the critical-race-theory narrative: white, patriarchal Western societies have created a "Cycle of Socialization" that has resulted in "racism, classism, religious oppression, sexism, heterosexism, gender oppression, ableism, ageism & adultism, and xenophobia."

The trainers make the case that, in the United States, "whites" are the racial group responsible for the "systematic subordination of members of targeted racial groups who have relatively little power." Whites are also guilty of "cultural racism," or the creation and maintenance of social structures that "overtly and covertly attribute normality to white people and Whiteness." By definition, no other group can be racist—"institutional racism" can only "create advantages and benefits for Whites."

Christians Now Represent an Oppressor Class

They have created "Christian hegemony," which "normalizes Christian values as intrinsic to an explicitly American identity," and have instituted a regime of "religious oppression" and the "systematic subordination of minority religions." Consequently, Christians must atone for their "Christian privilege," the training suggests, because of, for example, their "close-minded hatred, fear, or prejudice towards Islam and Muslims."

The training divides participants into "dominant groups" and "subordinate groups." Dominant groups—whites, men, Christians, heterosexuals—are told that they are at the apex of the "matrix of oppression," but if they submit to social-justice ideology, they can seek redemption through "identity development." They are told that they begin their journey as "selfish," unable to "see privilege," "not interested in the system," and hoping to "maintain the status quo." But the oppressor class can eventually overcome its nature and work to "consciously [use] unearned privilege against self" and "destroy the system."

Beyond training programs, DEI ideology at Florida State has also become pervasive in nearly every academic department. The business school has pledged to create an award for "DEI heroes." The classics department has released a statement in support of Black Lives Matter. The art history department has adopted a "land acknowledgement" that portrays white Europeans as illegal settlers. And the sociology department has created an entire course, "Critical Race Theory," that presents left-wing racialism as the gospel truth and assigns readings that traffic in overt racial hostility, such as "Whiteness as Pathological Narcissism," with no competing opinions anywhere to be found. "Do not let the constraints of the discipline stop you from being the radical you want to be," the syllabus reads.

At the administrative level, the DEI bureaucracy also serves as a filter to exclude anyone who does not commit to social-justice ideology. Some departments at FSU now require potential faculty to submit "diversity statements"—best understood as loyalty oaths to left-wing racialism—as part of the application process. Likewise, some academic programs also require graduate students to pledge allegiance to DEI in order to gain admission into the department.

The result of all these programs is a racial and ideological spoils system, in which groups are rewarded or punished based on their identity and political orientation, rather than their academic merit. Following this system of race-based judgment, Florida State even offers scholarships that explicitly exclude white students. The Delores Auzenne Assistantship for Minorities, for example, is designated solely for "African-American, Hispanic, Asian or Pacific Islander, and Native-American" graduate students—no European-Americans need apply.

The end goal of DEI ideology is to move everyone in the university's orbit toward partisan political activism. In the Social Justice Ally Training, the university makes its desire clear: participants are directly encouraged to engage in "structural change activism" and "lobbying for policy change," including "petition drives, picketing, performance art, teach-ins, vigils, overloading administrative systems, rent withholding, strikes, walk-outs, protests, marches, blacklisting, slowdowns, sit downs, dumping, [and] demonstrations."

Knowledge, it seems, has been displaced as the core mission of this university. At Florida State, the diversity commissars have busied themselves making radical politics—administrated by the bureaucracy and imposed downward on students, faculty, and staff—the highest principle.

The DEI Cult

The University of South Florida turns left-wing racialism into a psychological conditioning program as reported in the Christopher F. Rufo "DEI Cult" *City Journal* February 2023 article:

The University of South Florida has adopted a radical "diversity, equity, and inclusion" (DEI) program that claims America is a force for "white supremacy," encourages students to attend racially segregated counseling programs to address their "privilege" and "oppression," and promotes a variety of left-wing causes, including "reparations," "defund the police," and "prison abolition."

I have obtained a trove of public documents exposing the university's DEI programming, much of which, according to the Internet Archive's Wayback Machine, the university tried to delete from its website following Florida governor Ron DeSantis's recent request for information on DEI in the state's public universities.

Taken together, these materials paint a troubling picture. USF's sprawling diversity bureaucracy has turned left-wing racialism into a new orthodoxy and implemented an administrative policy of racial preferences and discrimination. It divides individuals into categories of oppressor and oppressed, presents "anti-racism" as the solution, and proposes "racial identity development"—which, in practice, resembles a form of cult programming—as the necessary method of atonement.

The first step in this programming is the condemnation of American society. Following the 2020 death of George Floyd, nearly every appendage of USF condemned the United States as fundamentally racist. Then-president Steven Currall published a statement denouncing the "systemic racism that continues to plague our nation." The English department attacked the United States for "centuries of normalized violence, structural oppression, and dehumanizing rhetoric that target Black, Brown, and Indigenous people."

The School of Interdisciplinary Global Studies blasted America for its "institutionalized, structural racism and white supremacy." The anthropology department assailed its own discipline for being "rooted in racism." The department of sociology pronounced on the "interlocking systems of oppression found throughout the institutions of our country." Literacy studies, women's and gender studies, engineering, medicine, nursing, pharmacy, public health, and other departments released similar statements.

University's DEI Administrators Offered the Solution: Racial Reeducation

In the aftermath of the ensuing George Floyd riots, the USF Counseling Center offered racially segregated counseling sessions for "Black & African American," "People of Color," and "White" students, providing a "healing space for POC to discuss unique impacts of systemic racism" and a "connecting space for allies to share experiences and identify ways to take action against racism." The goal of these psychological conditioning sessions, according to organizers, was to address "COVID-19, xenophobia, killings of unarmed Black people, systemic racism, privilege, oppression, and institutional challenges." In this kind of programming, individuals are subordinated to racial categories; ideology serves as a substitute for psychological health.

Meantime, the university's DEI officers reinforced the narrative and offered a battery of resources for racial reconditioning. The Office of Multicultural Affairs published an official guidebook, "Anti-Racist Resources: The Unlearning of Racism and White Supremacy," that promoted psychological approaches to "white identity development." The premise of these programs is simple: whites suffer from "white privilege," "white guilt," and "white fragility." And the solution is clear: whites must atone for their oppression through the process of "racial identity development" and "becoming an active anti-racist."

According to one of these programs, called "Scaffolding Anti-Racist Resources," whites must first admit their complicity in racism, which includes "being confronted with active racism of real-world experiences that highlight their whiteness." Whites will then enter the process of "disintegration," experiencing "white guilt" and thinking, "I feel bad for being white." Next, after their racial identity is broken down, they will enter a phase of "reintegration," thinking, "it's not my fault I'm white" and beginning to engage in left-wing political activism.

Finally, as whites move through the stages of "pseudo-independence" and "immersion," they will begin to "work against systems of oppression" and "use [their] privilege to support anti-racist work." At the end of the program, their psychology should conform entirely to political ideology. As the final step, whites must answer various loyalty tests. "Does your solidarity last longer than a news cycle?" the training asks. "Does your solidarity make you lose sleep at night? Does your solidarity put you in danger? Does your solidarity cost you relationships?"

The Endpoint of USF's DEI Programming Is Left-Wing Political Activism

As part of the university's official "anti-racist" guidebook, diversity officials included materials promoting "reparations," "defund the police," and "prison abolition." One resource, "97 Things White People Can Do for Racial Justice," instructs whites to "join a local 'white space,'" "donate to [their] local BLM chapter," "participate in reparations," and "decolonize [their] bookshelf." Another, "For Our White Friends Desiring to Be Allies," demands that whites "stop talking about colorblindness" and stop oppressing those "who do not believe in a white, capitalist Jesus."

Taken as a whole, USF's DEI initiatives resemble practices of cult initiation. The path of "racial identity development" does not take as its endpoint individual psychological health but the submersion of the individual into political ideology. Whites are designated an oppressor class, born with racial guilt that can only be expiated through elaborate rituals and commitments to left-wing activism, to the point that they are alienated from previous relationships and feel compelled to "change the way [they] vote," "denounce [President Trump]," and "change how [they] read [their] Bible."

At a more practical level, the implementation of DEI ideology at USF has already resulted in a system of widespread racial preferences and discrimination. The university openly promotes racial quotas in hiring and requires potential faculty to submit "diversity statements"—best understood as loyalty oaths to left-wing racialism—to be considered for employment.

The university's Office of Supplier Diversity administers a system of racial and sexual preferences in contracting, instructing its "Diversity Champions" to hire vendors and suppliers based on identity, rather than on purely economic concerns. The university also promotes a range of racially segregated scholarships that explicitly exclude white students—the only racial group that receives such treatment.

These "diversity, equity, and inclusion" programs are a farce. In practice, they promote ideological conformity, racial and sexual discrimination, and the exclusion of any group that finds itself on the wrong side of the identity hierarchy. Governor DeSantis, who recently pledged to defund DEI programs in Florida's public universities, should not hesitate in demolishing these offices, terminating the employment of their commissars, and restoring colorblind equality, individual merit, and scholarly excellence as the guiding principles of the academy.

Racism in the Name of "Anti-Racism"

The University of Central Florida adopts DEI programming that segregates students by race and encourages discrimination against the "oppressor" class as reported in Christopher F. Rufo's "Racism in the Name of 'Anti-Racism'" Substack page in February 2023:

The University of Central Florida has adopted radical Diversity, Equity, and Inclusion (DEI) programming that segregates students by race, condemns the United States as "white-supremacist culture," and encourages active discrimination against the "oppressor" class, characterized as "male, White, heterosexual, able-bodied, and Christian."

Officially, UCF reports that it has 14 separate DEI programs, costing in the aggregate more than $4 million per year. But this dramatically understates the reality, which is that the ideology of "diversity, equity, and inclusion" has been entrenched everywhere. The university's administration and academic departments have created a blizzard of programs, classes, trainings, reports, committees, certifications, events, documents, policies, clubs, groups, conferences, and statements pledging UCF to left-wing racialism.

These programs, long in the making, exploded into prominence following the death of George Floyd in 2020. As the administration signaled that it was endorsing the Black Lives Matter movement, the academic departments immediately fell into line. The sociology department pledged allegiance to BLM and blasted the "anti-Blackness at the heart of US white-supremacist culture." The physics department released a statement promising to address "systemic anti-Black racism in policing" and its own "power and privilege." The anthropology department published a statement denouncing white European "hegemonic systems" and vowed to "advocate for a more inclusive society based on the principles of cultural relativism."

University DEI Programming Follows the Basic Ideology of CRT

America is a racist nation divided between white oppressors and minority oppressed, and society, using the logic of "antiracism," must actively discriminate against the oppressors in order to achieve social justice. The great oppressor who occupies the "mythical norm," according to the university's official glossary, is "male, white, heterosexual, financially stable, young-middle adult, able-bodied, Christian." Other groups are "minoritized," or condemned by the "systemic and structural realities in place that push people and communities to the margins."

Following the George Floyd riots, the university's administrators and faculty renewed their dedication to the DEI narrative. Ann Gleig, an associate professor of religion and cultural studies, instructed whites on campus to begin "waking up to whiteness and white privilege," encouraging them to "educate [themselves] on systemic racism and white supremacy," "participate in anti-racist training programs," and "commit to having difficult conversations with white family and friends about systemic racism." She also directed students to a set of resources, including one that encouraged whites to attend racially segregated "affinity groups" to develop their white racial consciousness and "unravel their feelings and ways of understanding without hurting people of color."

At the same time, S. Kent Butler, a black professor of counselor education then serving as UCF's chief diversity officer, pushed the argument that minorities live in a state of constant fear and exhaustion. "Leaving the house is an action that may seem ordinary for some, but for individuals who deal with regular hatred and judgment . . . we live with anxiety and fear about walking into unwelcoming spaces," he said. The responsibility for reforming society, he explained in another interview, belongs to whites. "Racism comes from slavery, from when they used to have [Black] people swinging from trees," he said. "White people have to come to the forefront and stop the systemic system that's been put into play by white people."

How do DEI bureaucracies recommend solving these problems? Through active racial discrimination, or, to use their euphemism, a policy of "racial equity." The University of Central Florida has embedded such discriminatory practices in its programs, including faculty hiring, student activities, and scholarship opportunities.

Regarding faculty hiring, UCF has adopted the position that merit is a "myth" that advances racism and must be corrected through active discrimination on behalf of "minoritized groups." In its official guidebook, "Inclusive Faculty Hiring," the university recommends tilting the hiring process toward minorities by minimizing objective measures—dismissed as "problematic heuristics"—and peppering job announcements with left-wing buzzwords such as "racial equity," "social justice," "anti-racist," and "mention of specific group identities," with the exception of those of whites.

Equity and Inclusion Statements

To reinforce this ideology, administrators also recommend that departments require potential faculty to submit an "Equity and Inclusion Statement," which serves as a loyalty oath to left-wing ideology. At the end of the process, the university endorses explicit racial quotas. "University policy indicates that a successful search will result in a diverse pool of candidates for the final interview round that [includes at least one woman and one member of a minoritized group]," the guidebook reads [brackets in the original]. "If at the time final candidates are identified and the specified parameters are not met, the search should either be restarted or the existing candidate pool should be revisited with more equitable strategies in mind."

Students, too, must navigate a racial filter. The university has held minority-only graduation ceremonies, and its counseling center offers racially segregated "affinity groups" and psychological programs, such as "Exploring Vulnerability in POC Spaces," restricted to "Black-identified, Afro-Latinx and students from African-descent," as well as other racial-conditioning groups delineated for "Asian-identified students" and "Hispanic/Latinx students."

UCF also advertises racially discriminatory and racially segregated scholarships that intentionally exclude European-Americans and sometimes Asian-Americans. The Professional Doctoral Diversity Fellowship, Harris Diversity Initiative Scholarship, and NSF/Florida Georgia Louis Stokes Alliance for Minority Participation in Engineering & Science and National Action Council for Minorities in Engineering scholarships, for example, promise to discriminate on behalf of "underrepresented populations," a euphemism for "African American, Hispanic, or Native American" students. Others, such as the Minority Teachers Scholarship, are explicitly segregated by race. Candidates "must be a member of one of the following racial groups: African American/Black, American Indian/Alaskan Native, Asian American/Pacific Islander, or Hispanic/Latino." In other words, anyone but whites.

All these racially discriminatory scholarship programs violate Title VI of the Civil Rights Act. But university administrators have been silently embedding "racial equity" principles into every academic process. They operate with impunity because, until recently, no one has attempted to stop them.

This could change. Along with my Manhattan Institute colleague Ilya Shapiro, I have proposed a model policy that would outlaw these practices and abolish the DEI bureaucracy. Florida governor Ron DeSantis has promised to address the problem in the coming legislative session. It seems that Florida lawmakers have seen the DEI scam for what it is: an attempt to push left-wing racialist ideology in the guise of academic justice. As they prepare for action, state legislators should consider a maximalist position: demolishing the DEI bureaucracy down to its foundations and restoring the principle of colorblind equality to the Sunshine State's public institutions.

An Alternative to the 'Diversity, Equity, and Inclusion' Deception

From the George Leef "An Alternative to the 'Diversity, Equity, and Inclusion' Deception" National Review November 2022 article:

Over the last decade, an acronym has swept through most of American education — DEI, which stands for "diversity, equity, and inclusion." It doesn't have any exact meaning, but stands for a farrago of leftist notions that call for radical socioeconomic change. DEI is against the free market, against freedom of speech, and against evaluating people on their individual merits. DEI enthusiasts have been trained in our colleges and universities, usually in identity programs, schools of education, and other ideological fever swamps of "progressivism."

In this superb piece on *The Hill*, Robert Maranto, Michael Mills, and Catherine Salmon look at this disturbing phenomenon.

How bad have things gotten? The authors write, "For example, one-fifth of the advertisements for higher education faculty jobs (and more for prestigious posts) require applicants to write statements of allegiance to DEI. Academic employment often depends on DEI relevant presentations at scholarly conferences and publications in scholarly journals. Increasingly, scholars are required to explain in advance how their research supports DEI. Such litmus tests are traditionally associated with totalitarian regimes and, in America, with McCarthyism."

The DEI zealots act like a tribe that intends to exclude anyone from higher education who isn't in their group. Anyone who questions DEI is obviously defective in some way, probably a racist or a defender of capitalist exploitation. Not suited to work in education.

DEI is a lousy set of ideas, but as the old saying goes, you can't beat something with nothing, so Maranto, Mills, and Salmon suggest a new acronym: MFE (Merit, Fairness, and Equality). They write, "Under MFE, academic decisions are based primarily on academic merit, well validated standardized test scores, grades and, for faculty, publication and teaching records. Individuals are primarily evaluated on their achievements, not by their group identities. This respects individual dignity and promotes the primary mission of research in higher education: the production of knowledge."

Most Americans would strongly prefer MFE over DEI if the choice were explained to them.

13 – Critical Race Theory, Illiberal Diversity Programs, 1619 Fiction vs. 1776 Facts

shutterstock.com · 2016916802

This debate over the semantics of critical theory might provide an interesting basis for a panel at a scholarly conference, but it's of little use or interest for parents concerned that their children are being taught partisan nonsense. While technical differences exist between the various critical paradigms, virtually all of them share three baseline assumptions:

1) that racism is "everywhere," and supposedly neutral systems, such as policing or standardized tests, are set up to oppress minorities;

2) that to prove the existence of this oppression one need only note that large groups perform at different levels;

3) and that the solution to this problem is equity—or proportional representation of all groups across all endeavors.

As responded to in the Wilfred Reilly "What Is Critical Race Theory, Really?" City

Journal article in October 2021:

None of this is an exaggeration. The quote about racism being "everyday" and constant comes from Richard Delgado, one of the founders of critical race theory. The claim that group differences must indicate racism or other prejudice comes from no less a critical eminence than Ibram X. Kendi, who has famously said that the only possible explanations for such gaps are either oppression or literal genetic inferiority. Kendi has also proposed a federal-level Department of Anti-Racism.

Along with these core ideas of "systemic racism" generally come a basket of other woke concepts like white privilege, "cultural appropriation," "intersectionality," the Black Lives Matter take on policing, and the idea of constant interracial conflict and crime.

Parents reject most of this CRT package not because they are bigots or too complacent in suburbia but because they believe it is wrong. As analysts like Thomas Sowell have pointed out for more than 40 years, the idea that gaps in performance between large groups must be due either to racism or to genetics is absurd.

Groups of people who vary in race and religion also often vary across other cultural and situational traits. For example, the most common age for a black American, which could be fairly called the modal average, is 27; the most common age for a white American is 58. Simply adjusting for these differences in age (and thus work experience), and for a few other traits like the regions people live in and their scores on standard aptitude tests, closes black-white gaps in income to almost nothing. In fact, either seven or eight—depending on how you count South Africans—of the top ten income-earning groups in the United States these days are made up of "people of color."

Most of the ideas associated with the major critical paradigms collapse as easily and totally as their core concepts.

After years of flattering mainstream media coverage of Black Lives Matter, a large recent study revealed that the majority of "very liberal" Americans believes that in a typical year police kill anywhere from "about 1,000" to "more than 10,000" unarmed black men. In 2020, the year of the Floyd Riots, the actual number of blacks killed in this manner was 18.

Yes, the number is a mere 18!

A serious look at the data on interracial crime and conflict reveals similar patterns. Major papers run nonstop stories about cruel whites or mobs attacking minorities. Meantime, figures from the U.S. National Crime Victimization Study reveal that only about 3 percent of all serious crimes in a normal year, like 2019, are violent crimes involving a white perpetrator and a black victim or a black perp and a white victim. Further, 70 percent to 90 percent of these incidents are generally black-on-white, rather than the reverse.

Facts matter, but so does context. Critical theorists say some things that are essentially true, but meaningless—and likely to mislead unless one has a nuanced understanding of history or other disciplines. For example, it is undeniably true that slavery once existed in the United States. However, it is also undeniably true that almost every other powerful nation in history held slaves as well.

A trans-African slave trade run largely by Muslim merchants lasted far longer than even the trans-Atlantic slave trade, and it subjected far more people (about 18 million) to human bondage. The same amoral traders didn't hesitate to sell battle captives or shipwrecked sailors with pale skin: the conveniently forgotten Barbary slave trade shipped more than 1 million Caucasian slaves to Arab and black masters for centuries. Focusing lesson plans and curricula on the horrors of slavery without ever mentioning the universal nature of the practice or the fact that it was ended by Western countries is hardly "just being honest."

Just being honest: that phrase really sums up what parents demand—not, generally, a jingoistic system of education, but also not a reflexively critical one. Parents want an honest, fair, and reasonably apolitical curriculum that depicts the United States as it was and is, warts and all.

Biden Criminalizes CRT Dissent

As noted in the Christopher F. Rufo "Biden Criminalizes CRT Dissent" *City Journal* article in October 2021: In an official memo, Attorney General Merrick Garland has pledged to mobilize the FBI against parents protesting critical race theory in public schools, citing unspecified "threats of violence" against school officials.

Garland's memo follows a National School Boards Association (NSBA) request that the Biden administration investigate threats to school board members and classify sometimes-heated parent protests as "domestic terrorism." The NSBA suggested that some of these parents should be prosecuted under the PATRIOT Act and federal hate-crimes legislation.

The school board association letter, however, is riddled with falsehoods, errors, and exaggerations. It begins with the claim that "critical race theory is not taught in public schools," despite a vast body of evidence, including my own reporting, showing that the teaching of CRT is widespread in public schools. Even the national teachers' union has admitted as much and called for CRT's implementation in all 50 states.

The NSBA deliberately misrepresents debates at school board meetings as "threats" and sometimes-vociferous and angry speech as "violence." The letter refers to dozens of news stories alluding to "disruptions," "shouts," "argument," and "mobs," but, contrary to its core claim, cites only a single example of actual violence against a school official: a case of aggravated battery in Illinois, which is obviously condemnable, but hardly the justification for a national "domestic terrorism" investigation.

The association even fabricated entire storylines to support its political objectives. For example, the NSBA claims that a Tennessee school board official named Jon White resigned due to "threats and acts of violence;" the linked source, however, reports that White resigned for "concerns about too much time away from his family," with no mention of threats or violence. (In another local report, White complains about parents calling him a "child abuser" and other epithets, which, while harsh, are hardly the equivalent of an "act of violence.")

The administration has mobilized the FBI against parents who oppose critical race theory.

Still, despite the school board association's flimsy pretext, the Biden administration appears to be doing its bidding. Garland's memo instructs the FBI to coordinate with "federal, state, local, Tribal, and territorial law enforcement" to develop plans to "discourage these threats, identify them when they occur, and prosecute them when appropriate." NSBA director Chip Slaven and national teachers' union president Randi Weingarten immediately praised Garland's aggressive actions.

This is a deeply politicized and dangerous escalation in the debate about critical race theory in public schools. For months, critical race theory proponents, including teachers' unions, have struggled to respond to critics, and new survey data show that strong majorities among all racial categories oppose teaching CRT in public schools. But as its standing in polls has plummeted, the education establishment has turned to more heavy-handed tactics.

The purpose of mobilizing the FBI is not only to monitor dissent but also to subdue it. The suggestion that parents might be engaging in "domestic terrorism" is designed to suppress speech and assembly and to justify further federalization of education policy. In congressional testimony, Education Secretary Miguel Cardona refused to say that parents are the "primary stakeholders" in their children's education; this week, Attorney General Garland is attempting to drive an even bigger wedge between parents and public schools.

Parents should not let this overreach deter them from speaking out against critical race theory in schools. The Biden administration has raised the stakes, and the fight is no longer only about CRT; it is also about protecting the basic rights of free speech, assembly, and constituent control over the nation's public institutions. The grassroots revolt against critical race theory is proof that Americans still have the instinct for self-rule. They must not let the Biden administration crush it.

Disingenuous Defenses of Critical Race Theory

As revealed in the Christopher F. Rufo "Disingenuous Defenses of Critical Race Theory" *New York Post* article in July 2021:

In July 2021, *The New York Times* published an opinion piece by commentators David French, Kmele Foster, Thomas Chatterton Williams and Jason Stanley, who presented themselves as a heroic "cross-partisan group of thinkers."

They derided as "un-American" laws passed by states such as Texas, Florida, Idaho, Oklahoma, Arkansas and New Hampshire that prohibit public schools from promoting the core principles of critical race theory, including race essentialism, collective guilt and state-sanctioned discrimination.

These authors imagine themselves the steady hand in a grandiose morality play, defending liberal-democratic freedoms against the threat of illiberalism, wherever it comes from.

But in practice, they are enablers of the worst ideologies of the Left and would leave American families defenseless against them. Their three core arguments— that critical race theory restrictions violate "free speech," that state legislatures should stay out of the "marketplace of ideas," and that citizens should pursue civil-rights litigation instead—are all hollow to the core.

In reality, they would usher in the concrete tyrannies of critical race theory, which explicitly seeks to subvert the principles of individual rights and equal protection under the law. Despite the superficial ideological differences between the four authors, they serve a single function: to prevaricate, stall and run interference for critical race theory's blitz through American institutions.

Teaching Hate: An Example

As uncovered by the Christopher F. Rufo "Teaching Hate" *City Journal* story in December 2020:

Seattle Public Schools recently held a training session for teachers in which American schools were deemed guilty of "spirit murder" against black students. The United States is a "race-based white-supremist society," the training instructed, and white teachers must "bankrupt [their] privilege in acknowledgement of [their] thieved inheritance."

The Seattle school district claims that the U.S. education system is guilty of "spirit murder" against black children.

The central message is that white teachers must recognize that they "are assigned considerable power and privilege in our society" because of their "possession of white skin." Consequently, to atone for their collective guilt, white teachers must be willing to reject their "whiteness" and become dedicated "anti-racist educator[s]."

The trainers acknowledge that this language might meet resistance from white teachers. They explain that any negative emotional reaction to being denounced for "whiteness" is an automatic response from the white teachers' "lizard-brain," which makes them "afraid that [they] will have to talk about sensitive issues such as race, racism, classism, sexism, or any kind of 'ism.'" The trainers insist that the teachers "must commit to the journey," regardless of their emotional or intellectual hesitations.

In the most disturbing portion of the session, the teachers discussed "spirit murder," which, according to Bettina Love, is the concept that American schools "murder the souls of Black children every day through systemic, institutionalized, anti-Black, state-sanctioned violence." Love, who originated the concept, declares that the education system is "invested in murdering the souls of Black children," even in the most ostensibly progressive institutions.

The goal of these inflammatory "racial equity" programs is to transform Seattle schools into activist organizations. At the conclusion of the training, teachers must explain how they will practice "anti-racist pedagogy," address the "current social justice movements taking place," and become "anti-racist outside the classroom." They are told to divide the world into "enemies, allies, and accomplices," and work toward the "abolition" of whiteness. They must, in other words, abandon the illusion of neutral teaching standards and get in the trenches of race-based activism.

Unfortunately, this indoctrination is not an aberration—it reflects deep ideological currents within Seattle Public Schools. In recent years, the district has expanded its Department of Racial Equity Advancement and deployed "racial equity teams" in dozens of neighborhood schools. The stated goal is to "advance educational racial equity," but in practice, these programs often serve to introduce, perpetuate, and enforce a specific ideological agenda.

Subversive Education: An Example

Also uncovered by the Christopher F. Rufo "Subversive Education" *City Journal* story in March 2021: North Carolina's largest school district launches a campaign against "whiteness in educational spaces."

In 2020, the Wake County Public School System, which serves the greater Raleigh, North Carolina area, held an equity-themed teachers' conference with sessions on "whiteness," "microaggressions," "racial mapping," and "disrupting texts," encouraging educators to form "equity teams" in schools and push the new party line: "antiracism."

The February 2020 conference, attended by more than 200 North Carolina public school teachers, began with a "land acknowledgement," a ritual recognition suggesting that white North Carolinians are colonizers on stolen Native American land. Next, the superintendent of Wake County Public Schools, Cathy Moore, introduced the day's program and shuffled teachers to breakout sessions across eight rooms. Freelance reporter A.P. Dillon obtained the documents from the sessions through a public records request and provided them to *City Journal*.

At the first session, "Whiteness in Ed Spaces," school administrators provided two handouts on the "norms of whiteness." These documents claimed that "(white) cultural values" include "denial," "fear," "blame," "control," "punishment," "scarcity," and "one-dimensional thinking." According to notes from the session, the teachers argued that "whiteness perpetuates the system" of injustice and that the district's "whitewashed curriculum" was "doing real harm to our students and educators." The group encouraged white teachers to "challenge the dominant ideology" of whiteness and "disrupt" white culture in the classroom through a series of "transformational interventions."

Parents, according to the teachers, should be considered an impediment to social justice. When one teacher asked, "How do you deal with parent pushback?" the answer was clear: ignore parental concerns and push the ideology of antiracism directly to students. "You can't let parents deter you from the work," the teachers said. "White parents' children are benefiting from the system" of whiteness and are "not learning at home about diversity (LGBTQ, race, etc.)."

Therefore, teachers have an obligation to subvert parental wishes and beliefs. Any "pushback," the teachers explained, is merely because white parents fear "that they are going to lose something" and find it "hard to let go of power [and] privilege."

This isn't an aberration. In fact, the district's official Equity in Action plan encourages teachers to override parents in the pursuit of antiracism. "Equity leaders [should] have the confidence to take risks and make difficult decisions that are rooted in their values," the document reads. "Even in the face of opposition, equity leaders can draw on a heartfelt conviction for what is best for students and families." In other words, the school should displace the family as the ultimate arbiter of political morality.

The equity plan outlines this new ideology in chart format, announcing the district's commitment to a series of fashionable pedagogies, including "color consciousness," "white identity development," "critical race theory," "intersections of power and privilege," and "anti-racist identity and action."

What's Wrong With the 1619 Project?

Discussed in the Wilfred Reilly "What's Wrong With the 1619 Project?" Prager U video:

Have you heard of The 1619 Project? It was published by the *New York Times* in August of 2019. It won the Pulitzer Prize for Commentary in 2020. Its thesis: The United States was founded in 1619, when the first slave was brought to North America.

Wait—that brings up some questions…What happened to 1776? To July 4th? The Declaration of Independence? George Washington, Thomas Jefferson and James Madison?

According to The 1619 Project, the Founding Fathers pushed for all that "Life, Liberty and the Pursuit of Happiness" stuff to protect their slave holdings. Independence from England? That was just a smoke screen. To them, everything that's wrong with America is tied to her "original sin" of slavery: from segregation to traffic jams (yes—traffic jams!). For The 1619 Project authors, racism is not a part of the American experience; it is the American experience.

Is this true? Let's look at three of the project's major claims:

1.   Preserving slavery was the real cause of the American Revolution

If you asked the Founders why they no longer wanted to be a British colony, they would have given you a long list of reasons: Taxation without representation, conflicts over debts from the French and Indian War, and the Stamp Act would be just a few. Probably most important was the burning desire to be free—to chart their own destiny as a sovereign nation.

Protecting slavery? Slavery was not under threat from the British. In fact, Britain didn't free the slaves in its overseas colonies until 1833—57 years later, after the Declaration of Independence. Yes, the subject of slavery was hotly debated at the Constitutional Convention, but that was after the war was won.

2.   Slavery made America rich

Slavery made some Americans rich—true enough. Eli Yale, for example, made a fortune in the slave trade. He donated money and land for the university that is named after him. But the institution of slavery didn't make America rich. In fact, the slave system badly slowed the economic development of half the country.

As economist Thomas Sowell points out, in 1860, just one year before the Civil War began, the South had only one-sixth as many factories as the North. Almost 90% of the country's skilled, well-paid laborers and professionals were based in the North. Banking, railroads, manufacturing—all were concentrated in the North. The South was an economic backwater.

And the cost of abolishing slavery was enormous—not merely in terms of dollars (Lincoln borrowed billions to pay for it), but also in terms of human life: 360,000 Union soldiers died in order to free 4 million slaves. That works out to about one soldier in blue for every ten slaves freed. It's hard to look at that butcher's bill and conclude that the nation turned a profit from slavery.

And many things have happened since 1865. In the almost 200 years since the Civil War, the population of the country has grown almost 900% and our national GDP has increased 12,000%. Slavery did not make America rich.

3. Racism is an unchangeable part of America

This argument is more philosophical than scholarly, but it undergirds the entire 1619 Project. It's also pernicious because it suggests that the United States is an inherently racist country that can't overcome its flaws. Yet that's exactly what it's done.

Today, America is the most successful multi-racial country in history, the only white-majority country to elect a black President—twice. Of course, progress has not always been smooth. There have been terrible setbacks. But to compare American attitudes about race today to America a hundred years ago, let alone to 1619, is absurd.

Here's a fact that should be better known: Two million black Africans have come to America as legal immigrants—from countries like Nigeria—in the last 50 years, and have become one of the most successful groups in the country. Why would these folks move to what is often called an evil, racist country? Because, unlike many people lucky enough to be born here, they know that America is a land of opportunity for everyone.

It's also only fair to note that while blacks have heroically fought for our rights, often against great odds, we haven't done it alone. A vast number of decent whites have also advanced the cause of racial equality. To cite one of countless examples, the U.S. Senate that passed the landmark Civil Rights Act in 1964 contained 98 whites and two men of color (and they were Asian)

The great black leaders of the past—Harriet Tubman, Frederick Douglass, Booker T. Washington, Martin Luther King—never lost faith in America's promise that all people are created equal. None of them believed that racism was America's defining characteristic. They were right.

Shortly after The 1619 Project was published, a group of distinguished historians—almost all on the left—wrote a public letter condemning the work. They called it a "displacement of historical understanding by ideology."

They were right, too.

Kick the '1619 Project' Out of Schools

Per the David Randall "Kick the '1619 Project' Out of Schools" National Association of Scholars article in August 2020:

America needs to get the "1619 Project" curriculum out of its schools. Senator Tom Cotton (R-Ark.) has introduced a new bill that would go a long way toward that goal—the Saving American History Act of 2020 (SAHA 2020).

The *New York Times* introduced The "1619 Project" last August. The "1619 Project" mainstreamed the anti-American ideology of a new generation of woke activists, who have graduated from college radicalism to careers in progressive institutions such as the *Times*. The "1619 Project" seeks to rewrite American history with the claim that it is based on slavery and oppression, rather than on liberty and democracy, in order to delegitimize the American republic.

The "1619 Project" claims to be "revisionist" history—but many of the best scholars of American history swiftly demonstrated that it was nothing more than a shabby, fact-free polemic. Nikole Hannah-Jones, the Pulitzer Prize-winning mastermind of the "1619 Project," recently admitted that the effort never had a historical basis—and never even intended to be history.

"I've always said that the '1619 Project' is not a history," Hannah-Jones said in a series of tweets. "It is a work of journalism that explicitly seeks to challenge the national narrative and, therefore, the national memory. The project has always been as much about the present as it is the past."

Nevertheless, the "1619 Project" has had a profound impact on America's schools.

School districts in cities ranging from Buffalo to Chicago to Newark to Washington immediately announced that they would incorporate the "1619 Project" into their school history curriculums—using a "1619 Project" curriculum that the Pulitzer Center posted to the internet as soon as the *Times* published the special edition of its Sunday magazine. The Pulitzer Center claims more than 3,500 classrooms have adopted their curriculum.

Clearly, the project's creators of the "1619 Project" had coordinated with the Pulitzer Center and school district leaders to transform the nation's curricula immediately—without bothering to wait for input from parents, school boards, or historians.

The "1619 Project" was meant to be a revolution from above, imposed on America's children to teach them to despise their country.

But Cotton carefully tailored SAHA 2020 to avoid measures that would harm students who are the victims of woke administrators. No school lunch funding would be affected, nor would funding for students with disabilities—no funding would change except for these two specific funding streams.

Indeed, Cotton would be warranted in strengthening SAHA 2020 considerably, to deal effectively with the challenge posed by the 1619 Project curriculum. Cotton might amend SAHA 2020 to:

1. Define what is meant by the 1619 Project curriculum, by reference to the contents of the Pulitzer Center's the 1619 Project Curriculum.

2. Extend the federal government's financial sanctions to prohibit funding that supports any third-party organization or curriculum that incorporates substantial elements of the 1619 Project Curriculum, such as the Zinn Education Project or Facing History.

3. Extend the federal government's financial sanctions to prohibit funding that supports any state-level standardized assessment that incorporates substantial elements of the 1619 Project Curriculum.

4. Draft standard procedures by which individuals and organizations may

report to the Department of Education that a school district has adopted some or all of the 1619 Project Curriculum.

5. Require the Department of Education to report annually to Congress which school districts have adopted some or all of the 1619 Project Curriculum.

6. Restrict eligibility for further carefully defined Department of Education grants and programs to school districts that the Department of Education certifies as free of the 1619 Project Curriculum.

Credit: America's founding in 1776 - The Heritage Foundation.

Legislation to restrict the 1619 Project Curriculum should be as rigorous as possible. America's future depends on knowing our true past. We must get rid of the 1619 Project Curriculum to save our children from the anti-American lies of the woke establishment.

The 1776 Commission Report Reinvigorates the American Mind

Per the Mike Sabo "The 1776 Commission Report Reinvigorates the American Mind" National Association of Scholars article in January 2021:

Former President Trump's 1776 Commission has issued a report that summarizes "the principles of the American founding and how those principles have shaped our country." It will be the only such report—President Biden swiftly dissolved the Commission by executive order after being sworn into office.

Biden's decision is regrettable because "The 1776 report calls for a return to the unifying ideals stated in the Declaration of Independence," as Chairman Larry P.

Arnn, Vice Chair Carol Swain, and Executive Director Matthew Spalding said in a statement. "It quotes the greatest Americans, black and white, men and women, in devotion to these ideals."

The report rejects the teachings of historians such as Howard Zinn, the New York Times's 1619 Project, and other efforts aimed at fundamentally transforming how Americans view their country's history. Neither hiding America's flaws nor offering a triumphal account of American history, the 1776 Commission aimed to recover "our shared identity rooted in our founding principles"—which, its report argues, is "the path to a renewed American unity and a confident American future."

"Our country's founding principles are the key to a peaceful, self-governing people," Arnn stated, "and the 1776 Commission sets out to educate the American public about them. The Commission's report is an approachable introduction to the historical facts of the founding and the principles that animate it."

Beginning with an overview of American founding principles and the constitutional architecture that the Founders fashioned to secure them, the report then catalogues the various threats to republican government and proposes tools that Americans can use to recover a way of life conducive to republican citizenship.

Though not denying that America was founded by a particular people with a particular history, religion, and virtues, the report stresses that the nation was nevertheless founded on the universal principles enunciated in the Declaration. This is why Abraham Lincoln argued by implication in the Gettysburg Address that the United States celebrates its birthday on July 4th, 1776.

Appealing to both human reason and biblical revelation—for example, the Declaration's references to the Creator, Providence, and the Supreme Judge—the Founders justified the government on the basis of eternal, universal principles.

Frederick Douglass once described them as "saving principles" that were the "ring-bolt to the chain of" America's "destiny."

The Progressive movement rejected the idea of permanent truths in favor of constantly evolving group rights meted out by the administrative state, a fourth branch of government composed of independent agencies staffed with experts insulated from political accountability.

Today, identity politics strikes at the heart of republican government by demanding "equal results and explicitly sorting citizens into 'protected classes' based on race and other demographic categories." Even worse, the purveyors of identity politics see people of certain races as evil not necessarily because of what they've done but simply because of their skin color. The 1776 Commission report states unequivocally that identity politics "makes it less likely that racial reconciliation and healing can be attained" because it rejects "Martin Luther King, Jr.'s dream for America."

In order to preserve the blessings of liberty for future generations, families should raise "morally responsible citizens who love America and embrace the gifts and responsibilities of freedom and self-government;" state and local governments should produce curricula that convey an "enlightened patriotism" through reading primary sources; and songwriters, filmmakers, and social influencers should create content that speaks "to eternal truths" that "embody the American spirit."

In the words of Commission member Charles Kesler, the 1776 report intends to rebaptize American citizens in the Declaration of Independence and the Constitution, reinvigorating the American mind in the twenty-first century. President Biden's move to dissolve the Commission does not change this imperative. Indeed, as Arnn, Swain, and Spalding have declared: "The Commission may be abolished, but these principles and our history cannot be. We will all continue to work together to teach and to defend them."

14 – Yes, Critical Race Theory (CRT) is Being Taught in Schools: Stop Denying It!

Credit: Education Next.

Critical race theory is fast becoming America's new institutional orthodoxy. Yet most Americans have never heard of it—and of those who have, many don't understand it. This must change. We need to know what it is so we can know how to fight it.

To explain critical race theory, it helps to begin with a brief history of Marxism. Originally, the Marxist Left built its political program on the theory of class conflict. Karl Marx believed that the primary characteristic of industrial societies was the imbalance of power between capitalists and workers. The solution to that imbalance, according to Marx, was revolution: the workers would eventually gain consciousness of their plight, seize the means of production, overthrow the capitalist class, and usher in a new socialist society.

However, during the twentieth century, a number of regimes underwent Marxist-style revolutions, and each ended in disaster. Socialist governments in the Soviet Union, China, Cambodia, Cuba, and elsewhere racked up a body count of nearly 100 million people. They are remembered for gulags, show trials, executions, and mass starvations. In practice, Marx's ideas unleashed man's darkest brutalities.

By the mid-1960s, Marxist intellectuals in the West had begun to acknowledge these failures. They recoiled at revelations of Soviet atrocities and came to realize that workers' revolutions would never occur in Western Europe or the United States, which had large middle classes and rapidly improving standards of living. Americans in particular had never developed a sense of class consciousness or class division. Most Americans believed in the American dream—the idea that they could transcend their origins through education, hard work, and good citizenship.

Per the Christopher F. Rufo "The Courage of Our Convictions" *City Journal* April 2021 report: But rather than abandon their political project, Marxist scholars in the West simply adapted their revolutionary theory to the social and racial unrest of the 1960s. Abandoning Marx's economic dialectic of capitalists and workers, they substituted race for class and sought to create a revolutionary coalition of the dispossessed based on racial and ethnic categories.

Fortunately, the early proponents of this revolutionary coalition in the U.S. lost out in the 1960s to the civil rights movement, which sought instead the fulfillment of the American promise of freedom and equality under the law. Americans preferred the idea of improving their country to that of overthrowing it. Martin Luther King Jr.'s vision, President Lyndon Johnson's pursuit of the Great Society, and the restoration of law and order promised by President Richard Nixon in his 1968 campaign defined the post-1960s American political consensus.

But the radical Left has proved resilient and enduring—which is where critical race theory comes in.

Critical race theory is an academic discipline, formulated in the 1990s and built on the intellectual framework of identity-based Marxism. Relegated for many years to universities and obscure academic journals, it has increasingly become the default ideology in our public institutions over the past decade. It has been injected into government agencies, public school systems, teacher training programs, and corporate human-resources departments, in the form of diversity-training programs, human-resources modules, public-policy frameworks, and school curricula.

Its supporters deploy a series of euphemisms to describe critical race theory, including "equity," "social justice," "diversity and inclusion," and "culturally responsive teaching." Critical race theorists, masters of language construction, realize that "neo-Marxism" would be a hard sell.

Equity, on the other hand, sounds non-threatening and is easily confused with the American principle of equality.

But the distinction is vast and important. Indeed, critical race theorists explicitly reject equality—the principle proclaimed in the Declaration of Independence, defended in the Civil War, and codified into law with the Fourteenth and Fifteenth Amendments, the Civil Rights Act of 1964, and the Voting Rights Act of 1965. To them, equality represents "mere nondiscrimination" and provides "camouflage" for white supremacy, patriarchy, and oppression.

In contrast to equality, equity as defined and promoted by critical race theorists is little more than reformulated Marxism. In the name of equity, UCLA law professor and critical race theorist Cheryl Harris has proposed suspending private property rights, seizing land and wealth, and redistributing them along racial lines. Critical race guru Ibram X. Kendi, who directs the Center for Antiracist Research at Boston University, has proposed the creation of a federal Department of Antiracism. This department would be independent of (i.e., unaccountable to) the elected branches of government, and would have the power to nullify, veto, or abolish any law at any level of government and curtail the speech of political leaders and others deemed insufficiently "antiracist."

One practical result of the creation of such a department would be the overthrow of capitalism, since, according to Kendi, "In order to truly be antiracist, you also have to truly be anti-capitalist." In other words, identity is the means; Marxism is the end.

An equity-based form of government would mean the end not only of private property but also of individual rights, equality under the law, federalism, and freedom of speech. These would be replaced by race-based redistribution of wealth, group-based rights, active discrimination, and omnipotent bureaucratic authority. Historically, the accusation of "anti-Americanism" has been overused. But in this case, it's not a matter of interpretation: critical race theory prescribes a revolutionary program that would overturn the principles of the Declaration and destroy the remaining structure of the Constitution.

What Does Critical Race Theory Look Like in Practice?

In 2022, Christopher Rufo produced another series of reports focused on critical race theory in education. In Cupertino, California, an elementary school forced first-graders to deconstruct their racial and sexual identities and rank themselves according to their "power and privilege." In Springfield, Missouri, a middle school forced teachers to locate themselves on an "oppression matrix," based on the idea that straight, white, English-speaking, Christian males are members of the oppressor class and must atone for their privilege and "covert white supremacy."

In Philadelphia, an elementary school forced fifth-graders to celebrate "Black communism" and simulate a Black Power rally to free 1960s radical Angela Davis from prison, where she had once been held on charges of murder. And in Seattle, the school district told white teachers that they are guilty of "spirit murder" against black children and must "bankrupt [their] privilege in acknowledgement of [their] thieved inheritance."

Per Rufo: I'm just one investigative journalist, but I've developed a database of more than 1,000 of these stories. When I say that critical race theory is becoming the operating ideology of our public institutions, I am not exaggerating—from the universities to bureaucracies to K-12 school systems, critical race theory has permeated the collective intelligence and decision-making process of American government, with no sign of slowing down.

This is a revolutionary change. When originally established, these government institutions were presented as neutral, technocratic, and oriented toward broadly held perceptions of the public good. Today, under the increasing sway of critical race theory and related ideologies, they are being turned against the American people. This isn't limited to the permanent bureaucracy in Washington, D.C., but is true as well of institutions in the states—even red states. It is spreading to county public health departments, small midwestern school districts, and more. This ideology will not stop until it has devoured all of our institutions.

So far, attempts to halt the encroachment of critical race theory have been ineffective. There are a number of reasons for this.

First, too many Americans have developed an acute fear of speaking up about social and political issues, especially those involving race. According to a recent Gallup poll, 77 percent of conservatives are afraid to share their political beliefs publicly. Worried about getting mobbed on social media, fired from their jobs, or worse, they remain quiet, largely ceding the public debate to those pushing these anti-American ideologies. Consequently, the institutions themselves become monocultures: dogmatic, suspicious, and hostile to a diversity of opinion. Conservatives in both the federal government and public school systems have told me that their "equity and inclusion" departments serve as political offices, searching for and stamping out any dissent from the official orthodoxy.

Second, critical race theorists have constructed their argument like a mousetrap. Disagreement with their program becomes irrefutable evidence of a dissenter's "white fragility," "unconscious bias," or "internalized white supremacy." I've seen this projection of false consciousness on their opponents play out dozens of times in my reporting. Diversity trainers will make an outrageous claim—such as "all whites are intrinsically oppressors" or "white teachers are guilty of spirit murdering black children"—and then, when confronted with disagreement, adopt a patronizing tone and explain that participants who feel "defensiveness" or "anger" are reacting out of guilt and shame. Dissenters are instructed to remain silent, "lean into the discomfort," and accept their "complicity in white supremacy."

Third, Americans across the political spectrum have failed to separate the premise of critical race theory from its conclusion. Its premise—that American history includes slavery and other injustices, and that we should examine and learn from that history—is undeniable. But its revolutionary conclusion—that America was founded on and defined by racism and that our founding principles, our Constitution, and our way of life should be overthrown—does not rightly, much less necessarily, follow.

Fourth and finally, the writers and activists who have had the courage to speak out against critical race theory have tended to address it on the theoretical level, pointing out the theory's logical contradictions and dishonest account of history. These criticisms are worthy and good, but they move the debate into the academic realm—friendly terrain for proponents of critical race theory. They fail to force defenders of this revolutionary ideology to defend the practical consequences of their ideas in the realm of politics.

No longer simply an academic matter, critical race theory has become a tool of political power. To borrow a phrase from the Marxist theoretician Antonio

Gramsci, it is fast achieving cultural hegemony in America's public institutions. It is driving the vast machinery of the state and society. If we want to succeed in opposing it, we must address it politically at every level.

Critical race theorists must be confronted with the following questions and forced to speak to the facts.

- Do they support public schools separating first-graders into groups of "oppressors" and "oppressed"?

- Do they support mandatory curricula teaching that "all white people play a part in perpetuating systemic racism"?

- Do they support public schools instructing white parents to become "white traitors" and advocate for "white abolition"?

- Do they want those who work in government to be required to undergo this kind of reeducation?

- How about managers and workers in corporate America?

- How about the men and women in our military? How about every one of us?

There are three parts to a successful strategy to defeat the forces of critical race theory: governmental action, grassroots mobilization, and an appeal to principle.

We Already See Examples of Governmental Action

In 2020, one of Christopher F. Rufo's reports led President Trump to issue an executive order banning critical race theory–based training programs in the federal government. President Biden rescinded this order on his first day in office, but it provides a model for governors and municipal leaders to follow.

In the following years, several state legislatures have introduced bills to achieve the same goal: preventing public institutions from conducting programs that stereotype, scapegoat, or demean people on the basis of race. And I have organized a coalition of attorneys to file lawsuits against schools and government agencies that impose critical race theory–based programs on grounds of the First Amendment (which protects citizens from compelled speech), the Fourteenth Amendment (which provides equal protection under the law), and the Civil Rights

Act of 1964 (which prohibits public institutions from discriminating on the basis of race).

On the grassroots level, a multiracial and bipartisan coalition is emerging to fight critical race theory.

Parents are mobilizing against racially divisive curricula in public schools and employees are increasingly speaking out against Orwellian reeducation in the workplace. When they see what is happening, Americans are naturally outraged that critical race theory promotes three ideas—race essentialism, collective guilt, and neo-segregation—that violate the basic principles of equality and justice. Anecdotally, many Chinese-Americans have told me that, having survived the Cultural Revolution in their former country, they refuse to let the same thing happen here.

In terms of principles, we need to employ our own moral language rather than allow ourselves to be confined by the categories of critical race theory. For example, we often find ourselves debating "diversity." Diversity as most of us understand it, is generally good, all things being equal, but it is of secondary value. We should be talking about and aiming at excellence, a common standard that challenges people of all backgrounds to achieve their potential. On the scale of desirable ends, excellence beats diversity every time.

Similarly, in addition to pointing out the dishonesty of the historical narrative on which critical race theory is predicated, we must promote the true story of America—a story that is honest about injustices in American history, but that places them in the context of our nation's high ideals and the progress we have made toward realizing them. Genuine American history is rich with stories of achievements and sacrifices that will move the hearts of Americans, in stark contrast to the grim and pessimistic narrative pressed by critical race theorists.

Above all, we must have courage, the fundamental virtue required in our time: courage to stand and speak the truth, courage to withstand epithets, courage to face the mob, and courage to shrug off the scorn of elites. When enough of us overcome the fear that currently prevents so many from speaking out, the hold of critical race theory will begin to slip. And courage begets courage. It's easy to stop a lone dissenter; it's much harder to stop 10, 20, 100, 1,000, 1 million, or more who stand up together for the principles of America. Truth and justice are on our side. If we can muster the courage, we will win.

You can find a link to the "Critical Race Theory Briefing Book" in the Appendix:

Yes, Critical Race Theory Is Being Taught in Schools: Stop Denying It!

To what extent, if at all, are critical race theory (CRT) and gender ideology being taught or promoted in America's schools? With little data available, and no agreement about what constitutes the teaching of critical social justice (CSJ) ideas, the answer up to now has remained open to political interpretation.

However, a new survey of young Americans vindicates the fears of CRT's critics per the Manhattan Institute "Yes, Critical Race Theory Is Being Taught in Schools" *City Journal* October 2022 report:

Motivated by the work of Manhattan Institute senior fellow and *City Journal* contributing editor Christopher F. Rufo, many on the right allege that CRT-related concepts—such as systemic racism and white privilege—are infiltrating the curricula of public schools around the country.

Educators following these curricula are said to be teaching students that racial disparities in socioeconomic outcomes are fundamentally the result of racism, and that white people are the privileged beneficiaries of a social system that oppresses blacks and other "people of color." On gender, they are being taught that gender identity is a choice, regardless of biological sex. But are the cases Rufo and others point to representative of American public schools at large—or are they merely outliers amplified by right-wing media?

The response to these charges from many on the left has been to deny or downplay them.

CRT, they contend, is a legal theory taught only in university law programs. Therefore, what conservatives are up in arms about is not the teaching of CRT, but the teaching of America's uncomfortable racial history.

But strong connections exist between the cultural radicalism of CRT and the one-sided, decontextualized portrayal of American history and society that Democratic activists endorse. And these ideas have also influenced many Democratic voters. Indeed, according to a 2021 YouGov survey, large majorities of Democratic respondents support public schools' teaching many of the morally and empirically contentious ideas to which opponents of CRT object.

These include the notions that racism is systemic in America (85 percent support), that all disparities between blacks and whites are caused by discrimination (72 percent), that white people enjoy certain privileges based on their race (85 percent), and that they have a responsibility to address racial inequality (87 percent).

Whatever one thinks of these ideas, they are hardly "settled facts" on the same epistemic plane as heliocentrism, natural selection, or even climate change. To the contrary, they are a moral-ideological just-so theory of group differences, an all-encompassing worldview akin to a secular religion, whose claims can't be measured, tested, or falsified.

They treat an observed phenomenon (disparate group outcomes) as evidence of its cause (racism), while specifying causal mechanisms that are nebulous, if not magical.

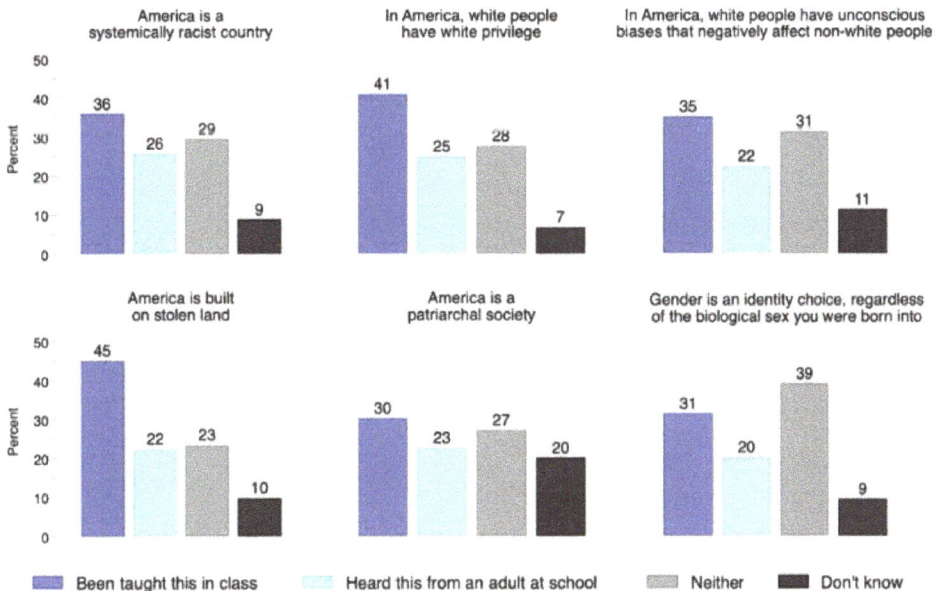

Credit: City Journal-Yes, Critical Race Theory is Being Taught in Schools. Chart # 1.

Their advocates have not refuted counterarguments; they've merely asserted empirically unverified statements about the nature of group differences. Publicly funded schools that teach and pass off left-wing racial-ideological theories and concepts as if they are undisputed factual knowledge—or that impart tendentiously curated readings of history—are therefore engaging in indoctrination, not education.

The question before us, then, is not whether or to what extent public schools are assigning the works of Richard Delgado, Kimberlé Crenshaw, and other critical race theorists. It is whether schools are uncritically promoting a left-wing racial ideology.

To answer this and other related questions, we commissioned a study on a nationally representative sample of 1,505 18- to 20-year-old Americans—a demographic that has yet to graduate from, or only recently graduated from, high school. A complete Manhattan Institute report of all the findings from this study will be published in the coming months; what follows is a preview of some of them. Our analysis here focuses mainly on the results for the sample overall rather than for various subgroups.

We began by asking our 18- to 20-year-old respondents (82.4 percent of whom reported attending public schools) whether they had ever been taught in class or heard about from an adult at school each of six concepts—four of which are central to critical race theory. The chart below, which displays the distribution of responses for each concept, shows that "been taught" is the modal response for all but one of the six concepts.

For the CRT-related concepts, 62 percent reported either being taught in class or hearing from an adult in school that "America is a systemically racist country," 69 percent reported being taught or hearing that "white people have white privilege," 57 percent reported being taught or hearing that "white people have unconscious biases that negatively affect non-white people," and 67 percent reported being taught or hearing that "America is built on stolen land."

The shares giving either response with respect to gender-related concepts are slightly lower, but still a majority. Fifty-three percent report they were either taught in class or heard from an adult at school that "America is a patriarchal society," and 51 percent report being taught or hearing that "gender is an identity choice" regardless of biological sex.

Perhaps it's wrong to assume that the teaching of these CSJ concepts necessarily amounts to ideological indoctrination.

After all, such concepts are salient on social and other media, and have also been uttered or invoked by prominent politicians. Perhaps, then, most teachers are merely using them as fodder for healthy classroom debate or presenting them as perspectives among other competing ideas.

Yet our data suggest that this is hardly the majority experience. Specifically, we asked those who reported being taught at least one of the listed concepts in a high school class what, if anything, they were taught about arguments opposing them. Unsapiently, 68 percent responded that they either were not taught about opposing arguments or were taught that there are no "respectable" opposing arguments. Importantly, this rate does not meaningfully vary by race, political orientation, or high school type.

Whites (30 percent) and nonwhites (34 percent), Democrats (29 percent) and Republicans (31 percent), liberals (29 percent) and conservatives (31 percent), and public (32 percent) and private or parochial (28 percent) schoolers were equally likely to report being told about respectable counterarguments. No evidence, then, suggests that this response reflects respondents' political biases.

Instead, the data suggest that large majorities in all groups have been given the impression that the concepts they were taught are beyond reproach. And these data hardly tell the full story: in our forthcoming report, we additionally show that the number of concepts respondents report being taught is positively related to the probability of being told there that opposing arguments are not "respectable."

If This Isn't Indoctrination—Unwitting or Otherwise—Then What Is?

The prevalence of students' classroom exposure to left-wing ideological concepts raises the question of its attitudinal effect. Are students who report receiving such instruction more "woke" than those who do not? Given the many other sources of attitudinal influence with which any effect of exposure must compete, there is ample reason for skepticism. At the same time, our respondents are in a phase of life in which, by some accounts, social and political attitudes are malleable.

The potential for exposure to shape related attitudes is plausible. In fact, in a dissertation chapter, one of us found that having white respondents read a short "racially woke" op-ed article led to eight- to 12-point increases (mostly via increases in collective shame and guilt) in support for race-based affirmative action, government assistance, and reparations to African-Americans. If attitudinal shifts of this magnitude can be produced over a span of just minutes, what might be the effects of more protracted exposure?

It's also fair to say that many educators incorporating such concepts into their instruction expect, or at least hope, that doing so makes a difference in the minds of students. Indeed, the notion that concepts like "white privilege" and "systemic racism" are solely taught for knowledge's sake strains credulity, especially when such instruction usually entails the omission or delegitimization of competing arguments. The hope instead seems to be that students will come to see white people as ultimately responsible for the creation and persistence of racial inequality; and that this realization will inspire support for race-conscious, "equity"-oriented policies.

Perhaps This Hope is Ill-founded, But Our Data Indicate Otherwise

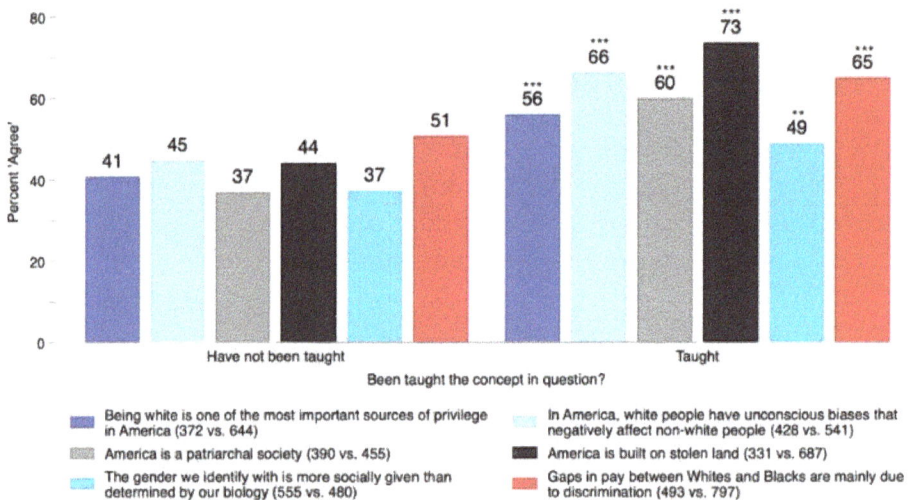

Credit: *City Journal-Yes, Critical Race Theory is Being Taught in Schools. Chart # 4.*

As an initial test, we examined whether those who report being taught a given concept are more likely to endorse it. For instance, relative to those who reported they were not taught the related concept, those who indicated they were taught it were 14 points more likely to agree that the black-white pay gap is mainly due to discrimination, 15 points more likely to agree that "being white is one of the most important sources of privilege in America," 23 points more likely to agree that "white people have unconscious biases that negatively affect non-white people," and 29 points more likely to agree that "America is built on stolen land."

These differences, all statistically significant at the 99.9 percent level, persist after adjustments for a host of theoretically plausible alternative explanations, including race, political orientation, county rurality, county partisanship, county racial liberalism, and county school segregation.

Our next analysis thus examines whether the volume of CRT-related classroom exposure—which we define as the total number of CRT-related concepts respondents reported being taught in school (from zero to five) affects attitudes toward white Americans and pro-black policies like affirmative action and race-based government assistance.

First, we consider whether exposure to a larger share of the five concepts increases agreement with the view that white Americans "are ultimately responsible for the inferior social position of black people." Per the survey results, this indeed appears to be the case. Support is lowest (32 percent) among those who didn't recall being taught any of the five CRT-related concepts (the "no exposure" group), and agreement rises—albeit non-linearly—to a high of 75 percent among those who report being taught all five concepts. Adjusting for alternative explanations has a minimal effect on this 43-point difference in attitudes between those taught no CRT concepts and those taught all five, which remains statistically significant.

We next consider whether exposure increases agreement with the broad-brush generalization that white Americans are "racist and mean"—an item one of us has previously tested and used as an indicator of collective moral shame among whites. Similar to the previous results, agreement with this statement begins at a low of 40 percent among those in the "no exposure" group and increases (again non-linearly) to a high of 72 percent for those who report being taught all five concepts. This difference remains significant when controlling for alternative explanatory variables.

If greater CRT-related classroom exposure increases the endorsement of negative moral appraisals of white Americans, we'd also expect it to boost support for group-based policies that afford preferential treatment to African Americans—even when descriptions of such policies explicitly speak to the risk of discrimination against whites (as our measure of support for affirmative action, adopted from the General Social Survey, does).

Consistent with this prediction, our data show that support for the preferential hiring and promotion of black people falls to a low of 17 percent among those who reported hearing no CRT, while reaching a high of 44 percent among those who reported being taught all five CRT-related concepts.

Similarly, the belief that the government should help black people (versus "our government should not be giving special treatment to black people") is endorsed by 35 percent of those in the "no exposure" group, compared with 43 percent of those who reported being taught one concept, 51 percent to 54 percent of those who reported being taught two to four concepts, and 72 percent of those who reported being taught all five concepts.

Again, a 30- to 40-point difference emerges between those who were not taught CRT material and those who received the maximum dose of it.

Here we should note that the above results are similar for white and non-white respondents alike—even if not always to the same degree. One relationship that is necessarily exclusive to whites, though, is that between exposure and white guilt,. Whereas 39 percent of whites who did not report any CRT-related classroom exposure indicated feeling "guilty about the social inequalities between white and black Americans," this share rises to about 45 percent among whites who reported being taught one or two CRT-related concepts, and to between 54 percent and 58 percent among whites who reported being taught three or more concepts.

These findings indicate that those reporting being taught more CRT-related concepts are more likely to endorse negative moral appraisals of and to view white Americans as responsible for black disadvantage. Among whites, greater CRT exposure is also linked to higher levels of guilt over racial inequality. Finally, and perhaps consequently, greater CRT exposure predicts a higher likelihood of both white and minority young people supporting race-conscious policies that afford preferential treatment to African-Americans.

The same is true for gender. Among those that were taught that gender is a choice, 53 percent say "the gender we identify with is more socially given than determined by our biology" compared with 40 percent of those who were not taught this, a significant difference. Those taught about gender as an identity are more likely to view it as detached from biological sex.

While we can't be certain that exposure causes attitude change—those with progressive attitudes could have had parents more likely to select into schools where CRT is taught (or to recall being exposed to it)—we used data from a person's zip code and county (rurality, diversity, education, voting patterns) that make such competing explanations unlikely. We can also rule out the possibility that these relationships are the product of alternative explanatory factors in our dataset.

While only scratching the surface of what will feature in the full report, our findings have several important takeaways.

First, the claim that CRT and gender ideology are not being taught or promoted in America's pre-college public schools is grossly misleading. More than nine in ten of our respondents reported some form of school exposure to at least some CRT-related and critical gender concepts, with the average respondent reporting being taught in class or hearing about from an adult at school more than half of the eight concepts we measured. Eight in ten reported being taught in class at least one concept central to CRT and contemporary left-wing racial ideology, with the average respondent reporting being taught two of the five we listed. A majority were taught radical gender ideas.

Given the sheer size of these numbers, the promotion and teaching of "white privilege" and "systemic racism" in America's public schools can hardly be regarded as a rare or isolated phenomenon. It is the experience of a sizeable share of pre-college students.

Second, educators are presenting CSJ ideas to students uncritically. If such concepts were presented only as perspectives—and in conjunction with competing others—then their introduction into the classroom could very well be defensible. But our data suggest that this is not the case. Instead, most are receiving them as undisputed "facts"—or at least facts only disputed by bigots and ignoramuses.

This is indoctrination, and governments should act swiftly to put a stop to it.

More-detailed policy recommendations must await the full report. But schools and teachers that wish to teach about these concepts should be given the option of either teaching the diversity of thought surrounding them or being barred from teaching them altogether.

Third, such biased instruction is effective. Our data show that those who report being taught CRT-related concepts are not only more likely to endorse them but are also more likely to blame white people for racial inequality, to essentialize white people as "racist," and to support "equity-oriented" race-based policies. Among whites, we also observe higher levels of white guilt among those exposed to more CRT-related concepts.

Overall, then, our data would appear to confirm many of the fears of anti-CRT activists about such instruction. Anecdotes are borne out by our representative large-scale data.

Critical race and gender theory is endemic in American schools. The vast majority of children are being taught radical CSJ concepts that affect their view of white people, their country, the relationship between gender and sex, and public policy.

For those inclined toward a colorblind and reality-based ideal, these findings should serve as a wakeup call. Unless sapient voters, parents, and governments act, these illiberal and unscientific ideas will spread more widely, and will replace traditional American liberal nationalism with an identity-based cultural socialism.

15 – The Progressivism Platform is Based on Lies, Bias, Deception & False Narratives

shutterstock.com · 1036576444

Central to the idea of Progressivism is the belief that every morally significant change from the status quo is necessarily progress. If you disagree with the change, you are morally "backward-looking." The presentation of morality as a historical development is powerful because it shuts down future debate. But is the status quo by necessity morally inferior to some inevitable future condition toward which we are being driven by the mysterious force of history?

For example, the army of social justice warriors takes frequent aim at the principles of the United States' founding. For them, progress is measured by how far consciousness can be raised in society to awareness of oppressive inequalities among human beings with regard to race, class, and gender as revealed in the Clifford Humphrey "The Myth of Change as Progress in Progressivism" *Epoch Times* February 2019 article:

Attacking the historicism of Progressivism, former President Calvin Coolidge noted that "it is often asserted … that we have had new thoughts and experiences which have given us a great advance over the people of [1776], and that we may therefore very well discard their conclusions for something more modern."

Coolidge contrasted such chronological snobbery with the "exceedingly restful" finality of the Declaration. He stated, "If all men are created equal, that is final. If they are endowed with inalienable rights, that is final. ... No advance, no progress can be made beyond these propositions. If anyone wishes to deny their truth or their soundness, the only direction in which he can proceed historically is not forward, but backward."

The Myth of Change as Progress in Progressivism

Opposed to the idea that some spirit in history determines what is moral is the belief that morality depends on something outside of time and is something human reason can discern.

On this idea, Leo Strauss, a notable 20th-century political philosopher, wrote: "All political action aims at either preservation or change. When desiring to preserve, we wish to prevent a change to the worse; when desiring to change, we wish to bring about something better. All political action is, then, guided by some thought of better or worse. But thought of better or worse implies thought of the good."

If both preservation and change are dependent on the good, then it is the supreme human endeavor to seek to understand what is good and the glory of a human being to make choices in accord with it. There is no escaping the often difficult task of exercising prudence to make our way through life's moral quandaries. This task cannot be outsourced to some vague notion of history.

The horrors of the 20th century easily belie the idea that history is the long story of the moral progress of mankind. Winston Churchill, through the force of his leadership, had a profound influence on limiting the spread of those horrors. He was well aware of the growing dominion that forces of technology and globalization would have over the scope of human action. Nevertheless, his reflections led him to retain hope in the vital role that statesmanship and choice played in influencing world events. He lauded "the profound significance of human choice and the sublime responsibility of men."

Citizens in a republic like ours have the sublime responsibility and profound significance of choosing our own rulers. First our choices and then theirs—not the spirit of history—will shape our future, for better or for worse.

Despite what Progressive politicians may presume, not every change is progress. Author C. S. Lewis put it well when he wrote, "We all want progress, but if you're on the wrong road, progress means doing an about-turn and walking back to the right road; in that case, the man who turns back soonest is the most Progressive."

How Progressives Are Retrogressive

Per the Philip Carl Salzman "How Progressives Are Retrogressive" *Epoch Times* January 2022 article: How often do we hear political commentators and Republican officials use the terms "liberal" and "Progressive" interchangeably when discussing Democrats? Yet the meanings of the two terms could not be more different.

Liberalism as a political philosophy emphasizes individual freedom, agency, and choice. Human nature, in the liberal view, is a mix of qualities: energy and sloth, selfishness and generosity, creativity and habit. Society exists to provide the maximum freedom to individuals, with the constraints necessary to limit the encroachment of one on another. Inequality in a liberal society reflects the differences in capabilities and motivations among individuals. Liberalism favors free elections of public officials and limited government. For liberals, economics should be based on contractual relations freely entered into by producers and consumers, entrepreneurs, and labor.

Progressivism emphasizes equality and rights. Human nature, in the Progressive view, is basically good, with vices resulting from imperfect and oppressive social arrangements. Society is perfectible, and the perfect society is one which guarantees equality and equal rights. The economy should be owned and run collectively, by society at large. The government must be strong, able to control all aspects of society. Political parties unjustly divide the society, and are unnecessary when the government represents all of the people.

The liberal vision supports liberal democracy and capitalism, while the Progressive vision supports socialism and government economic planning. It's no accident that some members of the Progressive caucus in the House of Representatives are members of the Democratic Socialists of America. The caucus favors collectivism, as seen in government control of all major institutions and programs, such as welfare support, pre-schools, education, medicine, and the organization of labor. Progressives prefer government monopolies in all of these fields, which is why they oppose school choice, labor choice, and medical choice (except abortion, which they love).

Progressives see liberal democracies as systems of unjust inequalities resulting from inherited privilege and oppression of the weak. Liberals see Progressives as crushing individual liberty by vesting all functions in an all-powerful government, and thus favoring authoritarian rule.

Progressivism rests on the idea of progress advanced by Karl Marx: a movement driven by class conflict from capitalism to socialism and then to communism.

In classic Marxism, classes are defined by economic position, by control over the means of production. The bourgeois class are the owners of the means of production, and the propertyless proletariat are the workers who must live on the pay provided by selling their labor.

In the classic socialist society, equality is advanced for most people, although the governing elite are all powerful and rank high above the multitude. While equality increases, and in the eyes of Progressives, justice is advanced, it's an equality of poverty and misery, because the all-powerful government's central economic planning fails to build the economy and stimulate innovation, motivation, and entrepreneurship. And, notwithstanding the century-long claim that "real socialism has never been tried," all of the socialist societies—the USSR, Soviet Eastern Europe, China, Albania, Cambodia, North Korea, Cuba, Venezuela—were or are oppressive authoritarian regimes and economic failures of stagnation and poverty.

Progressives in North America, with the exception of old-line socialists such as Bernie Sanders, have innovated in ideology, jettisoning the economic class struggle and replacing it with identity classes: gender, race, sexuality, religion, nationality, ableness. Now it's (allegedly) whites (including "white adjacent" Asians and "hyperwhite" Jews), males, and Christians who are oppressors, and people of color, women, LGBTQ++, Muslims, and the disabled who are the oppressed victims.

The Progressives' identity class conflict has not only not led to "progress" in any discernible form, but also has led to social regression, resuscitating ugly forms of prejudice and discrimination while undermining public order and national sovereignty.

With the "social justice" trinity of "diversity, equity, and inclusion," Progressives have returned us to the days of deep Jim Crow, with some races seen as virtuous and others as evil, the only difference being that the colors have changed. Progressive "inclusion" means including preferred races and genders, and excluding the others, as we see in hiring, college admissions, funding, promotions, and awards. The latest example is New York State ranking people for COVID-19 medical treatment according to their race.

Equity, meaning the statistical equivalence of races and genders, in practice means more of the preferred and fewer of the despised. Objective measures, such as standardized tests, and advanced education programs, are cancelled, because they don't produce the desired "equity" results. Now institutionalized racism and discrimination are regarded as desirable by Progressives, as long as preferred categories benefit.

Typical Examples:

Because certain racial minorities are heavily overrepresented among criminals (and victims), Progressives have advocated "justice reform" to alleviate the price that minority criminals pay. Progressives thus have advocated defunding and disbanding the police, handcuffing police operations, releasing prisoners from incarceration, a halt to holding the dangerous accused prior to trial by means of no-bail release, and district attorneys who refuse to prosecute criminals, because they view criminals as "victims of society" rather than as victims of their own bad choices.

The result, a surprise to Progressives but to no one else, is a major breakdown in public order, with violent and nonviolent crime surging, particularly in Democrat-led cities, but also more broadly. For Progressives, public safety is systemic racism, so they're happy to do without it. Even though the vast number of victims of violence are racial minorities, the Progressives continue to obsess over the tiny number of police killings rather than the victims of crime. Progressives prefer criminals to victims of crime. They even encourage people to engage in illegal acts, as when they encouraged rioters in 2020 to loot, burn, and assault police, and then bailed them out until Progressive district attorneys refused to prosecute them.

Progressives particularly favor illegal aliens who have, uninvited and against our laws, entered the country. For Progressives, illegal aliens are preferred to citizens, because many are people of color, because the country is "systemically racist," and the racial balance needs to be changed in favor of people of color, and because Progressives think that they can capture illegal aliens as future voters by plying them with privileges paid for by tax-paying citizens. Progressives have coddled illegal aliens with sanctuary states, cities, and universities, thus protecting the criminals among the illegal aliens, a two-for-one benefit for Progressives.

Progressives are not fond of fair elections, which they always have a chance of losing, so they favor "electoral reform," which means a federal takeover of elections, contrary to the Constitution, and wish to remove all safeguards against illegal voting. They particularly hate the voter ID requirement, which they label "voter suppression," although IDs are heavily supported by the public and in use in most democracies around the world.

When Progressives say, "voter suppression," they mean the suppression of illegal votes, such as those cast by illegal immigrants, or multiple votes by individuals, or votes inscribed by third parties. The manipulation and undermining of voting is another manifestation of Progressives' authoritarian tendencies. Progressives don't really like democracy; they prefer the dictatorship of the proletariat, or, in today's identity politics transformation, dictatorship of the "marginalized and underserved" minorities.

To sum up: Liberals favor individual freedom, limited government, public safety, and national sovereignty. Progressives favor some races and genders over others, criminals over victims, illegal aliens over citizens, and authoritarian rule over democracy. Progressives are about illiberal as they could be. Don't call them "liberals."

Critical Race Theory in Six Logical Fallacies

Logic is the friend of the wise person (a sapient being), and illogic is a snare to all (particularly Progressives). We ought to follow the logic and evidence wherever it leads as shown in the Douglas Groothuis "Critical Race Theory in Six Logical Fallacies" National Association of Scholars Summer 2022 report:

On those issues that matter most—questions about God, humanity, meaning, morality, and society—we dispense with logic to our own peril. Illogic can damage individuals and entire societies, as Marxism has done repeatedly and worldwide. Illogic is damaging America as well through the acceptance of and application of

Critical Race Theory (CRT), which has a penchant for fallacy production.

Some intellectual mistakes or fallacies are so commonly committed that they have been inducted into a canon of cognitive ignominy. Logical fallacies are divided into formal and informal fallacies. A formal fallacy is a blunder in a deductive argument, which invalidates the argument's form. We will instead concentrate on informal fallacies, which deceive in various ways, often through the use of irrelevant information, false assumptions, or incorrect or misleading uses of evidence. Let me define CRT and inspect its cognitive corruptions.

CRT is a neo-Marxist theory that grew out of Critical Theory (spearheaded by Herbert Marcuse). It was augmented by Critical Legal Studies and focuses more on racial and gender categories than on economic exploitation. Racism is everywhere and every white person is part of a system of racism that oppresses people of color (but mostly blacks). This system as a whole must be taken down and replaced by one that ensures "equity" (proportional representation for people of color) through socialism. Now to the fallacies.

Begging the Question

Begging the question assumes a conclusion without giving an argument. It substitutes an assertion for a logical case. "I am against capital punishment because two wrongs don't make a right," begs the question, since it assumes that capital punishment is another wrong in addition to the wrong of murder. A real argument against capital punishment requires reasoning that leads to the conclusion.

CRT lends itself to begging the question because it claims that its critics are animated by false consciousness, white supremacy, white privilege, or some other moral or cognitive impairment. The CRT advocate believes that those who disagree with CRT are not just wrong in a few ways, but are systemically deceived. Marxism originally applied this idea to economic actors, but it is now applied on a racial and gender basis by CRT. The oppressors are deceived; the oppressed are in the know (standpoint epistemology).

If someone begs the question and foreswears any counterevidence, then the idea becomes unfalsifiable. This is irrational. Every challenge to one's viewpoint can then be dismissed a priori. Proponents of CRT apply this idea to racism. White people are racists because they are part of systemic racism. No evidence to the contrary can exonerate them from this odious whiteness. When a claim is taken to be impervious to criticism, it loses rationality given its irrefutable dogmatism.

Things get worse when some CRT advocates claim that logic, critical thinking, appeals to standard logic, objective truth, objective evidence, normative grammar, and a linear approach to history and thinking in general are constitutive of the oppressor's ideology. If so, they can be denied. This denial leaves nothing to rationally argue with or to rationally argue from. But those who negate logic, truth, evidence, grammar, and linearity, quickly jettison their negations when arguing for their cases, since these elements are required for sharable discourse. They thus contradict themselves and disqualify themselves from rational discussion.

Argumentum Ad Hominem

This means "argument against the man." Instead of giving reasons against a position, those who hold the position are insulted as defective in some way that negates their view.

Of course, not all insults are fallacies. An insult can be justified by another's actions. Or an insult may be given that is unattached to any further claim. Saying "You are an idiot" or "You are a fascist," is true or false, but if it is unrelated to advancing another truth claim, there is no fallacy.

But, on the other hand, consider this indictment, "All who defend capitalism are racists." Of course, this statement might be true; however, a rational case needs to be made for it. One would have to demonstrate that (1) one thinks that a free-market system will disadvantage blacks, and (2) that (1) is a good thing. This case is not easily made.

If a white person advocates for merit-based admissions for higher education, this can be rejected as whitesplaining (due to false consciousness), since it supposedly favors whites over blacks. Whitesplaining means expressing a view based entirely on one's interests and privilege based on skin color. However, to advocate merit-based and race-neutral standards may have nothing to do with racism. It may simply be a color-blind endorsement of merit over race, whatever race benefits from it.

Consider sexual ethics. If you deem marriage to be a sacred and exclusive vow made between a man and a woman, this invites disparaging charges. You are homophobic since you are against gay marriage. You are also a religious bigot if your view is based on any sacred text or tradition. If you do not support some aspect of transgenderism, then you are transphobic.

The use of the term phobic is derived from psychology which uses it to refer to an irrational and pathological fear, such as agoraphobia (the fear of open places) or hydrophobia (the fear of water). Phobias are anxiety disorders. If you are homophobic, you have an irrational fear of homosexuals, which is a disorder. The question of moral judgment does not come up.

The label of phobic in these cases goes further. We pity or feel compassion for those who suffer from hydrophobia, but we resent or judge anyone who discriminates unfairly. Thus, this ad hominem vilifies people as both sick and immoral.

Admittedly, many are afflicted with phobias that impair their rationality and ability to judge fairly on diverse matters. However, to judge someone as phobic and thus untrustworthy in their judgments simply because they disagree with your views on moral matters is to commit the ad hominem fallacy.

In an essay called "Bulverism," C. S. Lewis exposed a new version of the ad hominem fallacy. Modern thinkers such as Freud and Marx have identified ways of discrediting ideas because they are "tainted at their source," either psychologically or politically. "The Freudians have discovered that we exist as bundles of complexes. The Marxians have discovered that we exist as members of some economic class." Ideas can be condemned and dismissed as stemming from psychological complexes or from one's economic class biases and prejudices. For CRT, ideas can be dismissed and condemned because those in "the dominant culture" (white) hold them.

Bulverists are right that many ideas are "tainted at their source," because of human prejudice, bias, turpitude, and other intellectual vices committed by our fallen race. However, if all ideas are tainted and thus unreliable, then CRT ideas are so affected. Thus, one could retort that, "You only say that because you are a Freudian." We could substitute "Marxist" or "CRT advocate" or anything else.

The Freudian and the Marxian are in the same boat with all the rest of us, and cannot criticize us from outside. They have sewn off the branch they were sitting on. If, on the other hand, they say that the taint need not invalidate their thinking, then neither need it invalidate ours. In which case they have saved their own branch, but also saved ours along with it.

To determine if a statement is true and reasonable, I need an argument to substantiate the claim. Everyone has biases and prejudices, but truth has neither biases nor prejudices, and finding truth through reason and evidence should be our goal. To Lewis again:

If you try to find out which [ideas] are tainted by speculating about the wishes of the thinkers, you are merely making a fool of yourself. You must first find out on purely logical grounds which of them do, in fact, break down as arguments. Afterwards, if you like, go on and discover the psychological causes of the error.

False Dichotomy

False dichotomy is a commonly committed fallacy. It is positively pernicious in CRT. It limits the options to two when, in fact, there are more than two options.

In some cases, there is a radical either/or. A person is dead or alive, not both. There are true dichotomies and false dichotomies, and the latter ought to be avoided. A true dichotomy is a binary such as: a woman is either pregnant or not pregnant. She cannot be both at the same time. The options are mutually exclusive and jointly exhaustive (covering all the possibilities). There is no third option. In computer coding, everything reduces to 1s and 0s. But life is more than computer coding.

Our use of the either/or may be fallacious. We may split life up by oversimplifying the case and then generating false dichotomies. In a semi-drunken stupor, a fool might say, "Look, you are either a Democrat or a Republican." This is a false dichotomy, since one might be a Libertarian or a Green Party member or something else.

The false dichotomy excludes genuine logical options, and this brings us to CRT. CRT assumes that if you do not accept CRT, then you think that racism is not a problem in America and would not want the history of slavery and Jim Crow to be taught in schools. This is a non sequitur because it is a false dichotomy. There is a third option: teach history without the ideology of CRT. One may reject CRT, and still believe racism is real, the disparities in black and white achievement need to be addressed (though perhaps not through socialism), and that America's troubled racial history should be taught, pondered, and rejected. But consider yet another fallacy.

Hasty Generalization

It is easy to be intellectually impatient and reach a conclusion hastily and without enough evidence. We are prone to this error, especially in the age of mediated electronic images. The image may lead one to think that a phenomenon is common and widespread when, in fact, it is the image that is common and widespread, not the phenomenon itself. A visceral image of a protestor being hit by a policeman, accompanied by persuasive commentary, supports the idea that police brutality is common and that the police ought to be "defunded" or otherwise censured. Similarly, a montage of images of unarmed blacks being shot by white police officers raises the ire of many and lends credibility to claims of systemic racism.

The adage that "a picture never lies" is false. It often lies when it is taken out of context and placed into a preset and ironclad narrative. If an innocent black man is wrongly killed or injured by the police, that is morally wrong and a fair trial should ensue. But there is more to be considered than merely a series of images, since so much can be left out, such as a violent resisting of arrest that occurred before the video images of the shooting. Getting the whole story about police violence against blacks requires hard statistics and social analysis about rates of violence and police policies. It is easier to react quickly than to reason carefully. If so, we commit the fallacy of hasty generalization.

The Use/Mention Fallacy

In our hypersensitive culture, one can get into deep trouble simply by speaking or writing a word or phrase deemed offensive. These terms are often epithets—words that sharply derogate others. However, one can mention an epithet without using it.

Consider a non-taboo epithet: Bill says, "John is a jerk." Here, Bill uses the epithet "jerk." That is, he is insulting John. Consider another case. Don says, "Bill said that 'John is a jerk.'" Here Don is mentioning the use of "jerk" by Bill. Don is not using the word "jerk" to describe John. He is reporting what Bill said. If someone said, "Don called John a jerk," he would be committing the use/mention fallacy in his error.

The stakes escalate quickly concerning racial epithets, such as the n-word. Neal A. Lester rightly says that the "word is inextricably linked with violence and brutality on black psyches and derogatory aspersions cast on black bodies." Thus, no one should use the n-word as an epithet.

It used to be safe to mention an epithet if it was clear that one was not using it. By mentioning it you are, as it were, putting quotation marks around the offensive term or phrase. In conversation, this can be indicated by making the scare quotes gesture. One might say with the proper gesticulation, "In the film, 'No Way Out,' several characters call the lead character a (they then say the n-word with all its original letters)." I do not advise saying or writing out the n-word, even in this context, but this person is not using the n-word in the sense I described. He is mentioning it. To say that this person used the term is to commit the use/mention fallacy.

This is simple, but some people are obtuse. Inside Higher Ed reports that "Augsburg University in Minnesota suspended a professor for using the n-word during a class discussion about a James Baldwin book in which the word appeared—and for sharing essays on the history of the word with students who complained to him about it." Professor Phillip Adamo was quoted in this piece as saying, "I see a distinction between use and mention. To use the word, to inflict pain or harm, is unacceptable. To mention the word, in a discussion of how the word is used, is necessary for honest discourse." Adamo, who is white, asked one of his students to read a quote by the black writer James Baldwin from his essay *The Fire Next Time* (1963), which used the n-word. In discussion, he mentioned the word himself.

The offended students should have taken issue with Baldwin himself, since he, a black man, used the word. Instead, they went after the Professor, who merely mentioned the word. The university suspended the Professor for two terms. Such is the power of fallacies.

A Newcomer: The Cancellation Fallacy

We end our sad tour of logical fallacies with a new fallacy. This fallacy is a team effort, a collection of at least five fallacies packed into one. I call it the cancellation fallacy. It is so commonly heard and so egregious that it deserves analysis.

The phrase "cancel culture" popped up in 2020 after the death of George Floyd.

Angry crowds felled and defaced statues of those deemed racist. Churches were vandalized. Some schools changed their names if their namesakes were deemed racist. Donald Trump and others have been deplatformed in social media purges. An entire platform, Parler, was removed from Apple and Google apps and effectively shut down. "Cancel culture" is an epidemic.

I will put the cancellation fallacy abstractly since it helps us see its basic structure.

- Someone (especially a POC) is offended by P (any statement, person, object, process, or event).

- Therefore (i), P is wrong.

- The moral wrong committed by one who holds P is racism, homophobia, transphobia, or the like

- Therefore (ii), whoever affirms P must be cancelled.

- Unless others denounce P, (iii) they too must be cancelled, since "Silence is violence."

- The cancellation fallacy is a synergistic and strenuous effort. It is a high achievement of sophistry. But it suffers from at least five errors:

- First, it equates taking offense with a proper moral judgment. Emotional reactions may be proper or improper.

- Second, it commits the ad hominem fallacy (discussed above). If you offend me, you are a bad person, and bad people cannot give good arguments, which is false.

- Third, the supposed wrongness is placed into a broad condemning category, such as racism, and thus commits the straw man fallacy. It may offend you that I don't want statues of Abraham Lincoln torn down, but that, in itself, does not make me a racist.

- Fourth, the threat of cancellation is a form of intimidation and means punishment if the threat is enacted. This commits the fallacy of argumentum ad baculum or "if you don't agree with me, I will hurt you. Therefore, agree with me." Today, this translates as: "Those critical of Critical Race Theory will be cancelled, which means losing your book contract, your employment, your social status, and more."

- Fifth, to claim that if I do not oppose P, then I must endorse P, commits the fallacy of the argument from silence. Not saying anything ("silence") cannot, in itself, be used to indict someone.

Statistical Disparities Among Groups Are Not Proof of Discrimination

Statistical disparities among groups are the norm in every facet of human life, including those in which discrimination cannot possibly play a role. To cling to a narrative that asserts racial discrimination as the only cause of statistical disparities turns a blind eye to reality and leads to harmful Progressivism policies.

From the Bradley Thomas "Statistical Disparities Among Groups Are Not Proof of Discrimination" Foundation for Economic Education (FEE) May 2019 report: In spite of this, however, perhaps the most prevalent pretext leftists have used for massive state coercion over the last 50 years is that disparities in outcomes between races, genders, or nationalities are de facto evidence of discrimination.

"Institutional" racism and sexism are the only possible causes of such disparities, the experts tell us. Society's prejudices and bigotry are so ingrained that only by growing the leviathan state can these negative results be corrected, they insist.

Does Disparity Entail Discrimination?

But if such disparities do arise absent discrimination perpetrated by "society," then assumptions about statistical disparities "lose their validity as evidence," Thomas Sowell notes in his book *Civil Rights: Rhetoric or Reality*:

There are many decisions wholly within the discretion of those concerned, where discrimination by others is not a factor—the choice of television programs to watch, opinions to express to poll takers, or the age at which to marry, for example. All these show pronounced patterns that differ from group to group.

The bottom line, Sowell concludes, is that "Statistical disparities extend into every aspect of human life" and that "statistical disparities are commonplace among human beings."

Income Inequality

Problems abound with how academics diagnose even seemingly straightforward measures like income inequality and discrimination.

The real issue is not with income inequality itself but with the processes put in motion in hopes of eliminating inequality.

For example, Sowell contends most income statistics are crude aggregates. The implicit assumption that the mere existence of income disparities is evidence of racial discrimination is unsubstantiated. Simply examining the average age differences among different demographics can explain away a portion of the income inequality that intellectuals proclaim exists due to discrimination. Those races and nationalities with older average ages would naturally boast higher average incomes due to being more experienced.

Adding factors like education level and personal career choices explains much of the rest.

The real issue, Sowell concludes, is not with income inequality itself but with the processes put in motion in hopes of eliminating inequality, which involve damaging government intervention and welfare programs.

Color vs. Culture

Moreover, when evaluating the "disparities are proof of discrimination" narrative, we can compare the levels of economic success among people of color. After all, a racist society just sees people of color and does not differentiate based upon different backgrounds.

As Sowell wrote, "Blacks may 'all look alike' to racists, but there are profound internal cultural differences among blacks."

As a result, comparing results for people of the same color but different culture is a valuable tool to provide an indication of other factors besides discrimination at work.

One source of data is a recent American Community Survey Report from the US Census Bureau that analyzes characteristics of selected Sub-Saharan African and Caribbean ancestry groups. Among these "ancestry groups," 60 percent or more are foreign-born.

Culture unquestionably plays a role in income and poverty disparities.

For instance, in 2012 the US poverty rate for Jamaicans was reported as 14.8 percent, Ethiopians 19.7 percent, and Nigerians 12.8 percent. All the rates were significantly lower than the rate of 28 percent for blacks as a whole.

Furthermore, the median income for Jamaican males was $41,969 and $39,155 for females; $34,018 for male Ethiopians and $30,253 for females; and $50,922 for male Nigerians and $44,874 for females.

Two of the three of these male ancestry groups noticeably out-earned the median rate of $37,526 for black males overall, while the same two groups outpaced the overall female black median income of $33,251.

Additionally, these three ancestry groups had significantly lower rates of poverty and higher median incomes than the Hispanic population.

How were these people of color, often without the benefit of growing up in America, able to clear the "barriers" of a discriminatory "system" far better than other people of color? Culture unquestionably plays a role in income and poverty disparities, even in situations comparing people of color where "discrimination" can be ruled out.

The Disparities Narrative Is a Pretext for Greater State Control

Nobody is arguing that racial or ethnic discrimination has been eliminated. But to cling to a narrative that asserts racial discrimination as the only cause of statistical disparities in measures such as income and poverty turns a blind eye to reality and leads to harmful policies.

Perhaps making matters worse is the promotion of the narrative of an all-powerful "system" that is structured unfairly and creates a sense of helplessness among those labeled "victims" of said barriers to economic prosperity.

"Why study and discipline yourself in preparation for the adult world if the deck is completely stacked against you anyway?" Sowell asked rhetorically.

Progressives like to lecture us about embracing diversity but then also deny that such diversity lends itself naturally to differences in outcomes. Instead, they choose to play identity politics based on faulty assumptions in pursuit of greater social control.

16 – Testing, Admissions, Training, DEI Programs, Diversity Training & Statements

SAT score distributions by race

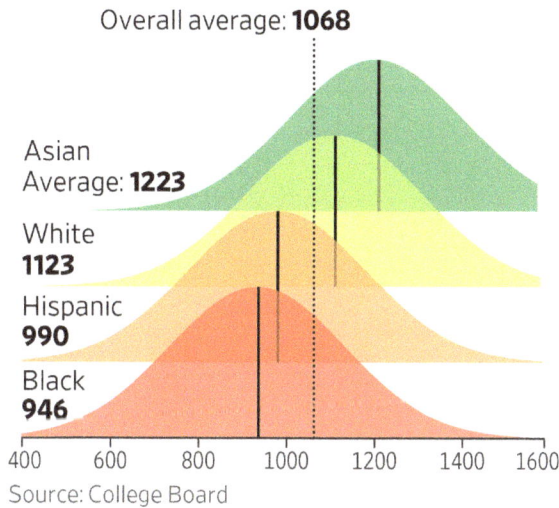

Overall average: **1068**

Asian
Average: **1223**

White
1123

Hispanic
990

Black
946

400   600   800   1000   1200   1400   1600

Source: College Board

Race and education data are from 2018 high school graduates.

It has been taboo to hint at the reason that the millions of dollars already expended on campus diversity initiatives have yet to engineer exact proportional representation of blacks in the student body and on the faculty: the vast academic skills gap. Now this truth will be even more professionally lethal to anyone who dares mention it.

The highest reaches of the university have declared as a matter of self-evident fact that systemic racism is the defining feature of American society, one that explains every inequality. Fighting against that racism has now officially become colleges' reason for being.

The prevalence of systemic racism in the U.S. is far from an established fact, however. Other credible explanations exist for ongoing racial disparities, including family structure, cultural attitudes, and individual behavior.

From the Heather Mac Donald "Conformity to a Lie" *City Journal* article in the Summer of 2020:

To declare from the highest reaches of the academy that racism is the defining and all-explaining feature of American society is to adopt a political position, not to state a scientific truth. That political position entails a host of unspoken assumptions about the world, themselves open to debate.

In aligning itself with one particular political position, the academy is betraying what Max Weber saw as its mission: to stay assiduously neutral and to teach "inconvenient" facts about the world that undercut received assumptions across the political spectrum. Political action was antithetical to scholarship, Weber argued.

SAT Math Scores Mirror and Maintain Racial Inequity

As per the Ember Smith and Richard V. Reeves "SAT Math Scores Mirror and Maintain Racial Inequity" Brookings Institute article in December 2020:

The race gap in test scores is far from a new phenomenon; Asian and white students consistently outperform their Black and Hispanic or Latino peers on the math and verbal sections of the SAT.

In 1996, the gap between the mean Black score and the mean white score was 0.91 standard deviations; by 2020, the gap had narrowed to 0.79 standard deviations. Despite a wide range of efforts to reduce inequality, the racial gap in SAT scores has scarcely narrowed during the lifetimes of the class of 2020. In 2002, the average white student's SAT math score was 106 points higher than the average Black student's (533 compared to 427); by 2020, the gap narrowed to 93 points. Still, nearly a third (31%) of white test takers scored above 600 on the math portion of the SAT, compared to just 7% of Black test takers.

Rising SAT participation and college enrollment

Test score gaps shrunk by a small margin in the last two decades, but other indicators show reason for optimism: the portion of students taking the SAT rose drastically over the last two decades, outpacing the increase in the number of public high school graduates from 2000-2020.

From 2000-2020, there was a 119% increase in the number of Black students taking the SAT and a 482% increase in Latino or Hispanic students, compared to a 36% and 185% increase in the number of Black and Hispanic or Latino students graduating from a public high school (reflecting, to a large extent, the increase in the size of the Hispanic population). SAT participation also rose dramatically among Asian and Pacific Islander students—136% compared to a 66% increase in the number of public high school graduates. By contrast, slightly fewer white students graduated from a public high school in 2020 than in 2000, but the number of white students taking the SAT increased by 28%.

As SAT participation gaps have shrunk, so have enrollment gaps. But significant gaps in graduation rates and test scores remain; representation is increasing, but success rates have yet to catch up. Half of Asian students and 45% of white students graduate college in 4 years compared to 21% of Black students, and 32% of Latino or Hispanic students. Default rates on student loans tell a similar story; Black and Latino or Hispanic students are much more likely to default within 12 years of graduation.

Beyond the score: effects of racial math score gaps

As our colleague Andre Perry has written, "Standardized tests are better proxies for how many opportunities a student has been afforded than they are predictors for students' potential." This is right. While attempting to measure college-readiness, the SAT both mirrors and maintains racial inequity. There is also evidence that test scores are a less accurate predictor of subsequent Black and Hispanic or Latino performance.

In 2019, the SAT developed an adversity score to contextualize students' scores to their school and neighborhood. Under pressure, the College Board then abandoned the single statistic in favor of an Environmental Context Dashboard, which provides information like the portion of students at a high school receiving free and reduced lunch, median family income, and advanced placement enrollment.

Nonetheless, SAT scores clearly capture important information about the academic position of the test taker; it is also clear that many fewer Black and Latino or Hispanic students are college ready, especially in math.

So, is it time to scrap the test? No. While unthoughtful use of standardized test scores certainly reproduces inequality, abandoning them altogether risks making matters even worse. Scrapping tests altogether in college admissions could result in colleges overemphasizing factors that privilege being rich just as much.

Furthermore, post pandemic, fewer than half of the students who applied early to college in the fall of 2022 submitted standardized test scores, according to an analysis by the nonprofit that publishes the Common Application.

How Admissions Officers Could be Setting Up Minority Students for Failure

Per the James Piereson and Naomi Schaefer Riley "Less Than Meets the Eye" *City Journal* story in May 2021:

Dropping the requirement that students submit SAT or ACT scores meant that admissions officers could rely only on grades, essays, and recommendations. Thus students with lower scores may have been more willing to apply to schools they otherwise would have considered a reach.

Despite the shift of public opinion against them, SAT scores remain fairly good predictors of not only how well students will perform in college but also the difficulty of the classes they'll take. "Students with high test scores are more likely to take the challenging route through college," University of Minnesota psychologists Nathan Kuncel and Paul Sackett maintain.

Too often, young people admitted to demanding colleges wind up switching to easier, less remunerative majors. According to researchers at the University of Texas at Austin, "More than a third of black (40%) and Latino (37%) [STEM] students switch majors before earning a degree, compared with 29% of white STEM students."

While the authors of that study suggest that the reasons for this discrepancy are social rather than academic, the truth, as Purdue University researcher Samuel Rohr discovered, is that "a higher aggregate score on the SAT helped predict the retention of science, technology, engineering, mathematics, and business students." He concluded: "For every point increase in SAT, there was 0.3% increase in retention."

In other words, admitting students with lower SAT scores to fulfill diversity quotas may prevent those students from achieving their academic and career goals—something they might have done at a lower-tier school. Indeed, it may prevent them from completing their degree at all. At the most elite schools, the likelihood is that students who didn't perform as well as their peers on the SATs will simply be shunted into easier but less remunerative majors. For schools farther down on the academic ladder, these efforts could mean lower overall graduation rates.

Admissions, Affirmative Action and Two Supreme Court Cases

As per the Andrew I. Fillat and Henry I. Miller "Diversity Smokescreen" *City Journal* report in March 2022:

The Supreme Court has agreed to hear two more cases challenging the use of race as a criterion in college admissions, as has allegedly happened at Harvard University (a private institution) and the University of North Carolina (public).

On the surface, the argument turns on whether the desire for a diverse student body trumps many laws and the Fourteenth Amendment to the U.S. Constitution, which prohibit discrimination and guarantee equal protection to all. The question applies to virtually all universities because they are either public or accept government money.

The main argument in favor of discrimination in admissions is that diversity enhances the educational experience. But is it true that a student body needs to parallel, even roughly, the demographics of the general population to ensure that students are exposed to people from diverse backgrounds?

In fact, we would argue that the very process of using affirmative action—read: "discrimination"—to enhance the numbers of designated identity groups can contribute to the tribalization of the student body rather than helping it cohere into a harmonious whole.

Furthermore, even after receiving an affirmative action boost, minority students sufficiently qualified for a given university are already likely to have similar backgrounds to non-minority students, thus limiting the diversity of viewpoints and experiences that affirmative action allegedly enhances.

Nevertheless, it has become an article of faith that affirmative action, by enhancing narrowly defined diversity, improves education.

Digging deeper into the issue raises a fundamental question about the mission of a university. We believe that universities—and especially the more selective ones—should prioritize the following, in order of importance: the development of critical reasoning skills; the acquisition of a greater knowledge base and certain professional skills; and socialization. These priorities reflect centuries of precedent, including at institutions of higher education throughout Europe and Asia. The net result should be to turn out more productive individuals who can both achieve personal success and contribute to social harmony and national prosperity.

Some schools shuffle the order of these priorities or even radically deemphasize some of them. Doing so can produce graduates overburdened with debt and with lower lifetime earning capacity—and uncertain what to do with their degrees in gender or ethnic studies or "Disruption." (Yes, such a major exists, at the University of Southern California, where the cost to attend is more than $77,000 per year.)

If universities stuck to their traditional priorities, the admissions criteria that matter most would be academic achievement and potential

Diversity of the student body would pertain only to socialization, the lowest of the educational priorities. Diversity of ideas and interests, however, contributes to higher-priority goals and thus deserves far more consideration than it gets. An applicant who designs robots or rockets, did an internship in an R&D lab, or wrote a published critical essay in high school should win extra points.

If racial preferences in admissions aren't furthering the mission of a university, what are they doing? They become, effectively, a form of reparations, providing the potential "ticket" of a diploma to individuals who would otherwise have been deprived of that benefit based purely on academic merit. After all, a degree, particularly from a prestigious university, confers a lifetime benefit in terms of economic and other factors.

Though the idea of reparations to persons who have been wronged, as in restitution for theft, may have some justification, current university practices are different. They are a form of compensation (to the less-qualified students admitted) for past injury, given at the expense of those who bear no responsibility for the injury (the more qualified but rejected candidates). This is not "social justice," or any kind of justice, which is correctly defined as the fair treatment of individuals.

The notion that a demographically representative college class makes for better education is a pretext for the real proposition: that certain people deserve reparations. The deeper question for the Supreme Court to decide in the battle over racial preferences is thus whether a university, private or public, should be allowed to dispense de facto reparations, even if existing law suggests that it is not permissible.

Modern Diversity Training Too Often Violates Martin Luther King's Vision of Racial Healing

From the Chloé Valdary "Reconciliation, or Grievance?" *City Journal* article in June 2019:

Diversity training has become a standard feature of American corporate culture. Its origins date to Title VII of the Civil Rights Act of 1964, which codified protecting employees against discrimination and resulted in numerous lawsuits filed with the Equal Employment Opportunity Commission, the agency created by the statute.

Underpinning Dr. Martin Luther King's philosophy was his belief in the sanctity of the individual and the "amazing potential for goodness" within human beings. "We do not wish to triumph over the white community," he wrote. "That would only result in transferring those now on the bottom to the top. But, if we can live up to nonviolence in thought and deed, there will emerge an interracial society based on freedom for all."

Unfortunately, most major institutions' diversity and inclusion programs ignore these lessons and betray King's vision. Robin DiAngelo, an academic and diversity consultant who counts Amazon, Unilever, the YMCA, and the City of Oakland, among others, as clients, coined the term "white fragility," calling it "inevitable" that whites are racist. "Racism," she states, "is the foundation of Western society." Though making such sweeping judgments would surely offend many whites, she concedes, this reaction is itself a "weaponized defensiveness that . . . functions as a kind of white racial bullying."

DiAngelo holds that all whites are complicit in racism by virtue of their skin color. To argue otherwise is racist; to object to the label proves that the label fits. This racial double bind negates King's belief in the capacity for human goodness. In

"The Current Crisis in Race Relations," King wrote that "the important thing about a man is not the color of his skin or the texture of his hair but the texture and quality of his soul." For DiAngelo, no distinction exists between skin and soul. She and other purveyors of such thinking embrace a reductive and repellent vision of racial guilt.

So...what is the aim of diversity and inclusion training? Should it embrace the beloved community and its transcendent vision of human beings working through conflict—racial or otherwise? Or should it bring about a hierarchical inversion, in which one group of people is favored over another, which is perpetually castigated for sins, real or imagined? How we answer this question may shape our institutions, and the workplace, for decades to come.

Diversity Statements Can Determine Who Gets Hired at Universities

From the McKenna Dallmeyer "Diversity Statements Can Determine Who Gets Hired at Universities" Campus Reform story in April 2022:

A 2021 study found that diversity statement requirements for applicants seeking university faculty jobs are common and on the rise. Campus Reform analyzed faculty job postings to evaluate their frequency. And they concluded:

According to a 2021 study, approximately one-fifth of university job postings require applicants to expound their dedication to diversity by submitting a diversity, equity, and inclusion (DEI) statement with their application materials.

The study conducted by the American Enterprise Institute (AEI) estimated the prevalence of requisite diversity statements in public higher education job postings. After analyzing 999 job postings, the study found that 19% required applicants to submit a diversity statement in the job application materials alongside the traditional requirements such as a resume and cover letter.

"We believe our coding schemes are conservative and, if anything, likely underestimate the prevalence of DEI statements," researchers James Paul and Robert Maranto conjecture. As a surprise to the researchers, STEM jobs were found to be just as likely to require a diversity statement from applicants as social science jobs.

"The most surprising finding of the paper is that these requirements are not just limited to the softer humanities. I would have expected these statements to be less common in math and engineering, but they're not," Paul told the *Washington Free Beacon*.

Offering an example, the study cites UC Berkeley's 2018-2019 Initiative to Advance Faculty Diversity, Equity and Inclusion in the Life Science Year End Summary Report. The report reveals that of the 893 job applicants who met basic qualifications, only 214 were able to advance to the subsequent round due to "contributions to diversity, equity and inclusion."

Paul and Maranto believe that DEI requirements have "grown rapidly in recent years" and will continue to become more prevalent in the future. "If policymakers do not intervene, DEI requirements are likely to grow substantially in the years to come," the authors state. Campus Reform analyzed several universities' job advertisements finding that diversity statements are, in fact, prevalent.

The Campus Diversity Swarm

Cultivating the imaginary grievances of an ever-growing number of "oppressed" groups, a costly administrative infrastructure threatens the goals of higher education. Per the Mark Pulliam "The Campus Diversity Swarm" report in the *City Journal* in October 2018, consider the following examples:

- The University of Michigan's diversity bureaucracy employs nearly 100 full-time employees, one earning more than $300,000 per year, at an annual cost of more than $11 million. More than a quarter of UM's diversocrats make more than $100,000 a year, far more than the average salary of assistant professors with doctorates. UM is not exceptional.

- The University of Texas at Austin employs a similar number of bureaucrats in its Division of Diversity and Community Engagement (boasting eight vice presidents), at an annual cost of $9.5 million. The head of UT's diversity bureaucracy makes over $265,000 a year, more than most tenured faculty.

- *The Economist* reports that UC Berkeley has 175 diversity bureaucrats, and nationwide, the trend is toward increased spending in this area. According to The Economist, "Bureaucrats outnumber faculty 2:1 at public universities and 2.5:1 at private colleges, double the ratio in the 1970s."

- Over the same period, tuition has soared. Ohio State's Richard Vedder estimates that more than 900,000 nonteaching administrators—most of them unnecessary—bloat university payrolls.

What do all these diversity administrators do? By one account, "Diversity officials promote the hiring of ethnic minorities and women, launch campaigns to promote dialogue, and write strategic plans on increasing equity and inclusion on campus." NADOHE Standard Six helpfully supplies examples of other "delivery methods" for diversocrats: "presentations, workshops, seminars, focus group sessions, difficult dialogues, restorative justice, town hall meetings, conferences, institutes, and community outreach."

Campus diversity officers also advocate progressive causes, which coincidentally justify an enlargement of their bureaucratic empire.

In this fashion, diversity bureaucracies—like a ratchet—grow ever larger. When laws or regulations impose new compliance requirements (sometimes at the urging of the diversity bureaucrats themselves), administrative ranks and budgets swell.

Diversity bureaucrats exist to service the grievances of an evolving—and potentially unlimited—number of supposedly oppressed groups recognized by postmodern identity politics. Thus, by promoting "social justice" and encouraging "marginalized" students to embrace victimhood, diversocrats ensure their own job security. The mission of campus diversity officers is self-perpetuating.

Unless the cycle of promoting and nursing imaginary grievances is ended, diversity bureaucracies will take over our colleges and universities, supplanting altogether the goal of higher education.

It's Time to Roll Back Campus DEI Bureaucracies

Per the Jay P. Greene and Frederick M. Hess "It's Time to Roll Back Campus DEI Bureaucracies" *National Review* article in September 2022:

Diversity, equity, and inclusion are admirable things. We're quite fond of diversity and inclusion, in principle, and equity sounds a lot like equality, which we rather like. Unfortunately, in higher education, "Diversity, Equity, and Inclusion (DEI)" has taken on an Orwellian aspect—becoming a tool of "groupthink, censorship, and exclusion." At too many colleges and universities, DEI administrative units now pose a profound threat to free inquiry and academic integrity.

More than a few reputable observers have suggested that we've reached "peak woke" and that the stifling threat to free thought is no longer ascendant. But the status quo is not acceptable. Unless the DEI infrastructure is rolled back, it will continue to quietly distort higher education.

Given the relatively recent provenance of campus DEI bureaucracies, many readers may be unfamiliar with just what they do. After all, they are not academic units (like gender- or ethnic-studies departments). Nor are they legal-compliance staff charged with overseeing civil-rights laws (as with Title IX officials). In fact, because DEI staff are not charged with conducting research, teaching classes, or avoiding lawsuits, they enjoy an amorphous charge and remarkable leeway.

Universities have expanded the ranks of this DEI political commissariat at an extraordinary rate. A review of 65 universities in the Power Five athletic conferences found that the typical institution has 45 diversity-staff members on its payroll. That is more than four times as many employees as are devoted to supporting students with special needs (even though accommodations for disabilities, unlike DEI, is something institutions are legally required to provide). In fact, the typical university has roughly one DEI staffer for every 30 tenured or tenure-track professors.

Again, this sentiment is admirable in theory.

In practice, there are big problems. For starters, there's little credible evidence for the claim that DEI staff strengthen identity and belonging in a way that promotes better outcomes. In fact, surveys of all students (as well as of minority students) which ask about how welcome they feel on campus tend to show worse results at universities with larger DEI staffs. What's going on? It's not complicated. A bigger, more aggressive DEI staff is better able to operate as an ideological commissariat, sowing division and distrust as it enforces campus orthodoxy.

This is exactly what Ryan Mills and Isaac Schorr found when they took a deep dive into DEI at the University of Michigan (U-M). As U-M more than quadrupled its DEI staff over two decades, from 40 in 2002 to 167 in 2021, the campus climate deteriorated: "Rather than make U-M a more tolerant place, there's evidence that its DEI push has instead created a more culturally rigid campus, the kind of place where woke students and staff are forever on the lookout for offenses against the politically correct orthodoxy." By signaling what views were "problematic" while helping to organize and amplify the voices of campus radicals, DEI staff stifled free inquiry and robust scholarly discussion among students and faculty.

At many campuses, the DEI bureaucracy started out as a humble "multicultural center," one which was later joined by a host of organizations focused on racial, ethnic, gender, and sexual identity. Over time, universities created centralized diversity offices to support all these entities and now have increasingly replicated these infrastructures across multiple academic units.

This has fueled bureaucratic bloat and rising costs. For example, Northwestern University's Office of Institutional Diversity and Inclusion boasts an "Assistant Provost of Diversity and Inclusion," a "Manager of Diversity and Inclusion," and a "Vice President & Associate Provost for Diversity and Inclusion & Chief Diversity Officer."

There is also an Assistant Director of Campus Inclusion & Community, an Associate Director of Multicultural Student Affairs, an Assistant Director of Native American and Indigenous Initiatives, and an Associate Director of the Women's Center. . . . Well, you get the idea. Similar positions are then replicated in the medical school, business school, and so forth.

17 – Student Outcomes vs. Family Backgrounds, Behavior, Income, Schools & Policies

Credit: Drobotdean.com.

From the Anna J. Egalite "How Family Background Influences Student Achievement" report in Vol. 16, No. 2 of Education Next:

On the weekend before the Fourth of July 1966, the U.S. Office of Education quietly released a 737-page report that summarized one of the most comprehensive studies of American education ever conducted. Encompassing some 3,000 schools, nearly 600,000 students, and thousands of teachers, and produced by a team led by Johns Hopkins University sociologist James S. Coleman, "Equality of Educational Opportunity" was met with a palpable silence. Indeed, the timing of the release relied on one of the oldest tricks in the public relations playbook—announcing unfavorable results on a major holiday, when neither the American public nor the news media are paying much attention.

To the dismay of federal officials, the Coleman Report had concluded that "schools are remarkably similar in the effect they have on the achievement of their pupils when the socio-economic background of the students is taken into account." Or, as one sociologist supposedly put it to the scholar-politician Daniel Patrick Moynihan, "Have you heard what Coleman is finding? It's all family."

The Coleman Report's conclusions (similar but more conclusive than the 1965 Moynihan Report titled The Negro Family: The Case For National Action concerning the influences of home and family were at odds with the paradigm of the day.

The politically inconvenient conclusion that family background explained more about a child's achievement than did school resources ran contrary to contemporary priorities, which were focused on improving educational inputs such as school expenditure levels, class size, and teacher quality. Indeed, less than a year before the Coleman Report's release, President Lyndon Johnson had signed the Elementary and Secondary Education Act into law, dedicating federal funds to disadvantaged students through a Title 1 program that still remains the single largest investment in K–12 education, currently reaching approximately 21 million students at an annual cost of about $14.4 billion.

So what exactly had Coleman uncovered? Differences among schools in their facilities and staffing "are so little related to achievement levels of students that, with few exceptions, their effect fails to appear even in a survey of this magnitude," the authors concluded.

How Family Background Influences Student Achievement

Coleman's advisory panel refused to sign off on the report, citing "methodological concerns" that continue to reverberate. Subsequent research has corroborated the finding that family background is strongly correlated with student performance in school. A correlation between family background and educational and economic success, however, does not tell us whether the relationship between the two is independent of any school impacts.

The associations between home life and school performance that Coleman documented may actually be driven by disparities in school or neighborhood quality rather than family influences. Often, families choose their children's schools by selecting their community or neighborhood, and children whose parents select good schools may benefit as a consequence.

In the elusive quest to uncover the determinants of students' academic success, therefore, it is important to rely on experimental or quasi-experimental research that identifies effects of family background that operate separately and apart from any school effects.

In this essay I look at four family variables that may influence student achievement: family education, family income, parents' criminal activity, and family structure. I then consider the ways in which schools can offset the effects of these factors.

Parental Education

Better-educated parents are more likely to consider the quality of the local schools when selecting a neighborhood in which to live. Once their children enter a school, educated parents are also more likely to pay attention to the quality of their children's teachers and may attempt to ensure that their children are adequately served. By participating in parent-teacher conferences and volunteering at school, they may encourage staff to attend to their children's individual needs.

In addition, highly educated parents are more likely than their less-educated counterparts to read to their children. Educated parents enhance their children's development and human capital by drawing on their own advanced language skills in communicating with their children. They are more likely to pose questions instead of directives and employ a broader and more complex vocabulary.

Estimates suggest that, by age 3, children whose parents receive public assistance hear less than a third of the words encountered by their higher-income peers. As a result, the children of highly educated parents are capable of more complex speech and have more extensive vocabularies before they even start school.

Highly educated parents can also use their social capital to promote their children's development. A cohesive social network of well-educated individuals socializes children to expect that they too will attain high levels of academic success. It can also transmit cultural capital by teaching children the specific behaviors, patterns of speech, and cultural references that are valued by the educational and professional elite.

In most studies, parental education has been identified as the single strongest correlate of children's success in school, the number of years they attend school, and their success later in life. Because parental education influences children's learning both directly and through the choice of a school, we do not know how much of the correlation can be attributed to direct impact and how much to school-related factors.

Teasing out the distinct causal impact of parental education is tricky, but given the strong association between parental education and student achievement in every industrialized society, the direct impact is undoubtedly substantial. Furthermore, quasi-experimental strategies have found positive effects of parental education on children's outcomes. For instance, one study of Korean children adopted into American families shows that the adoptive mother's education level is significantly associated with the child's educational attainment.

Even small differences in access to the activities and experiences that are known to promote brain development can accumulate.

Family Income

As with parental education, family income may have a direct impact on a child's academic outcomes, or variations in achievement could simply be a function of the school the child attends: parents with greater financial resources can identify communities with higher-quality schools and choose more-expensive neighborhoods—the very places where good schools are likely to be. More-affluent parents can also use their resources to ensure that their children have access to a full range of extracurricular activities at school and in the community.

But it's not hard to imagine direct effects of income on student achievement. Parents who are struggling economically simply don't have the time or the wherewithal to check homework, drive children to summer camp, organize museum trips, or help their kids plan for college. Working multiple jobs or inconvenient shifts makes it hard to dedicate time for family dinners, enforce a consistent bedtime, read to infants and toddlers, or invest in music lessons or sports clubs. Even small differences in access to the activities and experiences that are known to promote brain development can accumulate, resulting in a sizable gap between two groups of children defined by family circumstances.

It is challenging to find rigorous experimental or quasi-experimental evidence to disentangle the direct effects of home life from the effects of the school a family selects. While Coleman claimed that family and peers had an effect on student achievement that was distinct from the influence of schools or neighborhoods, his research design was inadequate to support this conclusion. All he was able to show was that family characteristics had a strong correlation with student achievement.

Separating out the independent effects of family education and family income is also difficult. We do not know if low income and financial instability alone can adversely affect children's behavior, emotional stability, and educational outcomes. Evidence from the negative-income-tax experiments carried out by the federal government between 1968 and 1982 showed only mixed effects of income on children's outcomes, and subsequent work by the University of Chicago's Susan Mayer cast doubt on any causal relationship between parental income and child well-being.

However, a recent study by Gordon Dahl and Lance Lochner, exploiting quasi-experimental variation in the Earned Income Tax Credit, provides convincing evidence that increases in family income can lift the achievement levels of students raised in low-income working families, even holding other factors constant.

Parental Incarceration. The Bureau of Justice Statistics reports that 2.3 percent of U.S. children have a parent in federal or state prison. Black children are 7.5 times more likely and Hispanic children 2.5 times more likely than white children to have an incarcerated parent. Incarceration removes a wage earner from the home, lowering household income. One estimate suggests that two-thirds of incarcerated fathers had provided the primary source of family income before their imprisonment.

As a result, children with a parent in prison are at greater risk of homelessness, which in turn can have grave consequences: the receipt of social and medical services and assignment to a traditional public school all require a stable home address. The emotional strain of a parent's incarceration can also take its toll on a child's achievement in school.

Quantifying the causal effects of parental incarceration has proven challenging, however. While correlational research finds that the odds of finishing high school are 50 percent lower for children with an incarcerated parent, parents who are in prison may have less education, lower income, more limited access to quality schools, and other attributes that adversely affect their children's success in school.

A recent review of 22 studies of the effect of parental incarceration on child well-being concludes that, to date, no research in this area has been able to leverage a natural experiment to produce quasi-experimental estimates. Just how large a causal impact parental incarceration has on children remains an important but largely uncharted topic for future research.

Family Structure

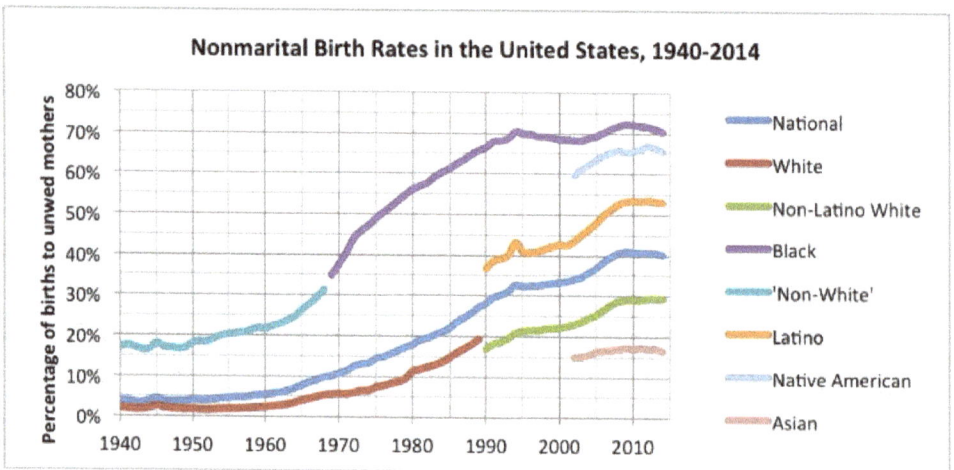

Credit: The Moynihan Report 2014 update.

While most American children still live with both of their biological or adoptive parents, family structures have become more diverse in recent years, and living arrangements have grown increasingly complex. In particular, the two-parent family is vanishing among the poor.

Approximately two-fifths of U.S. children experience dissolution in their parents' union by age 15, and two-thirds of this group will see their mother form a new union within six years. Many parents today choose cohabitation over marriage, but the instability of such partnerships is even higher.

In the case of nonmarital births, estimates say that 56 percent of fathers will be living away from their child by his or her third birthday. These patterns can have serious implications for a child's well-being and school success. Single parents have less time for the enriching activities that Robert Putnam, Harvard professor of public policy, has called "Goodnight Moon" time, after the celebrated bedtime storybook by Margaret Wise Brown.

The U.S. Census Bureau reports that 1- to 2-year-olds who live with two married parents are read to, on average, 8.5 times per week. The corresponding statistic for their peers living with a single parent is 5.7 times. And it's likely that dual-parent families in general have many other attributes that affect their children's educational attainment, mental health, labor market performance, and family formation.

More-rigorous quasi-experimental evidence also documents significant negative effects of a father's absence on children's educational attainment and social and emotional development, leading to increases in antisocial behavior. These effects are largest for boys.

Recent research by MIT economist David Autor and colleagues generates quasi-experimental estimates of family background by simultaneously accounting for the impact of neighborhood environment and school quality to investigate why boys fare worse than girls in disadvantaged families.

Comparing boys to their sisters in a data set that includes more than 1 million children born in Florida between 1992 and 2002, the authors demonstrate a persistent gender gap in graduation and truancy rates, incidence of behavioral and cognitive disabilities, and standardized test scores.

Policies to Counter Family Disadvantage

Policymakers who are weighing competing approaches to countering the influence of family disadvantage face a tough choice: Should they try to improve schools (to overcome the effects of family background) or directly address the effects of family background?

The question is critical. If family background is decisive regardless of the quality of the school, then the road to equal opportunity will be long and hard. Increasing the level of parental education is a multigenerational challenge, while reducing the rising disparities in family income would require massive changes in public policy, and reversing the growth in the prevalence of single-parent families would also prove challenging.

And, while efforts to reduce incarceration rates are afoot, U.S. crime rates remain among the highest in the world. Given these obstacles, if schools themselves can offset differences in family background, the chances of achieving a more egalitarian society greatly improve.

For these reasons, scholars need to continue to tackle the causality question raised by Coleman's pathbreaking study. Although the obstacles to causal inference are steep, education researchers should focus on quasi-experimental approaches relying on sibling comparisons, changes in state laws over time, or policy quirks—such as policy implementation timelines that vary across municipalities—that facilitate research opportunities.

Given what is currently known, a holistic approach that simultaneously attempts to strengthen both home and school influences in disadvantaged communities is worthy of further exploration. A number of contemporary and past initiatives point to the potential of this comprehensive approach.

Implications for Policy

Determining the causal relationships between family background and child well-being has posed a daunting challenge. Family characteristics are often tightly correlated with features of the neighborhood environment, making it difficult to determine the independent influences of each. But getting a solid understanding of causality is critical to the debate over whether to intervene inside or outside of school.

The results of quasi-experimental research, as well as common sense, tell us that children who grow up in stable, well-resourced families have significant advantages over their peers who do not—including access to better schools and other educational services. Policies that place schools at center stage have the potential to disrupt the cycle of economic disadvantage to ensure that children born into poverty aren't excluded from the American dream.

In opening our eyes to the role of family background in the creation of inequality, Coleman wasn't suggesting that we shrug our shoulders and learn to live with it. But in attacking the achievement gap, as his research would imply, we need to mobilize not only our schools but also other institutions.

Promise Neighborhoods offer cradle-to-career supports to help children successfully navigate the challenges of growing up. Early childhood programs provide intervention at a critical time, when children's brains take huge leaps in development. Finally, small schools of choice can help to build a strong sense of community, which could particularly benefit inner-city neighborhoods where traditional institutions have been disintegrating.

Back to Discipline

Per the Heather Mac Donald "Back to Discipline" *City Journal* article in December 2018:

A federal commission on school safety has repudiated the use of disparate-impact analysis in evaluating whether school discipline is racially biased. The Trump administration should go further, and extirpate such analysis from the entirety of the federal code of regulations, as well as from informal government practice.

Disparate-impact analysis holds that if a facially-neutral policy negatively affects blacks and Hispanics at a higher rate than whites and Asians, it is discriminatory. Noticing the behavioral differences that lead to those disparate effects is forbidden. In the area of school discipline, disparate-impact analysis results in the conclusion that racially neutral rules must nevertheless contain bias, since black students nationally are suspended at nearly three times the rate of white students.

In 2014, the Obama administration relied on this methodology to announce that schools that suspended or expelled black students at higher rates than white students were violating anti-discrimination laws.

To understand how counterfactual such an analysis is, consider Duval County, Florida, which has Florida's highest juvenile homicide rate. Seventy-three children, some as young as 11, have been arrested for murder and manslaughter over the last decade, according to the Florida *Times-Union*.

Black juveniles made up 87.6 percent of those arrests and whites 8 percent. The black population in Duval County—which includes Jacksonville—was 28.9 percent in 2010 and the white population 56.6 percent, making black youngsters 21.6 times more likely to be arrested for homicide than white youngsters. Nationally, black males between the ages of 14 and 17 commit homicide at ten times the rate of white and Hispanic male teens combined; if Hispanics were removed from the equation, the black-white disparity would be much greater.

Beneath Those Homicide Numbers is a Larger Juvenile Crime Wave

"The reason so many kids commit murder in Jacksonville is not because they are murderers, but because they are everything else: drug dealers, robbers, thieves, rapists and a bunch of other types of criminals whose crimes of choice has a great likelihood of leading to a murder," a teen murder convict, Aaron Wright, told the *Florida Times-Union*.

Fifty-nine percent of juvenile murder convicts from Duval County who responded to the paper's inmate survey reported that they were committing another crime such as robbery or burglary when they or their co-defendant killed their victim. Wright himself was robbing a woman when his fellow robber shot and killed her, making Wright guilty of felony murder.

The same family dysfunction and lack of socialization that create this juvenile crime wave inevitably affects classroom behavior.

Duval County Public Schools also have the highest number of violent campus incidents of any Florida school district. Nationwide, schools with the highest minority populations report the highest number of disciplinary infractions. Schools that are 50 percent minority or more experience weekly gang activity at nearly ten times the rate of schools where minorities constituted 5 percent to 20 percent of the population, according to the 2018 "Indicators of School Crime and Safety" report produced by the U.S. Justice and Education Departments.

Gang violence in schools with less than 5 percent minority populations was too low to be usable statistically. Widespread weekly disorder in classrooms was reported in schools with at least 50 percent minority populations at more than five times the rate as in schools with 5 percent to 20 percent minorities.

Disparate Impact Reflects Disparate Reality

More than four times as many high-minority schools reported weekly verbal abuse of teachers compared with schools with a minority student body less than 20 percent. Widespread disorder and teacher abuse at schools with less than 5 percent minority populations was again too low to be statistically reliable.

The "School Crime and Safety" reports produced during the Obama years contained identical disparities. And yet the Obama administration held that the only possible reason why blacks are disciplined in school more than whites is teacher and administrator bias. Never mind that teaching is the most "woke" profession in the country after social work, with education schools frantically indoctrinating their students in white privilege and critical race theory.

A substitute teacher who worked in Los Angeles's inner-city schools documents similar insubordination in his recent book, *Sit Down and Shut Up: How Discipline Can Set Students Free*. One student, recounts author Cinque Henderson, shoved a pregnant teacher in order to grab her laptop and watch a video. The dean then interrogated the teacher about why the student was not "jibing with her." An instructor from Miami-Dade County told Henderson: "It is virtually impossible to discipline a student. I know we are losing a generation of kids of color as a result of allowing them to run wild."

The *Times-Union* analysis identifies the biggest factor in juvenile violence: absent fathers. Eighty-four percent of the juvenile murderers who responded to the paper's survey had what the paper discreetly calls "divorced or separated parents"—the reality more likely being that their parents never married in the first place. "I believe that my life may have took a different turn . . . had my father been a man and raised me," a 61-year-old teen murderer and career criminal told the paper.

Excusing insubordination and aggression in the name of racial equity is not a civil rights accomplishment. The third-party victims of such behavior are themselves disproportionately minority—whether fellow classmates who cannot learn, or law-abiding residents of high-crime neighborhoods who have to worry about taking their children safely to school without being carjacked or caught in a drive-by shooting.

But the alleged beneficiary of a racial double standard in conduct is also a victim. Schools are usually the last chance to civilize children if their family has failed to do so. They accomplish that civilizing mission through the application of a color-blind behavioral code, neutrally enforced, that communicates to students that their behavioral choices have consequences.

A student who perceives that his race is an excuse for bad conduct will be handicapped for life. Pace the race advocates, it is this disparate-impact-induced state of affairs—not the supposed implicit racism of teachers and principals—that constitutes an actual school-to-prison pipeline.

A Nation Still at Risk

From the Chester E. Finn Jr. "A Nation Still at Risk" *Hoover Digest* article in the Winter of 2022:

Much as happened after *A Nation at Risk* was released in 1983, the United States finds itself facing a bleak education fate, even as many deny the problem. Back then, however, the denials came mostly from the education establishment, while governors, business leaders, and even US presidents seized the problem and launched the modern era of achievement-driven, results-based education reform.

There was a big divide between what educators wanted to think about their schools—all's well, but send more money—and what community, state, and national leaders were prepared to do to rectify their failings. Importantly, those reform-minded leaders were joined by much of the civil rights community and other equity hawks, mindful that the gravest education problems of all were those faced by poor and black and brown youngsters.

Today, by contrast, we're surrounded by denial on all sides, including today's version of equity hawks, and we see little or nothing by way of reform zeal or political leadership, save for a handful of reddish states where school choice initiatives continue to flourish. We certainly see nothing akin to the bipartisan commitment to better school outcomes, higher standards, reduced achievement gaps, and results-based accountability that characterized much of the previous forty years.

Yet today's core education problem is much the same as what the National Commission on Excellence in Education called attention to way back then:

The educational foundations of our society are presently being eroded by a rising tide of mediocrity that threatens our very future as a nation and a people. What was unimaginable a generation ago has begun to occur—others are matching and surpassing our educational attainments. Our society and its educational institutions seem to have lost sight of the basic purposes of schooling, and of the high expectations and disciplined effort needed to attain them.

That was 1983. Today we find continued signs of weak achievement, arguably more menacing because during the intervening decades so many other countries, friend and foe alike, have advanced much farther in education, while the United States, with a few happy exceptions, has either run in place or slacked off. If you don't believe me, check any recent round of results from the Trends in International Mathematics and Science Study (TIMSS) or the Program for International Student Assessment (PISA).

In American Schools, the "Rising Tide of Mediocrity" Keeps Rising

As other countries' children surpass ours in core skills and knowledge, we face ominous long-term consequences for our national well-being, including both our economy and our security. But what's even more worrying than the achievement problem is the loss of will to do much about it and the creative ways we're finding to conceal from ourselves that it's even a problem—and doing that without necessarily even being aware of the concealment. These strategies take five main forms.

First, we change the subject. Instead of focusing on achievement failings, academic standards, and measurable outcomes, we've been redirecting our attention and energy to other aspects of education and schooling, such as social-emotional learning, and to beefing up inputs and services, such as universal pre-K and community college.

Second, we've been denouncing and canceling the metrics by which achievement (and its shortfalls and gaps) have long been monitored, declaring that tests are racist, barring their use for admission to selective schools and colleges, and curbing their use as outcome measures (e.g., states scrapping end-of-course exams) without substituting any other indicators of achievement. I understand the ESSA testing "holiday" as COVID-19 raged and schools closed in spring 2020.

But why did the College Board abruptly terminate the "SAT II" tests that for many college applicants served as a great way to demonstrate their mastery of particular subjects? Combine what was already a teacher-inspired (and parent-encouraged) "war on testing" with the allegation that tests worsen inequity and you have a grand example of shooting the messenger.

Third, we've been tinkering with the measures themselves, usually in the name of making them "fairer" and broadening access to them. Policy makers have built innumerable workarounds for kids who struggle with high school graduation tests. The College Board has twice "renormed" the SATs to bring the median back up to 500, and that practice has been joined by other score boosters, such as the invitation to mix and match one's top scores from the verbal and math sections on different test dates rather than simply adding the scores that one earns on a given day.

Fourth, we're inflating grades and scores to make things look better than they are.

Grade inflation in high schools and colleges is widespread and well documented, now exacerbated by "no zero" grading policies and suchlike at the elementary- and middle-school levels. Standardized tests, too, can subtly be made to show higher scores—as many states did by setting their proficiency cut-points low—and even the National Assessment will gradually raise all boats as it supplies more "universal design" assists to test takers. (It may also artificially reduce learning gaps.)

Fifth and finally, we're scrapping consequences. In a no-fault, free-pass world that scoffs at both metrics and merit and practices the equivalent of social promotion and open admission for students, teachers, and schools alike, results-based accountability goes out the window. Out with it goes the central action-forcing element of standards-based education reform. Which is, in a sense, the ultimate erasure of achievement-related education problems and their replacement by an all's-well-and-don't-bother-telling-me-otherwise-much-less-doing-anything-about-it attitude. Which, let me say again, is pretty much what we faced from the education establishment after *A Nation at Risk*. The difference is that now it's coming from the political system, the culture, and many onetime reformers, too, and we don't appear to have any leaders pushing back against it. Instead, they're fussing about how many trillions more to pump into the schools.

18 – Progressivism Madness: Marxism Lite for Campus Radicals?

On the Heterodox Academy website, Dr. Jonathan Haidt explains eloquently why universities must choose one telos: truth or social justice. Furthermore, he elaborates that Aristotle often evaluated a thing with respect to its "telos"–its purpose, end, or goal. The telos of a knife is to cut. The telos of a physician is health or healing. What is the telos of university?

The most obvious answer is "truth"––the word appears on so many university crests. But increasingly, many of America's top universities are embracing social justice as their telos, or as a second and equal telos. But can any institution or profession have two teloses (or teloi)? What happens if they conflict?

Haidt believes that the conflict between truth and social justice is likely to become unmanageable. Universities will have to choose, and be explicit about their choice, so that potential students and faculty recruits can make an informed choice. Universities that try to honor both will face increasing incoherence and internal conflict.

Universities Must Choose One Telos: Truth or Social Justice

Truth is paramount to sapience, and the antithesis to sapience is modern progressivism. Not only does progressivism deny commonly held truths across all cultures of the world, today's progressivism has evolved to many degrees into a twentieth century version of Marxism lite—without the horrific calories of human sacrifice, failed regimes, and economic ruin.

When progressivism madness is incubated in the right condition on campus, illiberalism will follow, and when illiberalism follows, so do social justice warriors and campus radicals. Put simply enough by Haidt, "no university can have Truth and Social Justice as dual teloses. Each university must pick one. He shows that Brown University has staked out the leadership position for Social Justice University (SJU), and the University of Chicago has staked out the leadership position for Truth U.

Throughout *The SAPIENT Being* we sometimes use the phrase "so called" progressive. The reason is because so many of the left's and "current" liberal platforms, policies, and agendas are actually regressive in regards to developing sapience. They are the antithesis to sapience! Please note this and the important distinction between progressive vs. progressivism as follows:

Progressive: One favoring or advocating progress, change, improvement, or reform, as opposed to wishing to maintain things as they are, especially in political matters. Today, a conservative or Republican can be just as progressive as a liberal or a Democrat because they both advocate progress, change, improvement, or reform as well, but they have vastly different agendas and ideologies in this regard.

Progressivism: A political philosophy in support of social reform based on the idea of progress in which advancements in science, technology, economic development, and social organization are vital to improve the human condition. It would be safe to say conservatives and Republicans favor addressing political matters vs. social ones so most who favor and/or part of the progressivism movement will be liberals and Democrats.

Furthermore, there's also a misconception that professors are leading their student disciples towards a path of Marxist indoctrination. That's partially true and a lessor of two influences. But if professors are not swaying student opinions in the classroom, and the lessor of two influencers, what is making them more sympathetic to socialism and less tolerant of conservative views about free markets and limited government?

Unknown to many, the greater influence is from college administrators which will be discussed later in this chapter. It's demonstrably true that professors are overwhelmingly liberal and have become more so in the past three decades. Some observers blame leftist professors for the socialist connection. This makes sense on the surface because the renewed sympathy for socialism seems most pronounced among recent college graduates.

However, it's far from conclusive that this kind of classroom and dormitory indoctrination is driving students to the far left. If it's not—what is?

Why Are Young People Growing More Sympathetic to Socialism?

A new study finds that "Millennials are most likely to view socialism and communism favorably." Whereas 54 per cent of Baby Boomers and 71 per cent of mature adults hold a positive view of capitalism, only 42 percent of Millennials are favorably disposed toward it. We see from this study that, with each new generation, hypersensitivity to capitalism's perceived injustices grows.

According to a survey conducted recently by the Victims of Communism Memorial Foundation, a third of Americans and as many as 44% of Millennials would prefer to live under a socialist system than a capitalist one. This is more than a little puzzling at a time when socialism has proved a catastrophic failure in its remaining strongholds in Venezuela, North Korea, and Cuba. China is now a market based communist system that owes its economic success to a large dose of capitalism.

In a study published in 2009 of 7,000 students at 38 institutions across the U.S., professors Matthew Woessner and Dr. April Kelly-Woessner found that students' political beliefs did not change much during their college years. Even in cases where students' opinions changed, there was little correlation between the direction of the change and the political leanings of their professors. When contacted about these conclusions, Woessner confirmed that although campuses today might seem more radical, his current research suggests that those earlier conclusions are still true that students' political beliefs did not change much during their college years.

Oddly enough, author Lenore Skenazy has suggested that students' upbringings are a large part of today's overprotective parenting; which may make them have more acceptance of socialism and the nanny state, particularly on campus.

In her book *Free-Range Kids*, she argued that parents who try to protect their children from every possible threat or danger deprive them of the freedom to grow up. Naturally, when they arrive on campus as 18-year-olds, they look to professors and administrators to take over the parental role of protecting them from life's challenges. Thus, "helicopter parenting" yields "snowflake" students unable to tolerate uncomfortable opinions.

Extracurricular Activities on Campus as Opposed to Classroom Studies

While this may be true, there are nevertheless organizations and constituencies on the contemporary campus that are in position to gain from protest and unrest. In response to perceived slights, however artificial or exaggerated they may be, activists demand and often receive compensation: greater funding for their programs, promises to hire more members of victimized groups, the creation of programs and courses to promote diversity and multiculturalism on campus, and other concessions of tangible kinds.

In these efforts, there seems to be a synergy of students, diversity administrators and faculty members representing multicultural programs. These alliances are rarely formed in the classroom or in the traditional research disciplines. The growing radicalism on campus seems to originate instead in the broad category of student life that takes place outside the classroom.

A 2014 study, for instance, found that students who spent a greater number of hours on extracurricular activities on campus (as opposed to classroom studies) were more likely to see their politics move toward one extreme or the other, in most cases toward the far left.

Kyle Dodson, assistant professor of sociology at the University of California, Merced, looked at data from the UCLA's Freshman Survey and the College Senior Survey. He found that time spent in academic pursuits has a moderating influence on students' political views. Students who are occupied with classroom studies are less likely to engage in disruptive or illiberal activities on campus.

This is an encouraging conclusion as it suggests that students who are more serious about their academic work are more likely to think for themselves and less likely to be drawn into disruptive political activities.

College Students Spend Less Time in Classrooms and Academic Study

But there is a catch: College students are spending less and less time in classrooms and academic study. According to data from the Bureau of Labor Statistics analyzed by the Heritage Foundation in 2014, college students spend fewer than three hours per day on classroom-related activities.

Therefore, it's not surprising to find that professors have little influence on student political beliefs compared with the enormous sway of peers, "student life" administrators and activists who are in charge of campus extracurricular activities.

This should be a wake-up call for faculty and administrators who still believe that a college education should involve classroom learning and the exposure of students to important ideas. As faculty have stepped back from their roles as the primary intellectual guides for students—teaching fewer hours, spending more time on research and publishing for their colleagues in the field, requiring students to take fewer general education requirements—other adults and peers have stepped in to fill the void, much to the detriment of academic learning and liberal ideals on campus.

'Hypersensitivity' as a Cause of Violence on American Campuses

The public has yet to glean the psychological connection between the hypersensitivity studiously cultivated on campus and the inclination to commit violent acts. This point has been largely missed in the ongoing debate over whether many of the campus protesters come to college already hypersensitive or are made that way by faculty and administrators.

An example of this debate is Judith Shulevitz's *In College and Hiding from Scary Ideas*, which was responded to by Phoebe Maltz Bovy's *Don't Blame Students for Being Hypersensitive. Blame Colleges.*

Both Shulevitz and Bovy are largely right. American culture already makes K-12 students hypersensitive (think of how a young person accustomed to receiving "participation trophies" is likely to react later in life when finally confronted with struggle and failure).

But, once in college, the effect of safe spaces, censorship, etc., promises only to exacerbate any preexisting hypersensitivity. As Clay Routledge observes, "More and more colleges are creating 'bias response teams' that students can contact if they feel they have been victimized by microaggressions. There is an increasing demand for safe spaces and trigger warnings to protect students not from physical danger, but from ideas, course material, and viewpoints they may find offensive."

In sum, think of these colleges and universities as finishing schools for those bent on spending their lives competing in the "sensitivity sweepstakes." However, much of the commentary on campus censorship suggests that the only, or worst, effect of the new "therapeutic" education is the production of "little snowflakes," that is, weak individuals. Could it also be the opposite?

What has been missed is the role hypersensitivity can play as a cause of violence. This nexus is one of the themes of Roy Baumeister's *Evil: Inside Human Cruelty and Violence*. He identifies a number of individual psychological factors on whose basis it is possible to "begin to predict who is likely to be dangerous or violent. Hypersensitive people, who often think their pride is being assaulted, are potentially dangerous."

Turning Sensitivity Into Hypersensitivity

He goes on to explain how "hypersensitivity to insults also makes it possible to understand what might otherwise appear to be senseless violence... . Many violent people believe that their actions were justified by the offensive acts of the person who became their victim."

The hypersensitive person can become so irrational that subjectivity becomes all: "Even when a neutral observer would conclude that no serious provocation had occurred, it is still important to recognize that, in the perpetrator's own view, he or she was merely responding to an attack."

From this it is not difficult to see how what is taught at a growing number of our universities can turn sensitivity into hypersensitivity. After all, these schools defend their creation of safe spaces and their prohibition on free speech on the grounds that "oppressed groups" face "institutional discrimination."

In this light, the ideological agenda driving the rise of hypersensitivity on campus becomes clearer. It also becomes more frightening, given the demonstrated connection between hypersensitivity and violence.

In sum, sensitivity has been weaponized.

Campus Administrators' Bias and the Attack on Free Speech

Almost since the start of *Power Line* in 2002, American Council of Trustees and Alumni (ACTA) has reported with dismay the descent of American colleges and universities into a leftist bastion of illiberalism. Most of their focus has been on professors, and not without reason. They are the ones who have degraded the teaching of humanities through their obsession with identify politics and disdain for Western Civilization.

However, Dr. Samuel Abrams came away from an ATHENA Roundtable Conference believing that administrators, not professors, are the primary culprits on American campuses today. The ATHENA Roundtable Conference is a program presented by the American Council of Trustees and Alumni (ACTA). ACTA is an independent, nonprofit organization committed to academic freedom, excellence, and accountability at America's colleges and universities.

The threat posed by the ever-growing ranks of college administrators was pinpointed in an address by Abrams. He's a professor of politics at Sarah Lawrence College who has not only fought courageously for academic freedom, but also studied, as an empirical matter, the threat to it.

Abrams explained that, compared to administrators, college professors exert limited influence on the lives of students. They teach relatively light course loads, have limited visiting hours, spend most of the day on research, and then head home to their family (if any).

Administrators, by contrast, are embedded in their colleges. Some live in dorms where they adjudicate disputes that, in better times, students worked out for themselves. As Abrams puts it in his American Enterprise Institute (AEI) article:

Today, many colleges and universities have moved to a model in which teaching, and learning is seen as a 24/7 endeavor. Engagement with students is occurring as much—if not more—in residence halls and student centers as it is in classrooms.

Schools have increased their hiring in areas such as residential life and student centers, offices of student life and success, and offices of inclusion and engagement. It's not surprising that many of the free-speech controversies in the past few years at places like Yale, Stanford and the University of Delaware have concerned events that occurred not in classrooms but in student communal spaces and residence halls.

The Difference in the Attitudes of Student-Facing Administrators and Professors

Dr. Samuel Abrams surveyed the "student-facing" administrator class—those whose work concerns the quality and character of a student's experience on campus. He found that liberal staff members outnumber their conservative counterparts by a ratio of 12-to-one. Only six percent of campus administrators identified as conservative to some degree, while 71 percent classified themselves as liberal or very liberal. On New England liberal arts campuses, liberals outnumber conservatives by a 28-to-one ratio!

The leftism of this cohort is significantly more pronounced than that of professors, which is pronounced enough.

The difference in the attitudes of student-facing administrators and professors is even more stark when it comes to free speech. Samuel Abrams told us that somewhere around ten percent of professors participate in "shout down" style protests or encourage their students to do so. For the administrator class, the number is more than 40 percent. (These numbers are from Abrams's memory).

Less than twenty percent of professors believe these kinds of protests are a good idea. By almost a two-to-one ratio, student-facing administrators believe they are.

Radical students engage in aggressive protests, such as occupying the office of the college president. One of their demands is that the college hire more diversity coordinators, sex harassment specialists, etc. The college complies.

The new hires foment grievances and encourage new protests. The protests result in the hiring of still more agitator-administrators.

The problem of administrative bloat at colleges and universities is well recognized by Joe Asch who painstakingly documented the problem at Dartmouth. However, it wasn't until he attended the ATHENA Roundtable that he fully understood the relationship between the problem of bloat and the assault on academic freedom.

Colleges could ameliorate both problems by cutting back on diversity deans and other student-facing staff members. It's clear, however, that this isn't going to happen. If anything, the ranks of these grievance mongers likely will continue to swell, and free speech on campus likely will come under even more intense attack.

Marxist Professors or Sensitive Students?

Students should complain about professorial indoctrination, because it is real and it is loaded heavily on the left, most notably in the social sciences and the humanities. One recent ghastly example that received woefully inadequate press attention was a true thought reform program at the University of Delaware.

In this program, all 7,000 residents of the university's dormitories were required to attend coercive and unabashedly ideological "treatments" (the actual term administrators used) with the explicit goal of getting students to adopt specific points of view with regard to issues such as morality, environmentalism, and sexuality. Resident assistants were required to give students questionnaires on what races and genders they would date with the goal of getting students to be more open to dating other races or genders.

One student, who in one of these exceedingly creepy "one on one" sessions answered, "none of your damn business" to the question "When did you discover your sexual identity?" was written up by an RA and reported to the administration. That's only the tip of the iceberg and, shockingly, the Residence Life program at the University of Delaware still seems to believe this was a good program.

It is chilling that we are raising a generation of citizens who believe it is their right to mandate the appropriate views that other citizens should have. It's a formula for totalitarianism.

Why Today's Students Are Less Tolerant Than Before

The resurgence of influence of Herbert Marcuse's New Left, who argued in the 1960s that true "liberating" tolerance requires suppressing all non-progressive voices is problematic with Millennials and college students. Dr. April Kelly-Woessner shows the big split in American opinion on matters of free speech per her "How Marcuse made today's students less tolerant than their parents" Heterodox Academy article in September 2015:

Millennials and college students embrace Marcusian ideals much more than did previous generations, and it is this moralistic illiberalism that leads to the witch-hunts and ultimatums that are sweeping across American college campuses since Halloween 2015.

When Samuel Stouffer first wrote on political tolerance during the McCarthy era, he concluded that Americans were generally an intolerant bunch. Yet, finding that younger people were more tolerant than their parents, he also concluded that Americans would become more and more tolerant over time, due to generational replacement and increases in education.

However, Stouffer did not predict the rise of the New Left, which has reframed our collective notions about free expression, resulting in a significant decline in political tolerance among America's youth. Two months after Kelly-Woessner posted an essay confirming this bias, Pew research published strong confirmation of her argument: 40% of Millennials OK with limiting speech offensive to minorities.

Kelly-Woessner develops the argument from Stanley Rothman's last book, *The End of the Experiment*, (Rothman, Nagai, Maranto, and Woessner, 2015) that Millennials are less politically tolerant than their parents and her findings are outlined below.

Millennials Are Less Politically Tolerant Than Their Parents

First, Dr. April Kelly-Woessner makes the case that young people are less politically tolerant than their parents' generation and that this marks a clear reversal of the trends observed by social scientists for the past 60 years. Political tolerance is generally defined as the willingness to extend civil liberties and basic democratic rights to members of unpopular groups.

That is, in order to be tolerant, one must recognize the rights of one's political enemies to fully participate in the democratic process. Typically, this is measured by asking people whether they will allow members of unpopular groups, or groups they dislike, to exercise political rights, such as giving a public talk, teaching college, or having their books on loan in public libraries.

Americans have not, in fact, become more tolerant. Rather, they have shifted their dislike to new groups. For example, "Muslim clergymen who preach hatred against the United States" are now the least liked group included in the General Social Survey (GSS), followed by people who believe that "blacks are genetically inferior." Most importantly, compared to those in their 40s, people in their 30s and 20s actually show lower tolerance towards these groups.

According to the 2012 GSS, people in their 40s are the most tolerant of Muslim clergymen who preach anti-American hatred: 43% say a member of this group should not be allowed to give a public speech in their community. Among people in their 30s, the number who would prohibit this group from speaking climbs to 52%, and for those in their 20s it jumps to 60%.

Young people are also less tolerant than the middle aged groups toward militarists, communists, and racists. This is not true for tolerance towards homosexuals or atheists, because younger people simply like these groups more. (Political tolerance is not a measure of liking someone, but the willingness to extend political freedoms to those one dislikes).

Second, Kelly-Woessner argues that youthful intolerance is driven by different factors than old fashioned intolerance, and that this change reflects the ideology of the New Left. Herbert Marcuse considered "The Father of the New Left," articulates a philosophy that denies political expression to those who would oppose today's progressive social agenda. In his 1965 essay "Repressive Tolerance," Marcuse (1965) writes,

Sharp differences in partisan, ideological identification between younger and older generations

% of each generation who are ...

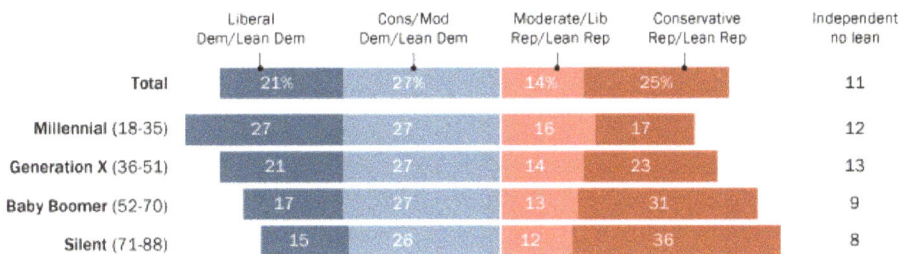

	Liberal Dem/Lean Dem	Cons/Mod Dem/Lean Dem	Moderate/Lib Rep/Lean Rep	Conservative Rep/Lean Rep	Independent no lean
Total	21%	27%	14%	25%	11
Millennial (18-35)	27	27	16	17	12
Generation X (36-51)	21	27	14	23	13
Baby Boomer (52-70)	17	27	13	31	9
Silent (71-88)	15	26	12	36	8

Note: Don't know responses not shown.
Source: Based on merged Pew Research Center surveys conducted in 2016.

PEW RESEARCH CENTER

"Tolerance is extended to policies, conditions, and modes of behavior which should not be tolerated because they are impeding, if not destroying, the chances of creating an existence without fear and misery. This sort of tolerance strengthens the tyranny of the majority against which authentic liberals protested… Liberating tolerance, then, would mean intolerance against movements from the Right and toleration of movements from the Left."

The Orwellian Argument of Liberating Tolerance

The idea of "liberating tolerance" then is one in which ideas that the left deems to be intolerant are suppressed. It is an Orwellian argument for an "intolerance of intolerance," and it appears to be gaining traction in recent years, reshaping our commitments to free speech, academic freedom, and basic democratic norms.

If we look only at people under the age of 40, intolerance is correlated with a "social justice" orientation. That is, I find that people who believe that the government has a responsibility to help poor people and blacks get ahead are also less tolerant. Importantly, this is true even when we look at tolerance towards groups other than blacks. For people over 40, there is no relationship between social justice attitudes and tolerance. I argue that this difference reflects a shift from values of classical liberalism to the New Left.

For older generations, support for social justice does not require a rejection of free speech. Thus, this tension between leftist social views and political tolerance is something new.

Third, Dr. April Kelly-Woessner states that intolerance itself is being reclassified as a social good. For six decades, social scientists have almost universally treated intolerance as a negative social disease. Yet now that liberties are surrendered for equality rather than security, the Left seems less concerned about the harmful effects of intolerance. In fact, they have reframed the concept altogether. For example, political scientist Allison Harell (2010) uses the term "multicultural tolerance," which she defines as the willingness to "support speech rights for objectionable groups" but not for "groups that promote hatred."

In other words, multicultural tolerance allows individuals to limit the rights of political opponents, so long as they frame their intolerance in terms of protecting others from hate. This is what Marcuse refers to as "liberating tolerance."

In fact, the idea that one should be "intolerant of intolerance" has taken hold on many college campuses, as exemplified through speech codes, civility codes, and broad, sweeping policies on harassment and discrimination. Students now frequently lead protests and bans on campus speakers whom they believe promote hate.

While this may have the effect of creating seemingly more civil spaces, it has negative consequences. In fact, tolerance for all groups is positively correlated. It is not simply the fact that leftists oppose the expression of right-wing groups. Rather, those who are intolerant of one group tend to be intolerant of others and of political communication in general.

When colleges fail to represent the full measure of political ideas, students are less likely to learn to tolerate those unlike themselves. This combined with the New Left's legacy of "liberating tolerance," creates an environment that values anger and orthodoxy over inquiry, debate and viewpoint diversity.

19 – The Leftist Madness of Campus Rage

Credit: The Epoch Times.

A recent 2017 issue of *The Wall Street Journal* ran an interview article featuring New York University professor Dr. Jonathan Haidt by Bari Weiss. The article is titled "The Cultural Roots of Campus Rage," and in it, Haidt shares his insights into what's happening on many a college campus across the nation. An unorthodox professor explains the 'new religion' that drives the intolerance and violence at places like Middlebury and Berkeley.

Haidt, a psychologist and professor of ethical leadership, along with Jordan Peterson at the University of Toronto, have become helpful guides to Scott Allen, the author of most of this chapter's content and point of view that the SAPEINT Being shares in understanding these very disturbing cultural trends. So, in Allen's own words (less a few sections edited out for continuity's sake plus impactful "madness" comments added), comes the rest of the content in this chapter.

"What I think is happening," Haidt says, is that "as the visible absurdity on campus mounts and mounts, and as public opinion turns more strongly against universities—and especially as the line of violence is crossed—we are having more and more people standing up saying, 'Enough is enough. I'm opposed to this.' " I too have been outraged and this reaction describes our inspiration for the SAPIENT Being movement on campus.

In introducing the leftist roots of campus rage, the fundamentalists may be few, Haidt says, but they are "very intimidating" since they wield the threat of public shame. On some campuses, "they've been given the heckler's veto, and are often granted it by an administration who won't stand up to them either."

The Berkeley episode illustrates the Orwellian aspect of campus orthodoxy. A scheduled February 2017 appearance by right-wing provocateur Milo Yiannopoulos prompted masked agitators to throw Molotov cocktails, smash windows, hurl rocks at police, and ultimately cause $100,000 worth of damage. The student newspaper ran an op-ed justifying the rioting under the headline "Violence helped ensure safety of students." Read that twice!

You cannot make a more un-sapient statement than that one—but read on—and you'll see more!

The Left Has Undergone an Ideological Transformation

Dr. Jonathan Haidt has observed: In the recent past, important social matters were settled though free and open discussion and debate using logic and reason. Our American civil order is predicated on this. It works well when those engaged share a conviction that universal truth exists—regardless of one's beliefs, feelings, and opinions.

For today's campus radicals, feelings have largely replaced logic and reason. A generation ago, social justice was understood as equality of treatment and opportunity. Per Haidt, "... If black people are getting discriminated against in hiring and you fight that, that's justice."

Today justice means equal outcomes. "There are two ideas now in the academic left that weren't there ten years ago," Haidt says. "One is that everyone is racist because of unconscious bias, and the other is that everything is racist because of systemic racism." That makes justice impossible to achieve: "When you cross that line into insisting if there's not equal outcomes then some people and some institutions and some systems are racist, sexist, then you're setting yourself up for eternal conflict and injustice."

Haidt is right. If the goal of this new social justice is equality of outcome, you are setting yourself up for eternal conflict, injustice, and ultimately social disintegration.

Equal outcomes can only be achieved through the tyrannical imposition of power and coercion, with a resulting loss of individual freedom. It results in human beings being objectified, manipulated, and otherwise treated unjustly.

Where it has been attempted—in places like Maoist China and the Soviet Union—the outcomes were utterly destructive. Millions were imprisoned and murdered. Millions more lost their families, livelihoods, and freedoms. These are the facts!

The Tyranny of Feelings

Authenticity, or "being true to yourself," means acting in accordance with strong emotions. The use of the phrase "I feel like" has become pervasive. Powerful emotions can be extremely dangerous when decoupled from reason.

This new religion—a toxic mix of postmodern relativism, Marxist social analysis, and a Nietzschean will to power—has taken this trend to a whole new level. Today, emotions have become "weaponized." They are used as blunt instruments to exert power and gain control like they were at Yale and elsewhere.

Political correctness (PC) is how most of us encounter the tyranny of feelings. PC is shorthand for speech codes (written or unwritten) that purport to protect the feelings of certain minority groups and avoid giving offense. They become blunt instruments of power by defining what is and is not acceptable speech, and by inflicting penalties on violators, including public defamation, shaming, fines, and even the loss of employment.

For selected groups (defined by the Marxist social analysis that underpins the new religion) claims of offense, "hurt feelings" or discrimination accrue power to silence opponents and force them to conform to the accuser's will. This conferring of power perversely incentivizes victimhood.

In this new religion, victimhood bestows an almost god-like status. It encourages people to cast themselves as fragile, aggrieved victims in need of "safe spaces." Dr. Jonathan Haidt observed that it incentivizes people to "respond to even the slightest unintentional offense, even going so far as to falsify offenses."

The Tyranny of Feelings is Incredibly Destructive

Thus, we have an explosion of so-called "microaggressions." The whole system is built upon the need to keep finding newer reasons to be offended, newer claims to victimhood.

As Haidt explains, "The goalposts shift, allowing participants to maintain a constant level of anger and constant level of perceived victimization … Some colleges have lowered the bar so far than an innocent question, motivated by curiosity, such as 'where are you from' is now branded as an act of aggression." Everyone walks around on egg shells, never knowing for certain if something they say might trigger an emotionally charged reaction, and a charge of racism, bigotry, or discrimination.

Reflecting on this in a recent *New York Times* op-ed, Molly Worthen writes, "Calls for trigger warnings and safe spaces … have eroded students' inclination to assert or argue. It is safer to merely 'feel' … Asserting that others must respond to your hurt feelings and sense of being offended is a way of deflecting (and) avoiding engagement with another person. You cannot disagree."

If you cannot disagree, dialogue is undermined. The attempt to understand all sides of an issue, to listen to arguments and alternative points of view truly and respectfully in a search for truth is undermined. This is the tyranny of feelings and it is incredibly destructive. If it continues to carry the day in our culture, the load-bearing pillars of our free society will inevitably collapse under its weight.

The Nietzschean Will to Power Demands It

As destructive as this is, it has gotten even worse over the last decade. Not only do feelings trump opinions, they now trump reality itself. We see this most clearly with the sexual orientation and gender issue where Progressivism is at its zenith of madness.

If I'm born biologically female, but "I feel like" I'm male (or really anywhere on the so-called gender spectrum), then I am a male. My feelings determine the reality. Postmodernism has empowered me to create my own reality—my own personal identity—without any reference to biological facts.

The Nietzschean will to power then kicks in, as I demand that others (and the society as a whole) affirm me in my personally created reality. If you fail to affirm me, I can wield power by claiming offense, pain, suffering, and discrimination. I can bash you as a hater and a bigot if you fail to let me use the bathroom or locker room of my choice based on my feelings about who I am at any given moment.

States have passed laws and ordinances to enforce the tyranny of feelings. In New York City, authorities now fine citizens up to $250,000 for the novel crime of "mis-gendering"—referring to people by any words other than their pronouns of choice (including newly constructed words such as zie/hir, ey/em/eir and co). Sexual madness!

Make no mistake: this new ideology is deadly serious. It is nothing less than a kind of acid, eating away at the central pillars of a free, open society. Yale University is supposed to represent dialogue and learning. What happens when we lose the freedom to openly dialogue, debate and discuss different viewpoints because we fear offending someone who may wield power over us by claiming our speech was "violence" leading to public shaming, fines, or loss of employment? Ideas have consequences. What kind of culture will this new ideology produce? What will be the fruit? Leftist madness!

How Progressivism Has Evolved by Redefining Words

One of the hallmarks of the new religion that is the focus of this series is how it redefines words. It has created a new dictionary. John Stonestreet of the Colson Center for Christian Worldview puts it this way: "We use the same words, but different dictionaries."

Some of the most important words in the English language have been redefined over the past 50 years. Words like marriage, freedom, love, compassion, and justice have taken on a new, culturally accepted meaning. According to Os Guinness, "there has been a subtle shift in the meaning of many Western ideas, so that once-strong Jewish and Christian (words) are now used in different ways that decisively change their meaning."

Why is this important? Because words matter. Words have the power to convey truth and help us rightly understand reality. Words and language are the basic building blocks of culture, and healthy, flourishing cultures are built on the truth. Vacating words of their meaning turns out to be incredibly destructive.

We can look, for example, at the word "violence" that was briefly discussed in previous chapters. According to the older dictionary, violence involves physical attack or abuse. The new dictionary defines violence as speech or language that is taken by a member of a self-described victim group to be hurtful or offensive. Paradoxically, this new definition has become a justification for acting out violently, as defined by the old dictionary.

So, violence is justified when it "ensures safety." Safety from what? From the "violence" of being exposed to offensive speech and language. This is free speech madness and a most un-sapient point of view.

Calling the speech and language of your opponents, not merely offensive, but "violent" is a way of appealing to emotions in order to prevail. Most people intuitively know that violence against innocent people is profoundly wrong, unjust, and even criminal.

The proponents of the new religion cleverly leverage this sentiment, and then twist it. Claiming that your opponent's speech is "violent" becomes an effective way of silencing them.

The problem is that the word "violence" is perverted in the process. People slowly lose a sense of its true meaning. Where does this perversion of language lead? What happens to a society when its people cavalierly redefine words in an effort to accrue power and silence opponents?

If offensive speech is now described as "violent," and violent acts have historically been illegal and criminal, it begs the question: Will certain speech now become illegal and speakers criminalized as well? Yes, it's already happening!

Postmodernist View of Words

Postmodernism, which holds that there is no objective, transcendent truth, or reality. Reality is "constructed" though words and language. Words have no objective meaning, but only a meaning that individuals or groups bring to them. According to Os Guinness, "Postmodern philosophies have untethered words from any clear content, let alone objective meaning, and can be used in any way the speaker likes."

This is sometimes referred to as "deconstructionism," a postmodern view of language championed by the philosopher Jacques Derrida (1930-2004) and concisely described in the ramblings of *Alice in Wonderland's* Humpty Dumpty:

"When I use a word, it means just what I choose it to mean—neither more nor less."

Winston Churchill observed: "words, which are on proper occasions the most powerful engines, lose their weight and power and value when they are not backed by fact or winged by truth."

Add to this postmodern view of language an overlay of Marxist social analysis, which sees the world as a zero-sum competition between "victims" and "oppressors." The "oppressors" use language to create a "reality" that is imposed upon so-called victims– often without them being aware of it– as a means of maintaining power and privilege. The "victims" can liberate themselves by "unmasking" these socially constructed realities.

Today, this form of Marxist thought is widely taught on college campuses under the rubric of Critical Theory. Critical Theory studies have mushroomed in the English, history, and social science departments of Western universities since the 1960s, completely replacing the older study of Western Civilization.

Words Are No Longer About Truth

Add to this the Nietzschean will to power, which seeks to manipulate or coerce others into using new definitions—even leveraging the power of the state as a means of attaining cultural supremacy. Now you begin to see the approach of the new religious orthodoxy towards language. Words are no longer a means of communicating truth. They are tools to control others, and ultimately to become master.

What kind of society emerges from the student's worldview assumption about group identity? Is it any surprise that we are experiencing ever-increasing social fragmentation, racial tension, and even hostility? Can there be any basis for unity—for America's founding creed, "E Pluribus Unum" –if the new religion fully replaces Judeo-Christian assumptions at the core of the culture?

We are already seeing troubling signs. On college campuses, black students are self-segregating. Other identity groups are following suit. In the past, our schools and universities taught "American history," but increasingly, this is being replaced with "black history" or "female history," or "gay and lesbian history." There is no single history we share. Any attempt to teach one is an act of cultural imperialism. Cultural madness!

Progressivism Madness by Way of Cultural Relativism or Multiculturalism

Scott Allen goes on to demonstrate how the next "core doctrine" of progressivism builds on the first. Postmodernism denies the existence of transcendent, objective truth or morality, so each identity group defines its own reality and morality, not subject to critique by outsiders. This is known as cultural relativism, or multiculturalism.

Even something as simple as enjoying food, clothing, or music from another ethnic group is taken to be an "act of oppression," or in the parlance of the new religion of progressivism, "cultural appropriation."

If a particular Muslim group practices female genital mutilation or honor killing, multiculturalism forbids any value judgment from outside that culture. After all, it is their culture—it is their reality. Who are we to judge? Somali-born Ayaan Hirsi Ali routinely challenges this belief.

At many American universities today, any critical examination pertaining to Islam, including Shariah and the treatment of women in Islam, is declared to be out of the realm of scrutiny. Examinations (i.e., freedom speech) frighten universities more than the litany of honor killings and wholesale abuse of women in so many parts of the Islamic world. Religion madness!

If some racial or ethnic groups suffer from higher rates of poverty, unemployment, drug addiction, or divorce, multiculturalism disallows laying blame on the beliefs or actions of those within the group. In keeping with the first "core doctrine" of group identity, individual belief or action isn't available for consideration. Justice madness!

Rather, the blame must, by default, lie in the larger historical, social, or structural forces. This is why the new religion is seemingly obsessed with "systemic or structural" oppression or racism. To attribute negative outcomes to the beliefs or actions of those within the community is "blaming the victim," *the* cardinal sin in the new religious orthodoxy.

Western Civilization as the Ultimate Source of Oppression

There is one major exception to the non-judgmental approach demanded by cultural relativism. The Judeo-Christian belief system comes in for very harsh critique, usually in the form of attacks against "Western civilization." Because America's history is part of the larger story of Western civilization, this explains the overwhelmingly critical view that adherents of the new religion of Progressivism have towards America and its history. American madness!

American history and culture, rooted in Judeo-Christian beliefs, is viewed as uniquely oppressive. That is the third "core doctrine," or unquestioned given of the new religion. If this seems inconsistent, it will make more sense when you realize that this particular view is grounded less in postmodernism, and more in a neo-Marxist ideology. We'll explore this further in the next section.

As Allen explains: To see the world through the lens of Marxism, either in its old or new form, is to see the world exclusively in terms of power relationships—a merciless, zero-sum world of domination, subjugation, and oppression.

In its original form, Marxism was framed in economic terms. The oppressors were bourgeois property owners and capitalists, and the oppressed were the subjugated "workers of the world." The newer form of Marxism thriving today on university campuses worldwide identifies Western civilization, rooted in a Judeo-Christian belief system, as the ultimate source of oppression. After all, it was this particular culture that gave rise to the capitalist economic system viewed by Marxists new and old as rapacious and destructive.

Western civilization (including the history and culture of the United States) is held by adherents of the new religion to be uniquely oppressive, imperialistic, colonial, racist, sexist, classist, and patriarchal. It has created (in the words of a student activist at Claremont's Pomona University), "interlocking systems of domination that produce the lethal conditions under which oppressed peoples are forced to live." Third World madness!

You might think he's describing life in North Korea, but you'd be wrong. He's talking about life for minorities in America, from his vantage point as a student at one of America's most elite institutions. Progressivism madness!

Redemption is Available, But Only Under Certain Conditions

If you happen to be a white, Christian (or Jewish), cisgender, heterosexual male, and you have anything positive to say about the contributions of Western civilization to human flourishing, expect to be labeled a "white supremacist." You are imbued with a deep-seated cultural superiority and subconscious racism, sexism, and host of "phobias." You have "privileges" that people of "marginalized identities" do not share, and you continue to enjoy these privileges at their expense. Racism madness!

You must confess and renounce your unconscious racism and white privilege. You must denounce America for her oppressive and violent history, and commit to working for her fundamental transformation, a sort of reverse pledge of allegiance to the flag (or at least a refusal to participate in that exercise which, for generations, marked the beginning of every school day). You must also actively "ally" with America's many oppressed victims. This is what was seen in the 2020 Democratic Party debates and primaries. Democratic Party madness!

Everyone who is not a white, Christian, heterosexual male, is by definition, an oppressed victim. Women, Muslims, "people of color," LGBTQ+ identity groups— all are victimized in a multitude of ways by the stealthy and diabolically oppressive systems and structures imposed by Western civilization. And while all non-white groups are oppressed, they are not oppressed equally. Diversity madness!

"Intersectionality" is the trendy new word coined to describe the complex matrix of oppression. A white woman is oppressed (because she is a woman), but she is not as oppressed as much as a black woman. A black woman who is also a lesbian is still more oppressed still.

According to The Hudson Institute's Heather Mac Donald, "individuals who can check off multiple victim boxes experience exponentially higher and more complex levels of life-threatening oppression than lower-status single-category victims." And because victimhood accrues a host of benefits, including status and power, there is a kind of perverse competition—a "victimhood Olympics"—to be seen as the most oppressed of all.

As with all worldviews, this new religion defines a source of evil—Western civilization. Fighting against it gives adherents a sense of purpose, a mission that brings meaning to their lives. That brings us to the final "core doctrine."

Academic Freedom and Cancel Culture

As noted in the Eric Kaufmann "Academic Freedom and Cancel Culture" *City Journal* November 2020 article: Only government action can protect speech and expression on campuses.

Ideological uniformity and political bias combine with academics' fear of being cancelled to create a toxic atmosphere, especially for conservative and, in the context of transgender issues, "gender-critical" dissenters.

The solutions, we point out, must involve proactive government oversight of universities' adherence to academic freedom in order to offset the influence of progressive pressure groups. The hope that moral exhortations will shift opinion, or that market-based solutions can address these threats are, we argue, unrealistic.

While the most egregious cancel-culture attacks sometimes make the news, everyday censorship usually permeates organizations below the level of public attention—especially at universities. The key relationship to grasp is the connection between political discrimination and self- censorship. When you fear that your utterances can harm your career, you silence yourself.

It's not that academics discriminate more, or cancel each other more, than people in other professions. The issue is structural. In our data, those on the left outnumber those on the right by a factor of six, rising to a factor of nine among current social-science and humanities faculty. In my U.S. data, the ratio is an even more extreme 14-to-1, in line with other studies.

Discrimination would be much less of a problem if the political ratio were more even. When each side is discriminating against the other at the same rate, but one side outnumbers the other by a factor of ten, the discriminatory effect is ten times worse for the Right. A known Brexit or Trump supporter is almost certain to face a biased assessor on a four-person panel, while a Remain or Biden supporter will be as likely to gain from discrimination in his favor as against.

The disparity also explains why most academics don't understand what the uproar is about. Most are progressive, so they don't experience discrimination.

The combination of political discrimination and intimidation restricts academic freedom and contributes to a steady narrowing of academic horizons. It's a prime example of what John Stuart Mill calls the "despotism of custom," which he identified as a greater impediment to free expression than government repression.

What happens on campus shapes the direction of the culture, adding urgency to the need for reform. Many conservatives and traditional liberals seem to believe that rational debate and the marketplace of ideas will solve the problem; good ideas will drive out bad ones, and consumers will shift their dollars to freer universities and away from repressive ones.

They ignore the first- mover advantage that established universities possess. Reputations, endowments, and powerful alumni with a vested interest in the high status of their alma mater give Ivy League schools, for example, a cachet that no upstart university can hope to match.

Meantime, powerful norms and internal pressure groups prevent universities from defying the social-justice agenda. These network effects mean that the only viable path back to open inquiry runs through the reform of existing institutions.

Viewpoint diversity on campus serves a vital purpose in an increasingly polarized society. While the leftward skew in academia is mainly the result of self-selection, discrimination is also likely playing a role. Our recommendation is for official university communications to be politically neutral, as they are in the U.K. school system. While scholars must have the right to espouse political opinions in class, official university communications should not do so.

This step may not solve the problem, though. A more effective measure to restore ideological diversity may be to require universities to show equivalence between policies promoting racial and gender equality/diversity and those addressing political discrimination and representation. This bypasses the problem of politicizing academia by allowing institutions to opt for as much or as little equality/diversity as they wish— provided they implement equivalent measures on political diversity.

President Trump's executive order ending the use of Critical Race Theory in diversity training in U.S. federal agencies—training that is compulsory, discriminates against whites, and brooks no dissent—is an important illustration of how democratic politics can change illiberal and discriminatory practices within elite institutions.

The administration's revised Title IX guidelines provide another example of government action putting a stop to forms of progressive overreach that persistently violate the due process rights of the accused. Any attempt by a Biden administration to reinstate the status quo ante will be viewed, correctly, as ideologically motivated.

Universities control immense resources, which they use to reinforce their status. Many are now in thrall to radical activist networks, which leverage powerful social taboos to amplify their power. The only way to limit them is by circumscribing the ability of fearful university administrators to punish dissent. Reformers who insist on libertarian purity and a non- governmental approach are just clearing the way for unchecked progressive activism, entrenching the illiberal status quo. The responsibility for upholding due process and free speech cannot devolve to individuals whose rights are already being abridged.

The only way for free speech to prevail over the progressive goal of emotional safety is for governments to apply the law to institutions proactively—that is, individual autonomy must be prioritized over institutional autonomy, even as we endeavor to safeguard as much institutional freedom as possible.

This is what the U.S. federal government did when it required southern universities to open their doors to black applicants in the early 1960s. It is also the strategy followed by the British government in dealing with Muslim-majority public schools that fell under the sway of Islamist leaders and were thus restricting the rights of their female students. Government should be limited—but this doesn't mean that it isn't sometimes required to protect people's rights.

In short, reform of the university system—meaning close government oversight— is the only realistic option.

20 – Mill vs. Marx: Free Speech Champions Rise Up Against Free Speech Suppressors

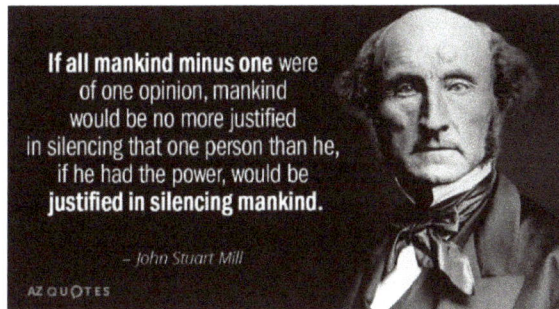

If all mankind minus one were of one opinion, mankind would be no more justified in silencing that one person than he, if he had the power, would be justified in silencing mankind.

– John Stuart Mill

AZ QUOTES

Today, Americans are deeply divided about the meaning of their country, its history, and how it should be governed. This division is severe enough to call to mind the disagreements between the colonists and King George, and those between the Confederate and Union forces in the Civil War. They amount to a dispute over not only the history of our country but also its present purpose and future direction.

Comprising actions by imperfect human beings, the American story has its share of missteps, errors, contradictions, and wrongs. These wrongs have always met resistance from the clear principles of the nation, and therefore our history is far more one of self-sacrifice, courage, and nobility. America's principles are named at the outset to be both universal—applying to everyone—and eternal: existing for all time.

According to the October 2021 "What Happens When Free Speech Dies" article by Judson Berger in the *National Review:* In the past years, the political and intellectual energy has been with illiberal movements. Too often, the advocates of free speech and free institutions have been passive, even fatalistic. It is high time for those of us who believe in these enduring ideals to stand up for our convictions.

In September 2021, the *Economist* featured "the threat from the illiberal left" on its cover as well. One article included this haunting line: "Belief in foundations of liberalism such as free speech declines with each generation." This is a demonstrable trend in America's generations.

Pew found that 40 percent of Millennials (also referred to as Generation Y) "say the government should be able to prevent people publicly making statements that are offensive to minority groups." Compare that with 27 percent for Generation Xers and 24 percent for Baby Boomers. Making the data even more alarming is that it was gathered in 2015; one can only presume that the percentage today, especially among Generation Z, is even higher.

What does our campus culture value? One recent survey found that a majority of college students support shouting down speakers with whom they disagree; 23 percent supported the use of violence toward this end. At some colleges, the percentage supporting such violence crept into the 40s.

That is not a culture that values free speech. It is a culture that values freedom from emotional, political, and intellectual disturbance of any kind. These shifts in attitude, which have escaped campus and are spreading quickly throughout America and the world –are a detriment to free speech and expression and an accelerant for free speech suppression and censorship.

The Moral Authority of the Campus Left is Starting to Dwindle

The campus left, in particular, is fiercely determined to forestall any expression of views that run counter to its preferred narratives, and to punish those who disobey. Shout downs are a blend of forestalling and punishing as noted by Peter Wood's article that is part of the July 2018 "A Tide Flowing Toward Free Speech on Campus" article inside the report *Free Speech in Peril: College—Where You Can't Say What You Think* by Peter Wood of the Minding the Campus organization.

The tactics used against Charles Murray at Middlebury College and Heather Mac Donald at Claremont College, to cite two of the most famous instances, were aimed at preventing speech but also at humiliating the speakers. The spirit of such disruption is theatrical anger in service of what the protester takes to be righteous indignation.

Those feelings are not going to evaporate like the morning dew. They have become ingrained among the protesters. And yet the protesters are losing the dark glamour they enjoyed when shouting-down, taking over, and spitting outrage seemed somehow authentic and cool.

The protesters seemed for a while to be immune to all the rules because leftist administrators just couldn't bring themselves to impose serious consequences for lawlessness in the name of "social justice." But something has changed.

The moral authority of the campus left is starting to dwindle. We see that in the sudden emergence of the "walk away" movement. A gay New York hairdresser, Brandon Straka, has given the movement its manifesto in a YouTube video. Straka denounced what he calls "liberalism" as "tyrannical groupthink," and described it this way: "For years now, I have watched as the left has devolved into intolerant, inflexible, illogical, hateful, misguided, ill-informed, un-American, hypocritical, menacing, callous, ignorant, narrow-minded, and at times blatantly fascistic behavior, and rhetoric." It is a system, he says, that allows a mob "to suppress free speech, create false narratives, and then apathetically steamroll over the truth."

I can think of any number of conservatives who could say (and have said) much the same thing, though perhaps focusing more precisely on the progressive social justice zealots, rather than liberalism per se. But Straka brings to the message the burn of a Carolina Reaper chili pepper.

The Fight for Free Speech

While free speech has been under attack, we are beginning to see some pushback. More than 12,000 professors, free speech leaders, and conservative-leaning organization leaders have signed "The Philadelphia Statement."

The 845-word document, as reported in the October 2020 "The Fight for Free Speech" article in The Daily Signal by Walter E. William says in part:

Similarly, colleges, and universities are imposing speech regulations to make students 'safe,' not from physical harm, but from challenges to campus orthodoxy. These policies and regulations assume that we as citizens are unable to think for ourselves and to make independent judgments. Instead of teaching us to engage, they foster conformism ('groupthink') and train us to respond to intellectual challenges with one or another form of censorship.

A society that lacks comity and allows people to be shamed or intimidated into self-censorship of their ideas and considered judgments will not survive for long. As Americans, we desire a flourishing, open marketplace of ideas, knowing that it is the fairest and most effective way to separate falsehood from truth.

Accordingly, dissenting and unpopular voices—be they of the left or the right—must be afforded the opportunity to be heard. They have often guided our society toward more just positions, which is why Frederick Douglass said freedom of speech is the 'great moral renovator of society and government.'

The recognition of the intellectual elite attacking free speech is not new. In a 1991 speech, Yale University President Benno Schmidt warned:

The most serious problems of freedom of expression in our society today exist on our campuses. The assumption seems to be that the purpose of education is to induce correct opinion rather than to search for wisdom and to liberate the mind

Tyrants everywhere, from the Nazis to the communists, started out supporting free speech rights. Why? Because speech is important for the realization of leftist goals of command and control. People must be propagandized, proselytized, and convinced.

Once leftists have gained power, as they have in most of our colleges and universities, free speech becomes a liability. It challenges their ideas and agenda and must be suppressed.

Attacks on free speech to accommodate multiculturalism and diversity are really attacks on Western values, which are superior to all others. The indispensable achievement of the West was the concept of individual rights, the idea that individuals have certain inalienable rights that are not granted by government. Governments exist to protect these inalienable rights.

It took until the 17th century for that idea to arise and mostly through the works of English philosophers such as John Locke and David Hume. And now the 21st-century campus leftists are trying to suppress these inalienable rights.

Don't let it happen. Resist at all costs. America's future depends on it.

Wesleyan President Roth Calls on Universities to Promote Intellectual Diversity

On May 11, 2017, Wesleyan President Michael Roth's statement about heterodoxy was published in *The Wall Street Journal* regarding the need for colleges and universities to proactively cultivate intellectual diversity on campus. While student protests over controversial speakers have dominated headlines of late, he writes:

The issue, however, isn't whether the occasional conservative, libertarian or religious speaker gets a chance to speak. That is tolerance, an appeal to civility and fairness, but it doesn't take us far enough. To create deeper intellectual and political diversity, we need an affirmative-action program for the full range of conservative ideas and traditions, because on too many of our campuses they seldom get the sustained, scholarly attention that they deserve.

Our present political circumstances should not prevent us from engaging with a variety of conservative, religious, and libertarian modes of thinking, just as they shouldn't prevent us from engaging with modes of thinking organized under the banner of progressivism or critical theory. Such engagement might actually lead to greater understanding among those who disagree politically, and it might also allow for more robust critical and creative thinking about our histories, our present and the possibilities for the future.

President Trump Signs 2020 Executive Order Protecting Freedom of Speech on College Campuses

One of those other critics is President Trump signed an executive order protecting freedom of speech on college campuses. At the signing, he was surrounded by student activists who have said conservative views are suppressed at universities.

Trump said he was taking "historic action to defend American students and American values that have been under siege" when he announced March 21, 2019 that he would make federal funding for universities contingent on assurances of free speech. Trump: 'People who are confident in their beliefs do not censor others'.

Trump strongly defended free speech on campus two years earlier after police at the University of California, Berkeley canceled a talk by the far-right agitator Milo Yiannopoulos amid intense protests by masked Antifa activists, who set fires and threw stones.

The order does not, on its face, make dramatic changes. But it was welcomed by people who say universities are fostering an unbalanced, liberal indoctrination of students—and condemned by those who say freedom of inquiry is a fundamental tenet of higher education, one the government should not be defining.

The president declared it the first in a number of steps the administration would take to defend students' rights. Universities have tried to restrict free thought and impose conformity, he said. "All of that changes right now," he added. "We're dealing with billions and billions and billions of dollars." Trump told the students that people can have different views, "but they have to let you speak."

What We Can Learn From the Campus Free-Speech War

Friends of liberty are few. But not as few as we might think according to the August 2021 "What We Can Learn from the Campus Free-Speech War" article by Isaac Willour in the *National Review*:

In July, free-speech advocates at the University of Connecticut took on a student body hellbent on destroying free speech on campus. A group of students pushed the university's student government to adopt the "UConn Statement," a petition for the university to uphold civil discourse on campus. According to the statement, UConn "has a solemn responsibility not only to promote a lively and fearless freedom of debate and deliberation, but also to protect that freedom when others attempt to restrict it."

Such attempts at restriction came swiftly and viciously. The simple move to promote the First Amendment on campus was met with stunning bigotry and intolerance from UConn's student body, and with it a barrage of hateful and violent threats. Students hurled accusations of white supremacy at UConn's student body president, an immigrant from Honduras. One of UConn's First Amendment advocates was harassed with racial slurs and even received a video of an ISIS beheading.

These students stared down an entire campus culture that had turned against them for their devotion to free speech. Though public sentiment remained negative and combative, people began voicing private support for UConn's free-speech warriors. Both faculty and students expressed agreement with the UConn Statement, and the First Amendment coalition on campus is moving forward with speaker events and increased activism. Free-speech debacles such as UConn's illustrate valuable lessons that advocates of conservatism would do well to bear in mind.

In my discussions with UConn students, both conservatives and those on the Left, I heard one description of the current political climate that piqued my interest. "Liberals give in to radicals too easily, and conservatives have some racism problems."

Innumerable members of the political Right cheer on the former characterization — the latter is met with defensiveness, skepticism, and a hearty chorus of "but look at the Left." This is why conservatives lose on the culture side. We know that the stereotype isn't true. But the culture doesn't, and we won't fix it by yelling. Segments of the modern American Right have embraced a reactionary response to conservatism's unwarrantedly negative cultural portrayal. But this tactic is not going to win over political moderates.

Visceral reactions are perfectly understandable in response to the far Left's blatant lies about conservatives. But we must change that tactic to persuade the persuadable. Moderates with deeply held biases against conservatism won't be won over by our most extreme and caustic voices and arguments. If we are to make cultural headway, our strategy must be responsive, not reactionary.

College students who advocate free speech are willing to do so with their ideological opponents, working with members of the opposite political party at institutions like UConn to advance the First Amendment. So should the movement more generally.

That's how we can fight back: With many allies by our side.

How To Keep Your Corporation Out of the Culture War

Dr. Jonathan Haidt and Greg Lukianoff wrote an afterword for *The Coddling of the American Mind* in the summer of 2021 with eight steps business leaders can take to prevent ideological pressure and political conformity in the workplace because business leaders from the corporate and non-profit sectors began contacting them about internal issues they are having with recent hires.

According to their December 2020 "How To Keep Your Corporation Out of the Culture War" article by Dr. Jonathan Haidt and Greg Lukianoff in Persuasion:

They told them that their youngest employees show increased levels of anxiety, depression, and fragility; a tendency to turn ordinary conflicts between co-workers into major issues requiring the attention of the Human Resources Department; and greater insistence that the organization must share and express their personal political values related to social justice.

Beginning around 2018, parts of the corporate world began to experience the same changes we saw in universities from around 2014. This makes sense once you realize that members of Gen Z began to arrive on campuses in 2013 and 2014—they spent four years within institutions that largely catered to their new needs and demands, and began to graduate from four-year colleges around 2017 or 2018.

A 2021 survey found that 48% of Gen Z respondents reported feeling stress all or most of the time, and the top source of worry among them was career prospects. As for the increased internal conflicts and tensions among employees, the title of a 2021 article on the front page of the business section of The New York Times sums it up well: "The 37-Year-Olds Are Afraid of the 23-Year-Olds Who Work for Them." Friction and punishment campaigns in the corporate world seem to be hyper-charged by Slack and other internal company messaging platforms.

The biggest change in the corporate world has been the explosion of social justice movements, employee political activism, and internal conflict about that activism since 2017, all playing out on social media.

Why Would Gen Z Have Any Meaningful Influence On Corporations?

But why would Gen Z have any meaningful influence on corporations during this turbulent period—2017 to 2020—when they had just arrived in the workplace and were present only in small numbers? The primary reason comes back, again, to social media.

Gen Z is the first generation where a critical mass of young people grew up as social media natives (with a 2018 survey finding 97% on at least one social media platform). This allowed them to organize and mobilize in a way that was simply not available to previous generations.

A single employee who is adept at using social media can create a PR nightmare for employers, often leading to nearly instantaneous public capitulation accompanied by a formulaic apology. Social media played a key role in the ouster of James Bennet from The New York Times in the summer of 2020, when many

NYT staffers tweeted that he "[put] Black @nytimes staff in danger" by running an op-ed by U.S. Senator Tom Cotton in favor of deploying military force during civil unrest—phrasing they were advised to use by their union due to the existence of employment protections for speech relating to workplace safety.

Five years ago, about three-quarters of Millennials said business was a force for good; at the time, Gen Z made up about five percent of the workforce. Today, Gen Z makes up about a quarter of the workforce, and fewer than half of Millennials say that business is a force for good—bringing them roughly in line with Gen Z. Whether the convergence came about by Gen Z influencing Millennials or because both generations responded in similar ways to the avalanche of social unrest since 2017 is unclear. But either way, Millennials seem to share Gen Z's skepticism about capitalism, and many of them share a willingness to prioritize social causes over company goals—to the detriment of free speech and expression.

Ever since they entered the corporate world in the early 2000s, some members of the Millennial generation (born 1982 to 1996) have pushed for being able to "bring their whole selves to work." Companies in the creative industries encouraged this shift, erasing boundaries between work life and private life. But as America became ever more politically polarized, the problem with this policy became evident: Some whole selves cannot tolerate working alongside other whole selves that have different political beliefs and voting patterns.

Corporate Social Justice and Cancel Culture Issues

On an everyday level, the move towards corporate social justice and the expectation of company-wide solidarity with specific causes can lead to what has (controversially) been dubbed "cancel culture." One of its defining patterns is that employees face calls for discipline or termination for expressing non-conforming opinions, even when those opinions are expressed away from the workplace or with no hostile intent.

Corporations, of course, have the First Amendment right of association and therefore can decide whom they employ—at least insofar as they comply with anti-discrimination law. Our fear, however, is that if too many corporations see themselves both as businesses and as participants in social movements, then employees who disagree face a stark choice: Keep your mouth shut, or express yourself and face possible termination.

For companies that wish to hire talent of all political stripes, or to reduce the frequency of campaigns to fire employees for political nonconformity, we offer the following advice.

- Expand your definition of diversity.

- Reconsider what colleges you hire from.

- Orientation: Be direct with candidates and new hires.

- Have a talk with the human resources department.

- Survey employees to see if there's a problem.

- If a social media firestorm demands that you fire an employee, slow down.

- Don't make firing a first or preferred punishment.

- Ask yourself "where does this end?

In conclusion: Many of the dynamics we described in *The Coddling of the American Mind*, which transformed college campuses beginning in 2014, are now spreading rapidly through the corporate world in the U.S.

The Free Speech Alliance

From L. Brent Bozell III, President, Media Research Center: "Voices are being silenced, opinions are being censored and conservative media are being suppressed. These tech companies claim they provide platforms to connect people and share ideas. However, when the only ideas permitted are from one side, any prospect of intellectual discourse dies. If these platforms merely serve as an echo chamber of liberal talking points, everyone loses."

And therein lies problem—conservatives, their ideals, and constitutional rights are under attack and are being sidelined on the intellectual playfield and marketplace of ideas. In today's America, conservatives face an existential crisis as social media giants in collusion with the radical left root out and silence conservative speech on their platforms and across the Internet.

This is the worst threat to free speech our country has ever faced and Dr. Michael Poliakoff, president of the American Council of Trustees and Alumni (ACTA), which also focuses on free speech and academic freedom, said he was happy the alliance was taking a stand.

The future of the conservative movement depends on our ability to communicate our message. If Facebook, Twitter, and Google censor conservatives on the Internet, the modern day public square, everything conservatives have fought for is at risk. The Left will control the narrative. The Internet is truly the new battleground for liberal media bias.

In April 2018, the Media Research Center released a groundbreaking report exposing efforts to censor conservatives and silence conservative speech from major online platforms. Our report was so impactful that US Representatives on the House Judiciary Committee cited it four separate times during a July 17, 2018 congressional hearing.

Our Project Reveals Two Concerns

Online censorship is a very real and dangerous problem, the ramifications of which are far more troubling than many conservatives realize. The problem is so dangerous that the MRC must take a stand against it.

Now—together with a Coalition of more than 90 conservative organizations—the MRC is letting tech giants know that we will not be silenced. We need the force of the entire conservative movement to win this battle.

The Free Speech Alliance protects the free speech of conservatives online. We fight for transparency on social media and demand equal footing for conservatives on Twitter, Facebook, Google and the other platforms. We defend the incredible and revolutionary ideal of free speech in which American democracy is rooted.

We actively work with tech companies to ensure that they are protecting conservative speech online and that the radical left does not contaminate the national online dialogue with their bias. For more information on how to join the alliance, please visit the Appendix under Free Speech Alliance.

The Alliance is calling on social media companies to address four key issues in order to begin to rectify their credibility problem and rebuild trust with conservatives:

1) **Provide Transparency:** We need detailed information so everyone can see if

liberal groups and users are being treated the same as those on the right. Social media companies operate in a black-box environment, only releasing anecdotes about reports on content and users when they think it necessary. This needs to change. The companies need to design open systems so that they can be held accountable, while giving weight to privacy concerns.

2) Provide Clarity on 'Hate Speech': "Hate speech" is a common concern among social media companies, but no two firms define it the same way. Their definitions are vague and open to interpretation, and their interpretation often looks like an opportunity to silence thought. Today, hate speech means anything liberals don't like. Silencing those you disagree with is dangerous. If companies can't tell users clearly what it is, then they shouldn't try to regulate it.

3) Provide Equal Footing for Conservatives: Top social media firms, such as Google and YouTube, have chosen to work with dishonest groups that are actively opposed to the conservative movement, including the Southern Poverty Law Center. Those companies need to make equal room for conservative groups as advisers to offset this bias. That same attitude should be applied to employment diversity efforts. Tech companies need to embrace viewpoint diversity.

4) Mirror the First Amendment: Tech giants should afford their users nothing less than the free speech and free exercise of religion embodied in the First Amendment as interpreted by the U.S. Supreme Court. That standard, the result of centuries of American jurisprudence, would enable the rightful blocking of content that threatens violence or spews obscenity, without trampling on free speech liberties that have long made the United States a beacon for freedom.

The Free Speech Alliance is made up of more than 90 organizations and individuals who oppose the silencing of conservative voices on social media. Members of the Free Speech Alliance are not affiliated with MRC and the MRC does not endorse any of the positions or opinions of the other members of the FSA.

21 – The Return of Freedom of Speech, Viewpoint Diversity, Intellectual Humility & Sapience

Credit: Talksub.

Leftist indoctrination is spreading well beyond academia, big tech, government, corporations, and educations organizations and we don't act now, it's only a matter of time before its oppressive and dysfunctional policies overtake all of America. Our treasured and God-given liberties, freedoms and way of life are at risk of being lost forever and an Orwellian wave of progressivism madness will overtake America from sea to shining sea.

Sapient individuals and organizations who understand the many blessings to humankind that are the direct result of American exceptionalism, Western European culture, and Judeo-Christian values—will not stand idly for this. As Dennis Prager so eloquently states, "I refuse to be forever labeled as 'the generation that lost America'—and I know you agree!"

To avoid that catastrophe, we must not merely double our efforts, but triple them and commit to educating our youth for the long haul. Humility, openness, engagement, a strong and maturing self that is always a work in progress; these are the necessary ingredients for a free society, and for shared progress, according to John Stuart Mill.

For far too long, sapient beings have failed to pass on their values to the next generation and to fight for them within the discourse of the marketplace of ideas. Clearly, we need to better market our successful, freedom-boosting values and ideas that will protect and nourish our republic—and deny those the opportunity who are intent on destroying it.

As strange as it may sound at first--that destruction starts with the addition and reinterpretation of words in the American lexicon.

The Pronoun Wars

Once upon a time and in a place very near America in a Canadian province called Ontario and its oh-so-proudly tolerant and diverse city called Toronto, on the campus of its celebrated and eponymous University, there was a professor, a clinical psychologist. And his name was Jordan Peterson as reported in the December 2021 Epoch Times' article "How the 'Cancel Culture' Mob's Attempt to Silence Jordan Peterson Backfired" by Rex Murphy.

It was at the beginning of what history now calls the Pronoun Wars, denoted by one sage observer, and the greatest nightmare grammarians have ever endured, and sparked by the emergence of the "trans" movement. A concentrated account must suffice. Dr. Jordan Peterson, a near anonymous figure in those days, objected to the idea that he could be mandated to use any of the glittering array of new-fangled (and frankly ridiculous) bedspread of invented pronouns.

It wasn't that he would not, in some person-to-person contact, agree to use a new "pronoun" to a student who requested it. His objection came from deeper sources: that the concepts behind the practice emerged from a mode of politics he regarded as pernicious. He emphatically declared that as either professor or citizen he would never submit to "compelled speech."

Skipping over much, a band of fevered students charged him with "transphobia"— not incidentally yet another term that has leaped into news and academic discourse, though you will not hear it much, even now, outside these progressive vaults. They interrupted Peterson's lectures, assailed him with contempt and insult, harassed him when he attempted to argue his case, brought noise machines to drown him out, and asked—demanded—he be fired.

The attempts to silence and ostracize Peterson failed in a divinely spectacular fashion. The woke, identity-politics mob—I'm going vernacular here—got its politically correct fat ass bitten as with the teeth of a monster crocodile—as he ascended into fame with supersonic speed, wrote the book "12 Rules for Life" that sold millions, and became the most famous academic in the world—a heralded icon to masses of people grateful for his advice, his multitude of Biblical and other lectures, and his articulated defiance of the bullying tactics and ideology of left dogma.

They tried to smother Peterson, and even his own University of Toronto was complicit in the early effort. But to their woe and heartburn resentment, unwittingly fed him Grade A oxygen and launched him to undreamt of fame and access to a worldwide audience. They had attempted to crush a sparrow and lo, they set a dragon in flight against themselves.

Sapient beings take notice!

Political Intolerance Among University Faculty Highlights Need For Viewpoint Diversity

Viewpoint diversity has become the bane of the academic elite per the "Political Intolerance Among University Faculty Highlights Need For Viewpoint Diversity" in the November 2016 *Forbes* article by Nathan Honeycutt:

It's an inconvenient reality: Universities are champions for diversity and inclusivity, except when it comes to viewpoint diversity. Supporting viewpoint diversity is certainly not "mainstream"—academics have proven predominantly resistant to research and discussions calling for this issue to be addressed.

Recently published research, though, suggests the lack of viewpoint diversity in our universities is neither a small nor trivial issue: It's widespread, impacting academia across disciplines. Further, the data clearly indicate that explicit political discrimination is widely endorsed.

Surveying faculty across all academic disciplines at four California State University campuses my coauthor and I found that overall 71% of respondents were liberal (15% moderate, 14% conservative). Liberals comprised an overwhelming majority in every academic area except for Agriculture where conservatives were a plurality, but not a majority.

Reporting on their experiences in the academy, conservative faculty were found to have experienced significantly more hostility than their more liberal colleagues. Additionally, nearly one-third of both liberals and conservatives expressed a willingness to discriminate in hiring decisions. These individuals explicitly reported that if presented with two equally qualified job candidates, they would choose the candidate that shared their political beliefs.

Given the symmetrical nature of expressed willingness to discriminate, it certainly would be inappropriate to label the liberal majority as the "bad guys" for not wanting to hire conservatives, as conservatives indicated they wouldn't be interested in hiring liberals. But stopping here and claiming there is no cause for concern is a tad too simplistic.

Conservatives clearly lack the means and opportunity to act upon their willingness to discriminate due to their small numbers. Given the sheer quantity of liberal faculty, and the willingness of a sizable number to make political ideology a "litmus test" for hiring, it's more realistic to expect that the number of politically conservative faculty on university campuses will continue to shrink.

This quickly becomes problematic on multiple fronts. As Dr. Jonathan Haidt of New York University has routinely argued, dismissing conservative (or non-liberal) views could lead scholars to overlook meaningful research questions, or even misinterpret the results of their research. Psychology and many other academic disciplines are working to maintain sure footing amidst a relative crisis of scientific integrity, characterized in part by incidences of fabricated data and influential studies failing replication. Scientific integrity has the potential to be bolstered by an increased commitment to viewpoint diversity.

Welcoming different perspectives allows ideas to be better refined, questions that may otherwise be avoided to be pursued, and data to have a better chance at being accurately analyzed and interpreted. It provides a natural check on research, preventing it from descending into what Philip Tetlock of the University of Pennsylvania dubbed "scientific hell," where scientific standards are clouded by political passions.

Volumes of research related to minority influence—such as that by Charlan Nemeth of the University of California, Berkeley—have demonstrated the benefits of welcoming divergent or underrepresented perspectives into the fold. Numerical minorities positively influence creativity and divergent thinking in problem solving and decision-making. Even if minority positions and ideas aren't adopted, their influence on the quality and quantity of thought still provides a positive boost for the quality of the group's end product.

Collaborations or coexisting with those who may see the world in a fundamentally different way is certainly not easy—it's a primary instinct to surround ourselves with like-minded individuals. Ultimately, though, it's counterproductive for academics to respond to research or ideas they don't agree with by stifling the research or the colleagues performing it. Rather, the best way academics can seek to answer difficult questions and understand perplexing phenomena is by openly debating the issues and conducting more research most accurately.

If universities and university faculty seek to support diversity and inclusivity, they cannot continue to apply it in selective or convenient ways. By welcoming those who think differently—perhaps coupled with a focus on superordinate goals such as the pursuit of truth—academics can become better stewards of the pluralistic tradition of our universities, and can correspondingly bolster scientific integrity in their work.

Ground Rules for Respectful Public Discourse & Behavior

Being concerned about growing incivility in our civic and public settings we can learn from the people of Utah to return to fundamental principles that will lead to greater civility and a new spirit of community. In 2008, they reaffirmed their "inherent and inalienable" Constitutional rights is the fundamental right "to communicate freely about our thoughts and opinions," and yet they are also "responsible for the abuse of that right" Constitution of Utah Article I Section 1. In that context they believe that there must be a renewal of respectful discourse and behavior in civic and public settings in Utah.

This is not an appeal for us all simply to get along. We recognize that there are profound differences among us, and that spirited debate is a vital part of American democracy. Participation in American civic and public life does not require us to sacrifice our deepest convictions; rather we best protect our own rights by protecting the rights of others and adhering to high ethical standards.

With that in mind lets propose the following ground rules of civic and public engagement that recognize the important place of the rights, responsibilities, and respect inherent in our civic and constitutional compact.

1. Remember the Importance of Rights and the Dignity of Each Individual. Our society is founded upon the proposition that all people are born free and equal in dignity and rights, and that freedom of conscience and expression are at the foundation of our rights.

2. Responsibly Exercise your Rights While Protecting the Rights of Others. Each of us should be responsible both in the exercise or our rights and in protecting the rights of others. Especially on matters of personal faith, claims of conscience, and human rights, public policy should seek solutions that are fair to all.

3. Respect Others. All people—especially our leaders and the media—should demonstrate a commitment to be respectful in discourse and behavior, particularly in civic and public forums. Respect should also be shown by being honest and as inclusive as possible, by mindfully listening to and attempting to understand the concerns of others, by valuing their opinions even when there is disagreement, and by addressing their concerns when possible.

4. Refrain from Incivility. Public discourse can be passionate while maintaining mutual respect that reaches beyond differing opinions. Intimidation, ridicule, personal attacks, mean spiritedness, reprisals against those who disagree, and other disrespectful or unethical behaviors destroy the fabric of our society and can no longer be tolerated. Those who engage in such behavior should be brought to light, held accountable and should no longer enjoy the public's trust.

5. Rekindle Building Community. Our social compact "of the people" and "by the people" is "for the people." Each one of us has a responsibility to build community. On divisive issues, areas of common ground should first be explored. Effort should be given to building broad-based agreement, giving due regard to the concerns of minority points of view.

Open Inquiry

A world-class academic community depends on an open society to thrive; it also models an ideal culture of discourse. Questioning and argument, weighing evidence and analyzing alternative interpretations—such values are at the core of teaching and scholarship.

Open Inquiry is the ability to ask questions and share ideas without risk of censure.

In an environment that is insufficiently open, facts can be corrupted or suppressed for the benefit of special interests. Important innovations can be set back or outright snuffed out. Avoidable problems can fester and spread. Personal and intellectual growth can be stunted.

Open inquiry is threatened on several fronts. Across the political spectrum there are people who make it their business to surveille and mob scholars who threaten their preferred narratives.

Expanding bureaucracies at many colleges and universities subject ever more of campus life to administrative oversight—and encourage people to resolve disputes through reporting, investigations, and academic reprisals rather than good-faith debate and discussion.

Concerns about placating donors, ensuring high enrollments or positive course evaluations can distort research and pedagogy—especially for the growing numbers of contingent faculty whose careers and livelihoods can be threatened by a single upset student, donor, or colleague.

And, of course, many fear losing the esteem of, or being ostracized by, one's peers for saying the "wrong" thing (a risk which is more pronounced in highly-homogenous environments). Even in the absence of formal sanctions, social and professional isolation can make academic life extremely difficult and unpleasant—and many reasonably prefer to self-censor rather than risk it. This is a significant concern among students, faculty, and administrators.

Academics worried about attacks on free speech have felt the need to respond, and they have articulated sound principles. Princeton professors Robert P. George and Cornel West recently attracted lots of supporters for a statement underscoring that "all of us should seek respectfully to engage with people who challenge our views" and that "we should oppose efforts to silence those with whom we disagree—especially on college and university campuses."

Trying to understand the logic of someone else's arguments is a core skill that schools should be paying more attention to, and it doesn't always require elaborate new programs. The group Heterodox Academy, which includes faculty from many universities and from across the political spectrum, has recently launched the "Viewpoint Diversity Experience," an online effort to combat "the destructive power of ideological tribalism." The aim is "to prepare students for democratic citizenship and success in the political diverse workplaces they will soon inhabit."

Such efforts are sorely needed, but they can succeed only if we do a better job of bringing underrepresented points of view into the mix. Simply relying on the marketplace of ideas isn't enough. We need an affirmative-action program for conservative, libertarian, and religious modes of thinking.

Restoring Free Speech on Campus

Restrictions on free expression on college campuses are incompatible with the fundamental values of higher education. At public institutions, they violate the First Amendment; at most private institutions, they break faith with stated commitments to academic freedom. And these restrictions are widespread.

The good news is that the types of restrictions discussed in this section can be reformed. A student or faculty member can be a tremendously effective advocate for change when he or she is aware of expressive rights and is willing to engage administrators in defense of them. Public exposure is also critical to defeating speech codes since universities are often unwilling to defend their speech codes in the face of public criticism.

Unconstitutional policies also can be defeated in court, especially at public universities, where speech codes have been struck down in federal courts across the country. Many more such policies have been revised in favor of free speech as the result of legal settlements.

Any speech code in force at a public university is vulnerable to a constitutional challenge. Moreover, as speech codes are consistently defeated in court, administrators cannot credibly argue that they are unaware of the law, which means that they may be held personally liable when they are responsible for their schools' violations of constitutional rights.

Censorship in the academic community is commonplace. Students and faculty are increasingly being investigated and punished for controversial, dissenting or simply discomforting speech. It's time for colleges and universities to take a deep breath, remember who they are and reaffirm their fundamental commitment to freedom of expression.

The suppression of free speech at institutions of higher education is a matter of great national concern. However, by working together with universities to revise restrictive speech codes and to reaffirm commitments to free expression, we can continue to stride toward campuses that truly embody the "marketplace of ideas" that such institutions must be in our society.

With these issues and goals in mind, in 2015, the University of Chicago convened a Committee on Freedom of Expression to do exactly that. The committee issued a statement identifying the principles that must guide institutions committed to attaining knowledge through free and open discourse. Guaranteeing members of the academic community "the broadest possible latitude to speak, write, listen, challenge, and learn," the statement guarantees students and faculty the right "to discuss any problem that presents itself."

The Chicago Statement (Committee on Freedom of Expression)

How should students and scholars respond when challenged by speech with which they disagree, or that they even loathe? The Chicago Statement (Committee on Freedom of Expression) sets forth the answer: "by openly and vigorously contesting the ideas that they oppose." Anticipating the push and pull of passionate debate, the statement sets forth important ground rules: "Debate or deliberation may not be suppressed because the ideas put forth are thought by some or even by most members of the University community to be offensive, unwise, immoral, or wrong-headed."

Perhaps most important, the Chicago statement makes clear that "it is not the proper role of the University to attempt to shield individuals from ideas and opinions they find unwelcome, disagreeable, or even deeply offensive." Laura Kipnis, Alice Dreger, and Teresa Buchanan would have benefited from this frank and necessary recognition.

"Because the University is committed to free and open inquiry in all matters, it guarantees all members of the University community the broadest possible latitude to speak, write, listen, challenge, and learn."–The Chicago Statement.

Since last year's report, FIRE has observed an increase in the adoption of free speech statements at colleges and universities inspired by the "Report of the Committee on Freedom of Expression" at the University of Chicago (better known as the "Chicago Statement"). As of May 2019, 63 institutions or faculty bodies have adopted or endorsed the Chicago Principles or a substantially similar policy statement.

Thousands more need to follow!

Adopting the Chicago Statement

All colleges that are seriously committed to free inquiry and robust debate should consider adopting a version of the Chicago Statement. In doing so, the college not only reaffirms its core purpose as a place for discourse and debate, but also encourages the campus community to engage in such expression. By actively prioritizing free speech in this manner, universities can outline a set of principles that will become the hallmark of the community they aspire to build.

As eloquently described in the Chicago Statement, "fostering the ability of members of the University community to engage in such debate and deliberation in an effective and responsible manner is an essential part of the University's educational mission." That is the type of campus community FIRE and HxA hope all colleges will aim to cultivate.

When institutional leaders wait until controversy erupts on campus to publicly endorse free speech, detractors often accuse well-meaning administrators of favoring one side over the other. A proactive endorsement of free expression principles effectively shuts down any criticism that the university is picking sides in the latest campus controversy. Why wait until a controversial speaker comes to campus or racist posters fill your residence halls to take a principled stand on free speech? Instead, consider adopting a free expression statement today.

The Chicago Statement Can Take Three Different Forms

As tracked by FIRE, endorsement of the Chicago Statement may take three different forms: official adoption by a university, approval by a governing board, or endorsement by a faculty body. Additionally, to ensure campus-wide engagement with the free speech issues raised by the Chicago Statement, many institutions choose to include several other stakeholders in the process, such as the student government and other campus community members.

Backed by a strong commitment to freedom of expression and academic freedom, faculty could challenge one another, their students, and the public to consider new possibilities, without fear of reprisal. Students would no longer face punishment for exercising their right to speak out freely about the issues most important to them.

Instead of learning that voicing one's opinions invites silencing, students would be taught that spirited debate is a vital necessity for the advancement of knowledge. And they would be taught that the proper response to ideas they oppose is not censorship, but argument on the merits. That, after all, is what a university is for.

Free speech and academic freedom will not protect themselves. With public reaffirmation of the necessity of free speech on campus, the current wave of censorship that threatens the continuing excellence of U.S. higher education can be repudiated, as it should be, as a transitory moment of weakness that disrespects what our institutions of higher learning must represent.

Say "No!" to Campus Mob Fascism

In response to the Berkeley riot incident in 2017, FIRE issued this statement:

No university may be considered "safe" if speakers voicing unpopular ideas on its campus incur a substantial risk of being physically attacked. A university where people or viewpoints are likely to be opposed with fists rather than argumentation is unworthy of the name. Granting those willing to use violence the power to determine who may speak on campus is an abdication of UC Berkeley's moral and legal responsibilities under the First Amendment.

Strong-arming one's belief onto others is just a form of mob fascism—no matter what side of a political spectrum you are coming from.

If the Chicago Principles support allowing any invited speaker, as the statement does, then great. We must value our wonderful educational space, framed by laws and policies on one side and supported by documents like the Chicago Principles on the other. We need students to feel free to offer any viewpoint and likewise to offer any challenge, both within the context of our curriculum and on campus, to open up a discourse, and to learn from the engagement.

Let's underscore that point at the beginning: the Chicago principles envision and protect both controversial viewpoints and protests against those viewpoints, with the proviso that protesters "may not obstruct or otherwise interfere with the freedom of others to express views they reject or even loathe."

Allowing Controversial Speakers on Campus

From the "Ron DeSantis seeks free speech resolution allowing controversial speakers at Florida universities" Emily L. Mahoney article in the *Tampa Bay Times* in April 2019:

Gov. Ron DeSantis said all of Florida's colleges and universities should adopt a resolution similar to the "Chicago Statement," a statement on campus free speech that declares that all viewpoints should be allowed to be discussed on college campuses, even if they are ones students may "loathe" or find "deeply offensive."

"We are here today to affirm our commitment to ensuring that all Florida's public universities and colleges and protect student speech and the open exchange of ideas on our campuses," DeSantis said during a news conference at Florida State University, flanked by the university's president, John Thrasher, Florida Commissioner of Education Richard Corcoran and Marshall Criser, chancellor of the state's university system.

Scores of colleges and universities across the country have already adopted a version of this resolution, including Eckerd College, a liberal arts school in St. Petersburg. According to the governor's office, all the state's other colleges and universities plan to adopt the Chicago statement

Notably, DeSantis addressed the topic of controversial speakers — an issue with which Florida is deeply familiar, after white nationalist Richard Spencer spoke at the University of Florida in October 2017 and had to cut his speech short after students in the audience drowned him out with chants like "Black Lives Matter."

"At an academic institution where you have a speaker expressing ideas, there's no room for a heckler's veto where you simply shout down or scream down a speaker so that they cannot articulate views," DeSantis said, later adding that in Spencer's case, the "best response" by students would have been "an empty auditorium."

He added that he's noticed "a trend" nationwide where universities have disinvited certain speakers that espouse controversial opinions, such as conservative pundit Ben Shapiro, who has said that the majority of Muslims have been "radicalized" and tweeted "Israelis like to build. Arabs like to bomb crap and live in open sewage."

"I think that's a sign of weakness on behalf of school administrators and I think that demonstrates a lack of commitment to free exchange of ideas," DeSantis said. "There can't be a safe space in the business world."

Experts in campus free speech emphasized that the Chicago statement doesn't have teeth, though it can be a positive first step in affirming institution's commitment to free speech regardless of the speech's content.

"It's unequivocally a positive step in the right direction for a public institution to affirm this is what they think about these issues," said Joe Cohn, legislative and policy director for the Foundation for Individual Rights in Education, which has done policy and legal work on behalf of students whose speech rights were infringed upon on campus.

"But they (universities) also need to do the hard work of comparing their policies to the principles reflected in the statement."

But Jonathan Friedman, the campus free speech project director for PEN America, a national group of writers and human rights advocates which has published a report on campus free speech, says that universities should not feel pressure to remain neutral on all issues in an effort to have open speech.

"Having a conversation about free speech alone ... without discussing the tensions that exist can inflame other issues like racism and hateful speech on campus," Friedman said. "If there's someone on campus promoting hate ... we would want the university to be able to say, 'We don't agree with this person and here are all the reasons why.'"

The announcement came as Florida lawmakers consider legislation (Senate Bill 1296 and House Bill 839) that would require each of the state's public universities, to conduct an annual "assessment" looking at "intellectual freedom and viewpoint diversity at that institution."

The bill's sponsor, Rep. Ray Rodrigues, R-Estero, has pointed to a University of Colorado survey as the inspiration for the proposal, which polled students and faculty on whether they felt the school promoted an environment respectful of all people of all identities and opinions. As part of that survey, students and faculty were also asked to anonymously identify their race, ethnicity, religious affiliation, sexual orientation and political party.

And just last month, President Donald Trump issued a broad executive order on the topic of university free speech, asking federal agencies to make sure that colleges or universities that receive federal grants "promote free inquiry." If not, those grants could be at risk.

When signing the order, Trump said "professors and power structures" are keeping students from "challenging rigid far-left ideology." DeSantis said that he agrees that university faculty tend to lean leftward, though he said that should not matter. "I've had liberal professors over the years who were very fair about putting forward the alternative viewpoints," he said.

22 – Freedom of Speech Models & Policies for America's Public-Private Institutions

Credit: Wallpaper Cave.

Though the Cold War ended 30 years ago, our nation is still in a war that has been brewing for decades—a war for America's soul. Nikita Khrushchev, who ran the Soviet Union from 1958 to 1964, openly predicted the destruction of the United States and said it would happen in the way that every society eventually collapses.

"We will take America without firing a shot," he said. "We do not have to invade the U.S. We will destroy you from within." He was talking about an entire system of Marxist indoctrination and takeover that had been refined and executed in country after country during the 20th century.

Soviet defector Yuri Bezmenov, a former KGB operative and high-level Russian propagandist, escaped to the West in 1970. He warned the United States about the KGB tactics used to subvert a nation that he witnessed firsthand in the Soviet Union. Those tactics amounted to a planned process of altering the way people think for a particular purpose, which is to affect a regime change.

Per the September 2021 "We Are in a War for America's Soul" article by Michele

R. Weslander Quaid of the *Epoch Times*: It's effectively the brainwashing of society—a slow, methodical transformation. Those who conduct that ideological subversion are very patient to employ the tactics over decades. This ideological subversion has four stages and follows the Hegelian dialectic, a tactic long exploited by Marxists and Fascists to control people.

Stage 1: Demoralization. This is the destruction of faith in the government and society. Believing that society is broken, systems are failing, and patriotism is evil are three key beliefs that are promoted to create guilt. This leads to the acceptance of radical new ideas because the current structure is believed to be harmful. Traditional Judeo-Christian morality, classical education, and U.S. patriotism are discarded.

Stage 2: Destabilization. With the decision-making ability of Americans negatively affected through demoralization, the next step takes a foothold—destabilization of the nation's foundations. Destabilization causes citizens to believe the worst of what they hear about their nation and form of government. Supporters of traditional values and foundational structures in the nation are ostracized and even demonized.

Stage 3: Crisis. The altered values of Americans cut to the root of the current systems. Upheaval presents opportunities for change. Once a society is destabilized, it begins to collapse into chaos. At that point, citizens want the government to provide stability.

We saw that recently as a demoralized and destabilized society responded with fear and panic when a "pandemic" faced our nation. Americans are willingly trading civil rights and freedoms for authoritarianism and overreach that they believe will keep them safe. The messaging in all of this is key. The mainstream media and their "tell-a-vision" programming play a key role in framing the prescribed narrative as truth.

Stage 4: Normalization. The "new normal" is a term we've heard constantly lately, and it's an accurate description of what the normalization stage is all about. When the government and societal structures have changed to restrict liberty, citizens are told the radical transformation is "the way it has to be." Ironically, it's described as normal when it's not normal at all. Normalization creates a new baseline for what a nation will accept, value, and promote. The cycle is complete.

The United States Could Be On the Verge of Collapse

Those steps are repeated over and over, bringing a greater result with each cycle, until there's a controlled collapse. The United States could be on the verge of collapse right now unless we collectively wake up to reality and take a stand to stop tyranny.

The Hegelian dialectic is the framework for guiding people's thoughts and actions into conflicts that lead them to a predetermined solution. The enemies of the United States are using that tactic to create fear, turn citizen against citizen, and divide our nation. A house divided can't stand.

If people don't understand how the Hegelian dialectic shapes their perceptions of the world, then they don't know how they're helping to implement the agenda, which ultimately is to advance humanity into a dictatorship—whether by the fascists, the communists, or the globalists and their New World Order. We must step outside the dialectic so that we can be released from the limitations of controlled and guided thought.

The most important thing about America is liberty. America is what has stood between power-hungry people and their goals of world domination. The true enemies of the United States are trying to convince us that we're each other's enemies and that big government and control of the lives of the many by a few is the cure for what ails us.

We must all recognize that they're weaponizing the crisis and that this narrative is a lie. Government bureaucrats are now labeling anyone who thinks that they've overstepped their constitutional bounds as enemies of the state—"patriot terrorists." What liberty-loving people are now combating is pure evil.

All it takes for evil to prosper is for good people to do nothing. As we reflect back on Sept. 11, 2001, one thing that stands out about that time following the terrorist attacks is that we forgot about the things that divided us. We united as Americans. There's no better example than what we saw in New York. We were united together in support of one another fighting a common enemy.

So many have sacrificed so much to secure our liberty and preserve it for future generations. Many of us have lost a loved one on a foreign battlefield or from a service-connected illness after they returned, or in the line of duty here at home.

How do we honor their sacrifice and that of so many others in our nation's 245-year history? We stand and fight to uphold liberty and our unalienable rights enshrined in America's founding documents. If liberty is to be lost, it won't be on our watch.

Free Speech Suppression Thrives Without Civics Literacy

It should be mandatory for all students to take courses relating to civic education and the U.S. Constitution. According to a recent study, only 18% of American colleges and universities require their graduates to take a foundational course in U.S. history or U.S. government.

But civic education should accompany these other mandatory courses. By the time they've graduated, all college students should have analyzed the text and history of the Constitution. They should have read the Federalist papers, Alexis de Tocqueville's "Democracy in America," and other important foundational documents: It's a matter of empowering our citizens by teaching them their rights and responsibilities.

"Knowledge will forever govern ignorance," said James Madison, "and a people who mean to be their own Governors, must arm themselves with the power which knowledge gives." We are failing to educate our students about American institutions and self-government. And this failure, if uncorrected, will lead to greater political ignorance, greater political polarization, and a greater disconnect between those with power and those without.

And as long as we fail to provide young people with a civics education, we are what we teach.

The First Amendment and Public Schools

Public schools embody a key goal of the First Amendment: to create an informed citizenry capable of self-governance and political debate. As many commentators have observed, a democracy relies on an informed and critical electorate to prosper.

On the eve of the Constitutional Convention in 1787, Benjamin Rush stated that "to conform the principles, morals, and manners of our citizens to our republican form of government, it is absolutely necessary that knowledge of every kind should be disseminated through every part of the Unites States."

Not surprisingly, universal access to free public education has long been viewed as essential to realize our democratic ideals. According to the Supreme Court in *Keyishian v. Board of Regents,* 1967:

The classroom is peculiarly the "marketplace of ideas." The Nation's future depends upon leaders trained through wide exposure to that robust exchange of ideas which discovers "truth out of a multitude of tongues, (rather) than through any kind of authoritative selection."

Schools must, of course, convey skills and information across a range of subject areas for students of different backgrounds and abilities. They must also help students learn to work independently and in groups and maintain a safe environment that promotes learning. Given the complexity of these responsibilities, school officials are generally accorded considerable deference in deciding how best to accomplish them.

Modern Supreme Court decisions have made it clear that the right to free speech and expression can sometimes be subordinated to achieve legitimate educational goals. (See discussions of *Hazelwood School District v. Kuhlmeier* and *Bethel School District v. Fraser.*)

A school is not comparable to a public park where anyone can stand on a soapbox or a bulletin board on which anyone can post a notice. While students and teachers do not "shed their constitutional rights to freedom of speech or expression at the schoolhouse gate" (*Tinker v. Des Moines*), speech is not quite as free inside educational institutions as outside.

This does not mean that students and teachers have no First Amendment rights at school. Quite the contrary. But within the educational setting, the right to free speech is implemented in ways that do not interfere with schools' educational mission. Students cannot claim, for instance, that they have the right to have incorrect answers to an algebra quiz accepted as correct, nor can teachers claim a right to teach anything they choose.

How Can I Bring the Chicago Statement to My Campus?

Any statement or policy that supports students' freedom of speech rights is welcomed. Below is an excerpt from the Chicago Statement as a reference if there is ever a question or push-back about allowing a controversial speaker on campus because someone finds some topic of inquiry distasteful.

"Because the University is committed to free and open inquiry in all matters, it guarantees all members of the University community the broadest possible latitude to speak, write, listen, challenge, and learn . . . . it is not the proper role of the University to attempt to shield individuals from ideas and opinions they find unwelcome, disagreeable, or even deeply offensive."

The "Chicago Statement" refers to the free speech policy statement produced by the Committee on Freedom of Expression at the University of Chicago. In July of 2014, University of Chicago President Robert J. Zimmer and Provost Eric D. Isaacs tasked the Committee with "articulating the University's overarching commitment to free, robust, and uninhibited debate and deliberation among all members of the University's community." The Committee, which was chaired by esteemed University of Chicago Law School professor Geoffrey Stone, released the report in January of 2015.

Here are several tips for ensuring that your university will be the next institution to stand in solidarity with the Chicago Statement's principles:

- Work to pass a student government resolution calling on the university to adopt its own version of the Chicago Statement.

- Reach out to faculty members and work with faculty governing bodies on campus.

- Build a broad coalition of students and groups, particularly across the ideological spectrum, to support the Chicago Statement and raise awareness on campus.

- Publish articles and op-eds in student newspapers and other outlets.

- Host events on campus, such as debates, speakers, and panels to discuss the principles supported by the Chicago Statement.

- Communicate and collaborate with members of your university's administration.

- Host a petition drive, asking students to pledge their support for the Chicago Statement's principles in a petition that will go to the administration.

- Work with other freedom of speech groups like the SAPIENT Being.

Campus Free Speech: A Legislative Proposal

In her 2016 convocation speech, Brown University President Christina Paxson explained that a reporter had recently asked school officials if Brown had established any "safe spaces" on campus. "What on earth are they referring to?" Paxson said. "Idea-free zones staffed by thought police, where disagreement is prohibited?"

Yes, precisely such spaces as detailed in the "Campus Free Speech: A Legislative Proposal" by Stanley Kurtz, James Manley, and Jonathan Butcher of the Goldwater Institute.

Sadly, this kind of challenge to campus free speech is now widespread. Surveys show that student support for restrictive speech codes and speaker bans is at historic heights. As both a deeply held commitment and a living tradition, freedom of speech is dying on our college campuses, and is increasingly imperiled in society at large.

Nowhere is the need for open debate more important than on America's college campuses. Students maturing from teenagers into adults must be confronted with new ideas, especially ideas with which they disagree, if they are to become informed and responsible members of a free society.

In order to protect the increasingly imperiled principle and practice of campus free speech, this brief offers model legislation designed to ensure free expression at America's public university systems. It is hoped that public debate over these legislative proposals will strengthen freedom of speech at private colleges and universities as well. The key provisions in this model legislation are inspired by three classic defenses of campus free speech: Yale's 1974 Woodward Report, The University of Chicago's 1967 Kalven Report, and the University of Chicago's 2015 Stone Report.

The model legislation presented and explained in this brief does several things:

- It creates an official university policy that strongly affirms the importance of free expression, nullifying any existing restrictive speech codes in the process.

- It prevents administrators from disinviting speakers, no matter how controversial, whom members of the campus community wish to hear from.

- It establishes a system of disciplinary sanctions for students and anyone else who interferes with the free-speech rights of others.

- It allows persons whose free-speech rights have been improperly infringed by the university to recover court costs and attorney's fees.

- It reaffirms the principle that universities, at the official institutional level, ought to remain neutral on issues of public controversy to encourage the widest possible range of opinion and dialogue within the university itself.

- It ensures that students will be informed of the official policy on free expression.

- It authorizes a special subcommittee of the university board of trustees to issue a yearly report to the public, the trustees, the governor, and the legislature on the administrative handling of free-speech issues.

Taken together, these provisions create a system of interlocking incentives designed to encourage students and administrators to respect and protect the free expression of others.

Free Speech is Under Siege on America's College Campuses

Freedom of speech, that cornerstone of our liberty and most fundamental constitutional right, is under siege on America's college campuses. Speakers who challenge campus orthodoxies are rarely sought out, are disinvited when called, and are shouted down or otherwise disrupted while on campus. Speech codes that substantially limit First Amendment rights are widespread. New devices like "trigger warnings" and "safe spaces" shelter students from the give-and-take of discussion and debate.

When protestors disrupt visiting speakers, or break in on meetings to take them over and list demands, administrators look the other way. Students have come to take it for granted they will face no discipline for such disruptions. Administrators themselves often disinvite controversial speakers and limit the exercise of liberty to narrow "free speech zones." Administrators also focus enforcement on silencing "offensive" speech and give short shrift to due process protections for students accused of saying the wrong thing to the wrong group.

University governing boards (boards of trustees) rarely act to curb these administrative abuses. Substantial sections of the faculty have abandoned the defense of free speech. The classic advocates of liberty of thought and discussion are rarely taught. Surveys show that student support for restrictive speech codes and speaker bans is at historic heights.

In short, as both a deeply held commitment and a living tradition, freedom of speech is dying on our college campuses, and is increasingly imperiled in society at large.

The Goldwater Institute has partnered with Stanley Kurtz of the Ethics and Public Policy Center to craft a model bill that will allow state legislatures to restore freedom of speech to our public university systems. As legislators introduce this bill across the country, a national debate on preserving campus free speech should influence both private colleges and the broader culture.

In 2016, the Goldwater Institute helped design a policy protecting free speech on Arizona campuses. Under HB 2615, community colleges and universities cannot create "free speech zones" that relegate free expression to narrow areas of campus. Rather, there is a presumption in favor of free speech and tailored restrictions to address legitimate time, place, and manner concerns are the exception.

The bill also "removes permissive language" in existing Arizona law that allows a "university or community college to restrict a student's speech in a public forum."

The model legislation presented in this white paper is patterned on recommendations contained in three reports widely regarded as classic statements on campus free expression: Yale's Woodward Report of 1974, the University of Chicago's Kalven Report of 1967, and the University of Chicago's Stone Report of 2015.5

Model Bill is Designed to Change the Balance of Forces

The model bill offered herein is designed to change the balance of forces contributing to the current baleful national climate for campus free speech. Administrators generally feel pressured to placate demonstrators who interfere with the free expression of others, so as to move campus controversies as quickly as possible out of the public eye.

Students who know they have little to fear in return for shouting down visiting speakers or interfering with public meetings feel free to protest in highly disruptive ways. In this atmosphere, students or faculty who disagree with current campus orthodoxies are left intimidated and uncertain of administrative support for their rights. Meanwhile, all students suffer for want of opportunities to hear the very best arguments on opposing sides of public questions.

The model legislation offered here challenges this balance of forces in several ways:

- First, it creates an official university policy that strongly affirms the importance of free expression, while formally nullifying any existing restrictive speech codes.

- Second, it establishes a system of disciplinary sanctions for students and others who interfere with the free-speech rights of others, while strongly protecting the due-process rights of those accused of such disruption.

- Third, it empowers persons whose free-speech rights have been infringed to seek legal recourse and recover court costs and attorney's fees.

- Fourth, it ensures that students will be informed of their university's commitment to free expression, and of the penalties for the violation of others' free-speech rights, during a special section of freshman orientation.

- Fifth, it authorizes a special subcommittee of the university governing board to issue a yearly report to the board itself, the public, the governor, and the legislature on the administrative handling of free-speech issues, including the application of disciplinary sanctions.

In sum, the model bill is designed to encourage public and institutional oversight of administrators' handling of free-speech issues, thus counterbalancing pressures on administrators to overlook interference with the free-speech rights of others.

Students will know from the moment they enter the university that they must respect the free expression of others, and will face significant consequences if they do not. An annual report on the administrative handling of these issues will either hold university presidents accountable, or be subject to public criticism for failing to do so. The overall effect will be to break the vicious cycle that has placed campus free speech in increasing peril.

The Model Bill Affirms Institutional Neutrality on Issues of Public Controversy

In addition to these provisions, the model bill affirms the principle of institutional neutrality on issues of public controversy. As articulated by the University of Chicago's Kalven Report of 1967, the institutional neutrality of universities on controversial public issues is the surest guarantee of intellectual freedom for individuals within the university community. When a university, as an institution, takes a strong stand on a major public debate, this inherently pressures faculty and students to toe the official university line, thereby inhibiting their freedom to speak and decide for themselves.

We see this issue at work today in the campaigns to press universities to divest their endowments of holdings in oil companies or companies based in the state of Israel. At any university, such divestment would tend to inhibit intellectual freedom. This is particularly true for state universities, which should reflect the diverse views of the entire population of the state that provides the university funding.

It's important to note, however, that the model bill's provision bearing on institutional neutrality is aspirational in character. Rather than undertaking the difficult task of identifying a clear boundary in law between issues on which there is social consensus and issues of public controversy, the bill simply affirms the basic principle of institutional neutrality and leaves its application in the hands of the university governing board.

Considered as a whole, the model bill presented in this report constitutes the most comprehensive legislative proposal ever offered to restore and protect campus free speech.

A Far Reaching Conclusion

Freedom of speech in America is facing the greatest threats since the Alien and Sedition acts of 1798, which unconstitutionally punished "false, scandalous, or malicious writing" against the United States.

Taken from Alan Dershowitz's "America's New Censors" Horizons: Journal of International Relations and Sustainable Development Summer 2021 article comes a sobering warning: Today's threats are even greater than during McCarthyism. This is true for three important reasons.

Today's censorship comes, for the most part, from so-called progressives, who are far more influential and credible than the reactionaries who promoted and implemented McCarthyism.

The current efforts to censor politically incorrect and "untruthful" views are led by young people, academics, high tech innovators, and writers—yes, writers! These self-righteous and self-appointed Solons of what is and is not permissible speech represent our future, whereas the McCarthyite censors were a throwback to the past—a last gasp of repression from a dying political order.

The new censors (Generations X Y Z) are our future leaders. They are quickly gaining influence over the social media, the newsrooms of print and TV, the academy, and other institutions that control the flow of information that impacts all aspects of American political life.

These censorial zealots will soon be the CEOs, editors-in-chief, deans, and government officials who run our nation. They are destined to have even more influence over what we can read, see, and hear.

If today's attitudes toward freedom of speech by these unsapient freedom of speech suppressors become tomorrow's rules, our nation will lose much of its freedom of thought, expression, and dissent. Those of us who cherish these freedoms must become more proactive in their defense.

23 – School Board & College Trustee Reformers Are Crucial for Education Reform

Credit: KATV.

Our Millennials and Zillennials know not the Founding Fathers, nor the Civil War and World War II, nor anything, really, about the world we live in. And that's true whether these young people come from poor or middle-class families and regardless of the types of schools or colleges they might have attended. Surveys conducted by NAEP and other testing agencies reveal an astonishing lack of historical and civic knowledge.

From the Sol Stern "Curriculum Is the Cure" *City Journal* article in December 2016:

Two-thirds of high school seniors were unable to identify the 50-year period during which the Civil War was fought; half didn't know in which half-century World War I took place. Over half couldn't name the three branches of government. A majority had no idea what the Gettysburg Address was all about. Fifty-two percent chose Germany, Japan, or Italy as "U.S. allies" in World War II. Such widespread ignorance is the result of adult malfeasance.

The next phase of education reform must include restoring knowledge to the classroom and fighting the ignorance it brings forth that also reminds us of a frightening premonition from Adolf Hitler, "Let me control the textbooks and I will control the state."

A solid body of scholarship has long been available showing that proven instructional practices were abandoned in the nation's schools beginning in the 1960s. Both sides of the school-reform debate ought to familiarize themselves with the education theories of E.D. Hirsch, Jr. Next year marks the 30th anniversary of the publication of Hirsch's seminal work, *Cultural Literacy*, which became an instant and surprise best seller.

Here's the essential discovery that Hirsch first made three decades ago, the missing link that explains why our schools spend more money than ever, yet produce increasingly worse academic results and increasingly ignorant Americans: starting in the 1960s, the nation's schools were subjected to a pedagogical upheaval fomented by self-styled "progressive" educators that succeeded in stripping away any semblance of a coherent grade-by-grade curriculum. The progressives resurrected romantic theories of child development dating back to Jean-Jacques Rousseau and then powerfully reinforced in the 1930s by the American philosopher John Dewey.

In the nation's education schools, future teachers were now instructed that children were capable of "constructing their own knowledge" and that the classroom teacher should be a "guide on the side" rather than a "sage on the stage." Most elementary schools concluded that it was more important for children to "learn how to learn" rather than to accumulate "mere facts" and useless knowledge.

New "Child-Centered" Pedagogy Turned Classroom Instruction Upside Down

In E.D. Hirsch's critique, this new "child-centered" pedagogy turned classroom instruction upside down, disrupting the transmission of civic values and traditions from one generation to the next. This was precisely a reversal of the Founding Fathers' insight that the nation's schools must follow a common curriculum in order to teach future generations the historical facts and general knowledge needed to sustain the Republic. But few teachers-in-training learn this civic wisdom. Instead, in their ed-school courses they are often urged to use the classroom to turn children into social-justice warriors.

Hirsch also showed how the new pedagogical doctrines harmed disadvantaged children and made it more difficult for schools to reduce racial-achievement gaps. The anti-equality effect of progressive education shows up in the early grades in the teaching of reading. Because of family and home influences, poor minority kids begin school lagging far behind middle-class children in vocabulary acquisition and background knowledge. The gap can be narrowed in the classroom, but only through explicit instruction, guided by a coherent, grade-by-grade, knowledge-based curriculum.

Relying on consensus findings in cognitive science and psycholinguistics, Hirsch showed that there was no such thing as "mere" facts—indeed, that factual knowledge was essential for students' ability to read and comprehend challenging texts. When, instead, progressive educators led schools into a curricular wasteland and decided that their students could create their "own knowledge," they effectively abandoned the very disadvantaged children they claimed to be championing.

Over the next several years, Hirsch published more books elaborating on the argument for explicitly teaching knowledge in the classroom. Meanwhile, progressive educators continued to dig in deeper. They also condemned the former English professor as an interloper and an elitist. Year after year, the progressives insisted that the schools didn't have to teach a "Eurocentric" curriculum, while promising that, with just enough funding for the public schools, their humane, child-friendly pedagogical methods would eventually prove effective in lifting up the children of the poor. Year after year, the results from national and international tests revealed something else.

Education researchers have concluded that the average reading score of high school seniors is among the most useful standards for evaluating a school system's effectiveness. Reading comprehension is the most accurate predictor of a high school senior's college preparedness and future economic prospects. Using this yardstick, American education has steadily stagnated since the progressives achieved hegemony in the classrooms.

Verbal Scores on the SAT Tanked in the 1960s and 1970s and Have Remained Flat Ever Since

The most recent long-term NAEP assessment of the reading proficiency of American 17-year olds revealed a steep decline, confirming the bad news from the

SAT tests. During the same period, American students' scores plummeted on various international assessments. In the 2015 Program for International Student Assessment (PISA) tests, the U.S. ranked 23rd in reading and 31st in math among the major industrial nations.

In his nineties, Hirsch has just published his fifth education book, *Why Knowledge Matters*. It offers a useful recapitulation of his critique of the failed ideas bringing down the nation's schools. Hirsch also cites new studies in cognitive science confirming that "the achievement gap is chiefly a knowledge gap and a vocabulary gap," as he puts it.

I see little chance that Hirsch's powerful new warning will provoke second thoughts among the stand-pat defenders of the public schools as they are, or the progressive education professors. After all, the progressives aren't unhappy with the qualities of mind of the young people that our knowledge-free schools are producing, including their political predilections and activism.

The Millennial and Zillennials generations now vote overwhelmingly for the progressive Left; they have been taught all their lives that personal feelings are more important than facts. They don't know anything about the history of socialism and don't recognize the names of Eugene V. Debs or Vladimir Lenin, but they believe that socialism is a good thing because it feels like a good thing, just as their favorite political candidate repeatedly told them in 2016.

The only realistic hope of restoring a knowledge curriculum in the schools rests with the reformers. I don't question the motives of the many philanthropic-minded billionaires (yes, they really are billionaires) who have spent enormous sums of money in recent years promoting charters and vouchers. The problem is that the donors have so far paid too little attention—and spent little money—promoting the teaching of knowledge in the classroom.

Since the choice movement is predominantly conservative in its political leaning, this is a classic case of shooting oneself in the foot. The success of the conservative vision for the country depends on broadly educated citizens and requires exactly what Jefferson called for—graduates of our schools "whose memories may here be stored with the most useful facts from Grecian, Roman, European, and American history." Will conservatives at long last begin working to restore a knowledge-based curriculum? We can only hope. The survival of the American republic is at stake.

E. D. Hirsch's Curriculum For Democracy

From the Sol Stern "E. D. Hirsch's Curriculum for Democracy" *City Journal* report in Autumn of 2009: Though educational progressives deride teaching facts, research shows that cultural literacy is crucial to educational success.

Hirsch was at the pinnacle of the academic world, in his mid-fifties, when he was struck by an insight into how reading is taught that, he says, "changed my life." He was "feeling guilty" about the department's inadequate freshman writing course, he recalls. Though UVA's admissions standards were as competitive as the Ivies,' the reading and writing skills of many incoming students were poor, sure to handicap them in their future academic work.

In trying to figure out how to close this "literacy gap," Hirsch conducted an experiment on reading comprehension, using two groups of college students. Members of the first group possessed broad background knowledge in subjects like history, geography, civics, the arts, and basic science; members of the second, often from disadvantaged homes, lacked such knowledge.

The knowledgeable students, it turned out, could far more easily comprehend and analyze difficult college-level texts (both fiction and nonfiction) than their poorly informed brethren could. Hirsch had discovered "a way to measure the variations in reading skill attributable to variations in the relevant background knowledge of audiences."

This finding, first published in a psychology journal, was consistent with Hirsch's past scholarship, in which he had argued that the author takes for granted that his readers have crucial background knowledge. Hirsch was also convinced that the problem of inadequate background knowledge began in the early grades.

Elementary school teachers thus had to be more explicit about imparting such knowledge to students—indeed, this was even more important than teaching the "skills" of reading and writing, Hirsch believed. Hirsch's insight contravened the conventional wisdom in the nation's education schools: that teaching facts was unimportant, and that students instead should learn "how to" skills.

Hirsch gave a lecture on the implications of his study at a Modern Language Association conference and then expanded the argument in a 1983 article, titled "Cultural Literacy," in *The American Scholar*. The article caused a stir, not so much in the academy (and certainly not in the ed schools) as among public intellectuals. William Bennett, then chair of the National Endowment for the Humanities, encouraged Hirsch to pursue his theme. Education historian Diane Ravitch urged him to get a book out fast and to call it *Cultural Literacy* as well.

Hirsch heeded the advice, and in 1987, the book landed on the New York Times's bestseller list, where it stayed for 26 weeks, resulting in a dramatic career change for the author. He kept researching and writing about how to improve the "cultural literacy" of young Americans and launched the Core Knowledge Foundation, which sought to create a knowledge-based curriculum for the nation's elementary schools.

A Content-Rich Pedagogy Makes Better Citizens and Smarter Kids

A wide range of scholars assisted him in specifying the knowledge that children in grades K–8 needed to become proficient readers. For example, the Core Knowledge curriculum specifies that in English language arts, all second-graders read poems by Robert Louis Stevenson, Emily Dickinson, and Gwendolyn Brooks, as well as stories by Rudyard Kipling, E. B. White, and Hans Christian Andersen. In history and geography, the children study the world's great rivers, ancient Rome, and the Constitution and the Declaration of Independence, among other subjects.

By the late 1980s, E.D. Hirsch had all but abandoned academic literary studies and become a full-time education reformer. His curriculum appeared at an opportune moment. Four years earlier, the U.S. government had released *A Nation at Risk*, a widely publicized report about falling SAT scores and the mediocre education that most American kids were getting. The report set off shock waves among parents, many of whom weren't thrilled, either, when they heard educators dismissing the report's implications. Parents saw Hirsch's call for a coherent grade-by-grade curriculum as an answer.

Like *A Nation at Risk*, *Cultural Literacy* came under fierce attack by education progressives, partly for its theory of reading comprehension but even more for its supposedly elitist presumption that a white male college professor should decide what American children learn. Critics derided Hirsch's lists of names, events, and dates as arbitrary, even racist.

Hirsch's next book, *The Schools We Need and Why We Don't Have Them* (1999), took the argument about core knowledge and educational equity to the next level by dismantling those faulty theories. Hirsch's early academic work on Wordsworth and the Romantics helped him in this project, since he could see how the progressives' education agenda was rooted in a deeply flawed understanding of child development that went back to Rousseau. "The Romantics were wonderful for poetry but wrong about life," Hirsch tells me, "and they were particularly wrong about education."

Romanticism's Triumph Was Complete

By the time E.D. Hirsch turned his attention to education reform in the mid-1980s, Romanticism's triumph was complete. European Romanticism, he argued in the book, "has been a post-Enlightenment aberration, a mistake we need to correct."

Influenced by the Romantics, progressive-education doctrine held that children learn best "naturally" and that we should not drill "lifeless" facts into their developing minds. Such views, which became prevalent in American teacher training by the 1920s, Hirsch shows, represented a sharp break with the Founding Fathers, who believed that children needed to learn a coherent, shared body of knowledge for the new democracy to work. Thomas Jefferson even proposed a common curriculum, so that children's "memories may here be stored with the most useful facts from Grecian, Roman, European, and American history."

Most public schools, for instance, taught reading through the "whole language" method, which encourages children to guess the meaning of words through context clues rather than to master the English phonetic code. In many schools, a teacher could no longer line up children's desks in rows facing him; indeed, he found himself banished entirely from the front of the classroom, becoming a "guide on the side" instead of a "sage on the stage."

More powerfully than any previous critic, Hirsch showed how destructive these instructional approaches were. The idea that schools could starve children of factual knowledge, yet somehow encourage them to be "critical thinkers" and teach them to "learn how to learn," defied common sense.

But Hirsch also summoned irrefutable evidence from the hard sciences to eviscerate progressive-ed doctrines. Hirsch had spent the better part of the decade since Cultural Literacy mastering the findings of neurobiology, cognitive psychology, and psycholinguistics on which teaching methods best promote student learning.

The scientific consensus showed that schools could not raise student achievement by letting students construct their own knowledge. The pedagogy that mainstream scientific research supported, Hirsch showed, was direct instruction by knowledgeable teachers who knew how to transmit their knowledge to students—the very opposite of what the progressives promoted.

The ed-school establishment has worked busily to discredit Hirsch. In 1997, the journal of the American Educational Research Association (AERA), the umbrella organization representing most education professors and researchers, launched an unprecedented 6,000-word dismissal of his work.

Hirsch shrugs off these slights and keeps working. In his nineties, he has written what may be his most important book, *The Making of Americans: Democracy and Our Schools*, which deepens his argument about the American Founders' support for core knowledge.

After Hirsch has memorialized early American education, you can almost hear his remorse as he surveys what passes for higher thinking today in the education schools and teachers' organizations. In *The Making of Americans*, Hirsch again shows how consensus science proves that "a higher-order academic skill such as reading comprehension requires prior knowledge of domain-specific content." But the ed schools' closed "thoughtworld" (Hirsch's term) has insulated itself from science.

For that matter, future classroom teachers must search far in ed-school syllabi to find a single reference to any of Hirsch's work—yet required readings by radical education thinkers such as Paulo Freire, Jonathan Kozol, and ex-Weatherman Bill Ayers are common.

From these texts, prospective teachers will learn that the purpose of schooling in America isn't to create knowledgeable, civic-minded citizens, loyal to the nation's democratic institutions, as Jefferson dreamed, but rather to undermine those institutions and turn children into champions of "social justice" as defined by today's America-hating far Left.

The Massachusetts Miracle

The "Massachusetts miracle," in which Bay State students' soaring test scores broke records, was the direct consequence of the state legislature's passage of the 1993 Education Reform Act, which established knowledge-based standards for all grades and a rigorous testing system linked to the new standards. And those standards, Massachusetts reformers have acknowledged, are E.D. Hirsch's legacy. If the Obama administration truly wants to have a positive impact on American education, it should embrace Hirsch's ideas and urge other states to do the same.

In the new millennium, Massachusetts students have surged upward on the biennial National Assessment of Educational Progress (NAEP)—"the nation's report card," as education scholars call it. On the 2005 NAEP tests, Massachusetts ranked first in the nation in fourth- and eighth-grade reading and fourth- and eighth-grade math. It then repeated the feat in 2007. No state had ever scored first in both grades and both subjects in a single year—let alone for two consecutive test cycles.

On another reliable test, the Trends in International Math and Science Study (TIMSS), the state's fourth-graders ranked second globally in science and third in math, while the eighth-graders tied for first in science and placed sixth in math. (States can volunteer, as Massachusetts did, to have their students compared with national averages.) The United States as a whole finished tenth.

It is hard to imagine in other states and school districts, that our students, in other states and thousands of school districts, particularly in grades 3–8, wouldn't have done much better if the schools had adopted the Hirsch solution of a content-rich, grade-by-grade curriculum and recognized that the way for students to achieve advanced reading comprehension is to master a broad range of background knowledge.

The most hopeful alternative to dead-end progressive education is still to be found in Charlottesville. The national headquarters of the Core Knowledge Foundation is located a block or two from the University of Virginia in a sprawling, two-story residential house with a wraparound porch. A staff of about 25 people is working on a new K–3 reading program and bringing the Core Knowledge K–8 curriculum up to date with the latest relevant subject matter. The staff also maintains contact with a network of about 1,000 Core Knowledge schools around the country (many of them charters).

Progressives Against Transparency

As per the Zaid Jilani "Progressives Against Transparency" *City Journal* article in January 2022:

In at least a dozen states, Republican lawmakers have introduced bills seeking to make instruction in public schools more transparent. Pennsylvania's bill, for example, would require public schools to post their curricula online. The ACLU joins Democratic politicians in opposition to making school curricula available to parents.

Democrats have largely opposed these bills, viewing them as the latest conservative salvo against critical race theory–inspired pedagogy. In vetoing the Pennsylvania legislation, Democratic governor Tom Wolf warned that the "legislation is a thinly veiled attempt to restrict truthful instruction and censor content reflecting various cultures, identities, and experiences."

Taken literally, Wolf's statement is false. Requiring schools to be transparent about what they're teaching does not inherently restrict instruction or censor content. But Wolf, like many progressives, is obviously concerned that if citizens knew what is being taught in schools, then they might demand a change in curriculum.

As debates over school curricula have raged for the past year, progressives have openly expressed anti-democratic views about how the education system should operate. Nikole Hannah-Jones, progenitor of the New York Times's 1619 Project, made her view clear during an NBC appearance. "I don't really understand this idea that parents should decide what's being taught," she said. "I'm not a professional educator. I don't have a degree in social studies or science. We send our children to school because we want them to be taught by people who have expertise in the subject area."

Meantime, Virginia Democratic gubernatorial candidate Terry McAuliffe arguably cost himself a second term in the governor's mansion by admitting that he didn't "think parents should be telling schools what they should teach."

Next Step for the Parents' Movement: Curriculum Transparency

Per the December 2021 James R. Copland, John Ketcham and Christopher F. Rufo "Next Step for the Parents' Movement: Curriculum Transparency" *City Journal* article:

In 2021, public school parents vaulted to the forefront of America's fractured political landscape. Around the country, parents objected both to Covid-related school closures and to racially divisive curricula. Parental frustration helped secure sweeping GOP wins in Virginia, highlighted by Glenn Youngkin's victory over former governor Terry McAuliffe. Youngkin has promised to rein in public-school radicalism and "ban critical race theory" on his first day in office.

Perhaps the central moment in the Virginia gubernatorial race was McAuliffe's comment during a debate: "I don't think parents should be telling schools what they should teach." Like most Virginia voters, we couldn't disagree more. Research shows that greater academic success follows when parents actively engage in their children's education.

To be sure, this doesn't mean that we should decide the finer points of curricular design by plebiscite; nor does it mean that a minority of objecting parents should dictate school pedagogy. But public schools are institutions created by "We the People" and should be responsive to the input of parents and the broader voting public at the state and local level.

At a minimum, parents should be able to know what's being taught to their children in the classroom. Transparency is a virtue for all of our public institutions, but especially for those with power over children. To that end, we have drafted a template—building on one of our earlier efforts at the Manhattan Institute and the work of Matt Beienburg at the Goldwater Institute—to inform state legislatures seeking to foster school transparency. The policy proposal is designed to provide public school parents with easy access—directly on school websites—to materials and activities used to train staff and teachers and to instruct children.

The last year and a half since 2020 has demonstrated the need for transparency measures. As many public schools migrated to "virtual only" learning in response to the pandemic, parents received a first-hand look at the divisive, racialist curricula being taught to their children. They learned that public schools were forcing third-graders to deconstruct their racial and sexual identities, showing kindergarteners dramatizations of dead black children and warning them about "racist police," and telling white teachers that they were guilty of "spirit murdering" minorities. These were not isolated incidents.

These revelations prompted parents to demand to know exactly what was being taught to their children. They felt that the public-school bureaucracies had been hiding controversial materials and exerting undue influence over their children, all in the service of fashionable left-wing ideologies.

Frustrated Parents Understandably Pushed Back

Frustrated parents understandably pushed back, protested at school board meetings, and, in some cases, forced the resignations of school superintendents who refused to listen to their concerns. School officials often responded to parents' concerns with resentment. Some were so agitated by the parental pushback that they sought federal intervention—including through a well-publicized (and since retracted) letter from the National School Boards Association comparing parents to "domestic terrorists."

Other school officials insisted that they, not parents and not voters, should be in charge of children's pedagogy. This is precisely backward. While government schools necessarily cannot meet every parent's demands, parents have a fundamental right, long recognized in law, to guide their children's education and moral conscience. To exercise those rights, parents need accurate information about the learning materials and activities their kids are encountering in government schools.

Our "A Model for Transparency in School Training and Curriculum" can be found in the Appendix.

It does not attempt to define specific concepts, methods, or ideologies. Nor does it seek to ban, restrict, or discourage any materials, activities, or pedagogies. Its aim is simply to provide parents with information about the curricula used in the classroom across all subjects—and to let families, teachers, and schools negotiate disagreements at the local level. If they cannot resolve their differences, parents have options: petition elected leaders or run for school board seats themselves, move to a different area, or remove their children from the public school system.

By focusing on transparency, our prescriptions sidestep arguments about "censorship" in public schools. (Realistically speaking, any school necessarily has to pick and choose what to teach among near-infinite options.

Openness will not necessarily engender trust. Parents will certainly disagree about pedagogy. There's no simple way to reconcile all competing perspectives. But the answer to these inevitable disagreements cannot be to hide from parents what's being taught to their own children. We believe that funding common schools in our democratic system requires information and engagement—and so we propose that public schools open their books and let parents see what's inside.

Bolstering the Board: Trustees Are Academia's Best Hope for Reform

Per the Jay Schalin "Bolstering the Board: Trustees Are Academia's Best Hope for Reform" The James G. Martin Center for Academic Renewal report in July 2020:

Higher education is approaching an existential crisis. It is in danger of rejecting its most fundamental value, the search for truth, and replacing it with political dogma and opportunistic careerism. Other problems abound, but none so serious as this one.

Indeed, in many departments on many campuses—even on campuses that seem well-ordered—the spirit of free inquiry is under attack. Irrational theories, such as the belief that race and gender are mere social constructs, are proliferating. Political correctness and corporate and government money are distorting scientific exploration. Many departments are dominated by adherents of fundamentally flawed philosophies, such as French post-modernism or communism.

Disturbed or hostile individuals are routinely hired, while conservative scholars "need not apply" to many departments. On occasion, even political liberals who express moderate views in public are hounded out of their jobs; one widely publicized incident occurred in 2018 at Evergreen State University when a liberal biology professor, Bret Weinstein, was forced to resign because of harassment from students after he refused to leave campus on a specified "day of absence" for white people.

Certainly, much of academia is still functioning at high levels, in technological research and STEM (science, technology, engineering, and mathematics) education, for instance. But the continued success of some programs merely provides cover for the erosion of standards and quality elsewhere in the Ivory Tower. In much of the humanities and social sciences, political dogma has already replaced objective inquiry. In some schools of education, for example, science is considered dependent upon the background of the individual instead of having universal principles for all, with indigenous myths considered equal to rigorous research methods.

It is still possible to get an excellent education at many universities, even in the humanities. But it is not likely to happen by chance; either a student must be intensely focused on a career path in the financial or empirical fields, or he or she will need considerable guidance and awareness to make it through the maze of nonsense. And the maze is getting increasingly difficult to maneuver.

How can this be happening in plain sight, without spurring a massive campaign for reform?

In a well-run higher education system based on the honest pursuit of truth, the marketplace of ideas would permit critics to attack, refute, and even satirize such ideas. The worst theories would be prevented from gaining even a tiny foothold; the rest would be condemned to some musty little corner while more reasoned ideas displaced them. But that is not the case; the free market of ideas is broken, replaced by a one-sided, dogmatic consensus.

At the heart of the problem is higher education's tradition of sharing governance functions and authority among the board, the administration, and the faculty. Few observers are willing to criticize it; it is truly a "sacred cow."

The prescriptions of experts for fixing higher education's problems call for more of the same practices that led to the crisis in the first place. That is, most of the acclaimed writers call for heightening the shared components of higher education governance, not reducing them.

But that may be the worst thing institutions can do. If higher education's governance practices are working, why then is academia increasingly struggling to protect its most important goals? To increase the shared component of governance by empowering faculty and administrators is to essentially do more of the same thing that causes the current failure to correct the problems.

For shared governance, by definition, inhibits reform

It is based on developing a consensus among widely differing constituencies, and therefore tends to clog and tangle rather than attack problems directly. If you wish to maintain the status quo, instituting a system with multiple layers and involved processes is the way to go. Of course, to maintain the status quo in academia doesn't mean that no change will occur. It means that the system will continue to move in the same direction: toward more politicization.

If, on the other hand, you wish to address problems aggressively, it is best to instill a hierarchical form of governance with a clear chain of command. And with the trustees in charge. Only boards can represent all interests. And the American system of higher education was intended to function with boards in charge.

To preserve the best of higher education, something more fundamental—a "Copernican revolution," or "Kuhnian paradigm shift," if you prefer—is needed to turn academia back toward the spirit of open inquiry. Such a paradigm shift is called for when the existing framework is no longer sufficient to explain or solve existing puzzles; a new perspective is needed with greater explanatory power.

Such a shift in higher education would require reordering power relationships, elevating the power of governing boards, the public, and the alumni while reducing the power of faculty and administrators.

To many, such a recommendation may seem drastic, even alarming

Most commentary on higher education remains within fairly narrow boundaries; much of the best-known literature tends to be written by former college administrators, who have the seeming advantage of being "inside" the system, or else written by policy professionals from professional associations that have risen to prominence within the current system.

But their insider status also tends to blind them to the overall picture. They may decry the gridlock that an outside observer will perceive to be the natural result of shared governance, but they blame it on the governing boards, whom they would prefer to keep at a distance and forego their legal and natural authority. More faculty involvement, a more powerful administration, more shared governance is their solution.

But to support the current system is to permit antagonistic forces to incrementally dislodge the best of the Western intellectual heritage from the academy. This must not be allowed to happen!

24 – Reversing America's 'D -' Grade Education System to an Ascendant 'A +' Grade

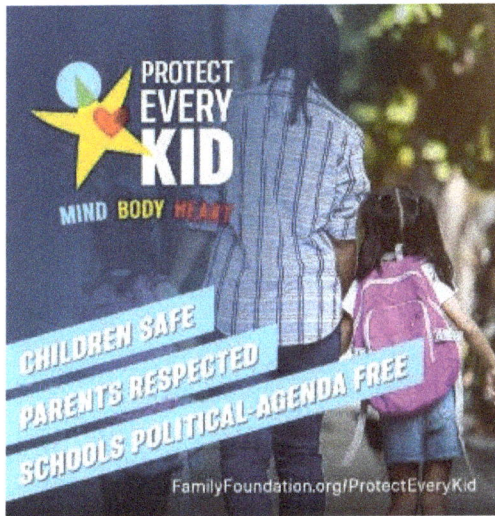

Credit: The Family Foundation – Parents' Bill of Rights.

Per the Jay Schalin "The Pushback Against Classroom Indoctrination Begins" The James G. Martin Center for Academic Renewal article in July 2022:

America is finally waking up to the fact that poisonous, divisive ideas are proliferating in public education, from pre-K to graduate school. The question is how to push back against such ideas, and recognize the damage that is being done to young minds. We must never downplay how serious this issue is as we consider another frightening quote, this one from Vladimir Lenin: "Give me four years to teach the children and the seed I have sown will never be uprooted."

Solutions are easier in K-12; primary and secondary teachers do not have the same protections of academic freedom that college faculty have, and the K-12 curriculum is more tightly controlled by state agencies. The issue is more complex in academia, where academic freedom reigns and the curriculum is controlled by a decentralized faculty.

The situation is also more dire at the college level: Higher education is where the bad ideas originate, and, for a long time, academia has seen little opposition to radicalization of public universities. While boards of trustees have the legal right to control curricula, they have almost universally relinquished that power to the faculty in practice.

In recent years, however, with the degradation of much of the academy reaching an advanced stage, state legislatures have begun to rise to the challenge and push back against radical encroachment on the public-college curriculum.

State legislatures have begun to push back against radical encroachment on the public-college curriculum.

The Pushback Against Classroom Indoctrination Begins

One such attempt is Florida's "Stop the Wrongs to Our Kids and Employees (WOKE) Act." This 2022 law statutorily prohibits discriminatory classroom teaching. It targets such divisive ideas as Critical Race Theory (CRT), which demands that members of a racial group must perpetually atone for injustices committed by members of their group centuries before, and that claims by aggrieved minorities against the offending groups should pass unchallenged.

It should be obvious that such a system of preferences and punishments along racial and ethnic lines will make a pluralistic society such as the United States unworkable without oppressive government control. Simply accepting the status quo of this biased indoctrination is no longer acceptable to the majority of Americans who, as taxpayers, provide many of the funds for public universities. Thus, the situation screams for reform.

But not everybody wants that reform, and the Stop Woke Act is a point of departure from many long-established academic practices. As can be expected, the law has received a hailstorm of criticism from faculty and civil-rights organizations that favor the status quo. A rapidly filed lawsuit intended to render the law unconstitutional was thrown out of a U.S. district court because the plaintiffs lacked the necessary "standing."

Much of the criticism depends on a fundamentally incorrect assumption about who "owns" the public universities and is therefore in charge of institutional policies such as who decides what and how to teach. Many academics and their supporters claim that higher education belongs to the faculty, deriving this notion of ownership from the formation of medieval universities in Northern Europe (especially England) as "guilds" of faculty.

Our public institutions of higher education were created by state legislatures explicitly for the benefit of the state and its residents.

But this self-interested claim—obviously advantageous to those making it—is false with respect to public universities in the U.S. Our public institutions of higher education were created by state legislatures explicitly for the benefit of the state and its residents; the residents, citizens, and taxpayers of the state are the rightful owners and express their control through their elected representatives. As such, they are the ones who should hold the ultimate power over classroom content. This fact was expressed in Florida by the legislature and governor when they enacted the Stop Woke Act.

Another wrong assumption in the critics' reasoning is the claim that academic freedom is a First Amendment issue. It is not; it is a matter of employment, not a matter of legality. Nobody's rights as a citizen or resident to express themselves are infringed by the Florida law; nobody will face criminal charges or civil fines for speaking their minds.

But even as a matter of employment, the Florida law does not silence faculty members from expressing their opinions. It is only concerned with classroom teaching, not with research or extramural comments, and these vehicles for speech are still protected by traditional academic-freedom conventions.

Even the oft-cited 1967 decision *Keyishian v. Board of Regents of the State University of New York*, from which faculty and others derive their claim that academic freedom is a First Amendment right, would not apply in this case. It concerns "membership in a subversive organization," not classroom teaching. Furthermore, even Keyishian's declaration that academic freedom "is ... a special concern of the First Amendment, which does not tolerate laws that cast a pall of orthodoxy over the classroom" does not apply here. The Florida law does not impose "orthodoxy" but attempts to remove from the classroom the imposition of orthodoxy in the form of one-sided discriminatory politics. It does so while protecting open discussion by encoding it within its text:

It is not the role of a professor to teach his or her opinion of racial preferences.

Florida Parents Take Back the Classroom

Per the Zach Weissmueller "Florida Parents Take Back the Classroom" *Reason* article in January 2022:

"It is a fundamental right of parents to direct the upbringing, education, and care of their minor children." That's the opening line of Florida's Parents' Bill of Rights, signed into law in June 2021. Similar bills have been proposed in Missouri, Kentucky, Texas, and even at the federal level.

"Our children do not belong to the government," says Patti Sullivan, state coordinator for Parental Rights Florida, which has pushed for legislation of this sort since 2013. But parental rights laws and anti–critical race theory bills can't end the curriculum wars. Only school choice can. "We do not co-parent with the government. And these entities seem to think that they are entitled to our children, and they are not," says Sullivan.

State bans on the teaching of critical race theory (CRT), which have swept the nation, are a more aggressive attempt to limit the discretion that teachers and administrators have over what's taught in school. They've been especially popular with voters.

Republican Glenn Youngkin ousted the heavily favored Terry McAuliffe in the Virginia governor's race after he campaigned against CRT in schools, and on his first day in office, he banned it from classrooms via executive order. Four other states have also banned CRT, and several more are considering similar bills.

However, opponents of CRT bans and more modest bills to force schools to post their curricula online say that "curriculum transparency bills are just thinly veiled attempts at chilling teachers and students from learning and talking about race and gender in schools," as the American Civil Liberties Union recently tweeted.

Parents have never had the "right to shape their kids' school curriculum," authors of a recent *Washington Post* op-ed argued. If that's what parents want, it says, they should opt out and "send their children to private or religious schools."

But why should families who can afford private school be the only ones who have a say in how their children are taught?

"I'm pretty skeptical of the government deciding what should be taught in any type of school," says Corey DeAngelis, national director of research for the American Federation for Children and a senior fellow at Reason Foundation (the nonprofit that publishes this website). He says public school parents should also have the right to choose the most fitting academic setting for their kids. The solution is to "fund students, not systems," giving families the choice to spend education dollars on the schooling of their choosing instead of the one-size-fits-all approach offered by traditional public schools.

"[CRT] bills are just a form of whack-a-mole, where your CRT battles of today were the common core battles of yesterday, and it'll be something else going forward because the reality is parents disagree about what kind of education they want their kids to have...And the better solution is the bottom-up accountability in allowing families to vote with their feet," says DeAngelis.

This has become such a hot-button issue because the pandemic gave parents direct exposure to exactly what their children were and weren't being taught.

"Parents are awake now that they have seen the curriculum," says Tina Descovich, a former Brevard County, Florida, school board member and co-founder of Moms for Liberty. "They now understand school district policies, which they had never looked at before. They are understanding the structure, who holds authority, and what types of authority, within the education system. I think that's vital, and it's something that's been lacking for a long time."

Florida Parents' Bill of Rights

In contrast to CRT bans, the Florida Parents' Bill of Rights broadly affirms that parents have a right to know what schools are teaching and providing to their children.

One of the most controversial aspects of the bill is how it applies to medical and mental health services. It establishes that any medical services provided without parental consent can result in misdemeanor charges.

Sullivan says some parents are particularly concerned that schools are counseling their kids on their sexuality and gender identity without parental consent. The parents of one student in a Tallahassee public school sued after the staff held a meeting without their knowledge to discuss accommodating their 13-year-old's shift to a nonbinary gender identity. They also noted in a file that the student's "privacy when [staff are] speaking to parents" must be considered.

"The law states that they must share all information with the parent," says Patty Sullivan. "I think that it's very important that we maintain the fact that these parents are entrusting their children to these [government] entities, and they are not qualified or equipped to make those decisions [regarding sexuality and gender]."

Corey DeAngelis maintains that the clash of values is best addressed through increased school choice.

"We force families into a one-size-fits-all, government-run school system, and these bills try to prohibit or encourage certain types of policies in that one-size-fits-all system," says DeAngelis. "The only way to move forward with freedom rather than force is to allow the money to follow the child to wherever they want to get an education that aligns best with their parents' values."

The pandemic-related school closures have bolstered the school choice movement, with 22 states expanding, improving, or implementing new school choice programs in 2021.

Florida is already far ahead of most states in providing parents with school choice, but DeAngelis says it should go further by offering universal vouchers and education savings accounts, which would truly empower parents and children to opt for any school of their choosing.

"What better way to assert parental rights are important than to empower them directly by allowing the money to follow their child to wherever they get an education? Funding students directly truly empowers parents when it comes to their kid's education. That is the best way to assert those rights," says DeAngelis.

DeSantis Introduces 'Stop WOKE Act' to Ban Critical Race Theory in Schools

From the Bethany Blankley "DeSantis introduces 'Stop WOKE Act' to ban critical race theory in schools" Just the News story in December 2021:

Gov. Ron DeSantis announced another bill for the legislature to consider when it convenes next year: a law banning so-called critical race theory from being taught in K-12 schools.

But the law goes beyond other similar CRT bans passed in other states in that it also protects employees from CRT training in the workplace and allows workers and parents to sue those that violate the ban.

DeSantis' "Stop WOKE Act," or "Stop Wrongs Against Our Kids and Employees Act," would statutorily ban the teaching of CRT in all K-12 schools in Florida. It would also prohibit Florida school districts, colleges and universities from hiring CRT consultants—and allow employees and parents to sue if they did.

"In Florida we are taking a stand against the state-sanctioned racism that is critical race theory," DeSantis said. "We won't allow Florida tax dollars to be spent teaching kids to hate our country or to hate each other. We also have a responsibility to ensure that parents have the means to vindicate their rights when it comes to enforcing state standards. Finally, we must protect Florida workers against the hostile work environment that is created when large corporations force their employees to endure CRT-inspired 'training' and indoctrination."

Critical Race Theory is broadly defined as a set of concepts used for "examining the relationship between race and the laws and legal institutions," according to Merriam-Webster's dictionary.

Thomas Lindsay, a distinguished senior fellow of higher education and constitutional studies at the Texas Public Policy Foundation, explains that CRT programs are "being instituted down to the third grade, where they're telling third-grade children that because of the color of their skin, they are oppressors, meaning that because of the color of their skin, they're bad."

"That used to be called racism," he said. "And unfortunately, critical race theory is the new racism."

According to the UCLA School of Public Affairs, CRT "is an outgrowth of Critical Legal Studies, which was a leftist movement that challenged traditional legal scholarship. It recognizes that racism is engrained in the fabric and system of the American society. The individual racist need not exist to note that institutional racism is pervasive in the dominant culture. This is the analytical lens that CRT uses in examining existing power structures. CRT identifies that these power structures are based on white privilege and white supremacy, which perpetuates the marginalization of people of color."

The new Florida law codifies the CRT ban issued in June by the state Board of Education. Because not all schools are necessarily following the department's ban, DeSantis implied, the legislation will give "parents a private right of action to be able to enforce the prohibition on CRT and they get to cover attorney fees when they prevail."

Parents' Guide to Children's Rights Aims to Save America's Public Schools From CRT

Per the Jack Fitzhenry The Heritage Foundation June 14, 2022 article "Parents' Guide to Children's Rights Aims to Save America's Public Schools From CRT":

The most important battleground in the fight to save our American republic is the public schools." So says Kimberly Hermann, general counsel at the Southeastern Legal Foundation, in the introduction to the foundation's guide for parents, "Your Child's Rights and What to Do About Them: A Parent's Guide to Saving America's Public Schools."

Hermann's outlook is increasingly common among anyone taking stock of the proliferation of lessons on critical race theory (a radical worldview that advocates for the primacy of racial identity) in public school curriculums. And her foundation, a national nonprofit law firm that has litigated numerous cases arising in public schools and universities, is ready to persuade anyone else who will listen.

Renewed interest in curricular content is not coming from conservative quarters alone—parents of various political stripes have been galvanized by their children's encounters with critical race theory-based lessons to oppose its dominance in classrooms. That's the audience the Southeastern Legal Foundation addresses in its guide—those who "have had enough."

Why should any parent feel they've had enough of critical race theory? To many parents, the theory's doctrines of "white supremacy" and black/brown victimhood are anathema to their civic or religious convictions on the nature of the person, his or her agency, and the sources of his or her goodness, guilt, and redemption.

To others, critical race theory is just a time- and resource-intensive distraction from their schools' persistent failure to bring students somewhere near a grade-level competence in reading and mathematics.

Fair-minded parents can and should be skeptical of the pedagogic value in a theory that dismisses "legal reasoning" and "rationalism" as mere instruments of white supremacy. After all, critical race theory-based impulses led the Smithsonian to opine that "objective, rational linear thinking" was only an "assumption of whiteness."

Yet for all the legitimate concern parents feel when they find this racialist thinking in their child's homework, there is often a gap between their desire to oppose critical race theory-based instruction and their ability to advocate effectively for that outcome. The foundation's guide is meant to bridge that gap with introductions to the core legal concepts in play when a public school introduces a critical race theory-based curriculum.

Gov. Youngkin Bans Critical Race Theory, But More Reform is Necessary

From the David Randall "Gov. Youngkin Bans Critical Race Theory, but More Reform is Necessary" National Association of Scholars article in January 2022:

The National Association of Scholars and the Civics Alliance are delighted that newly inaugurated Virginia Governor Glenn Youngkin has begun his term by declaring that he will make good on his campaign promises.

His Executive Order #1 directs the state administration to remove Critical Race Theory (CRT) from the public K-12 schools. His Executive Order #2 directs the state administration to remove the mask mandate from the public K-12 schools. We congratulate Governor Youngkin for moving so swiftly to redeem his promises—and to redeem Virginia's children from the authoritarian whims of the public school bureaucracy.

Yet the state of Virginia must do more, to institutionalize education reform in Virginia. Virginia's education bureaucracy, as education bureaucracies throughout the nation, remains deeply committed to CRT and other radical ideologies. We urge Governor Youngkin to address these priorities during his administration:

PARENTS' RIGHTS: Governor Youngkin rightly stated in his Executive Order #2 that "parents, not the government, have the fundamental right to make decisions concerning the care of their children." Virginia should pass laws that will give parents the power to enforce their rights to determine their children's education. These laws should include:

- An Academic Transparency Act, to require public schools to publicize transparently every category of document relating to schools' policies and procedures.

- A Financial Transparency Act, to require school districts to post immediately on a public website a transparent, detailed financial statement that itemizes all expenditures.

- A School Board Election Date Act, to shift school board election dates to the same day as the general election, and thereby improve education reformers' chances to win school board elections.

- A School Board Member Recall Act, to establish straightforward procedures by which to recall school board members.

Virginia's parents should not need to depend on Virginia's governor to find out what their schools are doing or to remove school board members devoted to indoctrination rather than education. These laws will give Virginia's parents real power to run their schools.

CRITICAL RACE THEORY AND ACTION CIVICS: Governor Youngkin's Executive Order #1 is good within its scope, but it should be expanded to be effective. Virginia should pass laws to remove CRT and action civics (which is used to provide vocational training in radical activism) entirely from the state's public K-12 schools. These laws should include:

- A Partisanship Out of Civics Act, to prevent teachers from giving credit to action civics or any other sort of public policy advocacy in history, government, civics, or social studies, and to bar civics classes from using the discriminatory ideology at the heart of Critical Race Theory.

- A Classroom Learning Act, to eliminate service-learning pedagogy from public K-12 schools.

- A Values Assessment Act, to prohibit public schools from assessing, rewarding, or punishing students, teachers, or administrators for their level of commitment to any value or attitude.

- A Contractor Nondiscrimination Act, to require contractors for school districts to prohibit the use of Critical Race Theory policies that require discrimination by race, sex, or other group identity.

REFORMED STATE STANDARDS: Radical education bureaucrats impose their ideology by distorting the state education standards as well as by explicit injection of CRT and action civics. Virginia should pass laws to restore proper education standards to its public K-12 schools. These laws should include:

- A Social Studies Curriculum Act, to mandate K-12 instruction in Economics, State History, United States History, Civics, and Western Civilization.

- A Civics Course Act, to mandate a year-long high school civics course, including requirements to study the primary documents of the American founding and bans on action civics and the components of Critical Race Theory.

- A United States History Act, to mandate a year-long high school United States History course, including requirements to study the primary documents of American history and bans on action civics and the components of Critical Race Theory.

- A Western Civilization Act, to mandate a year-long high school Western Civilization course, including requirements to study the primary documents of Western Civilization and bans on action civics and the components of Critical Race Theory.

- A Schools Nondiscrimination Act, to mandate that no one should be either included or excluded from our nation's content standards, curricula, trainings, textbooks, and other school materials on account of their race, sex, or other group identity.

- A Historical Documents Act, to mandate instruction in historical documents and the liberty to use historical documents.

- A Legislative Review Act, to require all existing academic standards, and all forthcoming revisions, to be submitted to the state legislature and the governor for review and possible veto.

HIGHER EDUCATION: Radical advocates have also seized control of universities, education schools, and teacher licensure. The campaign against CRT and action civics, if it is to succeed, must also include work to reform these institutions. Legislative priorities should include:

- A modified version of the Partisanship Out of Civics Act, to forbid administrative trainings and policies that inculcate CRT, but which incorporates recognition of the constitutionally established sphere of academic freedom in higher education.

- An American History Act, to add an American History and Government general education requirement to public universities.

- Dual-Course Credit. Virginia should make sure that the American History and Government course added to the public university General Education Requirements is also available as a dual credit course in public high schools. This dual credit course should possess rigorous standards, forbid action civics or activism, and have transparent syllabi.

- Reform Teaching Licensure. Education schools abuse their monopoly on teaching licensure to train teachers to teach social justice propaganda and action civics. States should establish teaching licensure pathways that allow teachers to avoid education schools and that establish a preference for subject-matter specialists over education majors. States should also require teachers in state public schools who teach English or Social Studies to pass six (6) survey courses in Western Heritage, American History, and American Government. These courses should include no action civics or activism.

We make these recommendations for a broad array of laws to institutionalize the prohibition of CRT, and to make sure it cannot return. We are aware, however, that education reformers do not yet possess a sure majority in Virginia's General Assembly. We urge Governor Youngkin and his administration to push for these laws both in hopes that they can secure immediate passage and to prepare the ground for legislation when a legislative majority can be secured.

We make these recommendations, and we make one further one of the utmost importance. Make sure the Virginia education bureaucracy enforces Executive Orders #1 and #2. Bureaucrats are past masters of the arts of noncompliance. We urge Governor Youngkin and his administration to make it a top priority that these Executive Orders actually go into effect, both in the state Education Department and in each public school district. We urge in particular that they take all necessary disciplinary measures to ensure that CRT advocates do not sabotage these reforms.

Governor Youngkin began his term very well. He will do even better by enforcing his Executive Orders. We urge him to ensure the long-term success of his agenda by passing a broad range of laws to institutionalize education reform.

The Greatest Education Battle of Our Lifetimes

Per the Stanley Kurtz "The Greatest Education Battle of Our Lifetimes" *National Review* article in March 2021:

With the 2021 introduction in Congress of the misleadingly named Civics Secures Democracy Act, we are headed toward an epic clash over the spread of extremely controversial pedagogies—Critical Race Theory and Action Civics—to America's classrooms

Because this new legislation is a backdoor effort to impose a de facto national curriculum in the politically charged subject areas of history and civics, the battle will rage in the states, at the federal level, and between the states and the federal government as well. The Biden administration's Education Department will almost certainly collaborate in this attempt to develop a set of national incentives, measures, and penalties that effectively force Critical Race Theory and Action Civics onto states and localities.

The likelihood of education controversies moving from third-tier to first-tier issues in federal elections has never been greater.

The Obama administration pushed the K–12 Common Core on states, but the founders of Common Core made a calculated decision to omit the controversial subjects of history and civics from that effort. They understood the dangers of mixing education policy with high-intensity culture war issues.

Now, however, in an attempt to complete the creation of a de facto national curriculum, the top supporters of Common Core (including, sad to say, a few conservatives) have formed an alliance with the top national advocates of Action Civics and Critical Race Theory. The result is what we see in the "Civics Secures Democracy Act"—and what we're likely to get very soon from the Biden administration—a de facto national curriculum in Action Civics and Critical Race

Theory.

And all of this is happening as woke culture is spilling out of the campuses and into the wider society. Once the reality of this new push for education "reform" comes into the open, we will see the culture war merge with the details of federal education policy in unprecedented fashion.

Critical Race Theory, of course, is antithetical to the classically liberal principles upon which our constitutional republic rests. Teaching it is actually a form of anti-civics. Yet that is what hundreds of millions of dollars disbursed by the "Civics Secures Democracy Act" is going to be used for.

The Civics Secures Democracy Act of 2021 is very much part of an effort to use NAEP to force a revisionist history and civics curriculum down the throats of unsuspecting states and localities. The bill would increase and regularize NAEP assessments in history and civics, facilitate state-by-state comparisons, and condition grants on the willingness of a state to participate in the history and civics portions of the test on a regular basis. Grant renewals would also be conditioned on statewide performance on the reorganized NAEP.

In effect, we are looking at an effort to impose a new federal Common Core in the politically explosive subject areas of history and civics. Worse, the program in each of these areas does more than just lean a bit toward the left side of the political spectrum. Instead, it sharply breaks with fundamental assumptions in American education, first by promoting illiberal Critical Race Theory, and second by turning what should be a politically neutral classroom into a training ground for leftist advocacy and lobbying.

All around us, the culture war has broken the bounds of the university and spilled into our day-to-day lives. Conservatives and traditional liberals are rightly up in arms about the woke assault on our most fundamental freedoms, extending to inculcating guilt and shame in elementary-school students for the color of their skin.

The Democrats in Congress, in league with the Biden administration and the leftist Action Civics movement, are about to supercharge this culture war by injecting it into the heart of federal education policy. Whether sooner or later, this is destined to become the greatest education battle of our lifetimes.

25 – Stopping America's Impending Destruction From Progressivism Madness

PEACEbuttons.INFO

As we've seen and discovered through the course of this book, attempting to find any semblance of sapience in today's Progressive arguments is as elusive as Big Foot, let alone facts, logic, and the truth. Furthermore, many Progressive policies are outright racist, unconstitutional, and Marxist based, at the very least. And finally, Progressives cannot admit they're wrong on so many issues, and continuously fail to produce logical arguments, provide proven results, and/or utilize unbiased data to back their ideology.

With so much going against today's Progressivism movement, the anti-Progressive long game must be focused on educational policies, legislation, and pedagogy that help wins the culture war by restoring conservative values, viewpoint diversity, and sapience to high school and college campuses—as well as enlighten their students, administrators, and faculty of the many blessings to humankind that are the direct result of Western European culture, American exceptionalism, and Judeo-Christian values.

This prudent approach, is a project of recapture and reinvention, enabling sapient beings, independents, libertarians, and conservatives the opportunity to finally to demonstrate an effective countermeasures against Progressivism's long march through the institutions. The Progressive Left's permanent bureaucracy will be dead-set against this gambit, but if it succeeds, a new era for higher education—and for the country—is possible.

This task will be monumental, yet critical, to America's survival and future, and this chapter, along with the others, provides the means and methods to enable the mission and vision of sapient beings to reverse the idiocracy and hypocrisy of the 'Regressivism' movement. Outlined in this final chapter are a number of successful strategies to help make this happen, like we showed in earlier chapters, particularly at the K12 parents and school board level and with college trustees and alumni intervention.

Woke Schooling: A Toolkit for Concerned Parents

The June 2021 Manhattan Institute report offers an excellent "Woke Schooling: A Toolkit for Concerned Parents" toolkit that provides most everything concerned parents need to know about every aspect of defeating the Progressivism agenda at their woke schools. For a link to this toolkit, please check out the Appendix.

The following advice is based on conversations with a number of activists, journalists, and others who have spent the past several years pushing back on critical pedagogy in their children's and others' schools. It is not meant to be comprehensive but rather a starting point—a way for you to begin thinking about how you can take an active hand in making your child's school a better place for him or her to learn.

What follows are a few principles to keep in mind before taking action.

Proportionality

We are all probably aware of the most controversial instances of critical pedagogy in classrooms: the Buffalo, New York, school district that told students that they must become "activists for antiracism" instead of focusing on their failing test scores, or the California model "ethnic studies" curriculum that speaks approvingly of Aztec human sacrifice, to name just two cases. That these incidents made it into the national news means that they are rarefied examples of critical pedagogy at its most expansive.

By contrast, maybe the problem you are dealing with is a single assignment that your child's teacher has handed out—something that might have been hastily scraped from a seemingly reliable website. You could respond by calling down the school board or launching a boycott—but doing so may induce the board to circle the wagons and force a conflict where a few simple words would have made the problem evaporate.

But at times, you do need to prepare for an extended fight. When resolving any problem—including the problem of dangerous falsehoods in your child's classroom—it's important to make your response proportional to the scale of the issue. Throughout the rest of this section of the guide, we'll cover solutions ranging from a polite conversation to total parent boycott. Remember: start small and think about the scale of the problem before you go nuclear.

The Minority Rule

There is rarely such a thing as a truly popular movement, and the spread of critical pedagogy is no exception. Most diversity initiatives at major schools are spearheaded by administrators, often in a specifically designated department of diversity, equlty, and inclusion (DEI); social media protests are often instigated by a small group of students or alumni, not a spontaneous and uncoordinated mass action.

The point is not about the legitimacy of these movements but about how they operate. A small group of people who demand something will generally get the compliance of the majority who are indifferent. This is what mathematician, investor, and social critic Nassim Taleb calls the "minority rule": the insight that majorities will follow minorities' preferences if the latter are intransigent and the former are "flexible."

This is a useful principle to understand not only because it allows you to focus on the minority of actors who are driving the change to which you object; it also makes you aware that you and other parents like you can together become an intransigent minority. If you're more stubborn than the most stubborn proponent of critical pedagogy in your school, you may win through intransigence alone.

Effective Persuasion

In every step of the process, it's important to keep in mind how you're communicating, which means keeping in mind with whom you're communicating.

Your fundamental goal is a change at some level, whether it be in your child's classroom or across the whole school. To attain that change, you need to convince someone—a teacher, a principal, a school board—and therefore you need to think about effective persuasion.

In general, being polite and conciliatory is the correct first move—you catch more flies with honey than with vinegar. No one thinks of himself as a bad guy, including a teacher teaching your child something you don't want your child to learn. If you go in guns blazing, you are more likely to elicit a defensive response, which will move you further away from your goal. Do not allow politeness to make you a pushover—your goal should be calm and reasonable but firm.

That said, do not discount the effectiveness of getting angry, particularly if you find that you need to escalate past a one-on-one conversation. Advocates of critical pedagogy have wrung huge changes out of administrations through pressure campaigns built on assertions of "righteous rage" and "justified anger." The squeaky wheel, as it were, gets the grease, and you should not be afraid to match your opponents' level of being demanding—after all, it has been successful for them.

Another insight that can be gleaned from paying attention to critical pedagogy advocates: a story is worth a thousand arguments. The persuasiveness of so-called critical race stories comes from their pathos—anecdotes are a powerful tool for swaying public emotion, and you should actively strive to use them. You can outline why you think critical pedagogy is bad; but actual stories of how these practices are hurting kids are far more effective in changing the minds of administrators—never mind the community at large.

Solving the Problem Yourself

As mentioned, it's important to adapt your response to the scale of the problem. Before you do anything, assess the level at which the problem is happening. Although curricular guidelines may be set at the school district or even the state level, day-to-day decisions about what your children are reading and learning are still mostly in the hands of teachers. So start by consulting with their teachers: Is their use of a critical pedagogy resource a one-off, or is it part of a deliberate learning plan? Are they incorporating a variety of perspectives, or only offering one view? You may find that a simple conversation can get you further than you would have thought.

If the original teacher is recalcitrant, it's time to move up the administrative ladder. In a public school, that might mean the head of the division, the principal, and then the district superintendent's office. Be calm and polite but persistent—administrators should see you as someone who demands to be taken seriously. In a private school, that might mean going to the head of the division, followed by the head of the school.

While you're still prosecuting your issue on an individual level, here are a few tips to keep in mind:

Document everything. Make sure to save e-mails and take notes after meetings. Consider recording conversations—but be aware that this may be interpreted as hostile before you need to become hostile. If you do record conversations, be aware of the laws surrounding recording in your state.

Consider whether you want to press for your child to be able to opt out of the objectionable lesson/content. Such opt-outs have long existed—for example, for parents concerned about the content of sex education classes. Rather than asking your teacher/administrator to change the curriculum for everyone else, consider the pros and cons of keeping it away from your own child.

Don't let yourself be bullied. A major feature of critical pedagogy is the way that it dispatches critics through personal invective and guilt by association—dissenters are tarred as "racists," "white supremacists," and the like. You should recognize that these assertions are nothing more than an attempt to intimidate you; do not let these words have power over you. If you hold firm, the most ardent critical pedagogy advocates will quickly discover that they've run out of ammo.

Getting Organized

Maybe your efforts to address the problem one-on-one have gone nowhere, or maybe the problem was too big for a one-on-one solution. Some schools have implemented large-scale critical pedagogy programs, with the full endorsement of the administration and associated staff. In situations like that, your complaint about one teacher isn't going to cut it. What you need, then, is to move from solving the problem yourself to working in concert with other parents.

In fact, operating as a lone wolf may make it easier for the administration to dismiss your concerns. Be wary of techniques designed to mollify you without addressing the problem: for example, offering you a teacher's aide position, or a favored teacher for your child next year, or bringing in the PTA to outnumber you.

Your first step is to identify other parents who are sympathetic to your concerns and skeptical of the school's new direction. This is easier said than done—in a school that has fully leaned in to critical pedagogy, those who speak out critically may find themselves ostracized. You may need to be the first person to step forward by speaking out publicly, such as at a PTA meeting or over a parent e-mail list. Alternately, if you observe others expressing discontent or being reticent, approach them.

Another approach is to give parents an anonymous forum to vent, and then form connections. At Los Angeles's Harvard-Westlake school, an Instagram page called "Woke at Harvard-Westlake" has documented critical pedagogy excesses over the past year. It includes a public-facing e-mail address and form so that parents and students can contact its anonymous administrator(s). Such an anonymous venue could highlight absurdities in your school as well as help build connections.

A key reality of establishing a group of parents is that the bigger the group becomes, the easier it gets. That's because another parent you bring in might know two more sympathetic parents. But it's also because the bigger the group becomes, the easier it is to be comfortable affiliating with it—knowing that five other people are on your side is exponentially more comforting than knowing that only one person is.

After you have more than two or three parents on your side, it may make sense to create a central venue for coordination. An e-mail list works well, as does a group chat application like WhatsApp or Discord. For those who are particularly concerned about privacy, encrypted apps like Signal or Keybase may be a better option.

Being aware of other parents' privacy concerns is paramount to organizing a successful group. Particularly in private schools, where enrollment is at the discretion of the administration, parents might fear that dissenting from pedagogical practices will hurt their kids' educational future. Giving parents a variety of options to disclose information about themselves to you might be a useful way to build their confidence and trust—ultimately producing a more cohesive group. Encourage parents to engage anonymously in a text chat, and then encourage an in-person meeting when they seem comfortable doing so.

Responding as a Group

Once you've organized even a small group of parents, you want to think about how to make your voice heard at school. Consider a similar escalation strategy to the one outlined above in "Solving the Problem Yourself"—approach a problematic teacher, and if that proves futile, work your way up. In general, at this stage, you have two goals: the ultimate goal of correcting the problematic behavior; and the instrumental goal of attracting more parents to your cause.

You should consider the medium by which you and your group of parents communicate your displeasure. Parents at the Dalton School in New York, for example, penned an anonymous letter to the administration condemning the school's turn toward critical pedagogy; parents in the Southlake, Texas, public school district pushed through an entirely new school board. But you could also consider asking for a sit-down meeting before moving to that step. Remember the principle of proportionality: only escalate if your less aggressive response is not getting the desired results.

You should consider the trade-offs of anonymity. As mentioned, some parents will be uncomfortable attaching their names to any opposition to the school's "diversity" agenda, particularly if you are in a private school where your child has no formal right to attend. At the same time, anonymity is inherently delegitimizing: the Dalton letter gives no sense of how many or which parents are opposed to your school's critical pedagogy agenda. This gives opponents an opportunity to dismiss you as a small, irrelevant group—or as not confident enough of, or committed enough to, your views to defend them publicly. Be aware that at a certain point, anonymity will no longer be tenable.

Once you have tried direct conversation and accepted the need to go public, many responses become available. You could consider organizing your group to write letters to the editor of your local newspaper (more on this in the next section), attend your local PTA or school board meeting en masse, and even organize a real-life protest, as parents did after D.C.-area magnet high school Thomas Jefferson High School dumped its race-blind admissions test.

If you are a private school parent, now may also be a time to consider talking about annual contributions to the school, one of the few points of leverage that such parents have over their schools' administrations that advocates of critical pedagogy usually do not. A group of parents can inform their school that they will not be giving annual contributions if divisive material remains in the curriculum. Doing so connects the issue to the school's bottom line and may instigate change.

To the extent possible, it pays to be aware of the diversity of the people presenting criticism of an ideology that has framed itself, however dishonestly, as promoting diversity and inclusion. To the extent that parents from different racial/socioeconomic backgrounds are genuinely represented in your group, their public expression of criticism helps make the case that the group's concerns are not rooted in racism but in a genuine concern that "antiracism" may make discrimination worse, not better.

You also should consider offering a range of ways for parents to get involved, so that even those who don't want to do too much can do something. Make it easy to write a letter to your school board or principal by offering a form outlining the specific problem, alluding to more general objections to critical pedagogy (consult the Glossary for more details), and emphasizing your investment as a parent in your child's right to an education that is free from racial and ethnic discrimination. Similarly, if you write a letter to the editor of your local paper (see the next section on working with the media), you can then ask fellow parents to sign it, which is relatively easy for them but helps make their support for your project public.

Offering a Positive Vision

Pushing back against critical pedagogy is a worthwhile and noble project, but it is also important and helpful to be positive. Some people who support (or believe they support) critical pedagogy in schools have strange beliefs about critics, thinking, for example, that skeptical parents do not want their children to ever face hard historical truths, or that they support a whitewashing of American history. That's not the case: critics of critical pedagogy are concerned that it defines America in an exclusively and simplistically negative light, not that it offers any criticisms of America at all.

One solution to emphasize—particularly in history and social studies curricula at the middle-and high-school level—is the importance of presenting a variety of perspectives on an issue and trusting students to sort out right from wrong. Parents and administrators are likely to be far more open to adding thinkers to the curriculum than subtracting them—consider floating the works of moderate (and even left-leaning) academic critics of critical pedagogy like John McWhorter,

Glenn Loury, Carol Swain, Erec Smith, Stephanie Deutsch, Peter Boghossian, and others.

A related strategy is to try to offset critical pedagogy's relentlessly negative account of ethnic relations with a more positive, affirmative story. Your student's school can use black history month to learn only about the "white supremacy" allegedly inherent in standardized tests or negative reactions to being called racist, or they can use it to celebrate great black Americans and try to respectfully build a better understanding of the many contributions of black people and black culture to America. Critical pedagogy's fixation on the negative can turn minority students into tokens of oppression—a more positive approach can help them celebrate who they are in school without dividing students into friend and foe.

Lastly, it is important to take seriously individual acts of bias and intolerance in schools. Regardless of critical pedagogy's claims, it's still the case that kids can be and often are cruel to each other—and parents should want an environment that minimizes and condemns bigoted bullying. Adopting critical pedagogy training and "antiracist statements" actually lets school administrators avoid the much harder work of treating acts of bigotry as a disciplinary problem. If you want to push back on these practices, make clear that you agree that racism should not be tolerated in your school—but critical pedagogy is the wrong way to go about reducing it.

Working With the Media

If your parent-group actions aren't working, or even if they are, you might consider bringing public attention to the problem. Even if your child's school is united behind the idea of critical pedagogy, much of the nation is not. Bringing your story into the spotlight can apply much needed pressure, highlighting unreasonable behavior in a way that can fix it.

If you've been carefully documenting your activities until this point, those details will be invaluable. Other parents should have been doing so, as well. You may want to organize those details in a common Google Doc or other online file-sharing service.

If your child is enrolled in a public school, you might want to familiarize yourself with your state's freedom of information laws. As government entities, public schools are generally subject to such laws, and administrators can be compelled to release everything from internal documents to the texts of their e-mails. For a guide to your state's public records law, consult a group such as the National Freedom of Information Coalition.

Note that compelling the release of, say, a principal's e-mails is a very aggressive action—so do so only if you're prepared to burn bridges. But if your child is a public school student, freedom of information laws exist to help hold public employees accountable, so don't be afraid to use them. For example, investigative journalist Asra Nomani (whose son attends Virginia's public Thomas Jefferson High School) used her state's freedom of information law to reveal a $20,000 contract (for a one-hour video presentation) between Virginia's Fairfax County Public School district and critical race theorist Ibram Kendi.

Whether you want to publish your personal story, the details of other parents' struggles against the administration, or something that you've uncovered through a public records request, you need to think about the platform on which you do it. Self-publishing allows you to spread your message quickly without relying on others, but it also limits your reach (unless you already have a large social media following). By contrast, working with local—or national—outlets gives you a bigger platform but also reduces your control over the story.

If you'd like to self-publish, a wide variety of platforms are now available that are easy to set up and use. Blogging services like Medium or WordPress allow you to set up a public-facing blog in minutes, while newsletter services like Substack enable you to produce similar output for a select list of subscribers. You might also consider using social media platforms like Twitter and Facebook to get the message out.

You can do only so much with such platforms, however, so you might want to approach the media. A good place to start is local media—your local paper or TV station—which are eager for local stories and, in general, less likely to be ideologically sympathetic to critical pedagogy than many large national outlets.

Before choosing to approach local media, consider whom you want to approach— a local television station, a local paper, etc. Take partisan slant into account—a right-leaning outlet will likely be more sympathetic but may give your opponents the opportunity to tar you as partisan yourself.

If you're not having success with the local media, or if you think that your message needs a broader audience, you might consider a news source with wider reach. A particularly clear-cut story of critical pedagogy–motivated wrongdoing may get traction at a national, left-leaning paper like the *New York Times* or *Washington Post*, but such outlets have evinced sympathy toward the goals of "antiracism," and thus might be less interested than you would hope.

Explicitly right-leaning outlets have the challenge of partisan tilt but are likely to be more sympathetic: consider sites like the Manhattan Institute's *City Journal*, *National Review*, the *Washington Free Beacon*, or the Daily Signal. Working with such sites will be more likely to connect you to a journalist interested in your story but may also make it harder for your story to have an impact with other parents skeptical of these outlets. Last, consider particular angles of your story: if, for example, you are dealing with critical pedagogy–inspired antisemitism, a site like Tablet, which focuses on Jewish issues, may be interested.

Before you approach anyone in the media, organize the information you want to present—a PDF of the most salacious documents you can share, a list of other parents with whom they can talk, for example. Giving a journalist something to work with makes him or her much more likely to take your story.

When talking to a reporter, be aware of journalistic norms around quoting and attribution. Unless you have explicitly stipulated that the conversation is "off the record," and your interlocutor has agreed, assume that everything that you are saying can and will appear on the front page of your local newspaper tomorrow, and conduct yourself accordingly. Be courteous and avoid personal criticisms of your opponents—your problem is with a failure of teaching, not with the people you may be butting heads with.

The trade-off of going to the media is that while your story will get a wider audience, it also becomes no longer your story to control. The journalist with whom you are working is free to quote you however he or she sees fit and is indeed professionally obligated to get the opinion of the "other side." This doesn't mean that you shouldn't approach the media, but you should be aware that your interlocutor's work product may not perfectly line up with how you imagined it.

While this guide advises speaking to the media only after you've tried internal recourse and sought to build connections to other parents, it's worth noting that a public story may have the effect of jump-starting those connections. Schools trying to push critical pedagogy over and above parents' objections have every reason to keep them in the dark and separated from each other, as many parents have experienced. A story about something crazy happening at your school can change the conversation, giving parents a concrete concern to discuss and coalesce around, and making the airing of thoughts socially permissible in a way that it previously was not.

Taking Legal Action

Critical pedagogy is not merely counterproductive and divisive, critics increasingly argue—it may also be illegal. The Fourteenth Amendment to the U.S. Constitution and the 1964 Civil Rights Act spell out certain rights to not be discriminated against on the basis of race, as well as certain guarantees of the right to free speech, even (in some cases) by students in public schools. Training and activities in public schools (and, potentially, private schools that have accepted federal funding) that divide students by race demean certain students as "oppressors" or inherently evil, or they compel students to profess certain beliefs that may run afoul of their state and federal rights.

These are the grounds for a number of lawsuits designed to fight back against critical pedagogy across the country. Although they are still in the early stages at the time of this guide's publication, they offer a promising approach for protecting students from discrimination, as well as a tool for you to consider when no other option is available.

Interested groups have, for example, sued the Santa Barbara Unified School District, the Democracy Prep Public Schools of Las Vegas, and Virginia's Thomas Jefferson High School. In these cases, plaintiffs have alleged that implicit bias training violates nondiscrimination rules, that compelled "antiracist" speech in the classroom is constitutionally impermissible, and that moves to end merit-based admissions to selective public high schools unconstitutionally discriminate against Asian-Americans.

Whether these arguments will be palatable to the courts remains to be seen. But parents should keep abreast of developments and consider whether their own situation could serve as a test case.

Whom Can I Ask for Help?

This guide is meant to be a starting point for parents looking to fight back against critical pedagogy in their school, but it's far from the only resource. Many national organizations—many brand-new—are interested in fighting various manifestations of critical pedagogy at every level of education, from kindergarten through college. They can help you connect to other parents, give you advice on organizing in your school, offer tips on talking to the media, and even help with lawsuits. Here are a few organizations:

Foundation Against Intolerance and Racism (see Appendix for link), a nonpartisan, centrist organization focused on responding to radicalism with a "compassionate anti-racism" dedicated to equal dignity and equality under the law. FAIR runs a membership organization, including local chapters, to help connect people from all parts of society skeptical of "woke" approaches that they term "neo-racism." It can also help connect parents like you to other parents and to professional and legal aid.

Parents Defending Education (see Appendix for link), a "national grassroots organization working to reclaim our schools from activists promoting harmful agendas," PDE is a school-focused group working to connect parents and provide resources to respond to critical pedagogy. It can help you find other parents in your local area and offer resources on how to respond effectively to your administration's agenda.

Foundation for Individual Rights in Education (see Appendix for link), has historically focused on repressive speech policing at the college level, however, FIRE has been expanding its work to K–12 education. Its high school network offers a free-speech curriculum, as well as resources for parents and students concerned about their voices being silenced.

Pacific Legal Foundation (see Appendix for link), a national nonprofit public-interest law firm focusing on civil rights issues. It has recently taken an interest in critical pedagogy discrimination in public schools, organizing the lawsuit against Thomas Jefferson High School. If you are considering legal action, or if you believe that you have a test case, this organization may be a useful resource.

Conclusion

It's important not to make a mistake in thinking about politics simply in terms of a Left versus Right dynamic. That dynamic is significant, but where the opportunity really lies today is focusing on a top versus bottom dynamic.

An elite class, representing a small number of people with influence in the knowledge-based institutions, are acting in their own interest and against the interest of the vast majority of the American people—those who are still attached to the idea that America is a force for good and who think, to take just one example, that young children should be protected from the imposition of radical gender ideology.

In terms of the top versus bottom dynamic, the choice today is between the American Revolution of 1776 and the leftist revolution of the 1960s. The first offers a continued unfolding of America's founding principles of freedom and equality. The second ends up in nihilism and demoralization, just as the Weather Underground ended up in a bombed-out basement in Greenwich Village in the 1970s.

Even those of us who are temperamentally predisposed to defense must recognize that offense—laying siege to the institutions—is what is now demanded. Now is the time to become involved and get to work, saving America's destiny from Progressivism madness.

Appendix

Beyond Red vs. Blue: The Political Typology – 11. Progressive Left: Pew Research Center. November 9, 2021. https://www.pewresearch.org/politics/2021/11/09/progressive-left/.

Censorship and the First Amendment in Schools – A Resource Guide: National Coalition Against Censorship. May 9, 2016. https://www.webjunction.org/documents/webjunction/Censorship_in_Schools_Learning_Speaking_and_Thinking_Freely_The_First_Amendment_in_Schools.html.

Civic Literacy Act: American Legislative Exchange Council (ALEC). www.alec.org/model-policy/the-civic-literacy-act/.

College Free Speech Rankings 2022: FIRE & RealClearEducation. https://www.thefire.org/news/just-released-2022-2023-college-free-speech-rankings.

Critical Race Theory Briefing Book: https://cplaction.com/wp-content/uploads/CRT-Briefing-Book-Rufo.pdf.

Foundation Against Intolerance and Racism: https://www.fairforall.org.

Foundation for Individual Rights and Expression (F.I.R.E.): https://www.thefire.org.

Free Speech Alliance: Media Research Center (MRC). https://www.mrc.org/freespeechalliance.

Heterodox Academy (HxA) & Programs: https://heterodoxacademy.org/. https://editor.wix.com/html/editor/web/renderer/edit/06d69a20-d6db-4ae0-a458-a22723ff3e41?metaSiteId=d68a3b84-6415-475d-818c-ab8cdd34b311

Institutional Neutrality – Blueprint for Reform: The James G. Martin Center for Academic Renewal. https://www.jamesgmartin.center/wp-content/uploads/2020/08/Blueprint-for-Reform-Institutional-Neutrality.pdf.

Is Intellectual Diversity an Endangered Species on America's College Campuses? Hearing before the Senate Health, Education, Labor & Pensions Committee: Senate Committee on Health, Education, Labor and Pensions. https://www.help.senate.gov/hearings/is-intellectual-diversity-and-endangered-species-on-americas-college-campusesd.

Journalism Code of Ethics, Practical Logic & Sapience Standards: https://www.fratirepublishing.com/books.

Model Freedom of Expression Resolution Based on University of Chicago Statement: F.I.R.E. https://www.thefire.org/research-learn/model-freedom-expression-resolution-based-university-chicago-statement.

Pacific Legal Foundation: https://www.pacificlegal.org.

Parents Defending Education: https://www.defendinged.org.

Prager U and Videos: https://www.prageru.com/.

S.A.P.I.E.N.T. Being Programs: https://www.sapientbeing.org/programs.
- Sapient Conservative Textbooks (SCT) Program.
- Free Speech Alumni Ambassador (FSAA) Program.
- Make Free Speech Again On Campus (MFSAOC) Program.

Spotlight on Speech Codes F.I.R.E. 2022: Foundation for Individual Rights and Expression (F.I.R.E.). https://www.thefire.org/resources/spotlight/reports/spotlight-on-speech-codes-2022/.

The Civics Alliance – A Toolkit: National Association of Scholars. https://www.nas.org/blogs/article/the-civics-alliance-a-toolkit.

The Critical Classroom: The Heritage Foundation. https://www.heritage.org/the-critical-classroom.

The Joy of Being Wrong (Video): John Templeton Foundation. https://youtu.be/mRXNUx4cua0.

Woke Schooling – A Toolkit for Concerned Parents: Manhattan Institute. https://www.manhattan-institute.org/woke-schooling-toolkit-for-concerned-parents.

Glossary

Academy – Is an institution of secondary education, higher learning, research, or honorary membership. Academia is the worldwide group composed of professors and researchers at institutes of higher learning.

Affinity Group – Is meant to be safe spaces for educators or students who share an identity, such as a common race or heritage, to discuss mutual concerns.

Antiracism – An illiberal term by Ibram X Kendi who argues unsapiently that the opposite of racist is anti-racist rather than simply non-racist, and that there is no middle ground in the struggle against racism; one is either actively confronting racial inequality or allowing it to exist through action or inaction.

Bourgeoisie – Are the people who control the means of production in a capitalist society; the proletariat are the members of the working class.

Cancel Culture – An intolerance of opposing views, a vogue for public shaming and ostracism, and the tendency to dissolve complex policy issues in a blinding moral certainty.

Capitalism – An economic system characterized by private or corporate ownership of capital goods, by investments that are determined by private decision, and by prices, production, and the distribution of goods that are determined mainly by competition in a free market

Chicago Statement – Refers to the free speech policy statement produced by the Committee on Freedom of Expression at the University of Chicago in 2014, with "articulating the University's overarching commitment to free, robust, and uninhibited debate and deliberation among all members of the University's community."

Civic Literacy – The knowledge and skills to participate effectively in civic life through knowing how to stay informed, understanding governmental processes, and knowing how to exercise the rights and obligations of citizenship at local, state, national, and global levels.

Civil Discourse – Requires respect of the other participants, such as the reader. It neither diminishes the other's moral worth, nor questions their good judgment; it avoids hostility, direct antagonism, or excessive persuasion; it requires modesty and an appreciation for the other participant's experiences.

Civil Rights Act of 1964 – Outlawed discrimination on the basis of race, color, religion, sex, or national origin, required equal access to public places and employment, and enforced desegregation of schools and the right to vote.

Colorblindness – Is a term that has been used by justices of the United States Supreme Court in several opinions relating to racial equality and social equity, particularly in public education.

Communism – A theory advocating elimination of private property and a system in which goods are owned in common and are available to all as needed

Confirmation Bias – Happens when a person gives more weight to evidence that confirms their beliefs and undervalues evidence that could disprove it.

Constructive Disagreement – Occurs when people who don't see eye-to-eye are committed to exploring an issue together, alive to their own fallibility and the limits of their knowledge—and open to learning something from others who see things differently than they do.

Critical Legal Theory (CLT) – A Progressive movement that challenges and seeks to overturn accepted norms and standards in legal theory and practice.

Critical Pedagogy – Is a teaching approach inspired by critical theory and other radical philosophies, which attempts to help students question and challenge posited "domination," and to undermine the beliefs and practices that are alleged to dominate.

Critical Race Theory (CRT) – Programs, based on a neo-Marxist ideology that originated in law schools a generation ago, purport to expose and correct "unconscious racial bias" and "white privilege" among their employees. Critical race theory treats "whiteness" as a moral blight and maligns all members of that racial group as complicit in oppression.

Critical Theory (CT) – A Marxist-inspired movement in social and political philosophy originally associated with the work of the Frankfurt School.

Cultural Relativism – Cultural relativism is the idea that a person's beliefs, values, and practices should be understood based on that person's own culture, rather than be judged against the criteria of another.

Deconstruction – Doesn't actually mean "demolition;" instead it means "breaking down" or analyzing something (especially the words in a work of fiction or nonfiction) to discover its true significance, which is supposedly almost never exactly what the author subconsciously intended.

DEI – Diversity, equity, and inclusion; a conceptual framework that promotes the fair treatment and full participation of all people, especially in the workplace, including populations who have historically been underrepresented or subject to discrimination because of their background, identity, disability, etc. However, 21st century Progressive regressive DEI programs have returned us to the days of Jim Crow, with some races seen as virtuous and others as evil, the only difference being the colors have changed.

Democracy – A government by the people; especially : rule of the majority b : a government in which the supreme power is vested in the people and exercised by them directly or indirectly through a system of representation usually involving periodically held free elections; a political unit that has a democratic government.

Disparate impact – Also called adverse impact, occurs when a decision, practice or policy has a disproportionately negative effect on a protected group, even though the impact may be unintentional.

Diversity – In today's Progressive regressive ideology, "diversity" is defined not by opinion, such as viewpoint diversity and heterodox thinking, but instead by race, ethnicity, or gender identity.

Dystopia – An imagined state or society in which there is great suffering or injustice, typically one that is totalitarian or post-apocalyptic.

Equality of Outcomes – It means that given the same opportunity and privileges two people should end up in the same position or at least equal position. But equality of "opportunity" does not promise equality in the "outcome." People have different levels of skill and put different amounts of effort into whatever they do. Only a totalitarian state can enforce equal outcomes, creating a state of dystopia.

Equity – In today's Progressive regressive ideology, "equity" is no longer the laudable goal of equality of opportunity, but the insistence on equality of outcome, meaning the statistical equivalence of races and genders. This in practice means more of the preferred and fewer of the despised (i.e., institutionalized racism and discrimination), a desirable goal by Progressives, as long as their preferred categories benefit.

First Amendment – States that "Congress shall make no law respecting an establishment of religion, or prohibiting the free exercise thereof; or abridging the freedom of speech, or of the press; or the right of the people peaceably to assemble, and to petition the government for a redress of grievances" and applies to every American citizen.

Frankfurt School – The Frankfurt School's biggest intellectual creation was Critical Theory, an approach to cultural analysis that focuses on criticizing existing social structures. It's founding members included Max Horkheimer, Theodor Adorno, Erich Fromm, Walter Benjamin, Jürgen Habermas, and Herbert Marcuse.

Groupthink – A phenomenon that occurs when a group of individuals reaches a consensus without critical reasoning or evaluation of the consequences or alternatives. Groupthink is based on a common desire not to upset the balance of a group of people.

Heckler's Veto – In American free speech, a heckler's veto is a situation in which a party who disagrees with a speaker's message is able to unilaterally trigger events that result in the speaker being silenced.

Hypersensitivity – Symptoms of hypersensitivity include being highly sensitive to physical (via sound, sigh, touch, or smell) and or emotional stimuli and the tendency to be easily overwhelmed by too much information.

Hypocrisy – Is the practice of engaging in the same behavior or activity for which one criticizes another or the practice of claiming to have moral standards or beliefs to which one's own behavior does not conform.

Identity Politics – Is a political approach wherein people of a particular gender, religion, race, social background, social class or other identifying factors, develop political agendas that are based upon these identities.

Idiocracy – An idiocracy is a disparaging term for a society run by or made up of idiots (or people perceived as such). Idiocracy is also the title of a 2006 satirical film that depicts a future in which humanity has become dumb.

Illiberalism – The 21st century term is used to describe an attitude that is close-minded, intolerant, bigoted and is a key attribute of the 21st century Progressivism movement.

Implicit Bias Training – Are programs purport to expose people to their implicit biases, provide tools to adjust automatic patterns of thinking, and ultimately eliminate discriminatory behaviors.

Inclusion – In today's Progressive regressive ideology, "inclusion" means including preferred races and genders, and excluding others, as we see in hiring, college admissions, funding, promotions, and awards.

Intellectual Humility – A mindset that encompasses empathy, trust, and curiosity, viewpoint diversity gives rise to engaged and civil debate, constructive disagreement, and shared progress towards truth.

Intersectionality – A term that refers to the "multiple social forces, social identities, and ideological instruments through which power and disadvantage are expressed and legitimized."

Jim Crow – Racial segregation laws up to 1965, that were enacted and enforced in the South in the late 19th and early 20th centuries by white Southern Democrat-dominated state legislatures to disenfranchise and remove political and economic gains made by blacks during the Reconstruction period.

Liberating Tolerance – Herbert Marcuse propounded this Orwellian and illiberal oxymoron in the 1960s that would involve "the withdrawal of toleration of speech and assembly from groups and movements" on the Right, as opposed to the aggressive partisan promotion of speech, groups, and Progressive movements on the Left.

Libertarian – An advocate of the doctrine of free will; a person who upholds the principles of individual liberty especially of thought and action; a member of a political party advocating libertarian principles.

Marcuse, Herbert – A German-American philosopher, sociologist, and political theorist, associated with the Frankfurt School of Critical Theory. Author of the *One-Dimensional Man: Studies in the Ideology of Advanced Industrial Society*, a 1964 best seller primarily known by the "power of negative thinking" became the standard for revolutionary speech in the movement he called the "Great Refusal." Marcuse distinguished between repressive tolerance, a form of tolerance that favors the already powerful and suppresses the less powerful, and a liberating tolerance, a form of tolerance that discriminates in favor of the weak and restrains the strong.

Marxism – The political, economic, and social principles and policies advocated by Marx and a theory and practice of socialism including the labor theory of value, dialectical materialism, the class struggle, and dictatorship of the proletariat until the establishment of a classless society.

Meliorism – Is the doctrine that the federal government should intervene in the market economy to improve the economic condition of citizens

Meritocracy – Is the only way a free people can create an efficient, prosperous, opportunity society. Without it, nobody has any incentive to innovate or work hard. The capable and hard-working become cynical and resentful, while the incompetent and the indolent know they don't have to step up, because they can live for free. This is the inherent flaw of Marxism, Communism, and Socialism.

Microaggression – It has entered the national conversation to mean brief, subtle verbal or nonverbal exchanges—often unintended—that send denigrating messages because of the recipient's group membership.

Multiculturalism – The view that cultures, races, and ethnicities, particularly those of minority groups, deserve special acknowledgement of their differences within a dominant political culture.

Nietzschean – A will to power with overflowing strength, both of mind and body, who must discharge this strength or perish, is the Nietzschean ideal.

Nihilism – Is a philosophy, or family of views within philosophy, that rejects generally accepted or fundamental aspects of human existence, such as objective truth, knowledge, morality, values, or meaning.

Open Inquiry – Is the ability to ask questions and share ideas without risk of censure.

Political Correctness – A term used to describe language, policies, or measures that are intended to avoid offense or disadvantage to members of particular groups in society.

Postmodernism – Is an intellectual stance or a mode of discourse that rejects the possibility of reliable knowledge, denies the existence of a universal, stable reality, and frames aesthetics and beauty as arbitrary and subjective.

Proletariat – Are the members of the working class in a capitalist society; and the bourgeoisie the people who control the means of production.

Progressivism – A political philosophy, in prior 19th and 20th centuries' periods, in support of social reform based on the idea of progress in which advancements in science, technology, economic development, and social organization are vital to improve the human condition. However, today's 21st century Progressivism has now devolved into a neo-Marxist and racist ideology founded on illiberal DEI principles.

Republic – A government having a chief of state who is not a monarch and who in modern times is usually a president; a political unit (as a nation) having such a form of government; a government in which supreme power resides in a body of citizens entitled to vote and is exercised by elected officers and representatives responsible to them and governing according to law.

Sapience – Also known as wisdom, is the ability to think and act using knowledge, experience, understanding, common sense and insight. Sapience is associated with attributes such as intelligence, enlightenment, unbiased judgment, compassion, experiential self-knowledge, self-actualization, and virtues such as ethics, benevolence, and critical thinking.

Scientific Method – A way of investigating a phenomenon that's based on the collective analysis and into interpretation of evidence to determine the most probable explanation. The five basic steps in scientific method: 1) statement of the problem, twenty collection of facts, 3) formulating a hypothesis, 4) making further inferences, and 5) verifying the inferences.

Social Justice – A political and philosophical theory which asserts that there are dimensions to the concept of justice beyond those embodied in the principles of civil or criminal law, economic supply and demand, or traditional moral frameworks.

Socialism – Any various economic and political theories advocating collective or governmental ownership and administration of the means of production and distribution of goods. A system of society or group living in which there is no private property. A system or condition of society in which the means of production are owned and controlled by the state. A stage of society in Marxist theory transitional between capitalism and communism and distinguished by unequal distribution of goods and pay according to work done.

Telos – Its purpose, end, or goal.

Tyranny of Feelings – A recurring problem in contemporary discourse is the tyranny of emotion over reason as a guide to behavior. Its simplest, crudest form is the insistence in certain dialogues that if one feels offended, then that emotion should be honored and not questioned.

Viewpoint Diversity – Viewpoint diversity occurs when members of a group or community approach problems or questions from a range of perspectives.

Virtue Signaling – Is the conspicuous communication of amoral values and good deeds. The term has negative connotations as it is commonly used to denote virtuous actions and statements are motivated by a desire for rank and satisfaction.

White Privilege – The set of social and economic advantages that white people have by virtue of their race in a culture characterized by racial inequality.

White Supremacy – The term "white supremacy" can be confusing because it can mean an actual belief in the superiority of white people, in which case it is despicable. However, it is nearly always employed to mean something much larger—anything from classical philosophers to Enlightenment thinkers to the Industrial Revolution.

Woke – Or wokeism, is a left-wing racialist ideology of attempting to achieve "critical consciousness," which is a neo-Marxist term, meaning awakening the subject to their own oppression, then recruiting them into left-wing revolution. In reality, per Progressive regressive ideology, if we use "woke" as a stand-in for an illiberal concept such as critical race theory, it literally means subverting the United States into an oppressor nation that divides classes along the lines of race and then endorses active discrimination in order to create racial equity or equality of group outcomes. Being woke is the opposite to being sapient.

References

Abrams, Samuel J. "Think Professors Are Liberal? Try School Administrators." *New York Times*. Oct. 16, 2018.

Allen, Scott. "Toxic New Religions at The Cultural Roots of Campus Rage**.**" 12 post series in 2017. www.darrowmillerandfriends.com.

Berger, Raymond M. "Marxism and Progressivism: A Play in Two Acts." *The Times of Israel*. June 2, 2018. https://blogs.timesofisrael.com/marxism-and-progressivism-a-play-in-two-acts/.

Berger, Judson. "What Happens When Free Speech Dies." *National Review*. October 29, 2021. https://www.nationalreview.com/the-weekend-jolt/what-happens-when-free-speech-dies/.

Blankley, Bethany. "DeSantis introduces 'Stop WOKE Act' to ban critical race theory in schools." Just the News. December 16, 2021. https://justthenews.com/nation/states/desantis-introduces-stop-woke-act-ban-critical-race-theory-schools?utm_source=ground.news&utm_medium=referral.

Buck, Daniel and Garion Frankel. "How Public Schools Went Woke—and What to Do About It." *National Review*. March 5, 2022. https://www.nationalreview.com/2022/03/how-public-schools-went-woke-and-what-to-do-about-it/.

Cass, Oren. "What Are Public Schools For?" *City Journal*. December 14, 2021. https://www.city-journal.org/parents-and-educators-disagree-on-purpose-of-public-schools.

Connor, Bill. "The increasing intolerance of the left must stop." *Charleston Mercury*. March 25, 2023. https://www.charlestonmercury.com/single-post/the-increasing-intolerance-of-the-left-must-stop.

Copland, James R., John Ketcham and Christopher F. Rufo. "Next Step for the Parents' Movement: Curriculum Transparency." *City Journal*. December 1, 2021. https://www.city-journal.org/how-to-achieve-transparency-in-schools.

Dallmeyer, Mckenna. "Diversity Statements Can Determine Who Gets Hired at Universities." Campus Reform. April 25, 2022. https://www.campusreform.org/article?id=19424.

Dershowitz, Alan. "America's New Censors." Horizons: Journal of International Relations and Sustainable Development. No. 19 (2021): 202–21. https://www.cirsd.org/en/horizons/horizons-summer-2021-issue-no-19/americas-new-censors.

Dershowitz, Alan. *Cancel Culture: The Latest Attack on Free Speech and Due Process*. Hot Books: New York. 2020.

Egalite, Anna J. "How Family Background Influences Student Achievement." Education Next. Vol. 16, No. 2. https://www.educationnext.org/how-family-background-influences-student-achievement/.

Ellwanger, Adam. "The Art of Teaching and the End of Wokeness.*" National Association of Scholars*. Winter 2021. https://www.nas.org/academic-questions/34/4/the-art-of-teaching-and-the-end-of-wokeness.

Fillat, Andrew I. and Henry I. Miller. "Diversity Smokescreen." *City Journal*. March 21, 2022. https://www.city-journal.org/diversity-is-a-smokescreen-in-college-admissions.

Finn Jr., Chester E. "A Nation Still at Risk." *Hoover Digest*. Winter 2022 No. 1. https://www.hoover.org/research/nation-still-risk-1.

Fitzhenry, Jack. "Parents' Guide to Children's Rights Aims to Save America's Public Schools From CRT." The Heritage Foundation. June 14, 2022. https://www.heritage.org/education/commentary/parents-guide-childrens-rights-aims-save-americas-public-schools-crt.

Goldberg, Zach and Eric Kaufmann. "Yes, Critical Race Theory Is Being Taught in Schools." *City Journal*. October 20, 2022. https://www.city-journal.org/yes-critical-race-theory-is-being-taught-in-schools.

Greene, Jay and Frederick M. Hess. "It's Time to Roll Back Campus DEI Bureaucracies." *National Review*. September 18, 2022. https://www.nationalreview.com/2022/09/its-time-to-roll-back-campus-dei-bureaucracies/.

Groothuis, Douglas. "Critical Race Theory in Six Logical Fallacies." National Association of Scholars. Summer 2022. https://www.nas.org/academic-questions/35/2/critical-race-theory-in-six-logical-fallacies.

Haidt, Jonathan and Greg Lukianoff. "How To Keep Your Corporation Out of the Culture War." Persuasion. Dec. 3, 2020. https://www.persuasion.community/p/haidt-and-lukianoff-how-to-end-corporate.

Haidt, Jonathan and Greg Lukianoff. *The Coddling of the American Mind: How Good Intentions and Bad Ideas Are Setting Up a Generation for Failure*. Penguin Random House: New York. 2018.

Haidt, Jonathan and Greg Lukianoff. *The Righteous Mind: Why Good People Are Divided by Politics and Religion*. Vintage Books: New York, 2012.

Haidt, Jonathan and Greg Lukianoff. *The Coddling of the American Mind: How Good Intentions and Bad Ideas Are Setting Up a Generation for Failure*. Penguin Random House. New York, 2018.

Haidt, Jonathan. "Why Universities Must Choose One Telos: Truth or Social Justice." Heterodox Academy. October 21, 2017. https://heterodoxacademy.org/blog/one-telos-truth-or-social-justice-2/.

Hanson, Victor Davis. "Universities Breed Anger, Ignorance, and Ingratitude." *National Review*. October 22, 2019. https://www.nationalreview.com/2019/10/universities-breed-anger-ignorance-ingratitude/.

Holmes, Kim R. "Intolerance as Illiberalism." The Heritage Foundation. July 16, 2014. https://www.heritage.org/political-process/commentary/intolerance-illiberalism.

Holmes, Kim R. *Rebound: Getting America Back to Great*. Rowman & Littlefield Publishers: Lanham. 2013.

Honeycutt, Nathan. "Political Intolerance Among University Faculty Highlights Need For Viewpoint Diversity." Forbes. https://www.forbes.com/sites/realspin/2016/11/21/political-intolerance-among-university-faculty-highlights-need-for-viewpoint-diversity/?sh=578e68a214b5.

Humphrey Clifford. "The Myth of Change as Progress in Progressivism." *Epoch Times*. February 20, 2019. https://www.theepochtimes.com/the-myth-of-change-as-progress-in-progressivism_2800152.html?utm_source=ai&utm_medium=search.

Jilani, Zaid. "Progressives Against Transparency." *City Journal*. January 26, 2022. https://www.city-journal.org/progressives-against-school-transparency.

Kaufmann, Eric. "Academic Freedom and Cancel Culture." City Journal. November 10, 2020. https://clips.cato.org/sites/default/files/Ekins_CJ_cancelculture.pdf.

Kelly-Woessner, April. "How Marcuse made today's students less tolerant than their parents." Heterodox Academy. Sep. 23, 2015.

Kurtz, Stanley, James Manley, and Jonathan Butcher. "Campus Free Speech: A Legislative Proposal." Goldwater Institute. https://goldwaterinstitute.org/wp-content/uploads/cms_page_media/2017/2/2/X_Campus%20Free%20Speech%20Paper.pdf.

Kurtz, Stanley. "The Greatest Education Battle of Our Lifetimes." *National Review*. March 15, 2021. https://www.nationalreview.com/corner/the-greatest-education-battle-of-our-lifetimes/?utm_source=recirc-desktop&utm_medium=homepage&utm_campaign=right-rail&utm_content=corner&utm_term=second.

Leef, George. "An Alternative to the 'Diversity, Equity, and Inclusion' Deception." National Review. November 8, 2022. https://www.nationalreview.com/corner/an-alternative-to-the-diversity-equity-and-inclusion-deception/.

Leroux, Robert. "Woke Madness and the University." National Association of Scholars. Winter 2021. https://www.NAS.org/academic-questions/34/4/woke-madness-and-the-university.

Lindsay, Tom. "New Report: Most College Students Agree that Campus Free Speech is Waning." Forbes. May 31, 2019. https://www.forbes.com/sites/tomlindsay/2019/05/31/new-report-most-college-students-agree-that-campus-free-speech-is-waning/.

Mac Donald, Heather. "Back to Discipline." *City Journal*. December 19, 2018. https://www.city-journal.org/disparate-impact-analysis.

Mac Donald, Heather. "Conformity to a Lie." *City Journal*. Summer 2020. https://www.city-journal.org/academia-systemic-racism.

Mac Donald, Heather. "The Cost of America's Cultural Revolution." *City Journal*. December 11, 2019. https://www.realclearpolicy.com/2019/12/11/the_cost_of_america039s_cultural_revolution_43606.html.

Mahoney, Emily L. "Ron DeSantis seeks free speech resolution allowing controversial speakers at Florida universities." Tampa Bay Times. April 15, 2019. https://www.tampabay.com/florida-politics/2019/04/15/ron-desantis-seeks-free-speech-policy-allowing-controversial-speakers-at-florida-universities/.

McWhorter, John. "Taking on the Woke Movement." *Newsmax*. November 12, 2021. https://www.newsmax.com/george-j-marlin/wokism-john-mcwhorter-antiwoke/2021/11/12/id/1044432/.

Mukherjee, Renu. "Without a 'Diversity' Leg to Stand On." *City Journal*. October 12, 2022. https://www.city-journal.org/affirmative-action-and-viewpoint-diversity-at-harvard.

Murphy, Rex. "How the 'Cancel Culture' Mob's Attempt to Silence Jordan Peterson Backfired." *Epoch Times*. December 14, 2021. https://www.theepochtimes.com/rex-murphy-how-the-cancel-culture-mobs-attempt-to-silence-jordan-peterson-backfired_4153530.html?utm_source=ai_recommender&utm_medium=a_bottom_above_etv.

Peterson, Jordan. "Who Is Teaching Your Kids?" Prager U Video. https://www.prageru.com/video/who-is-teaching-your-kids?gclid=CjwKCAiAqaWdBhAvEiwAGAQltp9fPSnUTfV7LNKBQnJBtl0vroG3F_pOIqW_YaZkaAXUYHd-t58OvBoCXLkQAvD_BwE.

Piereson, James and Naomi Schaefer Riley. "Less Than Meets the Eye." *City Journal*. May 4, 2021. https://www.city-journal.org/scoreless-admissions-set-minority-students-up-for-failure.

Price, Harley. "From Mao to Now: A 'Progress' Report on the New Millennium." *Epoch Times*. December 29, 2020. https://www.theepochtimes.com/from-mao-to-now-a-progress-report-on-the-new-millennium_3634981.html?utm_source=ai&utm_medium=search.

Pulliam, Mark. "The Campus Diversity Swarm." *City Journal*. October 10, 2018. https://www.city-journal.org/campus-diversity-bureaucracies-16223.html.

Randall, David. "Gov. Youngkin Bans Critical Race Theory, but More Reform is Necessary." National Association of Scholars. January 18, 2022. https://www.nas.org/blogs/article/gov-youngkin-bans-critical-race-theory-but-more-reform-is-necessary.

Randall, David. "Kick the '1619 Project' Out of Schools." National Association of Scholars. August 10, 2020. https://www.nas.org/blogs/article/kick-the-1619-project-out-of-schools.

Randall, David. "Social Justice Education in America." National Association of Scholars. November 29, 2019. https://www.nas.org/reports/social-justice-education-in-america/full-report.

Reilly, Wilfred. "What Is Critical Race Theory, Really?" *City Journal*. October 13, 2021. https://www.city-journal.org/what-is-critical-race-theory-really.

Reilly, Wilfred. "What's Wrong With the 1619 Project?" Prager U Video. https://assets.ctfassets.net/qnesrjodfi80/6pHowieMH6mlh35Bs5SqVX/f65d59b627651783162f5edcfe42ce0b/Reilly-Whats_Wrong_With_the_1619_Project-Transcript.pdf.

Rufo, Christopher F. "Banging Beyond Binaries." *City Journal*. May 17, 2022. https://www.city-journal.org/philadelphia-schools-tout-radical-transgender-conference.

Rufo, Christopher F. "Biden Criminalizes CRT Dissent." *City Journal*. October 6, 2021. https://www.city-journal.org/biden-criminalizes-critical-race-theory-dissent.

Rufo, Christopher F. "Disingenuous Defenses of Critical Race Theory." *New York Post*. July 9, 2021. https://nypost.com/2021/07/09/disingenuous-defenses-of-critical-race-theory/.

Rufo, Christopher F. "Radical Gender Lessons for Young Children." *City Journal*. April 21, 2022. https://www.city-journal.org/radical-gender-lessons-for-young-children.

Rufo, Christopher F. "Sexual Liberation in Public Schools." *City Journal*. July 20, 2022. https://www.city-journal.org/sexual-liberation-in-public-schools.

Rufo, Christopher F. "DEI Cult." *City Journal*. February 9, 2023. https://www.city-journal.org/the-university-of-south-floridas-diversity-cult.

Rufo, Christopher F. "Laying Siege to the Institutions." *Imprimis*. April/May 2022 Volume 51, Issue 4/5. https://imprimis.hillsdale.edu/laying-siege-to-the-institutions/.

Rufo, Christopher F. "Racism in the Name of 'Anti-Racism.'" Substack Email. Feb. 17, 2023. https://rufo.substack.com/p/racism-in-the-name-of-anti-racism?utm_source=post-email-title&publication_id=1248321&post_id=103110646&isFreemail=true&utm_medium=email.

Rufo, Christopher F. "Subversive Education." *City Journal*. March 17, 2021. https://www.city-journal.org/critical-race-theory-in-wake-county-nc-schools.

Rufo, Christopher F. "Teaching Hate." *City Journal*. December 18, 2020. https://www.city-journal.org/racial-equity-programs-seattle-schools.

Rufo, Christopher F. "The Courage of Our Convictions." *City Journal*. April 22, 2021. https://www.city-journal.org/how-to-fight-critical-race-theory.

Rufo, Christopher F. "The Highest Principle." *City Journal*. February 2, 2023. https://www.city-journal.org/florida-state-university-adopts-dei-programming.

Sabo, Mike. "The 1776 Commission Report Reinvigorates the American Mind." National Association of Scholars. January 22, 2021. https://www.nas.org/blogs/article/the-1776-commission-report-reinvigorates-the-american-mind.

Sailer, John D. and Ray M. Sanchez. "An Overt Political Litmus Test." *City Journal*. May 16, 2022. https://www.city-journal.org/california-community-colleges-impose-political-litmus-test.

Salzman, Philip Carl. "Hate and Fear Are Now Major Motivators on Campus." *Epoch Times.* October 11, 2022. https://www.theepochtimes.com/hate-and-fear-are-now-major-motivators-on-campus_4785439.html?utm_medium=search&utm_source=ai.

Salzman, Philip Carl. "How Progressives Are Retrogressive." *Epoch Times.* January 6, 2022. https://www.theepochtimes.com/how-progressives-are-retrogressive_4193422.html?utm_source=ai&utm_medium=search.

Salzman, Philip Carl. "National Suicide by Education." Minding the Campus. September 23, 2022. https://www.mindingthecampus.org/2022/09/23/national-suicide-by-education/.

Salzman, Philip Carl. "Safeguarding Our Republic From Progressivism Madness." *Epoch Times*. October 11, 2022. https://www.theepochtimes.com/hate-and-fear-are-now-major-motivators-on-campus_4785439.html?utm_medium=search&utm_source=ai.

Sanzi, Erika. "The Monster Is in the Classroom." *City Journal*. April 30, 2021. https://www.city-journal.org/elementary-schools-go-woke.

Schalin, Jay. "Bolstering the Board: Trustees Are Academia's Best Hope for Reform." The James G. Martin Center for Academic Renewal. July 14, 2020. https://www.jamesgmartin.center/2020/07/bolstering-the-board-trustees-are-academias-best-hope-for-reform/.

Schalin, Jay. "The Pushback Against Classroom Indoctrination Begins." The James G. Martin Center for Academic Renewal. July 20, 2022. https://www.jamesgmartin.center/2022/07/the-pushback-against-classroom-indoctrination-begins/.

Smith, Ember and Richard V. Reeves. "SAT Math Scores Mirror and Maintain Racial Inequity." Brookings Institute. December 1, 2020. https://www.brookings.edu/blog/up-front/2020/12/01/sat-math-scores-mirror-and-maintain-racial-inequity/.

Stern, Sol. "Curriculum Is the Cure." *City Journal*. December 12, 2016. https://www.city-journal.org/html/curriculum-cure-14897.html.

Stern, Sol. "E. D. Hirsch's Curriculum for Democracy." *City Journal*. Autumn 2009. https://www.city-journal.org/html/e-d-hirsch%E2%80%99s-curriculum-democracy-13234.html.

Stevens, Sean. "The Coddling of the American Mind: How Good Intentions and Bad Ideas are Setting up a Generation for Failure," www.heterodoxacademy.org, Sept. 11, 2018.

Stone, Geoffrey R. and Creeley, Will. "Restoring Free Speech on Campus." *The Washington Post*. Sep. 25, 2015.

Thayer, Bradley A. "Our 1776 Moment: Either a Liberal or Progressive America." *Epoch Times*. January 26, 2022. https://www.theepochtimes.com/our-1776-moment-either-a-liberal-or-progressive-america_4231197.html?utm_source=ai&utm_medium=search.

Thomas, Bradley. "Statistical Disparities Among Groups Are Not Proof of Discrimination." Foundation for Economic Education (FEE). May 21, 2019. https://fee.org/articles/statistical-disparities-among-groups-are-not-proof-of-discrimination/?itm_source=parsely-api.

Tolson, Patricia. "Statistics Show America's Education System is Failing: CRT and Lower Expectation Equals Fewer Literate Graduates, Expert Says." *Epoch Times*. January 2, 2022. https://www.theepochtimes.com/statistics-show-americas-education-system-is-failing-crt-and-lower-expectation-equals-fewer-literate-graduates-expert-says_4179014.html.

Traldi, Oliver. "Peak Woke?" *City Journal*. July 6, 2022. https://www.city-journal.org/have-we-reached-peak-woke.

Valdary, Chloé. "Reconciliation, or Grievance?" *City Journal*. June 6, 2019. https://www.city-journal.org/diversity-training.

Weissmueller, Zach. "Florida Parents Take Back the Classroom." Reason. January 28, 2022. https://reason.com/video/2022/01/28/florida-parents-take-back-the-classroom/.

Weslander Quaid, Michele R. "We Are in a War for America's Soul." *Epoch Times*. September 21, 2021. https://www.theepochtimes.com/we-are-in-a-war-for-americas-soul_4001263.html?utm_source=ai_recommender&utm_medium=a_bottom_above_etv.

Williams, Walter E. "The Fight for Free Speech." The Daily Signal. October 07, 2020. https://www.dailysignal.com/2020/10/07/the-fight-for-free-speech/.

Willour, Isaac. "What We Can Learn from the Campus Free-Speech War." National Review. August 22, 2021. https://www.nationalreview.com/2021/08/what-we-can-learn-from-the-campus-free-speech-war/.

Wood, Peter. "A Tide Flowing Toward Free Speech on Campus. Minding the Campus." July 16, 2018 (from Free Speech in Peril: College—Where You Can't Say What You Think – Minding the Campus). https://www.mindingthecampus.org/wp-content/uploads/2020/01/MTC-e-book.pdf.

Index

L

M

N

T

Y

Z

Author Bio

Corey Lee Wilson was raised an atheist by his liberal *Playboy* Bunny mother, has three Anglo-Hispanic siblings, a bi-racial daughter, a brother who died of AIDS, baptized a Protestant by his conservative grandparents, attended temple with his Jewish foster parents, baptized again as a Catholic for his first Filipina wife, attends Buddhist ceremonies with his second Thai wife, became an agnostic on his own free will for most of his life, and is a lifetime independent voter.

Corey felt the sting of intellectual humility by repeating the 4th grade and attended eighteen different schools before putting himself through college (without parents) at Mt. San Antonio College and Cal Poly Pomona University (while on triple secret probation). Named Who's Who of American College Students in 1984, he received a BS in Economics (summa cum laude) and won his fraternity's most prestigious undergraduate honor, the Phi Kappa Tau Fraternity's Shideler Award, both in 1985. In 2020, he became a member of the Heterodox Academy and in 2021 a member of the National Association of Scholars and 1776 Unites.

As a satirist and fraternity man, Corey started Fratire Publishing in 2012 and transformed the fiction "fratire" genre to a respectable and viewpoint diverse non-fiction genre promoting practical knowledge and wisdom to help everyday people navigate safely through the many hazards of life. In 2019, he founded the SAPIENT Being to help promote freedom of speech, viewpoint diversity, intellectual humility and most importantly advance sapience in America's students and campuses.

Some unsapient readers might be prone to ask why would someone raised as a wild-hippy-gypsy child of the Sixties would take the conservative point of view? Quick answer: In this day and age it's the reasonable, logical, and sapient thing to do—and by comparison there is little to nothing "sapient" about the Progressivism movement. To quote Ronald Reagan, "There's a flickering spark in us all which, if struck at just the right age, can light the rest of our lives" and that is indeed what happened by always keeping an open mind.

The SAPIENT Being has three programs: Make Free Speech Again On Campus (MFSAOC) Program, Free Speech Alumni Ambassador (FSAA) Program, and the Sapient Conservative Textbooks (SCT) Program—all working together to promote its mission and vision of sapience.

If you're interested in the MFSAOC Program and starting a S.A.P.I.E.N.T. Being club, chapter, or alliance on or off campus, please contact me directly with any question or request for information at https://www.SapientBeing.org/start-a-chapter, or e-mail SapientBeing@att.net, or call me at (951) 638-5562.

If you're interested in becoming a conservative campus advisor or free speech champion for right-leaning campus organizations as part of the FSAA Program from the S.A.P.I.E.N.T. Being, please e-mail at SapientBeing@att.net, or call (951) 638-5562 for more information.

If you're interested as an educator, administrator, or student in the SCT Program and their 40 MADNESS series of textbooks from the S.A.P.I.E.N.T. Being, please check them out at the Fratire Publishing website at https://www.FratirePublishing.com/textbooks for more information.

Hopefully, this book was enlightening and your journey through it—along with mine—made you aware of the issues and challenges ahead of us. If it has, your quest and mine towards becoming a sapient being has begun. If it hasn't, there's no better time to start than now. Come join us in creating a society advancing personal intelligence and enlightenment now together (S.A.P.I.E.N.T.) and become a sapient being.

www.ingramcontent.com/pod-product-compliance
Lightning Source LLC
Chambersburg PA
CBHW042332030426
42335CB00027B/3308